BUFFALO
Everything

BUFFALO *Everything*

A GUIDE TO EATING IN THE "NICKEL CITY"

★ **ARTHUR BOVINO** ★

The Countryman Press

A division of W. W. Norton & Company

Independent Publishers Since 1923

For information about permission to reproduce selections from this book,
write to Permissions, The Countryman Press, 500 Fifth Avenue, New York, NY 10110

 For information about special discounts for bulk purchases, please contact
W. W. Norton Special Sales at specialsales@wwnorton.com or 800-233-4830

Manufacturing by LSC Communications, Crawfordsville
Book design by Lidija Tomas
Production manager: Devon Zahn

The Countryman Press
www.countrymanpress.com

A division of W. W. Norton & Company, Inc.
500 Fifth Avenue, New York, NY 10110
www.wwnorton.com

978-1-68268-122-0 (pbk.)

10 9 8 7 6 5 4 3 2 1

To my son Augustus, my wife Angela, my family, friends, and the people of Western New York. Buffalove.

CONTENTS

PREFACE: WHY BUFFALO?

Meglio murí sazzio ca campà diúno.

Better to die full than live fasting.

—Old Neapolitan proverb that goes double for Buffalo

First, wings, yes, but also, Buffalo is a city full of *delicious* comfort food—the melting pot of comfort food if you will. Yup. And you're the one missing out if you don't think so. I've been asked "Why Buffalo?" more than a few times by perplexed New Yorkers, and friendly and appreciative, if slightly skeptical Nickel City restaurant owners, bartenders, writers, and denizens. (What, wait—wings isn't a good enough answer?) I typically get one sentence to answer that question before I lose folks who *haven't* sat down to a perfectly rare beef on weck or a bowl of wings that has taken at least 15 minutes to cook.

Wings have taken the country by storm over the past five decades since they were invented. And yet, because they seem so simple, because they've become so ubiquitous, and maybe because of perceptions of their middle-class beginnings and their Western New York origins (the Midwestern part of what's arguably the country's most cosmopolitan state), the artistry behind this beloved bar food and its blue-collar Mecca feel distinctly overlooked. Someone needed to eat all the wings and give this great city's food scene the attention it deserves beyond lip service to

Frank and Teressa Bellissimo, as great a story as theirs is. And I was hungry.

The longer answer to "Why Buffalo?" Pizza.

Pizza is a common response to (and solution for) many of my life's questions. I'm a New Yorker and a pizza guy who has written about the holy trinity of cheese, sauce, and crust in the City and across America for nearly a decade. When I learned years ago about Buffalo-style pizza (not Buffalo chicken pizza, which is another story), a pizza species in *my* state that I hadn't explored, I considered it a gap in my cred. I'd made pilgrimages to some of America's most storied pizzerias and even visited Old Forge, Pennsylvania, the self-described "Pizza Capital of the World," but I'd never eaten pizza in one of the most pizza-obsauced parts of my own state?

For shame. Someday, I was going to get to Buffalo and find out what it was all about.

As a food editor and writer, I've checked off my ever-expanding bucket list many of America's best restaurants and most iconic food trails: New Mexico's green chile cheeseburgers, San Diego's fish tacos, hot dogs in Chicago and Connecticut, Maine's lobster rolls, Texas barbecue, San Antonio's puffy tacos. But again, when I thought of the state I'm so proud to be from, I found a gaping hole on my list: Buffalo wings. (For the record, they're just chicken wings or *wings* in Buffalo.)

This wings and pizza two-fer made Buffalo a *huge* draw. So when a writer friend put me in touch with her agent who was interested in pitching a Buffalo-sauce cookbook, I'd finally found my ticket. Little did I know how much more there was to eat.

As I ate my research, I learned of at least eight other nationally uncelebrated delicious things that are nearly as beloved to locals as wings, even if not quite as iconic. And then there were the bars, the old-school Polish and Italian-American eateries, the Burmese restaurants, and the new-school restaurants tapping into the region's rich agricultural bounty.

So, that Buffalo-sauce cookbook turned into an effort to chronicle Buffalo wing culture beyond its two most famous spots, to seek out its best pizza parlors, celebrate its fish-fries, restaurants, and lesser-known but no less delicious foods, and to share some secrets. All in all, I visited more than 120 restaurants, conducted dozens of interviews with local food icons, and researched and reverse-engineered recipes to replicate the city's tasty foods at home, the latter of which you can find in this book's companion volume, *The Buffalo Everything Cookbook*.

And that's how I fell in love with Buffalo, quickly gained 25 pounds, and learned a great piece of advice for anyone who loves comfort food: if you're someone who *hasn't* yet shuffled off to Buffalo, take nothing else away from this book than its first sentence, and get yourself to the city ASAP.

INTRODUCTION

"We can take it on the chin in this town. We can take it. That New York grit, we have that too, but it's been earned through nature."

—*Christa Glennie Seychew*

Buffalo food writer

"To you guys, less is more. To us, more ain't enough."

—*Anthony Kulik*

Lovejoy Pizza owner

To the outsider trying to understand the city, Buffalo can be a series of contrasts and seeming contradictions. It was described by Frederick Law Olmsted, the landscape architect behind New York's Central Park, as America's best designed city. A metropolis dotted with Art Deco architecture, Buffalo's cityscape was laid out by Joseph Ellicott in 1804. Ellicott was inspired by Pierre L'Enfant, the French-American military engineer who designed the basic plan for Washington, DC, after the Baroque system of city planning, which centers on public squares, main streets, and a series of boulevards.

Buffalo is a six-and-a-half hour drive from New York City but just an hour and a half by air. To out-of-staters, it seems like Buffalonians could just take a quick drive to Manhattan for the weekend, but from New Yorkers' per-spectives, Buffalo's that place all the way across the state that may as well be in the Midwest or Canada (you will even occasionally see soda here called "pop"!). And in fact, New York state is nearly half as wide as Texas—far enough away for Long Island college freshman at SUNY Buffalo State to be conveniently within reach of home while also relatively safe from unexpected parental visits.

Once you're in Buffalo, it's a three-hour drive to Cleveland, a little more than four hours to Detroit, and just two to Toronto.

Buffalo is a city that invented a food that's famous across the country and around the world. Paris, Rome, London, Hong Kong, Rio—none of them have a food as synonymous with its city's name. To most who haven't been, Buffalo is that depressed place where it snows, where the chicken wing was invented, and that has that team that lost four consecutive Super Bowls. It's a city that proudly drinks Labatt Blue, a Canadian beer (okay, a Belgian-owned Canadian beer) and roots for the Buffalo Bisons, the Triple-A affiliate of the Toronto Blue Jays, when the Yankees' own Triple-A team, the Scranton/Wilkes-Barre RailRiders, comes to town. Is it a Midwestern city populated by Americans who have a dash of Canadian personableness, a pinch of New York City attitude, and a bit of Brooklyn self-boosterism? Nah, it's just Buffalo.

It's hard to imagine there was a time, as Calvin Trillin described in his 1980 *New Yorker* article, when Buffalonians wondered if they could ever profit from exporting their local delicacy to the rest of America. According to the National Chicken Council's annual report, Americans ate 1.33 billion chicken wings in 2017, up 2 percent (30 million wings) over 2016. Wings have been on the menus of major national pizza chains for decades, and wing-centric restaurants have taken flight, among them Hooters, Wingstop, Wing Zone, Atomic Wings, and East Coast Wings & Grill. CHD Expert, a food service market research company that tracks restaurant data, estimates that there are more than 3,200 restaurants in the United States dedicated primarily to chicken wings. And that doesn't include Buffalo Wild Wings ("B-Dubs" for short, which gets classified as a bar and grill), which serves wings with, at last count, 21 sauces at more than 1,100 restaurants in America, Canada, Mexico, the Middle East, the Philippines, and Panama, and has a goal of expanding to 1,700 restaurants across North America in the next 10 years.

In fact, I'd challenge you to name iconic foods from other cities that have so successfully interwoven themselves into the national food consciousness. And yet, while there are maps in New York City for burgers, ramen, and doughnuts, and while foodies regularly plan pilgrimages to Lockhart, Texas, for barbecue and New Haven, Connecticut, for pizza at Frank Pepe, Sally's, and Modern, outside the city, you rarely hear about a wing pecking order in Buffalo beyond Anchor and Duff's. If you think you like wings and you haven't been to Buffalo, go. They're so much better made in the city of their origin and there are so many other places and styles of wings there worthy of obsession. All over the city, as stated on menus and by waitstaff, you'll receive warnings that great wings can't be made in less than 12 minutes. And I can guarantee that all those great wings will ruin you for life—they'll never be as good anywhere else.

Still, Buffalo isn't just a city full of great wings that goes largely unbuzzed about. There's a great hot dog tradition, from Greek-originated

"Texas red hots" culture to year-round charcoal-grilling at Ted's that puts Manhattan's dirty water dogs to shame. This is also a city of great sandwiches. It's a place where capicola gets layered on grilled sausage, where sautéed dandelions traditionally make up the greens in a comestible called "steak in the grass," and where chicken fingers slip off children's menus and into soft Costanzo's sub rolls with provolone, tomato, lettuce, blue cheese dressing, and Frank's RedHot Sauce to become something truly *naughty*: crunchy, spicy, and messy—too naughty for kids. It's a town where the darkest, grittiest, falling-down, salt-of-the-earth bar with epic bathroom graffiti and broken-latch stall-sniffing has bartenders who also make epic steak sandwiches between pouring shots. A town with carving stations *dedicated* to beef on weck, a sandwich that should be up there with Pittsburgh's Primanti Bros., Los Angeles's French dip at Philippe the Original, and pastrami at Katz's in New York City.

Speaking of New York City, Buffalo has just as intense of a pizza culture and a tradition that goes back as far as at least 1927. Often described as somewhere between the styles of New York and Chicago, Buffalo's pizza is made for bracing you against the cold of football tailgating, more like a Detroit-ified grandma slice but with more cheese, a sweeter sauce, and always, always slices of cup-and-char pepperoni that are crisp along the edges and filled with wading pools of hot, spicy grease. If you think Buffalo loves its wings, just ask locals who makes the best pizza. And Buffalo's Italian food traditions don't stop there. There are Russian roulette–spicy

Paula's is most known for its peanut stick, a cake donut entirely coated in finely chopped peanuts and peanut dust.

Famous Doughnuts was founded in 1938 by Teddy Roehm, who was inspired to "make and serve a product that would never become dated in flavor or quality." Teddy's son, Richard Roehm, and his wife, Pamela, have been running the business together for more than 30 years.

There's nothing *fancy* about Famous Doughnuts, but their glazed doughnut is dipped in sugar and obsession.

banana peppers bursting with cheese and bowls of lightly sauced spaghetti parm covered with a thick, melted layer of mozzarella that guarantees a cheese-pull every time.

Fantastic peanut-studded cake doughnuts stuffed with sweet angel's creme draw morning and weekend lines at Paula's, and the fresh glazed rounds at Famous Doughnuts are more addictive than Krispy Kreme's.

Not only that, but Buffalo is a city with a food schedule and calendar. On Fridays, religion can sometimes intersect with chicken wings, when the Catholic-inspired fish fry tradition means no wings until the fryer oil can be changed after dinner. And it guarantees to keep its secrets unless you go to certain places on certain days and visit during different times of year. Consider sponge candy, a chocolate-covered toffee made with baking soda, and whose inside looks a little like a Butterfinger but tastes nothing like it. Its airy center crumbles away into sweetness and leaves behind a silky sweet chocolate exterior on your tongue. Some of its most-lauded makers won't produce it past Mother's Day because they think the heat interferes with it being as good. There are pastries called *fastnachts* that are only made from Ash Wednesday through Easter Saturday every year, and a Brigadoon sardine-studded *pasta con sarde* that's green with fennel, red with tomato paste, and that only appears on March 19th during the Sicilian feast of San Giuseppe (St. Joseph). Food-truck Tuesdays take over Larkinville from April through October, filling Larkin Square with dozens of food trucks and hungry, beer-toting eaters, and during Labor Day weekend at the National Buffalo Wing Festival, 40,000 people fill Coca-Cola Field to eat more than 20 tons of wings. Roadside custard, fried food, and hamburger stands are only open during the summer. Then there's the Tom & Jerry, a seasonally available frothy, rum-and-brandy-soaked cocktail laboriously made with eggs whose whites and yolks are whipped separately and folded together with sugar and spice, ladled out of a punch bowl on the back of the bar, meticulously layered according to the rules of the house, and subject to long drinking sessions frequently tied to the intensity of the weather. Imagine the best eggnog you've ever had and it doesn't even come close to how good this drink is.

So why's the food such a secret? Buffalo has admittedly had a bit of an image issue for a few decades. Its killer "b's"—blizzards, blight, and the Bills—haven't helped.

Buffalonians are quick to point out that Rochester and Syracuse get more snow. I myself can't speak to Buffalo's cold. But I remember growing up hearing about the Blizzard of '77, and there's no way of getting around Buffalo's average annual snowfall of 94 inches.

The blight *is* something that's been changing. It may be hard to believe now, but Buffalo was once America's eighth-*largest* city. And it was the nation's fifteenth-largest city as recently as the 1950s. Its reputation over the decades since has been one of a Rust Belt town. But it also happens to have once been one of the *richest* cities in America. In the late 1800s, it was said to have had 60 millionaires, more per capita than any American city! Joseph Dart's grain elevator allowed ships to unload in one day, and as business increased Buffalo came to boast the nation's largest capacity for grain storage, with more than 30 concrete grain elevators along the outer and inner harbors on the Buffalo River and Lake Erie. The Erie Canal also made Buffalo the logical place to mill the grain before shipping it, and the city's proximity to water drew manufacturing jobs as well. But the rise of the railway eventually made access to water less important, and then with the postwar decline of both rail *and* canal transport, the city went from being a titan of manufacturing and industry to a depressed urban center. Its population, once as high as 580,000, is 256,902 today.

The current population, though, is not a commentary on the present state of things in Buffalo. Back in 2004, a $300 million development transformed the lakeshore from a bunch of parking lots into Canalside, a place where tourists and Buffalonians gather year-round (water bikes turn into ice bikes) for more than a thousand annual festivals, concerts, and other events. Then in 2012 came the Buffalo Billion, Governor Andrew Cuomo's plan to invest $1 billion in the local economy.

All this has led way to the construction of the SolarCity GigaFactory at RiverBend, America's largest rooftop solar installer (subsequently purchased by Tesla), as well as to the creation of the Buffalo High Tech Manufacturing Innovation Hub at RiverBend (a $225 million facility to host clean energy businesses), the Buffalo Medical Innovation and Commercialization Hub (a $50 million biomedical research equipment and facilities center), the establishment of

Athenex high-tech drug research (a $200 million research facility in Dunkirk, NY, with labs in Buffalo), and 43North, a startup competition where winners vie for $5 million in annual prizes and then relocate to Buffalo for investment capital, incubator space, expert mentorship, and 10 years of freedom from state taxes. There's also a current effort to remove a stretch of the Robert Moses Parkway that has been a barrier to the waterfront and downtown Niagara Falls and an ongoing project to revitalize its downtown, and a second phase of the Buffalo Billion, a proposal to spend another $500 million to bolster the economy and reinvigorate civic spirit in Buffalo and throughout Western New York. Then there's the city's red-hot housing market, which didn't suffer from 2008 economic crash simply because the area was already depressed.

As for the Bills (technically, the only football team New York state can call its own), sports fortunes can change quickly. Terry Pegula, who bought the Buffalo Sabres in 2011, purchased the Bills in 2014 after the passing of the original owner and team founder Ralph Wilson.

Now the Bills don't look like they'll be moving anywhere, except maybe to a new stadium that could be built on the new land Pegula seems to be gobbling up. Meanwhile, in a modern era that has seen the Patriots go from laughing-stock to world champions, and the evaporation of curses on the Red Sox and Cubs that once helped give meaning and personality to Boston and Chicago—two cold, windy, winter cities—Buffalo can wear an epic four-year Super Bowl meltdown with pride.

Pride, civic pride in general, is something you're seeing more and more of in Buffalo. "I've spent my career trying to convince the people who live here that this is a great place," Christa Glennie Seychew explained to me. "But one of the blessings that accompanied our lack of development is that it's almost as if there was a glass cloche put down over the city back in the 1965 that kept anything from moving in. Now that's actually working in our favor because we didn't get all of that crappy '70's, '80s', '90's strip mall development that a lot of other places' downtowns have. Buffalo's downtown is free of it, and a lot of places can't say that. Look at Columbus."

More millennials are reportedly staying and returning to Buffalo, more folks are renovating houses, and more T-shirts are expressing self-love of Buffalo. And that's a really cool thing, both for Buffalonians and its visitors, considering the slings and arrows it has learned to shrug off from its cross-state "cooler" older sibling. It all adds up to a city on the rise with great food.

Anyone curious about what an American city would look like without the chain saturation that has strip-mall-ified the rest of the country can just visit Buffalo. While chains have taken over the suburbs, much of the city proper is still populated with generational mom-and-pop businesses. And when it comes to eating out, that translates to a city with a blue-collar appetite with the know-how to make comfort food really, really well. The wings are crispier, the pizza is cheesier, and the portions are bigger. Writers and restaurateurs will explain that if there aren't leftovers, customers don't think they got their money's worth. This is a town

where appetizers get turned into condiments to be put on *other* dishes.

Buffalo is a friendly city. It's the kind of place where you can go into a corner neighborhood bar, not know anyone, and sometimes with a little effort and more often without, leave buying someone a round after having been bought two. It's a city of *you-have-tos*: You have to have Lottie's pierogies at R&L Lounge. You have to eat a custard at a summer stand. You have to go to Bocce. You have to go to La Nova. You have to go to Eddie Brady's. You have to try the wings at Gabriel's Gate, and then the ones at Judi's. You have to go to Schwabl's for the weck. You have to eat the fish fry at Gene McCarthy's. You have

to get hazed at Mammoser's. You have to go to Blackthorn to understand Tim Russert. You have to see how pretty the plate of wings are at Nine-Eleven Tavern. And the list goes on.

"Personally, I think in the next ten years, we'll have a hot Portland moment here, but we're not ready for it, yet," Christa Glennie Seychew predicted to me. "We will be really cool, I think, for at least a year, sometime in the next decade. But we have at least one more growth cycle before we're ready for that."

So why *not* Buffalo? Anybody who visits Buffalo who loves good food, and especially comfort food, will recognize the city for what it is: a great place to eat. Now . . . let's dig in.

Some Important Inventions and Moments in Buffalo History

1825 The Erie Canal is completed, linking the waters of Lake Erie in the west to the Hudson River in the east.

1842 Joseph Dart and Robert Dunbar invent the steam-powered grain elevator in Buffalo to solve the problem of unloading and storing grain transported via the Erie Canal.

1850 The first patent for an American-made roll-top desk is given to Abner Cutler of Buffalo, NY.

1859 Frenchman Jean-Francois Gravelet (aka Emile Blondin) becomes the first daredevil to walk across Niagara Falls on a tightrope.

1881 Prominent Buffalonian Maria M. Love establishes Fitch Crèche, which will become nationally recognized as the first day care center for children of working women in the United States.

1884 Brothers Edmund, Frank, George, Lucius, and William Ball expand their wood-jacketed tin can business to include the glass home-canning jars that will make Ball a household name, and a stalwart of hipster restaurants nation-wide more than a century later.

1885 The former New Jersey-born Mayor of Buffalo and Governor of New York, Grover Cleveland, is elected President of the United States.

1898 The New York State Pathological Laboratory of the University of Buffalo, the first facility in the world dedicated specifically to cancer research, is founded.

1901 William McKinley, the 25th President of the United States, is shot at the Pan-American Exposition in Buffalo on September 6. McKinley dies on September 14, and Theodore Roosevelt is sworn in at the house of his friend, a prominent lawyer Ansley Wilcox in Buffalo.

1901 Hoping to translate fame into money to pay her bills, 63-year-old schoolteacher Annie Edson Taylor becomes the first person to survive a plunge over Niagara Falls in a barrel.

1902 Willis Carrier designs the first modern air-conditioning system for the Buffalo Forge Company to solve the humidity problem of a printing company in Brooklyn.

1917 The Tri-Continental Corporation (now TRICO) mass produces the first commercially available wiper blade.

1958 An assistant professor in electrical engineering at the University of Buffalo, Wilson Greatbatch designs the first practical implantable pacemaker.

1960 A 7-year-old boy survives the 180-foot fall trip over nearby Niagara Falls, becoming the first to do so without a protective device.

1967 Race riots paralyze the city for a week.

1977 The Blizzard of '77 tops the 37 inches of snow that had previously fallen that winter with another foot. Thousands of people are stranded and President Jimmy Carter declares all of Western New York a federal disaster area.

1991 Kicker Scott Norwood misses a 47-yard field goal attempt at the end of Super Bowl XXV to lose to the New York Giants (who call New Jersey home) by one point. The Bills will go on to make it to and lose the next three Super Bowls by 13, 35, and 17 points.

2004 A master plan, which involved considerable public participation, calls for considerable residential and commercial development of the Canal District, to be rebranded "Canalside."

2011 Natural gas and real estate mogul Terry Pegula buys the Buffalo Sabres.

2012 Nik Wallenda braves the thick mist over Niagara Falls to become the first person in recent history to cross over the actual falls.

2012 Governor Andrew Cuomo announces the "Buffalo Billion," a plan to invest $1 billion in the local economy.

2014 After Ralph Wilson, the franchise's founding owner, passes away, Terry Pegula reaches an agreement to buy the Buffalo Bills.

2014 The $172 million HarborCenter development opens, adding to the revitalization of Buffalo's Canalside.

2018 The *New York Times* names Buffalo as one of its "52 Places to Go in 2018."

CHAPTER ONE

BUFFALO WINGS IN BUFFALO

A World of Difference in Wings

Anchor vs. Duff's: Buffalo's Best Chicken Wings?

"People ask me, 'Which is better: Anchor or Duff's?' and I'm like, I've never set foot inside Anchor Bar and I'm proud of that. My favorites are at Gabriel's Gate in Allentown and Cole's on Elmwood. They're at the bars I used to go to that made great wings."

—John Marren

Owner, Buffalo's Famous, Brooklyn

Online lists of America's best Buffalo wings are published by national food sites annually. They seem to be written by people who've never stepped foot in Buffalo and they always include Anchor Bar and Duff's. For the record, Duff's beat Anchor on Travel Channel's *Food Wars* in 2010, and when President Obama visited the city, he visited Duff's (though I was told by none other than Duff's co-owner Jeff Feather that the visit had been more about its proximity to the airport than a predilection to one spot over the other). Anyway, Anchor is the originator, as the story goes, but Duff's now makes them better—"best in the city!" in fact. Not quite, I say.

Don't get the locals wrong: Anchor deserves recognition for having invented the food that put Buffalo on the map, and nobody begrudges Duff's success.

"That's a landmark stop," Lovejoy pizzeria co-owner Anthony Kulik tells me. "I'm not kidding, man, that dude's lot down the street is packed night and day. Night and day. Night and

day for an average chicken wing in Buffalo. You ask anybody in Buffalo about a great wing, those guys won't even be in the top 20, guaranteed. But that's because we live here, you know?"

It's like Buffalonian and Brooklyn Buffalo food restaurant owner John Marren says: For many Nickel City citizens, where you eat wings says as much about who your friends are, where you live, and where you're from.

The nuances of wing culture and history are more intricate than the casual Buffalo wing enthusiast can imagine.

A History of Buffalo Wings

Buffalo's connection to wings actually stretches back to *before* the Civil War. The Buffalo History Museum has century-old menus featuring variations on turkey and chicken wings with buttered noodles, rice and poulette sauce (a creamy sauce with mushrooms, lemon juice, and parsley and a base of stock, flour and butter). There's an especially interesting document at the library sure to pique any wing historian's interests, a menu dated July 1st, 1857, from the Clarendon Hotel. While Frank's RedHot wouldn't be invented until 1920, the Clarendon, one of the city's largest hotels before it burned down on Main Street (at South Division) in 1860, apparently served "chicken wings, fried" even then! No word, though, on whether the fire started in the kitchen with a batch of wings.

And that's not the only pre-Anchor reference. In an article for *Buffalo Rising*, Cynthia Van Ness, the director of library and archives at the Buffalo History Museum, cites a recipe from 1894 in the Buffalo Commercial Advertiser. It calls for the wings to be stewed then placed on top a puree of peas mashed with butter and thickened with

"Chicken wings, fried" circa 1857, 107 years before that fateful night at Anchor. CREDIT: THE BUFFALO HISTORY MUSEUM

flour. Another recipe, this one found by Van Ness in *The Modern Cook* by Charles E. Francatelli (11th edition, 1858) calls for wings to be deboned, filled with chicken forcemeat, boiled, then cooked in a pot with bacon herbs, onions, and broth before being drained and dressed with Allemande sauce (a veal, chicken or shellfish velouté thickened with egg yolks and heavy cream and accented with lemon juice). A lot of work for wings!

"Very few foods have as clear-cut a creation story as the wing," food and travel writer Larry Olmsted suggested just a few years ago in a two-part series on Buffalo wings for *USA Today*. As far as the *conventional* wisdom goes, he's right: Buffalo wings' journey from scrap to commodity began on a Friday night in 1964 at Frank & Teressa's Anchor Bar. But it turns out the story isn't *anywhere* near as straightforward as all that.

Details differ between reported accounts from Frank and his son Dominic Bellissimo, the two family members involved who *didn't* actually cook any wings that fateful night. From there, pulling on the thread of the true origins of this now-iconic American food leads to a neck-deep vat of mumbo sauce in Auburn Gresham, Chicago. Indeed, in his 1980 attempt for the *New Yorker* to compile a short history of the Buffalo chicken wing, American journalist, humorist, and food writer Calvin Trillin (who was perhaps one of the writers most responsible for raising wings to national consciousness) comes close to comparing his own quest to discover their origins to that of a "medievalist whose specialty requires him to poke around in thirteenth-century Spain." And that was just some 16 years after they were first invented! Trying to nail down all the details surrounding Buffalo wings creation is a bit like herding chickens doused in hot sauce.

Trillin gamely notes that Frank's version involved the divine providence of a mistaken delivery of wings instead of the necks and backs they used to make spaghetti sauce.

Italians and Italian-Americans have a rich tradition of working magic with marginalized and leftover ingredients out of necessity, so using chicken scraps to add flavor to spaghetti sauce isn't beyond the pale (though nobody in my Italian-American family did that while making our gravy when I was growing up). But the "real story" on Anchor's extensive menu, as explained by Dom "The Rooster" Bellissimo, leaves out the mistaken delivery and makes a more likely case as to what the wings were really meant to be used for: soup.

"Frank Bellissimo thought it was a shame to use the wings for sauce. 'They were looking at you, like saying, "I don't belong in the sauce,"' he has often recalled. He implored his wife, who was doing the cooking, to figure out some more dignified end for the wings. Teressa Bellissimo decided to make some hors d'oeuvres for the bar—and the Buffalo chicken wing was born."
—Calvin Trillin

"One Friday night back in 1964, I was working behind the bar (as I still do now). It was busy that night. My mother, Teressa, was in the kitchen cooking, and dad, Frank, was popping in the restaurant greeting customers. It was one of those good Friday nights. At about 11:30 PM, a group of my friends came through the door and they were starving! I told them to wait until midnight so they could have what they wanted. I served another round of drinks. By midnight, they were really hungry! I ask my mother, Teressa, to fix something for them. About 10 minutes later, she brought them out two plates and set them on the bar. They all asked, 'What is this?' and to tell you the truth, I also was curious to know what those things were! They looked like chicken wings, but I was afraid to say so! To make a long story short, yes they were chicken wings—she was about to put them in the stock pot (for soup). She looked at them and said, 'It's a shame to put such beautiful wings in a stock pot.'" —Dom Bellissimo

Sauce or soup? It's a just one of the many hazy details of Buffalo wing origin lore. But even though Ivano Toscani, who started as Frank's assistant and worked at Anchor for 40 years, became owner in 2015, the spirit of the Bellissimo family lives on with the countless plates of wings served to tourists and in the pictures and articles that dot the walls license-plate filled walls. (The license plate collection started when Dominic found one plate in the parking lot and hung it up on the wall.)

Dominic passed away in 1991, and there are still details about his wing-origin explanation that aren't on the current menu at Anchor. Speaking to the *New York Times* in 1985 after Teressa died, Dom said: "The true story is that I was tending bar, and a bunch of my friends were drinking." He noted that they were spending a lot of money at the bar, and asked his mother to make something to pass around for free.

End of story, right? Not quite. Buffalo wings'

original custodians may have all passed away, but up until a few years ago, there was one surviving eyewitness to Teressa's ingenuity that fateful night in 1964—Dom Zanghi. And he was interviewed on camera by documentarian Matt Reynolds, whose 2013 film *The Great Chicken Wing Hunt*, a quest to find the world's best chicken wing, is a must-watch for any wing fanatic. "She was a pistol, a pistol," Zanghi explains, describing Teressa Bellissimo in the film. "She used the F-word like you say 'hello.'"

To Reynolds, the creation story told over and over through the years feels like a simplification of the story Dom shared with him, one that adds back to the story some of the personality that Teressa seems to have lost in decades of its telling. It adds mythology to her eureka moment.

"Dom is saying, Frank and Teressa got this case of wings when they wanted chicken parts," Reynolds explains. "Wings then are something that are thought poorly of and discarded, so she's pissed off at the distributor. Apparently, she had a notoriously foul mouth. She's yelling. She's making a scene, and her husband is saying, 'Don't worry. Do something with it, do something with it. Make soup.' And she's screaming, 'How much soup can I make?'"

"With the F-word," Zanghi adds in the film.

Teressa's plan as of Thursday night when she goes to sleep is to send the wings back.

"She goes to bed upset," Reynolds continues, recounting Dom's story. "She can't sleep. She wakes up at 3:30 or 4 in the morning, and thinks, 'Hey, I got an idea. Let me try and see what I can do with this.' She had this cayenne pepper sauce handy. We don't know the exact sequence, if she was experimenting, or she woke up with the idea, but in the middle of the night, she comes up with this recipe."

The next night, Dominic's friends, including Dom Zanghi, visit the bar near midnight on Friday. Teressa asks them to come to the back room and tells them she wants them to try the wings and that she's thinking of putting them on the bar as a snack. "We sat there, no tablecloth, no nothing," Zanghi recounts. "We waited and waited."

Then, finally, Dominic brings out his mother's wings to his friends from the kitchen.

Zanghi and the rest of Dominic's friends devoured the platters, and the Bellissimos start giving them away at the bar for free instead of peanuts and pretzels. "All of a sudden, everybody wanted them," Zanghi says in *The Great Chicken Wing Hunt*. "And they're going off so big people weren't ordering lunch."

So Frank takes them off the menu until he can figure out what he can add to them to help justify turning them into something he feels he can charge people for. "He came up with that and that," Zanghi explains, pointing to blue cheese and celery. "And that promoted it even bigger. The new customers were this big in here," he said, raising his hands out to either side as far as they can reach while finishing his story at a crowded table in the Anchor Bar.

"To me it feels like the version that is told now by Anchor Bar, that they came in one Friday night and her son and his friends they were like, 'Mom make us something,' and she came up with this recipe, I feel like that could be the simplification, and a dumbing down of the original story

"He said, 'Sit down guys, I want you to go to town on this.'

He had a platter this big with something on it that he set there, and passed it around so the seven of us could enjoy it.

I says, 'What the hell are we eating? What is this?'

Donny says, 'Will you shut the fuck up and eat, before my father whacks you one?'

So we're eating the second platter. And we realized it was the chicken wings that they sent by mistake."

—Dom Zanghi

that Dom tells, but not the other way," Reynolds tells me, adding that he doesn't have strong feelings one way or the other about who remembered correctly what actually happened that night so long ago. "If what it says on the menu is literally true, then the Dom thing, it's like he just made all this stuff up."

By all accounts, though, Zanghi didn't seem the type to misremember the story. On the last stop of the documentary, Anchor Bar, he accompanied Reynolds and his band of wing judges to the place where everything started, noting, "I almost broke down and cried. I was so sentimental. They're all gone. I'm the only one left out of the seven." And after his first interview with Reynolds, before Reynolds sets out on his wing quest, Dom gave him a rosary to hold onto in an hour of need should the journey face difficulties (it did). Zanghi has since passed away and Reynolds dedicated *The Great Chicken Wing Hunt* to him.

I like Zanghi's story the most, not just because it's a filmed firsthand account, but because it adds dimension to Teressa as a person and gives *her* more credit for the eureka moment. After all, while everyone agrees it was Teressa who invented the dish, cutting each wing in half in

most versions of the story, both of the men in her life, Frank and Dominic, took credit for *telling* Teressa she should do something though neither knew *what* that thing should be. And it's *Frank* who was bestowed a proclamation from the city crediting "Mr. Bellissimo's tasty experiment" and declaring July 29, 1977, Chicken Wing Day! (Who knew they'd been mansplaining wings to us all these years!) As Calvin Trillin puts it in his *New Yorker* article, "The inventor of the airplane, after all, was not the person who told Wilbur and Orville Wright that it might be nice to have a machine that could fly."

In fact, I came to fall even more in love with wings by listening to firsthand accounts like Zanghi's and from George Schaeffer, whose stories about Frank singing at the restaurant at the bar to entertain customers, and about the stories Frank said he could have told about drunk politicians rowing a rowboat on the bar at their original restaurant before opening Anchor, might have been blackmail-worthy. Somewhere in all those stories, some true and some embellished, is a life, a life enriched by chicken wings.

Whether you want to quantify that life by the millions of dollars spent on wings every year, the effect on a multi-billion dollar poultry industry, or how "Buffalo" is a flavor that has become omnipresent, you have to admit that an Italian-American couple in Buffalo at least in some way, significantly changed the world.

"I was hoping that Buffalo would become the capital city of chicken wings," Frank told the *Buffalo Courier-Express*. "I want everyone to be happy. I want the business people to be happy. I want nothing but the credit for having started it all. . . . My wife . . . she is the one that done it. She put a million dollars in my life."

One wonders if there wasn't some Italian-born precursor to the Buffalo wing that Teressa might have drawn on for inspiration (the Bellissimos' framed immigration papers on the walls at Anchor reveal them to have been from Palermo, Sicily). After all, dishes in southern Italy's Abruzzo region are frequently accompanied by and flavored with red peppers that are dried and crushed, or crushed, dried, and soaked in oil. But Colman Andrews, author of *The Country Cooking of Italy*, notes that, "the Tuscans do fry rabbit and chicken in pieces, but there's no sauce involved—and certainly no blue cheese." And John Mariani, author of *How Italian Food Conquered the World*, is even less unequivocal, insisting, "Buffalo chicken wings were a wholly spur-of-the-moment creation."

Buffalo wings' iconic condiment pairings, however, *do* owe their origins to the Bellissimo's nationality. They served the wings with celery from Anchor's antipasto dish and the blue-cheese dressing that started out as a house dressing on their salads. It's true that no matter what celery is wonderfully crunchy alongside wings and that blue cheese is a delicious dip with a welcome cooling effect, but knowing their Italian-American origins offers a satisfying answer to what otherwise would be a baffling mystery.

They've Gone Chicken Crazy!

Once you leave Anchor Bar, Buffalo wings' history gets even murkier. One lesser-known origin story involves an African-American man who claimed, "I am actually the creator of the wing." In his Buffalo wing history, Calvin Trillin recounts meeting John Young on his last evening in Buffalo, before heading out to try the wings at Fat Man's Got 'Em (since closed) and Santora's (Buffalo's first pizzeria, founded 1927). "If the Anchor Bar was selling chicken wings, nobody in Buffalo knew it then," Young told Trillin. "After I left here, everybody started chicken wings."

All these many years later, Trillin doesn't quite remember how or where he ended up talking with Young. "He was certainly quite willing to talk about it, and I mean more than willing—he boasted that he was the inventor of the wings," Trillin explained to me. What a chance encounter!

"We were so poor during the War that all we could afford to eat was chicken wings, the feet, the necks and gravy. The chicken wing was a delicacy on our table. We never saw a chicken breast, leg, or thigh, not even a back. It wasn't until I came to Buffalo at the age of 13 that I learned that a chicken had other parts.

I, being the eldest son, had worked hard in the southern cotton fields, along with the rest of my brothers and sisters, to save train fare for my father and me to come north, where we believed there were riches and jobs. Our plan was to get good jobs and send for the rest of the family. We accomplished this in 1951. I worked in and out of restaurants for the next 10 years."

—John Young

Unlike the wings at Anchor, Young's were breaded and fried uncut so the flaps and the drumettes were still connected. His invention, he claimed, was the sauce that coated the wings, which Trillin called "mambo" sauce, but that Young called "mombo sauce" in an article he co-penned in the Buffalonian a year after Trillin's was published. Young, who said he was from a "small country town" called Stockton 35 miles northeast of Mobile, Alabama, was the fourth of 14 children. Young could pinpoint his first memory of eating chicken to being six years old, which in itself should give anyone pause about doubting his story. Who remembers their first experience eating chicken!

Young opened his own first restaurant in 1961 at the corner of Jefferson and Carlton, a 20-minute-walk east of the original Anchor Bar, just off NY 33, what is now the Kensington Expressway. "At that time the menu was ribs, chicken wings, steak, eggs, bacon, grits, and sausage." He moved his restaurant northward and away from Anchor twice, first to Jefferson near High Street

in 1964 (the year Teressa Bellissimo invented her wings), and then to Jefferson and East Utica, in 1966. It's that location, in 1966, two years *after* the eureka wing moment at Anchor where, in his own words, Young decided to make chicken wings his specialty, naming his spot John Young's Wings and Things, which he said he filed in the Erie County Clerk's Office that year.

"The business took right off," Young said. "We advertised 'Ten Whole Chicken Wings For One Dollar.' There were times when we would not be able to turn the crowd back."

Professional singers on tour in Buffalo and Canada would stop by to try Young's wings and mombo sauce. Joe Tex, after visiting Wings and Things, made a smash record in 1969, "They've Gone Chicken Crazy," which along with a few other hits earned him about $500,000 a year by 1970. Imagine a hungry James Brown obsessed with chicken and you have a pretty good idea of how catchy the song is.

By then, Young noted, "There were no longer chicken necks and feet on our family table." But despite the business's success, Young moved to Illinois in 1970. Family members attributed the departure to the race riots a few years earlier, saying he decided Buffalo was no longer safe for his family. When he returned to Buffalo 10 years later, just months before Trillin visited, he joined the chicken wing gold rush that took flight in his absence.

That part of the story is somewhat routinely noted as an aside in best-of lists and wing recipes as a possible alternate origin, but what comes next *doesn't* seem widely known.

With all parties long since departed, it's impossible to confirm with any of them if they ever visited each other's restaurants, and difficult to speculate about the likely cross-pollination of Italian-American and African-American denizens *and* dishes. But according to interviews with John's brother Paul Young and John's daughter Lina-Brown Young in the *Southwest-*

ern Law Review, that's exactly what happened. According to the family, Frank and John did casually frequent one another's businesses and it was not uncommon for visitors to talk to John in the kitchen of Wings and Things. Paul Young, John's brother, said this was where Frank saw John make Buffalo wings.

Asked if she'd ever heard from or about John Young or the Bellissimos visiting each other's kitchens, the *Buffalo News*'s former restaurant critic Janice Okun said she hadn't, but suggested it was a reasonable thing to believe. "They were very close," she explained. "And there weren't very many restaurants then, so it makes sense."

But the Bellissimo story was that Teressa came up with the dish, and you'd think that if it had been Frank's idea to make the wings, he would have claimed credit for giving her the idea at some point during the many times he recounted the story over the years.

As the Buffalo Wing Flies: Chicago via Washington, DC

"It hurts me so bad that other people take the credit," John Young told the *Buffalo News* in 1996.

Reading those words and looking at the woeful photo of him from 1981 proudly bedecked in a robe and crown after being written about by Calvin Trillin elicits a heavy pathos. But setting aside the fact that Young's wings were breaded

(something that's never done now to wings anywhere that wants to be taken seriously for them), Young's recipe, in turn, is the subject of some dispute. He alternately claimed to have created it and to have been inspired to open his own wing shop after hearing about their popularity at a local business in Washington, DC, something his brother claimed in an article published in the *Southwestern Law Review*, and that Young himself hinted at in an article by Okun for the *Buffalo News* two years before he passed away in 1998.

In the Okun article, Young said he decided to specialize in wings after a well-traveled boxer named Sam Anderson told him there was a restaurant in Washington, DC, that was doing good business with wings. And the "mumbo" sauce at the heart of Young's claim is served with fried chicken wings in Washington, DC, where along with the jumbo slice, the half-smoke, and Senate Bean Soup, it's arguably one of the capital's signature dishes.

In DC, mumbo sauce is a sweet-and-spicy ketchup-esque condiment (think sweet-and-sour sauce) found at Chinese carryout spots where it's paired with fries, wings, and, increasingly, as that city gentrifies, fancier fare at high-end restaurants nodding to the city's culinary traditions. But in an article for the *Washington City Paper*, Sarah Godfrey traced mumbo sauce's origins from Chinese-owned carryouts to African-American–owned wing shops.

In fact, as Godfrey writes, wings and mumbo sauce can be traced back to a restaurant on 7th and Florida Avenue in Northwest DC near Howard University, a restaurant thought to be Chinese-owned and run by African-Americans from 1962 through 1978. And its name, "Wings 'N Things," complicates any feelings of empathy for John Young's idea being co-opted considering "Wings and Things" is what he ended up calling his *own* place four years after the DC restaurant that seems to have inspired him opened.

Did he know that was the name of the spot?

Is that the place the boxer Sam Anderson was talking about when he told Young about the restaurant in DC that was doing gangbuster wing business? Did Young ever visit it? Did he taste that mumbo sauce?

All this is unclear. But if you keep sailing down this saucy thread, you end up nearly 700 miles northwest of DC in Chicago. That's where, in 1950, Argia B. Collins Sr., an African-American from Indianola, Mississippi, invented Mumbo Sauce at his restaurant Argia B's. A 1971 article in the *Chicago Tribune* quotes Collins as saying customers would come in to buy barbecue and would ask about buying the sauce for their own personal use. By 1957 Collins had a plan, loan, patent name, and label design to market his sauce. It would take six years to persevere in the face of what seems likely to have been a racially motivated game of "seasonal football" played by various stores against an African-American entrepreneur. Collins would be told by their buyers that he had to wait until next season "because by the time the buyers had their meetings and completed all the red tape procedures, they said it was too late" for his "seasonal product."

But by 1971, a determined Collins boasted the largest percentage of the barbecue sauce market in Chicago. His original store is long gone, but his sauce is still sold on Amazon and bottled with guidance from its creator's daughter, Allison Collins. (The ingredients include tomato paste, vinegar, spices, garlic powder, onion powder, paprika, hickory smoke flavor, and lemon juice.) But lest we digress, an article by Meathead Goldwyn (yes, Meathead) in the *Huffington Post* quotes Collins as saying that in addition to ribs, her father sold hot links, fish, shrimp, fries, and yes, *fried chicken*, all of it drenched in Mumbo Sauce, which was prominently advertised on the sign above the restaurant.

In a Word, er, Sentence . . .

So to recap: Unbreaded and halved wings drenched with a butter-based hot sauce were first served at Anchor Bar in Buffalo by Frank and Teressa Bellissimo, an Italian-American couple who paired them with their house blue cheese dressing and celery from an antipasto plate at their Italian restaurant and bar, and who *may* have been inspired to serve their wings after seeing the battered and fried sweet-sauce version served by John Young at his restaurant Wings and Things, where *he* was inspired to serve wings after hearing how well an African-American–run, Chinese-owned restaurant of the same name was doing selling them in Washington, DC, after the sauce made its way to the African-American community there from another one in Chicago.

Whew. That's America for you.

If your head is spinning but your curiosity is piqued about what John Young's original sauce tasted like, you have a few options depending on the level of authenticity you're seeking. None of John Young's restaurants nor the one run by his brother that served the sauce for some time are still open. And Young's mombo sauce recipe is a secret kept by his daughter Lina-Brown Young. However, Buffalo's "Wing King" and founder of the National Buffalo Wing Festival, Drew Cerza,

has tasted the sauce. Ms. Young made him a batch, which he described to Meathead thusly: "It was sweet. More of a sweeter—but a very good—sauce. A little spicy."

So you can beg Ms. Young. You can also visit DC, where that city's version of mumbo sauce has proliferated over the decades since it was first popularized. Or, you can order the sauce that was the likely origin of the success at the DC restaurant that may have ultimately been the inspiration for Mr. Young to begin with. Its ingredients? Foregoing the preservatives, they're: water, tomato paste, distilled vinegar, sugar, salt, soybean oil, corn syrup, spices, garlic powder, onion powder, paprika, natural hickory smoke flavor, and lemon juice.

The coda to bookend *this* history of Buffalo

"My interest in Buffalo wings stemmed from a piece I had done a year before in Baltimore about a woman who was sort of a professional food person. She was hired to scout out what kind of food should be in a development in Baltimore called Harborside. She was sort of a taster really, a professional taster. I'm pretty sure that that's where I first heard about Buffalo chicken wings."

—Calvin Trillin

wings belongs to the Calvin Trillin, whose story is cited pretty much any time someone writes about wings. I reached out to see if he'd heard any of these other theories, if any of it may have been mentioned to him by the original players, if there was anything he hadn't written about them that he remembered, and how he ended up in Buffalo in the first place.

Trillin said he'd long ago thrown out the notes he'd taken while researching his piece. He recalled Dominic as very peppy, "the sort of guy who you expect to greet you at the restaurant with a big smile." Memories of his Buffalo reporting were understandably a little fuzzy all these years later. He was certain though that neither the Bellissimos nor John Young mentioned visiting each other's kitchens, that Young didn't mention the boxer Sam Anderson, and understandably, he wasn't sure how he'd met Young in the first place, or if he'd tasted Young's wings. (Janice Okun told me Trillin asked her about Young, but she hadn't been his source.)

While that trip to Buffalo wasn't his last, he noted that besides eating some at a few Buffalonian-run spots in Florida, his original trip to the Nickel City pretty much marked the end of his wing-eating days. "That was it really. It was sort of like poutine, I ate a lot of poutine when I did a piece on it for the *New Yorker*. It's a similar sort of situation with poutine in Quebec."

In Buffalo, while talking with several people, there was a quote attributed to him that basically asserts that *the best wings and pizza were the ones closest to your house.*

"I don't think I ever said that," Trillin told me. "I'm not sure I've ever written this down, but a friend of mine in Louisiana had a theory about crawfish and boudin. A friend who lives in a Cajun part of Louisiana. I can't remember which one was which, but the saying was, 'People always think the best boudin place is the one that's closest to their house, and the best crab shack is the one that's far away.' But it might be the opposite . . ."

Unsurprisingly, Trillin, a humorist, had a wry assessment of his own role in wing history.

"As sort of a joke, I remember talking to somebody once about whether there was anything lasting in journalism, that I always thought if you give somebody a smile on the Madison Avenue bus that would be sort of the goal," he told me. "But somebody once said to me, 'The only thing *you've* actually done is popularize the Buffalo chicken wing.' I thought maybe I should change the subhead of my obituary, that instead of saying, *Monolingual reporter succumbs*, it would say, *Popularized Buffalo chicken wing."*

Why Frank's RedHot? And Are They Buffalo Wings If They Don't Use Frank's?

Which brings us to another mystery: Frank's RedHot Sauce. Along with butter, it's the key ingredient every red-blooded American food obsessive knows is used to make Buffalo sauce. Frank's itself claims that its Original Cayenne Pepper Sauce "was the secret ingredient in the first ever Buffalo Wings recipe." But how did that happen? And is it now?

Let's put aside the proliferation of wing flavors outside the spicy red ones that made the appetizer famous. First, what's up with Frank's RedHot Sauce? Where did that come from anyway? Jacob Frank founded the Frank Tea and Spice Company in 1896 near the banks of the Ohio River in Cincinnati, Ohio. In 1918, Frank partnered with pepper farmer Adam Estilette in New Iberia, Louisiana, to create a cayenne pepper-spiced sauce. The first bottle of Frank's RedHot Sauce emerged from Estilette's pickling plant in 1920.

The ingredients in Frank's original sauce are simple and few: aged cayenne red peppers, distilled vinegar, water, salt, and garlic powder. While it wasn't known as well nationally in the nascent '80s when Calvin Trillin and *New York Times* food editor Craig Claiborne visited Buf-

falo, these days, it's as omnipresent in Buffalo's bars and pizza joints as ketchup is across the country.

Trillin didn't note the brand of hot sauce in his article, and despite Claiborne's pleas, the Bellissimo's son Dominic wouldn't divulge details of the recipe to *him* either. But according to George Schaeffer, Buffalo historian and former Western New York district manager for Durkee Foods (Frank's RedHot was sold to Durkee Famous Foods in 1977), all anybody interested in replicating Anchor Bar's wings had to do was read the *Buffalo Courier-Express*.

At Anchor Bar, Schaeffer tells me he met and befriended the Bellissimo family in the summer of 1978 and would listen to Dominic tell stories about growing the business through franchising. "The 'Little Rooster' had visions of becoming the Colonel Sanders of the wing business," Schaeffer said. "At this time, their business was flat, as major construction on Main Street was keeping customers away. I suggested he tell the story of the 'secret sauce.'"

Dominic's response according to George? "Damned if I do, damned if I don't."

The story Schaeffer recounted to the *Buffalo*

Courier-Express tastes a bit of divine providence and reverse eponymity. "When Teressa concocted the recipe, she had gone to a supermarket and picked up a bottle of Frank's RedHot Sauce. There probably were a couple of other brands of hot sauce, but she chose Frank's. Why not? It was her husband's name!"

According to George, the 'secret sauce' was the worst kept secret in the area. "Many bars and restaurants thought that Frank Bellissimo invented the sauce," he said. "Places would not put wings on their menu so as not to support Frank Bellissimo and his secret sauce."

Maybe so, but the trend had caught on enough at that point that according to Durkee's figures at the time, more hot sauce was being sold to restaurants and foodservice in Western New York due to the popularity of Buffalo wings than in the rest of the country. Hot sauce sales had quadrupled from just 1972 to 1977.

The *Buffalo Courier-Express* shut down in 1982, but by then, the secret was known as far away as Manhattan, where Craig Claiborne eventually published a recipe in the *New York Times* that named Frank's as the secret ingredient, with the assurance of Janice Okun, who had spent weeks experimenting with her own attempt to replicate the original.

Funnily enough, these days neither Duff's nor Anchor use Frank's RedHot. "We started with Frank's," Duff's co-owner Jeff Feather explained, "but for about 15 to 20 years now we have a sauce produced with our recipe."

And Anchor bottles and distributes its own dump-and-toss sauce made with margarine (instead of the butter mentioned in the origin story), cayenne pepper concentrate, water, vinegar, salt and garlic. Bottles of Frank's RedHot's own dump-and-serve wing sauce (the one they sell) add paprika to the cayenne, vinegar, salt, and garlic powder mix, opting for canola oil and natural butter flavor to echo the original recipe.

So if authenticity is what you're seeking, technically you'll want to get a bottle of Frank's straight-up original hot sauce and make some wings yourself. Frank's recommends using two parts melted butter to three parts Frank's.

What *Is* Buffalo Flavor?

When it comes to Buffalo-izing America's favorite foods, there really are few limitations. When you think about it, you quickly realize that Buffalo flavor is something the folks who come up with fast food menus and snack food flavors have gotten increasingly savvy about. After taking over chicken and bar menus, and finding its way onto tables at international chains like TGI Fridays, McDonald's, and Pizza Hut, this classic flavor has become ubiquitous and gone way beyond wings, Buffalo-izing a dizzying number of other commercially successful products. There are Buffalo potato chips, Buffalo chicken nuggets, Buffalo and blue cheese cheese curls, pretzels, popcorn, cheese (cheddar, Monterey, curds), Doritos, dips, and sauces. There's even Buffalo wing soda!

Most products come in packaging picturing wings, blue cheese, and even celery, even when they're just chips or dips. Which begs the question: What *is* Buffalo flavor anyway?

True Buffalo flavor tastes like Paula's doughnuts. It tastes like fried bologna at The Pink at two in the morning. It tastes like chargrilled hot dogs at Ted's and beef on weck at Schwabl's, like stuffed Hungarian peppers at The Place and a Tom & Jerry at McPartlan's Corner. But when it comes to foods you'll find in national chains and grocery stores, Buffalo flavor usually means garlic and onion powder, dried cayenne pepper sauce powder, and *sometimes* chicken powder, paprika, and vinegar powder. Doritos' Blazin' Buffalo & Ranch features Swiss and cheddar cheeses and tomato powder, as well as sour cream powder and cream powder, presumably to impart that Ranch flavor. Sigh, ranch? Where's the blue cheese? As for the soda, well, with an ingredient list that includes carbonated water, sugar, citric acid, sodium benzoate, ester gum, natural flavor, yellow 6, caramel color, and red 40, who knows!

Buffalo wing lovers know the truth: Buffalo wing flavor means creamy, buttery tang and heat.

Medium IS HOT! Medium Hot IS VERY HOT! Hot IS VERY VERY HOT!

Carolina Reapers, Trinidad Moruga Scorpions, Naga Vipers, and perhaps most famous, the Bhut Jolokia (aka the Ghost Pepper): these are some of the super hot peppers that have fascinated the world over the past decade. And thanks to shows like the Travel Channel's *Man v. Food* and the Food Network's *Heat Seekers,* we know these peppers' Scoville units (the measurement used to convey the level of a pepper's heat) have been applied to many a food challenge across America.

But who started the fire-in-your mouth grada-tions of Buffalo wings? It's likely that the different levels of heat originated at Duff's, something they weren't shy about claiming. "We're the ones who developed the degrees of hotness," Jeff Feather told me. "Now, I think people have caught up with us in terms of the heat levels."

According to Feather, Duff's famous "Medium Is Hot" signs started because their wings were known to be much hotter than anyone else's. Louise Duffney founded Duff's as a gin mill in 1946, but they didn't start serving wings there until 1969, when according to Feather a place nearby that Louise's son Ron used to visit for their wings, closed. The owner prompted him to make his own and the rest as they say, is wingstory.

"Ron was big with signs and rules," explained Mr. Feather. "He had all kinds of rules, like 'Our tables are for meals only. French fries aren't meals.' And he would just write them down and put them up on the walls. But with the 'Medium IS HOT!' 'Medium Hot IS VERY HOT!' 'Hot IS VERY VERY HOT!' signs it got to be a bit ridiculous to have them all handwritten. So we eventually had the signs made up."

Duff's features eight different heat levels and a spicy version of their BBQ wings. But does that mean you have to eat the heat to be a *real* wing nut? If you believe comments like this one written on an article about the history of the Buffalo wing published by the Smithsonian—"A true Buffalonian would never eat a mild or medium wing"—you might be inclined to believe so. But signs aside, in talking with Buffalo natives, writers, and waitstaff, I didn't find that to be the case.

"That's not our experience," agreed Clark Crook, owner of The Bar Bill Tavern. "But there are people, certainly probably in all towns, that really like hot food. And really appreciate our hot, because it's flavorful."

Wing King Drew Cerza was of the same school of thought. "You know, the hot wings, not so much in Buffalo, the heat thing," told me. "You don't hear about that too much around here."

During the month I spent eating Buffalo wings all over the city over the course of two trips, the heat level I was most frequently advised by waitstaff to order for a representative example of their wings was medium. And lest you think

waiters were concerned about a customer who couldn't take the heat, medium was the same answer given when asked what the most popular heat level was.

Take a look at the wing options at just a sampling of Buffalo's most well-known and beloved wing spots and tell me what you notice:

ANCHOR
Mild, Medium, Hot, Spic y Hot BBQ, Suicidal

BAR BILL TAVERN
Mild, Medium, Medium Hot, Hot, Extra Hot, Suicidal, Sicilian, Honey Dijon, Zesty Honey Pepper, Teriyaki, Cajun (Medium and Hot), Honey Butter BBQ, Hot & Spicy BBQ, Spicy Asian

BOCCE
Buffalo-Style, Hot, Medium, Mild; Over-the-Pit Grilled Wings, BBQ, Honey Mustard or Cajun

DOC SULLIVAN'S
Smitty Style, Hot, Medium, Mild, BBQ or Southie Gold BBQ

DUFF'S
Mild, Mild Medium, Medium Light, Medium (IS HOT), Medium Hot (IS VERY HOT), Hot (IS VERY, VERY HOT), Suicidal Sauce, Death Sauce, BBQ, Spicy BBQ

DWYER'S IRISH PUB
Dwyer's (Mild or Medium); Buffalo (Mild or Medium); Hot or Extra Hot; Raspberry BBQ, Honey BBQ, Hot BBQ, BBQ, Strawberry BBQ, Jameson BBQ, Suicide BBQ, Creole, Garlic Parmesan,

Suicide, Honey Garlic, Hot Honey, Honey Mustard, Spicy Sesame, Zesty Orange, Zesty Garlic, General Tso, Teriyaki, Bourbon, Italian, Sweet Chili, Chili Lime, Caribbean Jerk, Wasabi Plum, Cajun (Hot, Medium, Mild)

ELMO'S
Hot, Medium, Mild, Cajun, BBQ, Honey Mustard (Single, Double, Triple-Play Wings)

GABRIEL'S GATE
Cajun, BBQ, Suicide, Sriracha, Italian

GENE MCCARTHY'S
Mild, Medium, Hot, BBQ or Tangy BBQ, McCarthy's (Sweet & Spicy BBQ with Crumbled Bleu), Thai Chili and Garlic, Honey Mustard, Sheffield (Dry Rub with Cajun, Oregano and Other Spices)

KELLY'S KORNER
Mild, Medium, Hot, BBQ, Garlic

LA NOVA
Mild, Medium, Hot, Inferno, BBQ "from the PIT," Italian Style, Hot BBQ, Honey Mustard, Roasted Garlic BBQ, Honey Dipped (Hot, Medium,

Mild), Honey Sesame, Sweet Chili, Teriyaki, Ghost Chili, Hot 'N Spicy, Golden BBQ, Kickin' Bourbon Molasses, Kickin' Honey Garlic, Sweet 'N Spicy

LENOX GRILL
Mild, Medium, Hot, Suicidal, Barbecue or Korean BBQ, Honey Sriracha, Pineapple Jerk

THE NINE-ELEVEN TAVERN
Mild, Medium, Hot

Sure, without exception, everyone serves mild, medium, and hot. And most do serve an extra hot or suicidal option for yahoos, tourists, and folks who need a challenge after they've had a few too many. But forget heat for a second as representative of how a true Buffalonian orders their wings and consider the flavor options. You think you're a wing aficionado? Aside from a few outliers, most places offer incredible variation of *flavor*. There's a spectrum that ranges from the traditional Frank's base to "Italian" (typically a garlic-Parmesan mix) or sweet-and-spicy flavors that include things like raspberry, lime, Jameson's, Sriracha, General Tso's, teriyaki, Cajun, wasabi, and honey mustard.

Wingspan: The Size and Cost of Wings

So many places do wings today, you wonder if that hurts the bottom line of places that are primarily wing-oriented. "Look, wings were such a good profit business that people added them to boost their profits," Duff's co-owner Jeff Feather told me. "Now, I think they'd rather get rid of their wings because the cost is so high."

They can't. Buffalo would revolt. It's even hard for restaurants to raise the price on an order even when wings costs climb up to $2.60 a pound. The same way that New Yorkers obsess over the cost of a slice, Jane and Joe Buffalo have an idea of how much an order should cost. The days of turning a discarded item into a profit are gone. There may not be futures contracts like there are for hogs and cattle, but wings *are* a commodity. Wing tips, which even Teressa Bellissimo threw away, are a business. Chicken producers decide whether it's more profitable to export them to Asia where they're deep-fried and eaten as snacks, or to put them back into rendering. That can change, on a weekly basis, depending on demand.

In the business, buyers commonly refer to wing count by the pound (four to six pieces per pound, six to nine pieces per pound, etc.), but generally, wings come in four sizes:

SMALL	LARGE
from a bird 4.25 lbs and under	from a bird 6.26 lbs to 7.75 lbs
MEDIUM	**JUMBO**
from a bird 4.26 lbs to 6.25 lbs	from a jumbo bird 7.76 lbs and up

Chickens have gotten increasingly heavy as geneticists have engineered bigger birds for bigger breasts. According to the National Chicken Council, in the 1920s, the average chicken weighed 2½ pounds. Today, they weigh an average of 6 pounds! Currently, the geneticists are up against a toughening phenomenon called woody breast that has

stalled growth. But who *knows* how long these weight ranges will hold.

Calling wings "small," "medium," "large," and "jumbo" is not necessarily official. "What was considered 'jumbo' 5 to 10 years ago isn't necessarily jumbo today," explains Terence Wells, a poultry market reporter for business publisher Urner Barry. "Size matters, and everyone has a different opinion of size. Some restaurants might like a bigger wing (four to six pieces per pound or six to nine pieces per pound), some might want a smaller wing (9 to 11 or 11 to 13), and some might just go for whatever is cheaper."

What size do Buffalonians serve? Restaurant and bar owners usually have an idea in their head of what their perfect wing looks like size-wise. But they don't always get what they ask suppliers for. Some run with what they get, adding extras to orders if they're running small. It's something the waitstaff will tell customers when they order. That's how closely Buffalonians watch their wings.

"We buy jumbo wings," Bar Bill Tavern's owner Clark Crook told me. "But every day, we're sorting and eliminating wings that don't meet our size criteria or may be janky in some way. They could have bones sticking out or tips hanging on them. But you'll notice when your wings are delivered, they're fanned out, five drums and five flats. Presentation's important. If there's a janky wing, it's going to make our presentation look bad. Suppliers presort, and they'll give you a size count for their sorting, so we will order what would be the smallest count, which is supposed to be the largest wing, and we're still rejecting 15 percent."

Here you thought it was as simple as throwing

wings in the fryer and tossing them in Frank's and butter, huh? Still, the glass of Genesee *can* be half full. Size fluctuation has led to innovation.

"Our chicken wing pizza is made with real Bar-Bill chicken wings," Clark explains. "We cook chicken wings and then we rip the meat off and put *that* on the pizza."

Why do wings vary in size even when restaurants and bars request a specific size? Why have prices been up well over $2 per pound? I turned to Bill Roenigk, the ex-senior vice president and chief economist for the National Chicken Council, a national, non-profit trade association and the answer was straightforward: demand!

"You need more chickens to have more wings," Roenigk explained. "Unless you're locked into a contract paying a specific price, the supplier is going to send you the best that they have."

Another result of price fluctuation is the proliferation of "boneless wings." "Good for children and old people missing teeth," professional eater Crazy Legs Conti told me. "That's about it. Mostly, I think of them as Frankenstein food."

Crazy Legs may have a point. According to Bill, boneless wings are really just pieces of chicken breast flavored to taste like a bone-on wing. "When it comes to wings, consumers want the bone and skin on," Bill said. "The rest of us who want to save some money, it's straight down to the boneless skinless."

Freezing Wings: Fresh vs. Frozen

It was heartening to hear the fresh-versus-frozen refrain as a constant from Buffalo's most storied wingmakers. But you wonder: *is* there a difference between fresh and frozen wings when it comes to flavor and texture? The consensus is that you should avoid your grocer's freezer. Frozen chicken, including the skin, can retain moisture, which translates to soggy wings with rubbery skin.

"The consumer doesn't know whether it's fresh or frozen," Bill Roenigk told me. "Take them to someone who is a skilled taster and say, 'Which was frozen, which was not?' In many cases, not all cases, that educated taster, can say, 'This one was fresh and that one is frozen.' If you take the same wing and you put your seasonings, your spices, you do whatever you do to it, and cook it, even the most sophisticated taster will not be able to tell."

Bill's right. I froze some wings for a few months, bought fresh ones, thawed the frozen ones on the same day and fried them all for the same amount of time. Only a third of my taste-testers could tell the difference.

"If you do a slow freeze, what you're essentially doing is damaging the product," Bill explained. "Then the sophisticated or maybe even some regular tasters can notice a flavor difference. Properly frozen and then seasoned, marinated, whatever, I've never seen any science to say that anybody can tell the difference. Frozen wings may be slightly dryer."

The good news? As Bill explains, "Most people are getting fresh wings because it *costs* money to freeze wings. In today's market, where the price is over $2, there's little incentive to freeze a wing because you're going to put it in storage and hope for what? That's the market's going to go $2.20, instead of $2.10? It's like when you buy stock: you'll never lose money by taking a profit."

There are restaurateurs who swear by integrating freezing, and refrigerated air-drying into their process. On *Serious Eats*'s "The Food Lab," J. Kenji López-Alt quotes New York and San Francisco Mission Chinese chef Danny Bowien as saying that he fries his wings twice: "Once the day before, after which they'd go straight into the freezer, and the second time the next day (or whenever he needed to), straight from the freezer into the fryer."

And I've heard unverified stories that Anchor Bar used to hang wings in their walk-in above buckets to wick away the moisture so they'd be extra crispy.

The truth is, if it's not part of their normal procedure, there's little reason for folks to freeze wings. And most restaurants that serve wings who freeze them are pretty skilled at it. Where some get in trouble is, because they don't have the space, they'll cook their wings to a point and then pull them out of the cooking process, sometimes cooling or freezing them. Then when demand hits, they'll finish cooking them. Depending on how well they've done it, that *can* result in an off flavor.

Drums vs. Paddles:
Which Has More Meat? Which Has More Flavor?

Some people swear by flats, others by bats. But what's the science behind the flavor of unsauced wings?

According to competitive eater Crazy Legs Conti, if you're looking for the part of the wing that has the most meat, the answer may not be what you think. Curious himself, he once tested a hundred wings to discover the meat-to-bone ratio of paddles and drums.

"I replicated eating by stripping the meat off with my hands, but knowing what a wing looks like when you've stripped it with your mouth," he said. "Then I weighed the meat in batches of 20 five times to figure out the ratio of meat to bone. People think drumsticks have more meat, but I discovered it was .49 meat-to-bone on the drumstick and .66 on the paddle."

Pure amounts of meat aside, if you consider that much of the flavor we love comes from fat, you're going to look to the part of the wing that has the most of that.

"The drum head or the first joint has considerably more meat and skin and fat than the mid-joint," Bill Roenigk weighed in. "What they call the first joint, or the mid-joint and the first joint closest to the cavity of the body, tends to have the most muscle and the most fat. With that combination of mean and fat, that tends to be where people, if they're going to choose a part of the wing, that's the part that they like and they seem to gravitate towards."

Donnie Burtless, who in 2009 launched the influential Nickel City food blog *Buffalo Eats* (buffaloeats.org) with his now-wife Alli Suriani, noted that regardless of which part of the wing has more meat, there is definitely a big divide of people in Western New York who are either bat or flat people, adding that the difference is part of the glue that holds the fabric of the community, or at least relationships, together. "I honestly feel like relationships are strengthened because partners have an agreement that one will eat the drum and the other will eat the flat," he told me. "That's how me and my wife Alli work at least."

I Can't Believe It's Not Butter: "Butter Taste . . . and Better"

Let me put on my late-night infomercial ShamWow voice for a second and ask: *What if you could spend just 43¢ per serving on butter instead of $1.99 and make another $1.56 per order? What if it also meant skipping the step of melting the butter? What if I told you I had a pourable product that tastes like butter, requires less work, no refrigeration, works well when cooking with high heat and costs less? You can use it in sauces, roux, and marinades. You can grill with it, sauté with it and pan fry too! Would you make that substitution?*

The keys to great wings are Frank's and butter, right? When it comes to Frank's, as we know, the answer is historically correct and contemporarily true *sometimes*. When it comes to wings, here's the dirty secret. Butter is expensive. And while it may not sound like much, the difference of a dollar or even a few cents per order for a wing-centric business can be the distance between "remember that place" and becoming a neighborhood fixture.

That's why many bars and restaurants swap out butter, use butter-flavored *oil* and pocket the difference. There are several different brands, but the one that came up time and again was Whirl (credit the tip to Christa Glennie Seychew and chef Edward Forster).

If you scour the Internet, you'll find culinary insiders like the imposingly named user Formaldehyd3 on Reddit who back up the claims with testimonials like these: "I live two hours south of Buffalo and am actually known as the best 'wing girl' in my county. Honestly, this shit is what we in Erie and Chautauqua County use, mixed with Frank's. Yes butter is better, but that is why you're running into the not sticking problem. The Whirl is a thick butter substitute and when mixed, one part Whirl to three parts Frank's RedHot, will give you medium sauce. One to one gives you mild, and one to five yields hot sauce. If you disagree, please tell me why."

The company, Stratas Foods, which manufactures the oil in plants in Georgia, California, Texas, and Illinois, knows its customers. The advertising copy on their website (emphasis mine): "Whirl butter flavored oil adds delicious butter flavor to everything you make, without the hassles of butter or margarine. Whirl's authentic butter flavor makes it great for brushing on pizza crusts and breadsticks *and as a replacement for butter or margarine in wing sauces. Best of all, Whirl is up to half the cost of butter!*"

We'll get to what these butter-flavored oils actually are in a second. Let's do some quick cocktail napkin math first. At the risk of sounding like a Buffalo wing SAT question (wouldn't formal testing be so much more interesting though?), a gallon of Whirl (256 tablespoons) costs $39.99. You can buy four sticks of Land O'Lakes for $6.38 at Walmart. Which means every tablespoon of Whirl costs 16¢, 4¢ less than a stick of butter. The number of wings per order varies depending on where you get them, but let's say a single order of Buffalo wings comes with 10 wings. If we agree that you need about a tablespoon of butter or Whirl to appropriately cover a wing, that means that for each order of wings, substituting Whirl can save a restaurant 40¢. Wing prices vary due to several factors, but let's

say that it costs $2 per pound at 8 to 11 wings per pound and that you're charging $9.75 for an order. Without accounting for the cost of oil filling the fryers—some places replace it daily, others every few days—the labor to *make* wings, pay rent, electricity, and the other lovely expenses restaurant owners have, they're already out about $3.99 per order.

"You gotta watch your expenditures," Lovejoy co-owner Anthony Kulik explained to me. "To use real butter completely—I'd love to but I can't. But I use a combo of real butter with the liquid butter, and it gives me a great finish. I'm proud, and I can live with it. Believe me, in a perfect world, I'd use 100 percent real butter with all the ingredients. But it's just not cost effective."

What *is* this stuff? It's an opaque, bright yellow, tiny bubble-filled liquid with the consistency of a Caesar dressing and it smells just like movie theater popcorn. The oil features a label with small print that cites soybean oil, hydrogenated soybean oil and notes that it contains 2 percent or less of salt, soy lecithin, artificial and natural flavor, beta carotene (color), hydrolyzed soy protein, and autolyzed yeast extract.

"Hydrogenated oils in any amount are a big no-no, as they contain harmful trans fats, which contribute to inflammation in the body and increase your risk for heart disease. Even though the nutrition facts label says '0' for trans fat, there can still be less than half a gram of it in one serving of the product. We know that because we can see 'hydrogenated oil' on the ingredients list. Butter contains a bit of trans fat, too, but it's natural trans fat and is not harmful. The hydrogenated trans fats are synthetic. It also contains artificial flavors and hydrolyzed soy protein. Yuck! Autolyzed yeast extract contains glutamates, or MSG (monosodium glutamate) and many people are sensitive to it. The organic grass-fed butter is still the best choice, with regular butter coming in second. Compare this ingredient list to the ingredient list for organic butter, which is simply 'butter.'"   —Beth Reinke

Predictably, the nutritionists and dieticians I contacted weren't thrilled about Whirl. Beth Reinke, a registered dietitian, didn't trash it, but she was clearly in butter's corner.

Okay, but how does it taste? And can you really tell the difference? I ordered Whirl to find out. A first experiment went poorly. You can't use it the same way as butter, warming it on low heat over the stove then adding Frank's. The result is a thin "sauce" that wouldn't emulsify and runs off the wings. No seasoning or flavor adheres. A recipe buried on Stratas' website reveals you need to take a different tack, one that at first, feels a little Frankenfood-ish and odd in that it requires *no* heat at all, but does require a half hour of waiting.

The result is thicker sauce that's much more difficult to tell visually, and flavor-wise, apart from the original butter-sauce mix. When I conducted a taste-test of butter versus Whirl, everyone preferred the wings prepared in the butter-based sauce. Interestingly, only one out of

three folks could tell which was which. The ones who *were* able to noted that the Whirl sauce had a distinct sheen that made it resemble and taste more like supermarket salad dressing. More fat seemed to be on the surface of the wings made with butter. The granulated garlic the recipe calls for also acted as a thickener, giving the sauce a grainier texture. So if you are planning on using Whirl and you're not into graininess, keep that in mind.

I asked Christa Glennie Seychew, who has judged more wing competitions than she'd care to remember, for advice for anyone interested in the telltale signs it's been used:

If you're already eating wings, you're probably giving yourself the night off from counting calories (if you care about that). But in the spirit of the more you know, each tablespoon of Whirl carries with it an additional 18 calories. That means an additional 180 calories over an order of wings whose sauce was made with butter. Considering that according to the calorie counter

"If you're a butter lover, you'll likely notice upon first bite. There's just no substitute for the real thing. But kitchens using all manner of butter-flavored substitutes, including Whirl, are taking a shortcut I can't get behind. Google 'diacetyl' if you need more reason to care than just flavor. Anyway, I've found servers are usually fine with asking the kitchen on my behalf, and I've never gotten what I think is a false answer, so I think asking is a good move. Otherwise, I'd say sauce that is anything but glossy and translucent is a dead giveaway; the sauce on wings should never be opaque or cloudy. This isn't foolproof, since food scientists are improving fake food all the time, but if it's cloudy, drop the wing and run."

—Christa Glennie Seychew

and diet tracker Fat Secret, a small fried skin-on chicken wing totals 81 calories, that's the caloric equivalent of eating two more wings without real butter. I'd rather eat an extra wing!

It's an estimate based on talking with bar owners and restaurateurs, but it's a safe bet that at least half of the joints you visit anywhere don't use real butter. And that's conservative.

Buffalo Mother Sauces: Blue Cheese Dressing

So here's something that may (or may not) surprise you about the blue cheese dressing you get with your wings in Buffalo: it's not likely to be homemade. Many places even serve wings with a small, foil-sealed container of blue cheese dressing. And even if it's not coming from an individually packaged, commercially branded container, you may just as likely be getting brand stuff portioned out from larger containers from Sysco. Many places in Buffalo, probably 85 percent or higher, don't make their own. And you can argue that there's nothing wrong with that. "You're already eating something that's not

exactly healthy," the argument goes, "what's a little soybean oil and corn syrup?"

There's a time and a place for store-bought

stuff. Some restaurateurs even claim that folks complain if wings arrive with anything but a container of "Buffalo Bleu Cheese" with its iconic blue-rim and signature Ken's Steak House logo. And that's unequivocally better than dipping your wings in ranch dressing (what kind of animal are you!?). Christa Glennie Seychew put it bluntly: "Sysco blue cheese sauce NO. Ken's is acceptable."

There are two keys to blue cheese dressing being great. First, you don't want a dressing that's too thin (or too thick) or you won't get proper adherence of creamy, soothing dressing to crispy wing that's already drenched in hot

sauce. Second, ideally, the dressing will have blue cheese nuggets throughout. A thin dressing without any blue cheese niblets? That's a sin.

Kind of Bleu . . .

Who invented blue cheese dressing? What's *in* it? And which spelling is correct, blue or bleu?

Whoa, slow down. If you think Buffalo wings' origins as recent as the '60s are murky?! We don't have enough pages to go down the blue-cheese-dressing rabbit hole, but we know there was a recipe for it in *The Boston Cooking-School Cook Book* from 1896 that today's cooks would recognize (mayo, vinaigrette, Roquefort, and Worcestershire sauce). That recipe was accompanied in the same book by another one that was near identical to a recipe in the self-published version of Irma Rombauer's *Joy of Cooking* in 1931. It's thought that blue cheese

dressing became a recipe standard in the late '20s.

If preservatives aren't being added when blue cheese dressing is made in a factory, the recipe is usually a mixture of blue cheese, mayonnaise, and a combo of some or all of the following: sour cream, buttermilk, milk, yogurt, half and half, Worcestershire sauce, lemon juice vinegar, onion powder, and garlic powder.

As for *blue* or *bleu*, Patricia T. O'Conner and Stewart Kellerman have written five books about the English language and have more than 50 years of experience as writers and editors at newspapers. They claim "blue cheese" showed up in English 150 years before the Frenchified "bleu," and that "blue cheese" may have appeared in *English* before "fromage bleu" did in French! "Blue cheese" first appeared in the *Oxford English Dictionary* in 1787. "Bleu cheese" first turned up in the 1940s and "fromage bleu" in 1821. They add that besides Roquefort (French), the two best-known blue cheeses are Gorgonzola (Italian) and Stilton (English). Why would you call either of those cheeses by the French "bleu"?

The rising prices of wings (a scrap turned commodity) mean that margins can be tough. So you can pity folks for buying batches of something they'll spend money on twice: once for ingredients and once for the time to blend them. But how long does it take? And there are at least three benefits of bars making their own dressing besides the fact that you're more likely to be eating buttermilk, mayonnaise, and sour cream instead of soybean oil and corn syrup (if food service companies labeled it "Soybean Oil and Corn Syrup Dressing," would folks who love the brand stuff really love eating it?).

First, the prepackaged stuff is usually sweeter. You're looking for blue cheese dressing not blue cheese dessert topping, right? Second, you usually get more and bigger crumbles, which adds complexity and delicious cheesy funk to each dressing-dipped bite of hot, crispy wing. Third, it shows the place cares. I'll opt for a homemade dressing every time. There were a handful of places (count Doc Sullivan's among them) who told me they were proud to say they made their own blue cheese dressing. The Nine-Eleven Tavern, one of my favorites, makes theirs with huge blue cheese crumbles. It's a beautiful thing.

What's a Boston Steakhouse Got To Do With Wings from Western New York?

The irony about Ken's Bleu Cheese Dressing is a footnote about its history.

Ken's Food Service is a food company launched in 1958 by Frank and Louise Crowley. According to their website, the company was started in their kitchen to bottle a version of the house dressing served in Ken and Florence Hanna's Framingham, Massachusetts restaurant, Ken's Steak House.

A photoshopped image of New England Patriot quarterback Tom Brady at Mooney's.

Consider this: in an era where the Patriots top the AFC East and the Bills typically anchor it and in a part of America with a long Yankees–Red Sox rivalry, the Hannas shouldn't have dreamed of sending their dressing from Massachusetts to a city in New York state that invented the greatest bar food to eat while watching sports. But they did it, and folks now regularly dip their iconic food in a dressing invented 45 minutes west of *Boston*! Go figure.

From what I can tell, there *was* once an original Buffalo blue cheese dressing made by Pfeiffer Salad Dressings, which originated in a restaurant called the Marine Grille where Samuel Pfeiffer developed a dressing for his popular chef salad. At least one Buffalo bar won't serve anything else with wings.

"Let me tell you, if I run short, on Pfeiffer's Blue Cheese Dressing, and I switch to a different brand, the customers complain," Mammoser's owner Peter Dimfle told me. "It's a little bit more expensive blue cheese, but it is a better quality blue cheese."

Not every wing connoisseur buys into blue cheese dressing as essential.

"You know how I like my blue cheese to look?" Wing King Drew Cerza asks me at Elmo's, one of his favorite spots, pointing at an untouched container of dressing. "Like that. It's a rookie move to dip."

But after taking a sip of beer one night at Founding Fathers, Donnie Burtless, co-founder of local food blog *Buffalo Eats* smiles and confides, "I think that's just a Drew thing."

Extra Crispy and Easy on the Sauce, Please!

Decades of wing culture mean that Buffalonians order their wings with a degree of sophistication that rivals the way many Americans order steak. Wing snobs might note that the same way steak-lovers would say the right way to eat steak is medium-rare, crispy, medium and not too saucy is the way proper wings should be served. (Anchor's wings are often criticized for being overly sauced and runny.) And people are so picky about their wings and so devoted to their favorite places that many people are actually in the practice of making

two stops, one for wings and one for pizza, even though the two things are sold together at almost every pizzeria in Buffalo.

Even though many places have a wing-pizza deal, wing-lovers' preferences frequently lead them on multi-stop trips home with takeout. "You buy 20 wings, you get a large pizza," explains owner Peter Dimfle of the bar Mammoser's on Buffalo's outskirts. "Maybe that customer will just go with the wings that they have there, but I have to say, I have a lot of customers that come in specifically for wings, who are picking up food at other restaurants or other pizzerias. They're still coming in to get Mammoser's wings."

This was something I heard from many of the city's wing enthusiasts and the city's foremost pizza expert, an anonymous slice blogger who goes by the name SexySlices.

The choices are just so endless that it's easy to see why people make more than one stop based on their preferences. Do you want traditional wings (hot sauce-based) or pit-roasted? The menu at Bar Bill Tavern advises you to "Please specify if you want extra saucy." Elmo's allows you to "Double Dip" your wings and mix two different sauces (think Cajun BBQ or Hot Cajun wings). And Lenox Grill warns that "It takes approximately 20 minutes to cook wings," or nearly the same amount of time it takes to make a French soufflé and in a not dissimilar way that the waiters at fancy restaurants that serve those delicate desserts would mention at the beginning of your meal that if you'd like one, you should order it *then*, thank you very much!

"I have two daughters and they were, I don't know, six and eight, right? I came downstairs in the morning and they're both sitting on the couch. And they go, 'Dad, you talk in your sleep.' I'm, like, 'Really? Alright, I'll bite. What do I say?' And both of them in unison went, 'Extra Crispy.' I left it right there. I didn't want to know about anything else."

—Mark Gress, Nine-Eleven Tavern

Can You Get Good Wings in Under 15 Minutes?

The 15-minute lunch guarantee Buffalo Wild Wings announced in 2016 shows how far the chain has strayed from the technique espoused by many of Buffalo's great wing technicians. *"Designed to show time-strapped Guests that they don't have to sacrifice quality, value or variety for speed at lunch time. From the time a Guest orders a meal off the B-Dubs® Fast Break Lunch menu, Buffalo Wild Wings guarantees it will be at their table within 15 minutes, or the meal plus a fountain soda is free."* Why is guest capitalized? (Shudder) "The bad news is we don't plan on taking longer than 15 minutes," one radio ad brags.

If we're going to assume it takes at least two minutes to walk to a POS to enter an order and at least two minutes to pick them up from the pass and bring them to your table, that means your wings are being cooked, and I'm being generous here, in 11 minutes. There's no way they're going to be done well and crispy in a restaurant with busy fryers unless they've been par-cooked, which probably means you're eating wings that have been sitting around.

Interview with Duff's Owner Jeff Feather

At last count, there were 11 Duff's locations: five in the immediate Buffalo area, one in Rochester, three in Toronto, one in Texas, and one in Georgia. To wing lovers these days, Duff's is just as synonymous with wings as Anchor. But that wasn't always the case. Jeff Feather, who co-owns Duff's with founder Louise Duffney's son, Ron, said the turning point came in 1982 when then–*Buffalo News* restaurant critic Janice Okun gave them a positive review. Suddenly, families started coming and they had to open earlier to accommodate the lunch crowd. Duff's had become a destination.

Over the years, Duff's has become the counterweight to Anchor, the place you hear that locals prefer. There's even the perception of a rivalry between them, an idea that may have

To wing lovers these days, Duff's is just as synonymous with wings as Anchor.

been popularized with the 2010 broadcast of a head-to-head wing-off in the premiere of Travel Channel's *Food Wars*. Duff's, which opened in 1946, started serving wings in 1969, five years after Anchor. I didn't see much evidence of a rivalry and as I've said, you'll meet plenty of people in Buffalo who haven't been to either Anchor *or* Duff's because they think their own *local* place is better. What I *did* find while sitting down with Jeff were other interesting details, namely regarding how Duff's makes their wings, and the possibility that it was them who hotheads have to thank for originating the idea of making wings extra hot.

You'll hear about all of that stuff in the following interview with Jeff in his own words, but before reading on, take *my* word on his recommendation and order Duff's grilled cheese. Gooey with cheese and butter—griddled inside-out, with that salty-sweet crunch on the outside—it's one of the best restaurant renditions of this classic that I've ever had, and their technique has now forever changed how I make them at home.

How did wings get their start at Duff's?

My partner started the business in 1946. His mother, Louise Duffney, and her husband used to have a bar in Niagara Falls. It was a gin mill. It was just originally the dining room. There was a piano and his mother used to play it. Anyway, Frank and Teressa put wings on the menu and then not too long after, a place down the street started doing wings too. Ron used to go there and get the wings because he just loved to eat them. They were closing and the owner said to Ron, why don't you put wings on the menu at your place? So he did.

TV shows and articles often note a rivalry between Duff's and Anchor. Is there one?

The rivalry between Duff's and Anchor is really just the perception of everyone else. There are so many places with wings now that if you had a rivalry with everyone you'd waste your life away.

How'd you get your start at Duff's?

I started in 1981. I was a cook at Denny's and my brother worked at Duff's. They were shorthanded and he asked if I could help. Ron asked me to just stay up at the front and man the hosting station. There wasn't much going on, so I left it to help with this and that and he told me to stop and to get right back to my spot. "I really like how you work," he said. And I said to him, "But I was just sitting there." And he said, "Yeah, but you sat really well."

BUFFALO WINGS IN BUFFALO   49

Is Ron still involved with Duff's?

He's still around. He shows up every day. You'll see him sweeping the parking lot and cleaning the bathrooms.

After all the articles over the years, what do people still not know about Duff's?

The thing people don't know is how good the other food is. The burgers are real good. And we make one of the best grilled cheeses around. It's reverse-griddled and made with a blend of mozzarella and American cheeses. And there's enough variety of other things around.

How has wing culture changed over the years?

When I started, we didn't open until 7 PM. Wings were for before drinking and after drinking. Now, they're for lunch. For anytime. It used to be that the kids were the ones who were eating them, and now it's senior citizens too.

Your wings seem a little crispier than some other places in town. What's your secret?

We tend to do 'em crispy. They're also generally bigger here, though chicken wings change in size from week to week. I personally think the smaller ones are better tasting. We use a soy-based fry oil, which we change every other day. We get two days out of it and then use a whole new batch. We just strictly fry them here, but we're experimenting with some non-traditional ways of making them too. We're experimenting with baking at our location that has a brick oven. We'll see.

How do you make your sauce?

We have a basic sauce and we use margarine to cut it down. A medium wing will have less margarine than a hot wing.

How do you like your wings?

When I eat 'em hot I eat 'em with blue cheese. But I eat 'em cold too and when I eat 'em cold I don't eat 'em with blue cheese. In Texas they use ranch. I don't care what people use as long as they buy the wings!

How do you make your sauce? Do you use Ken's?

We use a Kraft base and we mix it with some other ingredients for a unique flavor. We've worked with Ken's to try to duplicate a sauce for our franchises but haven't come close yet to our satisfaction to what we do in the restaurants. We started with Frank's, but for about 15 to 20 years now we have a sauce produced with our recipe. Consistency and control is important to us.

Does the wing business that pizzerias do hurt your bottom line?

I love the variety of great independent restaurants we have in Buffalo. We have all the chains but we have all these new restaurants that are independently owned. Look, wings were such a good profit business that people added them to boost their profits. Now, I think they'd rather get rid of their wings because the cost is so high. They'd probably rather just do pizza.

Besides your trade secrets, is there something unique about Duff's that sets it apart from other wing joints?

We're probably the only wing place that's closed on Super Bowl Sunday. We probably could stay open now, but decided to keep it this way. When there was only one Duff's, we had too many people who would order them and we couldn't do them justice. People were getting mad at us so we just said, "Let's just close." We do special projects.

If there's one thing you'd like this interview to accomplish what would it be?

Hell, for people to order the grilled cheese.

You Say Flattie, I Say Flat: A Buffalo Wing Vocabulary

Drumette The drumette (aka "bat," "drumstick," "mini-drumstick," the "first section" or "first segment") is the humerus bone (and its meat and skin), the part of the wing that attaches it to the chicken.

BBQ wings BBQ wings have *nothing* remotely to do with the low-and-slow techniques practiced by pitmasters, but instead refer to wings that have been fried, tossed in sweet barbecue sauce and then thrown "on the pit," which here just means the grill, for char marks.

Blue cheese dressing A dipping condiment served with Buffalo wings made using mayonnaise or sour cream mixed with blue cheese and seasoning that sometimes also includes ingredients like Worcestershire sauce, dry mustard, onion powder, cayenne, white pepper, lemon juice, vinegar, garlic, and parsley.

Boneless wings Usually, white meat chicken that is lightly breaded and fried.

Buffalo-style Unbattered or floured wings or drumettes that are fried then tossed in a mixture of butter or margarine and hot sauce, traditionally Frank's RedHot and spices, then served with blue cheese dressing, and often celery and/or carrot spears.

Chiavetta's A watery, vinegar-based barbecue marinade and dipping sauce made with spices and garlic that originated at Chiavetta's, a Buffalo catering company started by poultry farmers Thomas and Eleanor Chiavetta. Chiavetta's bottled sauce can sometimes be found on area menus as at Mister Pizza, as a flavoring given to wings off the pit.

Double dip A saucing technique most well-known at Elmo's in Buffalo, where wings are dipped in one sauce, then another to create a new flavor combination.

Genny Short for Genesee, Genny is an American adjunct lager style—a category of thin malt beers that are low on bitterness and contain a moderate amount of alcohol—made with barley malt, corn grits and hops from the Yakima Valley by the Genesee Brewing Company in Rochester, NY, since 1878.

Genny Cream Ale A light bodied, cold-fermented ale brewed by Genesee that's neither fruity nor hoppy and that is primed for carbonation with wort instead of sugar.

Gurgitator A competitive eater.

Ken's A prepackaged "Bleu Cheese Dressing" manufactured by Ken's Food Service, a food company launched to bottle the house dressing served in Ken and Florence Hanna's Framingham, Massachusetts restaurant Ken's Steak House.

Mambo Sauce A spicy ketchupesque condiment with roots in Buffalo, DC, and Chicago and that is part of the disputed origins of Buffalo wings.

Medium The baseline wing heat level. The most frequently ordered heat level in Buffalo.

"Natural butter flavor" The traditional Buffalo sauce recipe calls for butter, but some restaurants use margarine and other oil-based substitutes flavored with diacetyl, acetylpropionyl and acetoin, three natural compounds found in butter (along with beta carotene for the yellow color).

Meat Shrapnel   Uneaten bits of meat left behind on the bone by a haphazard eater.

Niblets   With the skin removed, drumettes are sometimes called chicken niblets.

Nugget   Yes, chicken nuggets, but also a term used to describe large crumbles of blue cheese in blue cheese dressing.

Pit-roasted   Sometimes also called "BBQ pit wings," but in this case "barbecue" refers to the sauce applied to wings that are sauced and seared on a grill.

Smitty Style   Named after the style of wings served by Smitty's, the bar that occupied the space that now houses Doc Sullivan's. Instead of the traditional Frank's, the secret Smitty Style butter-based sauce is thought to include garlic and spices like cinnamon, nutmeg, ground cloves and celery salt.

Suicidal   Typically, the highest level of heat offered sauce-wise in Buffalo's wing joints.

Pizza Logs   Pre-fried oven-ready appetizers consisting of very thin dough rolled around cheese, sauce and pepperoni.

Wings   (aka "flats," "flatties," "paddles" or "wingettes") The part of the wing consisting of the radius and ulna bones between the humerus (drumstick) and the phalanges (the tip of the wing).

The Accoutrements:
What's Up With the Carrots and Celery?

Anticipation builds during the 18 to 20 minutes it typically takes for wings to be done right at any of Buffalo's famed spots, and whether you're with company and have a beer or not, any wing spelunker worth his or her sauce will likely start seeking insight and patterns in the place setting that typically arrives before the bats and paddles do. At the first five spots I visited, I'd count the number of napkins and Wet-Naps with the intention of a tea leaf-reader as they were set down on the table by servers.

Three napkins at Anchor. Would that mean they'd only be a little saucy? There'd be a thin film of sauce on the bottom of the oval plate. Napkin dispensers on the tables at Duff's—would these wings be super saucy? Well, there was a little puddle of sauce at the end. Some places serve their wings in wax-lined baskets, some on plates, some in wooden bowls. Some come with buckets or bowls for discards, some expect you to send the bones back on the plates they came on. There are places that toss their wings in a pile on foil, and another joint that alternates them precisely with celery sticks around a cup of blue cheese, a Buffalo wing star on a plate that's fit for celestial pondering.

That is to say, everyone does things their

own way, and examining these details may get you as far as trying to foretell your future by examining your picked-bare bones after a few beers.

There *are* several truths though. There *will* almost always be celery. Big honking half-moon slices at some places, slender slivers at others. Carrots only *occasionally* appear. Sometimes they're baby carrots, sometimes only a few times thicker than shavings. You'll always get blue cheese, sometimes homemade, but often prepackaged. I didn't and would never, but you *can* ask for ranch if you want it and usually, as evidenced by observing others doing so, get it quickly and without attitude. If you're one of those folks who insists on doing things the wrong way, like putting ketchup on a hot dog or ordering your steak well-done (wink, wink) and doesn't mind immediately being identified as an out-of-towner or someone who doesn't know better, go ahead and get yourself some ranch.

While some folks might agree, typically carrots are an added, undue expense. And while some customers see them as both their God-given wing right, they also seem to regard sacrosanct the privilege of ignoring them entirely.

Given tight margins, many owners explained that after seeing enough carrots return to the kitchen untouched one too many times, they stopped serving them to avoid throwing money away.

Capsaicin Salvation: Do Carrots, Celery, or Blue Cheese Beat the Heat?

There are those who suggest that the benefit, intended or just fortuitous, of Buffalo wings' traditional accoutrements are their handiness in cooling off your mouth between bites of spicy wings that are also hot from the fryer. Certainly a cool cup of blue cheese dressing and the crisp crunch of carrot or celery have been handy saviors for chilling the tongues of many an impatient eater over the decade, but is there any truth to claims that they have an effect on reducing the spiciness of an order of wings whose heat level exceeded the tolerance of the cocksure person who ordered them?

As you'd expect, the interwebs are full of conflicting opinions on the matter of which of these condiments are the most effective in neutralizing capsaicin. Casein, the fat-loving protein found in dairy (particularly that glass of milk often pointed out as the antidote to any spicy dish), binds with capsaicin oil, then helps dilute the heat by washing it away. Well, there's plenty of that in blue cheese, buttermilk, sour cream, and yogurt, the ingredients frequently used to make blue cheese dressing, right? "That's *why* it's served with wings!" some claim. Actually, as we've noted, blue cheese dressing comes with wings because that was the tradition Anchor started when they served them with their house dressing and celery from their antipasto dish. But maybe!

Others cry fowl (rimshot! I get one of those) positing that the carrots and celery might be better for helping to neutralize wings' spicy heat. But water is noted as one of the *worst* things you can use to counteract the effects of capsaicin because it spreads the heat around! Given that water makes up 95 percent of your average celery stick and 88 percent of carrots, you wouldn't think they'd be helpful. While capsaicin is not soluble in water, it *is* highly soluble in fats and ethanol. So how about beer? The Mythbusters have gone on record to say there's not enough alcohol in beer to conquer the burn. And while you're not likely to be in this situation anytime soon, you might have to drink about 10 ounces of 70-proof tequila to dissolve one ounce of concentrated capsaicin. That's more than six shots!

Who better to settle the matter than the Chile Pepper Institute at New Mexico State University in Las Cruces, New Mexico? I reached out to ask for the definitive *scientific* truth about the usefulness of neutralizing capsaicin with the traditional accompaniments of spicy Buffalo wings. And while they hadn't conducted their own experiment, the institute's co-founder and director, Dr. Paul Bosland, suggested the criteria for carrying one out.

Dr. Bosland theorized that there would be enough casein in blue cheese dressing to help but that milk would be the fastest remedy, and that water, celery and carrots would have the same effect: little to none.

There was only one way to tell, so in the name of the kind of useless knowledge perfect for back-pocket bar bets, I invited eight friends over to eat wings, and recorded the time each remedy took to work.

But I included a few tweaks. I added beer, tequila (a likely accompaniment at a bar), and milk (for its reputation as a remedy). Then, given that folks' heat tolerances vary, I asked each person to try *all* of the remedies to attempt to increase the results' consistency.

Frank's RedHot's Xtra Hot Cayenne Pepper Sauce was used (of course), and each wing was submerged in sauce. The guinea pigs—er, participants—cleansed their palates with saltines between each experiment. For authenticity's sake, the Rochester-brewed Buffalo stalwart Genesee was the beer of choice.

One thing that was near unanimous was the heat tolerance. Perhaps using remedies in between each wing lessened any cumulative effect, but nearly everyone pronounced Frank's Xtra Hot Sauce to be mild (on a scale of one to ten, ten being unbearable, the average score for the sauce's heat level was under four). Two things were clear. Milk was most effective. For perspective, the baseline for the heat to disappear *without* a remedy was between 40 seconds and two minutes. Milk halved the effect, making the burn disappear between 17 seconds and a minute. On the other hand, tequila made things worse than no remedy at all.

It was hard to pin down a universal truth about the usefulness of carrots and celery. At least one person felt that doing nothing was better than eating carrots. And blue cheese, while yearned for throughout for its flavor, wasn't useful. Celery, surprisingly, was. It elbowed out blue cheese *and* carrots. But beer is even more useful (a sentence that should be said more). It reduced the heat quickly and by about a third of the time.

Unless you plan on going full Lebowski and drinking White Russians (the Dude abides), milk may not be the most enjoyable libational remedy. Data suggests you'll want a beer and blue-cheese dipped celery for relief. Shots should happen quickly and before wings are eaten or after the heat disappears. Carrots are just a crunch crutch if your wings aren't well fried. Unconvinced? Gather a group. It's a fun experiment. Ah, science.

Lessons on Wing Eating with Competitive Eater Crazy Legs Conti

CREDIT: CHRIS CASSIDY

When it comes to wing-eating tricks, who better to learn them from than a competitive eater like Crazy Legs Conti, a man who said, "I consider Buffalo to be the greatest bar food city in the world."

According to Major League Eating, Legs got his start in 2002 at Acme Oyster House where he set an Acme endurance record while watching Super Bowl XXXVI. He downed 34 dozen oysters in a little more than three hours. Since then, he's participated in dozens of contests, including "too many wing-eating competitions to count." His personal best is 125 wings in 12 minutes. He's participated in the National Buffalo Wing Festival in Buffalo seven times since his first time in 2003.

What's the most wings that you've ever eaten in one sitting?

125 wings in 12 minutes. Major League Eating does it by weight. They weigh the wings before and after. Sometimes, that can mean close to 4½ pounds of meat.

Which is your favorite wing-eating competition that you competed in?

The National Buffalo Wing Festival in Buffalo. The community just comes together. Not only every Buffalo wing sauce maker from around the nation, but an incredible outpouring of support from Buffalo. All the greats are there. Wings are ubiquitous around the nation in terms of being a gold standard for the amount a normal person can eat. An order might be 10 or if you're really hungry, 20. So to see gurgitators putting down over 100 in a short amount of time is pretty amazing. The thing that I like even as a casual diner is I can go and hit Gabriel's Gate and eat the baked Parmesan wings at Cole's, which is in a class by itself. It's like if you've only dated blondes and brunettes and then you see a redhead, you don't even know what it is. There are all these wings in different categories.

What's special about the community in Buffalo?

The people. Maybe because winter's so brutal, they celebrate summer in such a great way, whether it's at free concerts or Wednesdays on the square where it's $2 Molsons. They have this notion that "We're just going to have as good a time as possible and we're going to eat the foods of our culture." I consider Buffalo to be the greatest bar food city in the world. Beef on weck, Buffalo wings—they have distinctive foods that aren't available elsewhere. They just do bar food better.

Where do wings place in your list of favorite things to eat competitively?

Very high. I love crawfish and oysters, but Buffalo wings, the thing that separates them from other contests is it's a technique food.

Which do you prefer: flats or drumettes?

I have a slight disdain for the drumstick when I'm casually dining. When I see a big plate of paddles, I get a little more excited.

Why?

I scientifically tested 100 wings to find the meat-to-bone ratio. I replicated eating by stripping the meat off with my hands, but knowing what a wing looks like when you've stripped it with your mouth. Then I weighed the meat five times in batches of 20 to figure out the ratio of meat to bone. People think drumsticks have more meat, but I discovered it was .49 meat-to-bone on the drumstick and .66 on the paddle.

What do you do with that information as a competitive eater?

You eat more during a contest when you eat more paddles. In Buffalo you have to finish your tray before you move to the next one. If you focus on paddles you stand a better chance of gaining more weight per consumption. There was one year I thought I could eat paddles and try to catch these guys who are a little faster than me.

During a contest they throw in both, right?

It's a hodgepodge. You never know what you're going to get.

So technique is probably the most challenging part of competitively eating wings?

Capacity comes in a little bit. There's flavor fatigue. As delicious as wings might be, 12 minutes of eating the same thing is pretty tough. There was a guy named the Fourth Tenor, because he had a long Italian name, and he brought a brownie that he ate halfway through a bratwurst contest, which was ridiculous. Why would you add food to a food eating contest? But he wanted to get over flavor fatigue. With wings, sauce can factor in. If they're heavily sauced they're slippery and harder to deal with. But if they're dryer then it's kind of a bummer. That's the only time when eating contests get into the lower poundage and you find people frustrated that they can't get into a rhythm and they can't get a lot of meat off the bone.

Does sauce affect technique?

In a competition, you tend not to have spicier sauces, but it does affect you after awhile. You can feel the tingling on your lips. Because you're eating in such great quantity it can't be helped. But you'll ignore everything and breathe through your nose.

Does sauce flavor vary in your experience?

We haven't done many flavors other than Buffalo. I don't think anything can compete with the perfection of Buffalo flavor. I'm not disappointed by that. Buffalo is the only way to go.

Is flavor fatigue different for wings than for eating other foods competitively?

Flavor fatigue is less for Buffalo wings than a lot of foods on the circuit. You feel it around eight or nine hot dogs, but with wings you might go a whole contest and then feel satiated, but not gross. It's one of those foods that is perfect for competitive eating because it has a bone, so you can't just shovel it in like grits. Your limitations are your technique and your speed.

It's been said you could save three minutes and 30 seconds for every dozen wings by employing these techniques. What do you suggest folks do with that time?

That's dessert time. Dessert is the one food where it's like, "We're just going to stop time and just enjoy." I endorse speed eating to save time and multi-task, but with dessert I like people to just kick back and enjoy the sweetness of life. Yeah.

Lightning round: Best spot in Buffalo for beef on weck?

Cole's.

Favorite Buffalo spot for wings?

Gabriel's Gate if I had to name just one for the traditional Buffalo wing.

Non-traditional?

Cole's for the baked Parmesan wings.

Jim's Steakout. Favorite sandwich?

I would know it if I saw it, but I'd have to be like nine beers in.

Favorite place to drink when you're in town?

It's got to be the Old Pink.

How To Eat a Wing: Is There a *Right* Way?

You have a bowl of wings set down in front of you. What do you do? Pick up a wing and start eating it? Dip it in blue cheese dressing first? Do you double-dip? Does it matter if your next bite is carrot or celery? *Is* there a best way to eat a Buffalo wing in terms of the order "wing, blue cheese, celery, carrot," or is it just dig in and do what comes naturally?

Asking these questions of owners of Buffalo's greatest wing joints earned me more than a few side glances and laughs. Almost like I was some kind of alien culinary anthropologist who'd never eaten wings. Believe me, I get why. "Of course, there's no right way," you're saying with an eye roll. "You just start eating." And assuming you're shar-ing an order and you don't mind whoever you're eating with double-dipping in the blue cheese, you're probably right: there are few if any rules.

"I'm not opinionated on that one," Gene McCarthy's owner Bill Metzger told me. "I gener-ally will go right to the wing and dip it into the blue cheese sauce because I really love blue cheese. I get to that before anybody else can."

But when something is so obvious as to make the question sound nutty, it *can* lead to discovery.

One of the problems when you're dipping wings into blue cheese is that it doesn't always stick to the wing. If you're painting it on with the celery, you probably get better coverage of blue cheese dressing.

"My stepfather used to make an art out of eating a chicken wing. He would take a celery stick and he would use the celery stick like a paintbrush. He would paint the blue cheese onto the wing. I've only seen a handful of people ever do that, ever! That was my stepfather. Most people just dip right in. Some people order extra hot sauce on the side. Sometimes they'll order medium wings and they want a little extra hot sauce so they'll paint it on with a celery stick."

—Manmoser's owner Peter Dimfle

The Moves

If when it comes to eating wings you have the need for speed, consider the following moves.

Bullet-holing Where you push the paddle through the middle into your mouth with your tongue or fingers.

Cluster Targeting In which the eater identifies areas on the flats and bats with bunches of meat and bites those as appropriate.

The Typewriter Involves rotating the wing while eating the meat crosswise as one might an ear of corn.

The Meat Umbrella According to Major League Eating, the meat umbrella was developed specifically for drums by former wing-eating champion, Cookie Jarvis. It requires the eater to hold the flat (or the drumette by the bone end) and push down against the plate, forcing the meat off the bone like an umbrella being opened.

The Bone Splitter Also known as "wishboning." With this move, you hold the flat at its tip and insert the whole thing in your mouth while pulling apart the hinge and using your teeth to pull the meat off in one smooth motion.

The One-Armed Bandit This move is used on the flats, where you open the bones using one hand, remove one bone and eat the meat off the remaining one.

According to a study conducted through the research division of Major League Eating's governing body, the International Federation of Competitive Eating, certain methods are more effective than others:

4.9 seconds—Cluster Targeting

4.4 seconds—The Bullet Hole

4.3 seconds—Meat Umbrella

4.2 seconds—The One-Armed Bandit

2.5 seconds—The Typewriter

2.3 seconds—Wishbone/The Bone Splitter

In Search of Buffalo's Best Wings

Ask a Buffalonian about the best wings and as with pizza and weck, you get balkanized responses. There are the places they *know* they have to shout out, the famous places. But Buffalo is New York state's second-most populous city. There are nearly a quarter-million residents and nearly another million in the surrounding metropolitan area. And while there are central corridors and neighborhoods with restaurants and bars, as of writing, taxis were rare and expensive and Uber had just arrived. The result is a city of small towns, each with their own civic pride and institutions. When it comes to two of Buffalo's most loved foods, pizza and wings, the nearest quality spot to home is often, "the best."

"If you did a straw poll, you're likely to put these at the top: Duff's, Gabriel's Gate, Bar Bill Tavern, and Gene McCarthy," suggests Brian Hayden, Visit Buffalo Niagara's communications manager. "Once you get past those four, each neighborhood will tell you something different."

An informal poll during the course of my visits revealed La Nova, Gabriel's Gate, Bar Bill, and Nine-Eleven Tavern as locals' picks. If you're a First Warder, the best wings are probably at Gene McCarthy's. If you're from or live in South Buffalo, you probably fight about which are better: Smitty's Wings at Doc Sullivan's or the ones at Nine-Eleven Tavern, if you're not intimidated by its dive décor. Anchor doesn't enter the picture—folks don't want to go out of their way to hang with tourists. And while Duff's is great (you could argue it's the Anchor to this generation's other wings spots), there were at last count 11 locations: five in and around Buffalo, one in Rochester, three in Canada and one each in Georgia and Texas where Ron Peddicord and his two partners persuaded Duff's to franchise.

Still, you have to establish a baseline. And Anchor and Duff's are it. The quickest way to get Frank's RedHot Sauce into your veins is to just start eating. So minutes after landing, I dropped my bags off, was back in my rental car and off to Anchor and then Duff's for my first two wing stops. My count would eventually reach higher than 220 wings over the course of a month. That ended up being about seven wings a day in between bites of Buffalo-style pizza, beef on weck, sponge candy, fried bologna, sips of Genny, Tom & Jerrys, and the city's other delicious specialities.

List-making is no joke. Ask any restaurateur who has been featured on local news or a cable food show. People will drive miles out of the way after hearing on the radio about a place just announced to a list of the best burgers, pizzas, hot dogs, wings, you name it. Given that, as far as I'm concerned, *irresponsible* listicle-makers should be seated at a special table in hell reserved out of view of both kitchen and staff where nobody will serve them and the only thing they should have any hope of ever eating would be cold food.

Over the years, I've developed a methodical system for seeking out Platonic food ideals. It's pretty simple, but it rarely fails me. I may get into trouble for saying this, but given the fact locals often skip tourist traps and stick to their favorites, if you do these things, I find that you'll likely glean an even more informed perspective than folks who have been eating their native specialty for decades.

> ★ Research online sites and existing books.
> ★ Get recommendations from trusted travelers, experts and passionate locals.
> ★ Establish a baseline and criteria.
> ★ Take serious notes.
> ★ Go to more places than should be humanly possible or gastrointestinally healthy in as short a period of time as you can to keep comparisons fresh in mind.
> ★ Always order that one thing that really stands out or that you've never seen or heard of.

If you're looking for an overview of the Buffalo wings *in* Buffalo, there have, of course, been some best-of lists written. Food writer Larry Olmsted wrote one for *USA Today* in 2015, but online guides published by *Buffalo Eats*, the *Buffalo News*, *Step Out Buffalo*, and Visit Buffalo Niagara offer great local insight into what Buffalonians' look for. I cross-referenced these lists to create a to-do list. But I have to give a shout-out to local Buffalo food writer extraordinaire Christa Glennie Seychew for her tireless quest to wrangle some of the Queen City's wing experts to compile *Buffalo Spree* magazine's 2015 best wing brackets. Christa pitted 30 of the city's most well-known wings spots against each other in a competition that—spoiler alert—crowned Bar Bill Tavern as the king of the roost. While it's sure to be a collector's item for wing obsessives, unfortunately, the issue is not online. I'm indebted to Christa, *Buffalo Spree*, and wing judges Jeff Biesinger, Donnie Burtless, Donny Kutzbach, Alli Suriani, Nina Barone, and Wendy Guild Swearingen for giving me a pool of the city's best wing spots from which to embark on the comprehensive wing primer that follows.

The Criteria

It's not enough to be armed with a list of places, you need a list of criteria to establish a thorough, honest appraisal. For wings, that means picking one style and one heat level—medium—not requesting the wings to be cooked to a specific degree of doneness, and then judging wings against the following:

- ★ Overall appearance of each wing
- ★ Crispness of the skin
- ★ Spiciness and flavor of the sauce
- ★ Application of heat (tossed, brushed, sprinkled, rubbed, etc.)
- ★ Tenderness of the meat
- ★ Ancillary to that? Overall plating, the condition of the condiments, and the quality of blue cheese dressing.

I visited 30 of the city's most vaunted places and narrowed down my top 20. Given the hundreds of restaurants and bars that serve wings in Buffalo and the surrounding area, if you're *from* Western New York, there will doubtless be a few favorite spots missing. A few of these picks may be controversial, others less so, but at all of them, you're likely to have better wings than you've ever had elsewhere in your life. Without further ado, here are Buffalo's wings I found most worth squawking about.

Buffalo's 20 Best Wings

#20 Anchor Bar

1047 Main Street, Buffalo, NY 14209 | 716-886-8920
anchorbar.com | Mon–Thu 11 am–10 pm,
Fri 11 am–11 pm, Sat 12 pm–11 pm, Sun 12 pm–10 pm

There are other Anchor locations (and as of writing, one planned for Manhattan, finally), but if you're passionate about wings, let's be real: Mecca is this big red barn of a building on a lonely corner north of downtown Buffalo at the intersection of Main and North. It's probably technically a hood called Hospital Hill and it's Ground Zero for wings. There's a parking lot in back where as soon as you exit your car, you're hit by the scent of "fry" wafting out through a back door to the kitchen. There's a door in the front that takes you directly to the horseshoe-shaped bar surrounded by license plates on the walls.

But the side entrance sets you up better for the experience. It's guarded by a wooden totem of Teressa Bellissimo, Buffalo wings' inventor, who once presumably held a plate of her wings but are now since long gone.

When Calvin Trillin wrote his history of chicken wings in 1980, he could only find

one article in the libraries of Buffalo newspapers that dealt with the Bellissimos and their restaurant—a piece in the *Buffalo Courier-Express* in 1969, five years after the invention of the chicken wing, that talked about the musicians who had appeared at Anchor over the years. That music tradition continues. Thursday through Sunday, you'll be treated to live music. It's Sinatra on Thursday (7 PM to 9 PM), live jazz on Friday and Saturday (9 PM to 11 PM), then an unspecified style for Sunday (5 PM to 7 PM).

The checkered black and gray tiled dining room is packed with wooden chairs and tables lined with red tablecloths covered with glass. A large painting of Christopher Columbus, patron saint of Italian-Americans, welcomes guests impassively. Everywhere you look is a window to time travel, an article, a document, or a picture related to Anchor's claim to fame and glory days. With the lilting music, the chandelier and stained glass lamps hanging from the ceiling, framed photos of musicians, wrestlers, football players, and the Bellissimos, the place feels a lot less like a tourist trap than the gift area out front implies.

The menu is one of those comically big near foot-and-a-half long ones you can hide behind with "The Real Story" printed inside with a picture of Teressa. While it's known as a bar, by all accounts Anchor began as an Italian restaurant, so along with other iconic Buffalo foods like beef on weck, stuffed hot peppers and fried bologna, and American comfort classics like chicken fingers and twice-baked potatoes, you'll find homemade pastas and various Parmed things. Buffalo flavor has proliferated across Anchor's menu—there's wing soup, a Buffalo burger, crispy chicken salad, a breaded and Buffalo-ized cubed chicken breast entree and a deep fried Buffalo chicken wing "style" sandwich. You almost want to see them go all out with a Buffalo chicken Parm or raviolis stuffed with blue cheese and doused with Frank's and butter.

Some may call my pizza cred into question, and it wouldn't be the reason to visit, but for a town that loves its pizza, Anchor's is actually a surprisingly good take on the city's style. It comes standard with pepperoni with a few other toppings to choose from, though no Buffalo chicken, unfortunately. It's thinner than most other places in town and enjoyably greasy with a sweet sauce and a cornmeal edge with puffy bubbles. It's extremely pliable with a crust that breaks when it's folded. It's a great sloppy drinking pie.

But you're here for the wings. They come mild, medium, hot, or spicy hot BBQ and they're available by the single order (10 wings, $13), double (20, $21) or bucket (50, $44). Suicidal wings ("if you dare!") are a dollar or so more. "The original style is medium," the waitress will sweetly advise. They arrive resembling some kind of Anchor wing mascot, a chicken wing turtle with glistening orange wings poking out from a small wooden bowl they're huddled under thin, three-inch long celery sticks. Turning over the bowl for discards releases wing steam and a welcome vinegary heat. There's a side cup of blue cheese dressing that's pretty smooth, almost like sour cream sweetened with blue cheese crumbles. The wings are plump and juicy, not shrunken and both the wings and the drums are slightly crispy in places but not shatteringly so. While medium brings a kick, the wings are not incredibly hot—the spice fades within a few minutes. There's a thin film of sauce coating most of the entire surface of the oval plate, but your wings require no more than the three napkins and the heat is nothing a Flying Bison beer won't take care of.

In the pantheon of wings, these are likely still better than most of the ones you've eaten on average through the rest of your life, but they're only a hint of the wing greatness Buffalo has to offer. File this one under the category of "got the T-shirt and thanks, Teressa."

#19 Wiechec's Lounge

1748 Clinton Street, Kaisertown, 14206

716-823-2828 | facebook.com/Wiechecs

Mon–Sat 11 AM–11 PM, Closed Sun

A pebble-studded concrete facade, windows filled with beer neon, the corner tavern on Center Street, the main drag in Kaisertown, a narrow slice of Buffalo between William Street and the Buffalo River, is something straight out of central casting for a late-'50s bar. A shingled eave bears the lounge's name above the door in simple white cursive: Wiechec's. And you need look no further for *the* prime example of where religion intersects with chicken wings than behind the faded silver and black sticker letters affixed to its glass front door.

Pronounced "Weechex," the cash-only neighborhood institution has been around for so long that local publications seem to have given up on documenting its origins, instead seeming to point to it as *the definition* of "old-school" Buffalo. Just eyeballing the distance between it

and Houghton Academy, the PK–8 public school across the street, you suspect that whenever it was founded it had to have been grandfathered into its foundation before there were rules against establishments selling liquor within 200 feet of a school. The lounge, founded by Henry Wiechec, and still operated by the family—his son Mike runs it now—goes back to 1964.

Inside on a Saturday afternoon, the long bar is filled mostly with gray hairs watching golf and the Yankees in high padded chairs. It's all vinyl tile floor and drop ceiling with a pool table and scattered Formica four-tops. At the end of the bar there's a wide archway to a dining room filled with booths and tables surrounded by wood-paneled walls outfitted with waitress buzzers from

decades long gone. There's a projection screen a few feet long hanging from the ceiling at the back of the long room for communal sports watching. You get the feeling you're about to settle into a church basement or the equivalent of the neighborhood living room.

Wiechec's is famous for their Friday fish fry. And that Catholic tradition has a direct effect on the menu, because whether that means fish that's breaded, broiled, beer-battered, or Cajun-blackened (all served with macaroni salad, potato salad, coleslaw, and fries), the fryers are otherwise occupied. So local wing-lovers know that as the menu notes, chicken wings are *not available Fridays between 11 AM and 9 PM.*

When wings are on the offer, they come with Ken's blue cheese dressing and nice big, thick sticks of celery in single (10 wings, $8.50), double (20, $16.95) and triple orders (30, $24.50) with 10 sauces to choose from: mild, medium, hot, BBQ, hot BBQ, honey BBQ, Cajun, honey Cajun, Garlic & Parm (Sox), or Red Sox. It costs an extra $1 to split flavors, but seemingly nothing to double-dip them, which is exactly what that last flavor does. And while every fiber of any diehard Yankee fan will scream out for them not to do it, the last two are *the* flavors to order, wings that will get them to say two words anathema to them: Go Sox.

Why the mixture of garlic Parmesan with hot sauce would be called "Red Sox" wings deep in Yankee country in a lounge with the Bombers' iconic bat-in-hat logo neon-lit in the front window and the game on above the bar isn't at all clear. And the waitress asked doesn't know why.

It's a persisting curiosity, but one that disappears into exultation when the wings arrive. An order of medium wings have an audible crack when bitten and are so hot temperature-wise that even on a summer day, steam can be seen rising out of them after one bite. The Red Sox wings are especially well-sauced—there has to be a ratio of 2 tablespoons of sauce to each wing. The wings look like they've been confetti-coated with cheese then slathered with butter and Frank's. They're even more cheesy than medium garlic Parm wings at Bases Loaded. It's hard to imagine there could be a way to saturate this sauce with more cheese without turning it into a paste. But there's no need to mess with the ratio anyway. They're tangy and spicy with a consistent garlic presence and at least two

sneezes worth of hot sauce and spice. Each wing leaves behind about a quarter- to a half-tablespoon of sauce on your fingers after you pick up a wing.

And Wiechec's self-described cook, bartender, manager ("When someone needs to say they're the manager when the real one isn't there") and 11-year veteran Matt Klopfer ("Everybody calls me Matty K.") sets the record straight: "Our regular garlic Parmesan wings are called 'socks' because they smell like sweaty socks or like a gym bag. That just became a nickname. So when you order wings you would say, 'I want 10 socks.' And everybody knows what that is. When I started working here and eating wings, I would ask for a side of hot sauce. So one day I was like, 'Well, why don't I just frigging put the hot sauce in with the socks?' And I'm actually a Red Sox fan so I thought it would be really funny to name something 'Red Sox' in a Yankees bar."

In other words, he's really looking to twist the knife. "Yeah," he said, "It really does hurt people to order them, but they order them anyway 'cause they're good."

#18 Bases Loaded

3355 Lakeshore Road, 14219 | 716-823-0158

Mon–Sat 11 am–4 am, Sun 12 pm–4 am

I must have passed Bases Loaded in Blasdell off Lake Shore Road (Route 5) about a half dozen times on the way back and forth from Buffalo to Hamburg and other points south where I'd been researching custard, hot dogs, pizza and wings. This squat little brick-faced, vinyl-sided joint was on my to-do list, but for some reason I kept

putting it off. That's not true. I know exactly why I didn't go in. It looks like an epically local blue-collar bar. And while that's a pure draw, as much as I'm a gamer for soloing in places where people are so well-known they may as well be glued to their stools, every time I passed by the small, neon-lit "Bases Loaded" sign with a little pipe-smoking, beer-toting Leprechaun leaning on his baseball bat, I knew the energy it could take to photograph wings in what essentially would be someone's living room. But as I passed by with the clock winding down on a second research trip, I finally pulled over. And boy, am I glad I did.

Bases Loaded is set between about a 10-minute drive south of downtown Buffalo and New Era Field where the Bills play. It's on Lake Shore Road, a stone's throw from where it intersects with Mile Strip Expressway (NY-179) and set between the Republic Steel Mill and Ford's stamping plant. You could walk five minutes west from the bar and wade right into Lake Erie.

Inside, on an early afternoon, a few women are chatting at the bar. Its gold glitter surface makes it look like someone took a '70s bowling ball and turned it into a countertop. There's a pool table, a dart board, an arcade machine, a

popcorn machine, and a TV is dedicated to *Quick Draw* and a countdown to the next drawing. The sunken dining room has windows that look out onto the busy highway, but the blinds are down, and with only cracks of light showing through, it may as well be any day and any time of the day as long as it's time to drink.

Unless it's Wednesday, when it's 40¢-wing night, the menu says they come in orders of 10 ($8), 20 ($14) or by the bucket (50 for $32) in mild, medium, and hot. It's $1 extra for BBQ and garlic Parmesan. Sauce recommendations come fast from around the bar. "Try the new honey mustard wings," one woman offers. "Medium garlic Parm," insists another. She has the persuasiveness of Obi-Wing Kenobi. "You need to have the medium garlic Parm wings."

These are the wings you're looking for. You can go about your business . . . as long as it's medium garlic Parm wings.

Recs are tricky. It's all about trust. Sometimes you get steered right, sometimes you drive off the cliff, and sometimes, someone's charm can lead you to culinary greatness. That was the case with Bases Loaded, where the medium garlic Parm wings are one of the great successes of the more than 250 or so dishes I ate at more than 120 restaurants in Buffalo.

There are only five other people in the bar besides me but the wings are still made to order—they take more than 15 minutes to arrive.

The medium garlic Parm wings have a very wet Frank's base, but one that's been completely saturated with at least a few tablespoons of both garlic and shredded Parmesan. The cheese almost even seems like it has somehow melted *into* sauce if that's possible. The result is a much wetter wing—one that still maintains a crisp crunch—that has a funky zest and a brings a constant tingle to the lips. This is a sauce that demands you to defy all propriety or to insist on not sharing an order. Party rules *do* not apply! Whatever sauce is left behind that you have already tried to sop up with your bitten-into wing is something you may feel compelled to lick off the foil. If you've ordered another batch of medium regular wings too (no slouch either: they're just as wonderfully crispy with a classic Frank's tingle) they're going to end up being used to mop up that medium garlic Parm sauce.

Owner Ernie Jewett is friendly, if nonplussed, by my overflowing enthusiasm for his wings. But he does point proudly to a sign above the bar that names Bases Loaded a finalist in *Buffalo Spree*'s 2015 search for the city's best wings (they lost out only to the winner: Bar Bill Tavern). He says they started doing this double-dipped sauce style in late 2014. He and the rest of the regulars call the medium garlic Parm wings "stinky wings" because they know his feelings about them, "I'm

not a Parmesan guy. I think garlic goes a long way too. It took a lot to get the kitchen to start making those, but once we started selling them a lot of people ask for them."

The secrets to the Bases Loaded wings? They get a 16-minute bath in the fryer. The blue cheese dip is a pre-made dressing doctored with blue cheese. "We use Frank's, as well as a mixture of our own spices," Ernie confides. "We try to use butter, but we use a little margarine as well."

And then they just cook them from scratch. "You order 'em, sometimes you gotta wait a little longer but that's just the way we do business here. Again, our regulars understand that. And most people when they come in understand that it's worth the wait."

Yeah, they are.

#17 Doc Sullivan's

474 Abbott Road, 14220 | Phone 716-436-3302

Mon–Sat 11:30 AM–3:30 AM, Sun 12 PM–3 AM

Just south of the Buffalo River and five blocks away from one of the city's best sponge candy shops, a staple pub in the city's Irish Heritage District has gotten a refresh. The awning and bright green paint outside are gone, as is Doc Sullivan's name in cartoon font above the entrance, replaced with big capital letters spotlit by lamps. While there's new flooring, hanging filament bulbs and a fresh coat of paint, it's still *Doc Sullivan's*, the neighborhood go-to for local stag parties where folks help friends with cash for upcoming weddings. Mondays and Tues-

days are 50¢ wing nights. The original shuffleboard table is there, and the Loser Boys League, a group of locals who gather to drink beer and take turns sliding, embrace their wives' nickname for them. Doc Sullivan's is clean and bright, the kind of place where a stroller and a banh mi burger don't feel out of place at lunch, which it's now open for. Most important for wing enthusiasts, Doc's is still the home of the Smitty-Style wing.

The 2015 remodeling is a result of new ownership, when local firefighter Jerry Sullivan and his wife Bonnie retired from the bar they opened in 1999. But South Buffalo–born owners Tommy Cowan and Justin Steinwandel made sure the large South Buffalo bar stayed true to its local roots. Good thing. Tavern tradition is strong at 474 Abbott Road, reaching back to the '30s when it was known as Smitty's, a bar Tommy said was owned "by the Smith family," said to have been known to bestow free drinks and train fare to servicemen during World War II. There's some serious wing tradition too, given the 50-year tradition carried on here for the tangy wing

recite said to have been created in the 1960s by Carol O'Neill.

Tommy's personal touch extends to Doc Sullivan's wings. Carrots are soaked in ice water so they're extra wet and cold to maximize their crunch, the kitchen melts Land O'Lakes butter for the sauce, and the wing baseline is wet and crispy, because that's how Tommy likes them. "We're known for a nice crispy wing," he explains. "We cook them for 18 minutes."

But he hasn't messed with the homemade blue cheese dressing or the essential recipe for the Smitty Wing, both passed on by the previous owners. The sauce is a matter of some curiosity. Tommy says the secrecy around its ingredients has led to the proliferation of "South Buffalo Style," wings in the neighborhood with places like Potter's Field and Blackthorn trying to replicate it. The *Buffalo News* speculates it involves nutmeg, celery seed, ginger, cinnamon, and ground cloves, but Tommy's having none of it. "That's a deny," he tells me. "They're not even close on that. There are some places around town that use cinnamon, nutmeg, and cloves, but that is not our recipe at all. A lot of people think

they know it but they don't. It's not a huge secret. But there are a few things that I wouldn't want to share."

So what *is* Smitty Style then? "A butter-based sauce with about a dozen ingredients, mixed with hot sauce, and that's it," Tommy explained. "But the butter and seasoning make up a recipe that has to be about 40 or 50 years old now."

These are some of the crispier wings in Buffalo. They're fried to the point that the skin on the flats seems like it's crackled away from the meat and when you bite, the skin tears in a way to leave near translucent shards sticking out. Tommy may like his wings saucy, but when I order them, there's little more than a tablespoon of sauce under each pile. Smitty sauce has a salty edge in a good way. Of the wings that leave the kitchen, Tommy says 95 percent are Smitty Style. But there's another signature style, Southie Gold BBQ wings, which don't look that much different. They taste a bit like Carolina mustard barbecue sauce with a sweetness reminiscent of McDonald's honey mustard, but in a good way.

Folks on the south side are proud of places closer to their neck of the woods and if you ask, you'll leave with lots of recs: Bada Bing for sesame-crust pizza topped with stuffed hot peppers, Charlap's in Hamburg for custard, Ballyhoo "for links and craft drinks," Ko-Ed for "Buffalo's best sponge candy." But there's some other worthwhile fare on Doc's own menu. Everything has a little bit of a fussed-up touch without being fancy. But perhaps the most indulgent is the Wardynski's fried bologna, which comes nearly two fingers thick, covered with sauteed peppers and onions and drenched in homemade queso the way Texans might smother chicken fried steak.

#16 Gene McCarthy's

Hamburg Street, First Ward, 14204 | 716-855-8948
genemccarthys.com | Mon–Fri 11 AM–12 AM,
Sat 11 AM–1 AM, Sun 11 AM–12 AM

Gene McCarthy's is a local's local, an Irish bar that's reportedly been an anchor for grain shovelers, lawyers, and politicians alike for more than 50 years. As an out-of-towner, the only way you'd find it if you weren't looking for it would be to get lost. The simple, two-story house is on the corner of an intersection deep in the First Ward just south of the Niagara Thruway (I-190) and a block from a bend in the Buffalo River where train tracks head off in three directions and grain elevators stand guard over Lake Erie. Given its blue collar roots, this 100-year-old building might not seem like the first place you'd expect to find craft beer and an experimental riff on wings. But inside, past and present meld.

Crusty regulars sipping Molson and Labatt Blue bend elbows with patrons there to try the latest creations of the Old First Ward Brewing Company.

The craft beer is the influence of co-owner Bill Metzger, the publisher of the *Brewing News* newspapers, who took over Gene McCarthy's with his partner Matt Conron with the idea of starting their own brewery. Metzger and Conron, who met when Conron was head brewer of Breckenridge Brewing in downtown Buffalo, purchased a brewing system from a pub in Burlington, Vermont and used it to start Old First Ward Brewing Company next door. They began producing under the OFW name in 2014 and have become one of Buffalo's most well-regarded craft beer institutions.

The details behind Gene McCarthy's origins are sketchy. Bill says that it was a bar named Julia's run by a Polish woman before it was taken over by the man who it would become named for. "Joe McCarthy, we call him 'the boss,' was a local bigwig," Metzger tells me. "He bought the bar and Gene, his younger brother from a family of eight, ran the place. Gene and Mary McCarthy started

it in 1963. It was reputed to be a gambling outfit. Mary ran the kitchen and Gene ran the bar."

McCarthy retired in 2006, and sold to Gerhardt Yaskow, who turned the keys over to Metzger in 2012. Bill said he became acquainted with it when he moved to the neighborhood in 2007, "It was four blocks from where I live."

If Bill is right, Gene McCarthy's is late to the wing game. Yaskow told him he started doing them sometime after he took over for Gene and Metzger remembers them being on the menu in 2007. Interesting then that in addition to the traditional mild, medium, and hot, and a few of the standard off-Frank's sauces, there are two inventive flavors idiosyncratic to the bar. The Sheffield employs a dry rub with oregano and Cajun spices (along with a few other secret ingredients) as well as a pairing you don't frequently see: barbecue sauce with crumbled blue cheese. "That was one of our inventions," Bill explained. "We named it after Gene. When we walked in there all there was was hot, medium, and mild. That was it."

As with the "Bleu Bayou" wings at Abigail's, the Waterloo restaurant two hours east of Buffalo that won the title of world's best from the wing documentary, *The Great Chicken Wing Hunt*, the blue cheese is built *right into* the spicy sauce that coats Gene McCarthy's eponymous fried flappers. Mixing blue cheese's umami funk into wing sauces is a seriously underemployed move and you have to wonder why. It's a serious flavor enhancer that solves the problem of trying to adhere blue cheese dressing to a wing that's already slick with hot sauce. And it saves the step of dipping celery or carrots. I have to guess it's likely out of deference to blue cheese haters (sigh). Two places doing this may not be a trend, but maybe it's a sign of things to come. There are two major differences between these blue-cheese-embedded styles: first, Gene McCarthy's doesn't use Frank's, instead employing a sweet and spicy barbecue sauce; and second, the blue cheese isn't pulverized into the sauce. Instead, tiny crumbles of blue are folded into the sauce and tossed with the wings and scattered on top. The Gene McCarthy's and the medium are the bar's top sellers. An order of traditional wings arrives with blue cheese, celery, and carrots and come 10 to an order ($10.50); the namesake wings, along with the bar's other specialty flavors, Thai chili and garlic, honey mustard, Sheffield, and garlic Parmesan cost an additional $1.25.

"We have not done any of that par-cooking yet and I'm of the opinion that it's about 20 minutes from start to finish," he explained. "When people come in and it's a crowded and busy day, whether it's a Friday, fish Friday, or whether it's just a busy day in general, our servers know to warn people because look we're a little backed up, the kitchen is small, it's going to take 40 minutes, not 20."

Forty minutes for wings? It could be that long, especially if you're there on Wednesday or Friday, when after 5 PM they use two of their three fryers to serve one of the city's best fish fries (they keep one dedicated to cooking wings). More time to sample one of the eight or so OFW creations on tap or if you're there on the third day of the week, participate in Trivial Tuesdays from 7 PM to 9 PM.

Bill's take on beer and wing pairings is that hops go well with heat. "Our pale ale is very good with just a regular wing. The hops for some reason counteracts the heat. In terms of the Gene McCarthy's wings, I don't think there's any one particular thing that would match it. A dark beer, an oatmeal stout, would be really nice just because you've got that blue cheese thing going on and the barbecue. Or just a basic lager. The lagers that we make really match well with food, period. They're very easy drinking and if there's some spice in something they'll tone it down."

There's also a very easy drinking beer they named Gene's Lager ("We try to give Gene some credit," Bill said), but their most popular beer is the Notta, short for "This is Not a Pale Ale" that Bill described as "a very hoppy pale ale," adding,

"We blow through that, people just love that beer. Probably half of it is drunk by my partner."

#15 McPartlan's Corner

669 Wehrle Drive, 14225 | 716-632-9896
mcpartlanscorner.com | Mon–Thu & Sat 10 AM–11 PM,
Fri 10 AM–12 AM, Sun 10 AM–10 PM

At the corner of Wehrle Drive and Beach Road, there's no demarcation between where the road stops and the parking lot surrounding McPartlan's begins. As you approach the squat, green-capped white stucco building in your car, it feels as though you could just softly break into a slow roll and in one uninterrupted motion, continue it out from behind the wheel and right into the old-school Irish tavern as if turning over in bed. Inside, it seems that's what Amherst locals do, long-time couples trading gentle nudges and barbs at the bar over which pie to order with just as much familiarity as if they were sitting on the sofa in their own living room.

Inside, there's a tiled dining room filled with four-tops and the kind of chairs that would seem just as at home in a church basement. Left of it, FOX News plays on the TV above the bar where near the entrance, a steady stream of people come in to pick up orders to go. "We're only here to break even and make friends," the bartender quips when someone asks to settle up.

Jim and Louise McPartlan opened McPartlan's in 1955 after she urged her husband to use the money he'd been saving to buy a car to instead follow his dream of owning a restaurant (he learned to cook while serving with the Army during World War II). It was originally

a south Buffalo bar, moving once in 1961 to a spot just south of the Buffalo River and then in 1971, migrating to its Amherst home on Wehrle Drive at the bend in I-90 where it turns eastward toward Rochester.

Orders of wings come in two sizes: 10 ($10.69) or 20 ($15.99). The menu says they're served with carrots and blue cheese, but wings arrive piping hot with thin shavings of celery too. McPartlan's wings are perhaps a little bigger than the average ones around town. While their baseline is not on the crispier end of the spectrum, and they're not very saucy, they're fresh and juicy with a consistent heat and an intense, vinegary tang that's particularly tasty.

McPartlan's may be best known in town for their fish fry, which as you can tell from the clippings on the walls of the vestibule has topped many a list over the years. It's a lightly floured haddock served with fresh coleslaw and your choice of potato, though the German potato salad is the most popular. It's the kind of dish where the potato salad seems like it's been portioned out with an ice cream scoop and a squeeze of lemon is about all you'll need. But they make a fantastic Tom & Jerry with long drizzles drip-

ping down the side, and they're one of the few places in town still serving them into February. Between every few creamy sips there are patches of granulated sugar chunks that haven't dissolved completely into the mix and that provide a welcome slight crunch that melts pleasantly into the gulp. There's a fairly strong beef on weck on the offer for a place that doesn't have a dedicated carving station in the dining room (ask for the rarest slices they have). Theirs is a beautiful, milky-white bun that's enthusiastically but not overly studded with salt and about a teaspoon scattering of caraway seeds.

And those pies! The dessert section on McPartlan's menu reads, "Ask your server for our new dessert menu." That may be the biggest understatement on the city's dining scene. McPartlan's has a special pie lady who makes about a dozen different homemade cream, crumb, sour cream, and meringue pies. While the owners politely declined to share any details about who she was, they did say that she arrives about 4 PM to make her delivery. That's a good time to shoot to arrive if you want first dibs. And you do. Because while all of them sound delicious, certain pies sell out fast. The pineap-

long folks from Western New York can expect to be able to settle into a barstool their grandfather once kept warm, where they can be greeted by someone who knows their drink and their name.

"We've had a good run," the soft-spoken Joe McPartlan tells me during a break from behind the bar. "We've had a good run."

Keep running.

#14 Dwyer's Irish Pub

65 Webster Street, North Tonawanda, 14120
716-692-4837 | dwyerspub.com | Mon–Thu 4 PM–2 AM,
Fri–Sat 12 PM–3 AM, Sun 12 PM–2 AM

I've no sooner parked out front of Dwyer's Irish Pub nose first and introduced myself to owner Greg Stenis than he's taken me next door to see the functioning Wurlitzer Organ inside the majestic, near-century-old Riviera Theatre. Stenis is a thick, friendly guy with a shaved head who has been an auxiliary member of the North Tonawanda Police Department. It takes 15 minutes for the old organ to warm up, but soon Greg has pressed a few buttons to raise it out of its pit and it's playing a song that sounds like something quite a bit older than I am. I hadn't expected it when I woke up, but here I am backstage, climbing up and around narrow ladders affixed to the wall to cram myself inside the closets the organ pipes, equipment and electronics are enclosed in. In between tidbits of local Tonawanda history, he's telling me about his raspberry barbecue sauce, and the pitfalls places outside Buffalo fall into.

"Nobody cooks wings enough," Greg tells me when I ask him about how wings are made out-

ple sour cream, filled with tender shards of the sweet fruit, may be the most popular. There's a thin, barely salted, flaky nod to a crust on the bottom, just enough to make you feel as if you're eating something besides whipped cream and the half-inch of filling under it. Often, pies can be victimized by being made too sweet. These come close to the opposite—just sweet enough to allow you to really enjoy their actual flavor. They may be some of the best slices of pie I've ever had.

McPartlan's is still a family business (it's run by Jim and Louise's sons), but when you think of old Buffalo and what of it will persevere, it's hard not to wonder how long an old-school place like this on the edge of town will stick around, how side of Buffalo. "I was watching TV and saw someone make them in four minutes. There's no way they're crispy. There's no way they're cooked. They're always crispy here. We cook them 14 to 15 minutes. I think that's the biggest mistake the rest of the country makes."

While there are places in Buffalo that do branch out from the traditional mild, medium, and hot sauces, there's an argument to be made that compared to other towns in Western New York, elsewhere in the state, when it comes to sauce, the city's bars and restaurants take a more traditional approach. "Buffalo is a bit more conservative, actually," *The Great Chicken Wing Hunt*'s director Matt Reynolds tells me. "I find that they are a bit more of the Frank's and butter school. In Syracuse, they'll add garlic and peppers. You get a lot of places where there's a bar with a guy in the back with a big pot of sauce. There's a tradition, at least in the part of the state where I'm from, of people experimenting with sauces."

Not so at Dwyer's Irish Pub on Webster Street, a quiet thoroughfare in Tonawanda, a seemingly sleepy town about a 20-minute drive north of downtown Buffalo. The menu declares itself "famous for our wings." Around Buffalo, their wings are referred to in a way that makes them sound more peacock than chicken. "It's the Disneyland of wings," Greg tells me proudly with a laugh.

Wing orders come with blue cheese and celery in perhaps more denominations at Dwyer's than anywhere else in Buffalo. You can get them in increments of 10 ($8.99), 15 ($12.99), 20 ($16.99), 30 ($23.99), 50 ($38.99), and 100 ($77.99). At last count, it served wings with 34 styles of

sauces. For context, that's 14 more than Buffalo Wild Wings serves, and their 20 seasonings and sauces were the most of any national chain I came across. Wing Zone has 16, Wingstop and Atomic Wings have 11 and East Coast Wings & Grill has eight sauces which it can serve at nine levels of heat (Hooters only has four). Stenis says that one sauce started them all.

Dwyer's opened in 1997 after Greg quit a job he was determined to make the last one where he'd have to work for someone else. "I was adopted," Greg explains, "and my birth name was John Paul Dwyer. So that was the name that I picked for the bar rather than Greg Stenis's. Stenis is Dutch. I don't know of many Dutch pubs. We'd have a whole different theme—wooden shoes and windmills. It would totally not be the same sort of place."

Greg, who orders wings from Dwyer's under an anonymous name once or twice a week to test out their quality, said he uses a butter substitute instead of the real thing, noting that he doesn't think most people can tell the difference and has never had someone even ask. But he *is* a Frank's man. "I haven't found one yet that's dead-on for Frank's," he told me. "People come in all the time and try to sell me on their sauce, but nothing comes close. It just has the right balance of not being too hot and having lots of flavor."

He does two versions of Frank's-based wing sauces: Buffalo style and Dwyer's style. In addition to a few secret ingredients Greg wouldn't share, the key difference is the addition of vinegar to the Dwyer's style. The Suicide sauce doesn't use any vinegar, but does include a pound of habaneros.

Dwyer's first non Buffalo-style sauce was raspberry barbecue. He had been using a bottled sauce and then one day it wasn't available anymore. Unwilling to part with a style that had become popular at the bar, he had to come up with his own version.

It was the opening of Greg's creative floodgates. If you're a barbecue-sauce wing lover, you've found Mecca. Dwyer's serves seven different kinds of barbecue flavors including esoteric sauces that include raspberry, strawberry, and Jameson Irish Whiskey. In addition to common non-Frank's flavors like Creole, garlic Parmesan, honey garlic, honey mustard, and teriyaki, there are more customized sauces like spicy sesame, zesty orange, and wasabi plum. And yes, you can even order General Tso wings.

Wings come in a plastic, paper-lined basket with four pieces of celery (carrots, Greg says, are just one more thing to stock that he doesn't have any other use for), a sealed container of Ken's blue cheese dressing and enough napkins and Wet-Naps to imply you're about to take a bath in the three tablespoons of sauce that collect in the basket underneath. Fair enough—both the flats and drumsticks are pretty wet.

The Dwyer's-style wings are fairly crispy on the edges with skin on the sides revealing big, white, beautiful scald patches. "People ask for them crispy, but ours are generally crispy already," Stenis says, noting that he cooks them at 350°F. Medium tastes more like mild with just a hint of spiciness. But the wings *are* tangy, really juicy under the crispness of the skin with enough sauce to flavor the meat on the inside on a second bite, a terrific ratio you don't always find.

If you're into flavor experimentation, double-dipping Dwyer's 34 sauces allow for more exponential combinations than you're likely to have time for. Greg singled out one regular's standby of honey garlic and barbecue as one of the most successful. As for purists who might cringe at a Baskin-Robbins slogan approach to wings? Stenis is unphased. "You know, somebody will be writing about chicken wings, and they'll say, '*That's* not a true chicken wing!' Well, okay. Well it is now."

#13 Bocce Club Pizza

4174 Bailey Avenue, 14226 | 716-833-1344
Sun–Thu 10 AM–11 PM, Fri–Sat 10 AM–12 AM

La Nova is widely credited in Buffalo as being the originator of barbecue wings "from the pit" in 1971, but the Nickel City's most famous pizzeria is no slouch when it comes to wing lineage. Bocce, which founder Dino Pacciotti opened in 1946 after returning from World War II (check out the chapter on pizza for more about Bocce's epic trim-surrounded pies), started serving their wings in the mid-'80s, about the time they added subs and started delivering.

At Bocce, orders come in 10, 20, and 30 pieces, or by the 50-piece bucket. You can have them either Buffalo-style (mild, medium, or hot) or grilled "Over-The-Pit" with a choice of barbecue sauce, honey mustard, or Cajun seasoning. (Pit wings cost about a dollar more per order than conventional Buffalo flavored ones.) Like many of Buffalo's venerated pizzerias, Bocce is mostly a takeout joint.

Since it's not fair to judge wings that travel (the Styrofoam containers steam the skin soft) that makes judging their wings a parking lot affair. That also means that it's at this takeout machine, where your wings go from the pit pretty much directly to you right away, you have a good chance of eating the hottest, crispiest wings you'll ever have. Glistening with a thick, deep red, sticky-sweet sauce, Bocce's pit wings are stone-cold, messy-face napkin killers. They come super hot and crunchy, the zesty barbecue sauce giving just a glimpse here and there of the fried skin underneath that's been branded with beautiful black grill marks. While still juicy, the extra heat from the pit roasting seems to cook the meat inside just slightly more, allowing it to pull off in tender chunks that are less wet than usual.

Even though Bocce does delivery, Dino's son Jim notes that a tremendous number of folks prefer to do their own takeout. That's the kind of thing that makes sense after eating their wings because even if you love the starving friends and family waiting for your return, these are worth sneaking a few solo in the car before leaving the lot. Just don't forget the Wet-Naps or the secret's out.

#12 The Place

229 Lexington Avenue, 14222 | 716-882-7522
theplacebuffalo.com | Mon 4 PM–2 AM,
Tue–Sun 11:30 AM–2 AM

Flynnie's Thinnie, Thanksgiving dinner every Wednesday (all year), and Buffalo's most storied spot for a Tom & Jerry—these are all things you hear about The Place, which is probably also the restaurant that the city's most nostalgic about. What I didn't hear as much about were the wings. And after tasting them, I have to ask: Can it be that The Place, arguably, one of Buffalo's most famous restaurants, also serves some of the city's most underrated wings? I'd argue yes.

For those who don't know, The Place is *old-school* Buffalo. Co-owner Jason McCarthy, who

took it over with husband-and-wife partners Kevin and Elizabeth Brinkworth, traces the building back to the 1870s, when Jacob Beier opened a saloon at 229 Butler in a rural intersection north of the city on a dirt and plank road before the street was named Lexington. Other owners followed, Edward Donnelly and Christoph Piller, who ran "Piller's Cafe" during Prohibition (when it was said to have been raided by federal agents who found nearly $15,000 of booze). But it was Bernie Flynn, who opened The Place two weeks before the bombing of Pearl Harbor in 1941, who is credited for many of its traditions, including its décor; its Tom & Jerry cocktails; its ham, Swiss, and onion on rye sandwich (Flynnie's Thinnie); and even its name.

"I heard that Bernie would say, 'I'm going to the place. I'm going to the place. I'm going to the place to work,'" Jason explained. "So it just became, "Why don't we call it The Place?'"

Edward "Buddy" Flynn (no relation), worked with Bernie at The Place before taking it over and passing it on to his own nephew Kenny Moriarty (Buddy Flynn's nephew). It's Kenny, who supposedly started working there at the age of 5, who most of Buffalo associates with The Place. He took it over in the '90s and could be found working there until he retired in 2015. And that's just the thing, The Place is *something* to everyone. "You have three or four generations of families that come through here," Jason told me. "They might just do it at different points of the night."

Daniel Okrent, the writer and the inventor of the fantasy baseball game Rotisserie League Baseball, told me, "The Place is [was] my idea of the perfect neighborhood restaurant."

New ownership brought some changes with it: the removal of the wall in the front, an extension of the bar and a whole new back bar, and a new porch out front for outdoor dining. But The Place is still The Place. And Rochester-born chef Chris Machols makes a mean plate of wings. They come 10 to an order, in mild, medium, hot, or BBQ ($12). They're spartanly sauced crispy wings made the classic way ("We use Frank's, absolutely," Jason said). They leave just a trace of red butter left on the plate and are served with a jumble of four clean and fresh carrot and celery logs, and a small ramekin of blue cheese sauce that Jason says they make from scratch: "I think the chunks of good, crumbly blue are important. You go to a pizzeria—it's always just very milky and not quite there, but the thickness of it, the chunks of blue cheese, that's what gives you that extra flavor when you get the wing and the cheese."

#11 Mammoser's

16 S Buffalo Street, Hamburg 14075
716-648-1390 | Mon–Thu 11:30 AM–11 PM,
Fri–Sat 11:30 AM–12:30 AM, Closed Sun

Mammoser's is a cozy, welcoming ramshackle place that emits a light and life that makes you wish to be a part of it in a Dickensian, Ghost-of-Christmas-Present kind of way. It's a narrow dive with a long bar, a few stained glass lamps, an Arachnid arcade dart machine and two wobbly high-tops along the wall. There's another room to the right when you first walk in but the life of the place is on the narrow left side at the bar underneath a low ceiling with exposed beams,

where a few beads of water dripped down from the ceiling on a night with no rain. It's the kind of place where not only does that not bother you, but you're kind of happy about it.

Mammoser's was actually born in 1937 across the street from its current location. Owner Peter Dimfle says his grandparents Earl and Mary Mammoser had to move in 1948, when another business in the building wanted to expand. "The building originally in 1840 was a stable," Dimfle explains. "If you look at the ceiling, you can see all the hand-cut beams. It was a stable and it was converted into a home, and then it was converted into a bar. I tell everybody, 'It started as a barn, then they just knocked the N off of it and turned it into a bar.'"

Dimfle's mother and stepfather bought Mammoser's in 1975 ("That's why my name's different," he tells me), and he took over in 2003. But their sauce has its origins with his mother in the '70s. They had a big garden and his mother was into spicy foods, and one day she just sat down and started mixing up some stuff for a wing sauce. It's a cayenne-based sauce, which Dimfle claims makes the heat stick to the wings better, and they don't use butter or margarine. At one point, he says they were mixing it with a drill motor in five gallon buckets, but they've been getting their recipe bottled since 1978.

"Wing sauce has really kept us alive," Dimfle tells me, noting the demise of Buffalo's post-shift, shot-and-beer days when the steel plants were still open. "When my mom and my stepdad bought the business from my grandfather, he told them, 'Forget about this kitchen, you're never going to make any money back there.' Honestly, if they would have done that, and didn't go into the food trade the way they did, we probably wouldn't be having this conversation."

Dimfle's goal when he took over was to be able to look down the bar anytime during the day or evening and see everybody at the bar sitting there eating. So he borrowed money, well over 100 percent of the original purchase price, to put in outdoor patios, outfit the bar with a walk-in and freezer, redo the kitchen, and expand into drafts and beers from micro-breweries. "I want everybody with a plate in front of them. That was my goal and that's what I've accomplished."

Wings come in orders of 10 up to 50, and are served with thin, short celery sticks, baby carrots ("We used to cut our own celery, but I had a cook put a knife through his hand and that's when we decided we were going to start buying baby carrots"), and a seven-stack of napkins, presumably to help just as much with keeping clean as for the scalp-sweating even the medium wings can cause.

You notice something more to these wings on the first bite. Definitely the cayenne, and it's a dryer wing than what you're used to. There's no runny sauce or film on the bottom of the plate. It almost seems like it's just a rub, but the more bites you take, the more it feels like a thicker, sticky powder. The drumsticks are pretty crispy along the edge, not juicy inside but not dry at all, and while there's a crispness to the flats, they're not necessarily *crispy* along the sides. And yet they're not wet either.

You'd be able to tell these apart blindfolded from any others in town. This might help you in matters of self-protection, because touching your eyes after touching these babies would *not* be smart.

#10 Kelly's Korner

2526 Delaware Avenue, 14216 | 716-877-9466
Sun-Thu 10 am–2 am, Fri-Sat 10 am–3 am

You're likely to drive right by many of Buffalo's best wing places. Except Anchor, whose signs outside proclaim it "home of the original Buffalo chicken wing," there's little indication outside of most of the best places that there are even wings being served. That's especially true of Kelly's Korner in North Buffalo, which, sitting on the corner of Delaware Avenue and Hartwell Road, looks like a local bar if there ever was one.

Sure, it says "Food & Spirits" in big black letters on the side of the building that look as though someone painted them over white stripes on a shaky ladder. And if you look closely as you whiz by, you might make out "Beef on Weck" highlighted in yellow below the green awning above the door. But none of that implies the urgency anyone looking for good food should feel driving by this spot founded in 1967 by Bob and Marge Kelly. Because what's not necessarily true elsewhere that *is* here is how tremendous the wings are and how great the beef on weck is too. If you only have time to hit one place for these two icons, this cash-only spot is it.

Inside, Kelly's Korner has the feeling of the kind of place you go when you need a few quick rounds of shots and chasers to get the night going. There's a dart machine, skeeball, a small bar topped with trophies and surrounded by a few Formica tables and a row of three weathered booths against the wall that feel well-sunken into.

Look no further for the menu than on the wall by the booths above a bright red Budweiser sign usually advertising beef on weck. The short menu is spelled out in small white letters like you

see on felt boards at church or in funeral homes: roast beef sandwich, hot beef and gravy, meatloaf with potatoes, turkey sandwich, chicken sandwish [sic], french fries, ham sandwich, kielbasa, homemade soup, chili, and mashed potatoes. The wings are served with both carrots and celery and come either mild, medium, hot, BBQ, or garlic in orders of 10, 20, 30, and 50.

A local at the bar recommends the garlic and proclaims the BBQ wings the best in town. "That's because you don't like cayenne," the bartender retorts, noting the spice as a key ingredient in their homemade house hot sauce.

As soon as they're set down, you notice the homemade touch applied to the wings. You get the sense someone really took care with them. There's no Frank's red sheen on these wings. Instead, you see flecks of red pepper seeds in a sauce that clings to the cracks, crevices, and corners of every fried surface and that pools in a small puddle of one or two tablespoons under the wings on the plate. There's a pale beige fry on the sides of the wings with crispy ends, and a pleasant, cayenne burn with little to no vinegary tang.

#9 The Lenox Grill

140 North Street, 14201 | 716-884-1700

lenoxgrill.com | Sun–Thu 11 AM–2 AM, Fri–Sat 11 AM–4 AM

The Lenox Grill has the look and feel of a dive bar that's been around forever. That probably has something to do with the fact that it's in the basement of the Lenox Hotel, an eight-story Allentown fixture built in 1896 that's said to be Buffalo's longest operating hotel. But the space has actually housed various restaurants over the years, most recently North, which replaced Leopold's Eatery before settling in as a cozy pub generally known around town for having Buffalo's largest variety of beer (nine pages of more than 500 bottled beers, craft beers, ciders, and meads at last count). Lenox Grill also proudly warns that it takes approximately 20 minutes to cook wings, the longest cooking time I saw declared on *any* menu in Buffalo (*Can't find better wings!?*).

A few steps down from the street, The Lenox Grill has the neighborhood character and sense of life that most hotel bars only dream of. If it's a weekend, you need to reserve ahead if you want

F. Scott Fitzgerald is said to have lived with his parents as a child in an apartment in the Lenox while his father was a soap salesman with Procter & Gamble.

to sit in the dining room. Don't get me wrong. It's not fancy. In fact, it's even been compared to a hobbit house. A low ceiling, a working fireplace in the dining room, and a stuffed goose on the wall (one of the trophies said to belong to owner Anthony Trusso) makes that case, but it doesn't quite feel like the kind of place to kick back with Gandalf to smoke some pipe-weed. The crowded pink neon-lit bar area up front is a dark, lamplit, and wood-paneled area with four TVs playing the news and whatever three sporting events are most Buffa-relevant. And there are a few tables where you can comfortably get a two-beer buzz on in friendly, no-frills confines where you can blend in with locals while you wait for wings.

Wings come single (10, $10.90), double (20, $17.20), triple (30, $24.70), and by the bucket (50, $38.20) with mild, medium, hot, suicidal, barbecue, Korean BBQ, honey sriracha, or pineapple jerk sauce. Korean BBQ is one of the Lenox Grill's most highly regarded sauces, but you do well to ask if there's anything off the menu in the works

too. They've been known to do daily specials of the chef's creations, like sesame teriyaki.

Twenty minutes is enough time for plenty of anticipation to build as well as the preceding preparation of a plate, two bowls, five napkins, and a Wet-Nap, all of which indicate you might be informed of some formal eating ceremony to come, or at least some very saucy wings. In fact, though, the wings arrive glistening and well-sauced but not particularly wet. Two thin celery sticks and three carrots have been hewn into spears, and there's a thin blue cheese dressing that has the consistency of yogurt and almost no crumbles of blue cheese to speak of. The sides of the flats get crisp attention, similar to the ones served at Gabriel's Gate. They're crispy, crunchy, and tangy, and their medium is a light heat with a buttery finish that you don't find everywhere in town.

Settling in on a Monday when they do 64¢ wings (as long as you buy a drink), and opting for the burger or one of three styles of steak sandwich—Pittsburgh-style topped with coleslaw and fries; "Leaded" with sautéed peppers, onions, and mushrooms; or "In the Grass" with sautéed spinach—may be one of the best deals to start the week in town.

#8 Duff's

3651 Sheridan Drive, Amherst Street, 14226
716-834-6234 | duffswings.com
Mon-Thu 11 am-11 pm, Fri-Sat 11 am-12 am,
Sun 12 pm-10 pm

Conveniently for anyone flying in or out of the Nickel City, Duff's locations form a Buffalo wing

triangle northwest (Amherst), northeast (Williamsville), and directly south (Depew) of Buffalo Niagara International Airport. There's also an Orchard Park Duff's and one in Niagara Falls. But the Amherst location is *it*, the original, and it's Buffalo's *best* most-famous wing spot.

The original is a squat, long white building with red letters that spell out "DUFF'S" on the right side. Inside, it's well-lit and cozy with brick walls, big windows, and stucco white pillars and arches on either side of the dining room. It's super clean and smells fresh. The black Formica tables are shining and ready for a good saucing.

I arrive late one night in February, just after leaving Anchor Bar. Whereas Anchor was noisy with live music and packed with wing-hungry

tourists waited on by a sweet if zigzagging staff, Duff's is winding down for the night, quiet. It's nearing closing time and there are only a few tables full. It lends an Edward Hopper "Nighthawks" effect to the place that seems to imply that Duff's is some suburban roadside pilgrimage, a temple to drums and flats that's somehow more serious about their wings. But subsequent visits to Duff's earlier in the day paint a much busier picture, and in the relative quiet I find that even in Buffalo you can't escape Brooklyn or best-of lists. Two college-aged kids who sound like they're from Long Island make me cringe, one describing Greenpoint, Brooklyn as a 'badass neighborhood' that's "close to everything and the rent's not bad for New York and what you get." His friend listens attentively and asks the waitress for ranch, a sin against wings. A waitress obliges without judgement (external, that is). Thankfully, native high-school kids provide Duff's with local cred. Over some picked over bowls of wings, they're discussing a recent list of the cities with America's favorite pizza published by *Travel + Leisure* where Buffalo ranks third, and how good Buffalonians have it when it comes to pizza.

Just to recap a few important details about Duff's that I've said scattered in a few other places: Louise Duffney founded Duff's as a gin mill in 1946 and started serving wings in 1969 five years after Anchor Bar. Duff's sauce started out being made with Frank's, but these days, they have their own recipe. Duff's beat Anchor on Travel Channel's *Food Wars* in 2010 and also won out on the Obama derby (when President Obama visited Buffalo, he hit up

Duff's). Duff's famous "Medium Is Hot" signs started because their wings were known to be much hotter than anyone else's, something that may have inspired the proliferation of heat levels applied to wings.

These days, Duff's wings come served with honking big celery sticks, baby carrots, and Duff's thin, slightly sweet blue cheese in orders of five ($6.79), 10 ($11.79), 20 ($20.79), 30 ($30.79), and 50 ($45.79) and at eight levels of heat: mild, mild medium, medium light, medium (IS HOT), medium hot (IS VERY HOT), hot (IS VERY, VERY HOT), suicidal sauce, death sauce, BBQ, and spicy BBQ. "'Medium is hot' is the most popular," the waitress says. They arrive with two wooden bowls, a plastic discard bucket, and no limit to the napkins. There's a dispenser right there on the table, which is a good thing because these are some pretty wet wings.

These are also some very crispy wings. They're less plump and juicy in a head-to-head with Anchor, but what you lose on that front is more than made up by the higher crunch of their fried skin. In truth, "Medium (IS HOT)" really just tastes like a slightly spicier and very vinegary-tangy medium, a really pleasant, low-key burn. They may not be quite as plump and juicy, but they're really well cooked with more Buffalo flavor and crunch than at Anchor with a little puddle of sauce left in the bottom of the bowl that gives you plenty of chances for double-dipping if you're eating alone or with someone who won't care.

#7 La Nova

371 West Ferry Street, 14213 | 716-881-3303
lanova-pizza.com | Sun–Thu 10 AM–11 AM,
Fri–Sat 10 AM–12 AM

La Nova wasn't the first place to serve pizza in Buffalo, (though neither was Bocce—that honor goes to Santora's), but it does claim to be the first *pizzeria* to start serving *wings*. In fact, they trace the introduction of their "Bar-Be-Que" wings ("from the Pit") to when Papa Joe Todaro moved the restaurant from its original location in Tonawanda to the intersection of Delaware and Tacoma in North Buffalo in 1971.

So they've developed some expertise over the years, and the accolades to go with it. In fact, if I didn't mention La Nova whenever I was asked where I'd been for wings so far, I heard the same refrain: "Oh, well that's a major gap. You *have* to go to La Nova." It's true, given its longevity (it was founded in 1957) and the role it plays in the city's pizza landscape (it may be even more famous than Bocce around town), if you leave Buffalo without eating pizza and wings at La Nova, you haven't done it right. La Nova has even taken the local success of their business (they've been reported to have annual gross sales of $5 million) and in 1994, turned it into a wholesale business, selling pre-cooked, heat-and-serve wings to other restaurants.

Not that heat-and-serve wings are what you're going for at La Nova. You'll get them fresh off the grill you can hear searing off order after order back behind the counter where row after row of deck ovens turn out some of the city's favorite pizza.

La Nova's Buffalo wings are some of the least sauced around town. There's plenty of flavor. But the medium was fairly mild, and the wings, even despite the relative lack of sauce, were on the tamer side of crispy. Don't get me wrong, they're good and probably the wings you want if you actually want to taste the chicken, but I wouldn't crave them the way I dream about their sesame-crust pizza. The pit wings on the other hand were something special. They're completely sauced but not dripping and they have dark ends and long black streaks of char on all sides from a few turns on the grill. These wings seem slightly smaller than ones they do Buffalo-style, though whether that's from them being cooked an extra way or because they started off smaller is impossible to know.

What you do know is that they're crunchy and crispy with a sour-sweet tang. And because La Nova is one of the rare pizzerias in town that has a big dining room, there's space to enjoy them right there at their prime with a fresh slice.

#6 Lovejoy Pizza

900 Main Street, Allentown, 14202 | 716-883-2323
lovejoypizza.com | Mon–Thu 11 AM–9:30 PM,
Fri–Sat 11 AM–10 PM, Sun 12 PM–9 PM

If there's a case to be made for wings made using liquid butter, co-owner Anthony Kulik is making it at his Lovejoy pizzeria. Truth be told, Kulik (pictured opposite) doesn't make his sauce with the liquid stuff full-on but says he cuts the real thing with the liquid to help offset the cost of butter. And I have to say, I'd be hard-pressed to tell his superior wings from a sauce made with straight butter.

Lovejoy's been on the rise in recent years. Their subs garnered the attention of the *Buffalo News*'s food editor Andrew Galarneau—particularly the Lovejoy Street chicken finger sub with sliced stuffed peppers. And Galarneau's colleague Emeri Krawczyk has argued in print that Lovejoy should be added to the list of the city's iconic area pizzerias; also, it beat out the famed La Nova in *Buffalo Spree*'s 2015 best wings bracket.

Both the Lovejoy and downtown locations do great wings using a simple, straightforward approach. "You need a fresh-cut wing, a wing

that's big, but not too big," Kulik tells me. "You shouldn't have to take more than three bites of a wing. The thing should be done within two to three bites."

After that: Frank's. ("We're Buffalo kids, so Frank's RedHot," Kulik says.) And clean oil. "Some guys in this city, they don't change their frigging oil for a month," he adds. "I'm changing this oil every two days. And that's the difference. You gotta have good quality oil, otherwise you're dead."

Per usual, medium is the most popular Buffalo-style ordered, with mild, medium, and hot coming in orders of 10 ($9.75), 20 ($17.50), 30 ($27.00), and by the bucket (50 for $36.00). Lovejoy largely keeps their experimentation to their wings from the pit. They serve Asian wings (a hoisin-based sauce), "Char B-Q Wings" (their take on standard pit wings, which Kulik says are a close second to his medium wings), honey garlic, honey sriracha, honey mustard, garlic-Romano, and his sleeper hit, Louisiana Cajun wings, for a dollar or two more.

"I have the greatest wing in the whole city on my menu," Kulik claims. "But it rarely gets picked. But the people who do find it, man, they order it all the time. And it's my Cajun chicken wing."

Like many pizza joints around town, Lovejoy's is primarily a takeout situation. There are just a few stools inside. And while they do vent the to-go containers with four holes to help prevent them from steaming (if a place doesn't, can they really be considered serious about their wings?) these

are wings that are so good you're going to want to eat them right away. In warmer months, you can sit at the picnic table outside the downtown location, but hanging out by the counter after ordering might be your best bet. Typically, if Kulik's there and he sees you waiting for your food, he's likely to offer you a taste of whatever he's most in love with at the moment. The two times I swung by, that meant tasting the Asian wings and the wildflower honey sriracha wings—both sticky, crispy, and delicious.

As for the classics? Kulik is right about their size. These are plump, crunchy wings that may be just a touch smaller than some around town. They're amply sauced with medium crispness and a heat that has a slow burn. They're more on the medium-hot range for a medium wing. What do they say about it ain't being bragging if it's true? In this case, Lovejoy's wings are worth crowing about.

#5 Judi's Lounge

2057 Military Road, Niagara Falls, 14304
716-297-5759 | judisbarandgrill.com
Mon–Sun 11 AM–2 AM

Judi's Lounge is a great wing stop on the way to or back from Niagara Falls. It's about a 20-minute drive from the *Maid of the Mist*, and about 45 minutes north of downtown Buffalo.

Judi's is one of those places actually named for the owner: Judi Justiana, who opened the

lounge on Military Road with her husband Tom in 1980 before it was widened and when the Outlet Mall was still King's Plaza. It's a dimly-lit, cozy little carpeted bar on the side of a busy four-lane road in a little strip mall with a nail salon, a computer repair shop, and a barber. Inside there are trophies and baseballs above the ATM alcove and bathrooms, since Judi and her husband have sponsored hundreds of local sports teams over the years. There's also a pool table and a few booths along one mirrored wall in the back. And on every table, you'll find New York Lottery's *Quick Draw* and condiment cages filled with salt and pepper, A1, ketchup, mustard, and, of course, Frank's RedHot Sauce. There are a few younger folk in their 20s and 30s, but twice that many in their 40s, 50s, and 60s. This is the kind of bar where you can hear yourself talk.

Judi's says they only use trans-fat-free oil, and their wings are served in three sizes with a very smooth blue cheese dressing and celery: regular (10 wings, $9.95), large (16, $14.50) and super (26, $22.50). You have your choice of mild, medium, hot, BBQ, Honey BBQ, Honey Garlic, "Sting'n" Honey Garlic, Cattleman's Tangy Gold BBQ Sauce (French's Carolina-style mustard sauce), Cajun dry seasoning, Cajun seasoning with wing sauce, Citrus Chipotle BBQ, Butter Garlic Parmesan, and in a rare move, Salt and Pepper.

The wings at Judi's are C-R-I-S-P-Y. Even the "sting'n" honey garlic, which the bar's staff notes as the most popular flavor outside the traditional sauce, which is thoroughly doused with a transparent and thin but very sticky varnish, maintained an impressive crunch. (Their buzz was worse than their bite however, there was a lot of sweet without much sting.) You may be tempted, and you'd be wise, to order wings with several different sauce applications here, starting with an understanding of the *lack* of sauce. The salt-and-pepper application is something you typically see applied to shrimp and pork chops in Chinatown. And here it means that if you're a crisp fanatic, you've found your happy place. It's all chicken flavor and crunchy skin on wings that haven't been

Traditional and "sting'n" honey garlic wings at Judi's.

soggied with sauce or spent even a minute out of the fryer before they're set in front of you. It's a preparation you wish you'd see more often. So too the Cajun dry seasoning, which can also be applied here *with* hot sauce, a tactic where wings are coated with Cajun spice and then sauce-tossed. The result is a peppery blast to the tongue that's a bit like licking a five-o'clock shadow.

But you always have to establish a baseline, and at Judi's the medium and hot wings are some of the best you'll find in town. Trying to dissect how they're made, local wing judge and expert Christa Glennie Seychew called it a *strangely* good sauce. She was right about that. Ten minutes after polishing off the medium wings, there was a pool of sauce at the bottom of the checkered-paper lining the bowl. The sauce had clearly separated the way hot sauce and butter falls apart when they've been heated too much. "It's definitely not Frank's and butter," she speculated, "I think it's homemade."

#4 Bar Bill Tavern

185 Main Street, East Aurora, 14052 | 716-652-7959
barbill.com | Sun 12 PM–2 AM, Mon–Sat 8 AM–2 AM

If you're serious about understanding Buffalo's wing scene—like mathematician, engineer, insane artist serious—you actually need to drive 24 minutes southeast of downtown on the Aurora Expy (NY-400) to visit the Bar Bill Tavern in East Aurora. (At the time of writing, a new location a half-hour north and around the corner from a Duff's and Brennan's Bowery Bar had just been announced.) The building has been there for 150 years, has been a bar for 50, and has been

getting attention for wings since 1983, when Joe Giafaglione added them to a menu that heretofore had only served beef on weck. Bar Bill Tavern is the Modern Apizza to Frank Pepe's in New Haven—it frequently tops the area's best-of lists (it topped *Buffalo Spree*'s most recent best wings bracket) and is routinely mentioned by folks as the place that locals actually go for wings.

There are plenty of theories about the place's name, but "Bar Bill" actually comes from the original owners, Barb and Bill Korzelius, who took over a small ice cream shop called The Cantina in 1967 to open their own tavern. Joe Giafaglione bought the bar in 1977, closing on it on a historic day in Buffalo—January 28th, the day of the Great Blizzard, when President Carter had to declare a state of emergency in New York.

"Joe was not a restaurateur," Clark Crook, the current owner of the Bar Bill tells me. Joe's niece Katie and her husband Clark bought the bar from Joe in 2011. Joe "was a mechanical engineer at Bell Aircraft. What he did was meticulous, maniacal, and anal: he brought engineering practices to his restaurant business."

For this type of business, that sounds promising. Clark said Joe used the scientific method to test and retest his weck and wing recipes to hone his ideal versions. Then, as Clark said, he documented his processes so that he and his staff could be the models of consistency. Joe decided the best wings needed to have sauce *painted* on them.

It's something you can catch a glimpse of if you sit in the back of the restaurant at one of the high-top tables against the wall within eye-shot of the kitchen. Servers paint the wings with a brush, dipping it into one of the many plastic cups on a counter by the door, each filled with a different sauce. It's mesmerizing to watch, and impressive, but you'd think this exacting methodology must really gum up the amount of time it takes to serve wings.

The other thing that happens is that the wings don't get soggy, especially the ones at the bottom of the plate that are laying in the sauce at most joints. A single order at Bar Bill is served with the wings arranged in a tray in a circle around their homemade blue cheese dressing like spokes of a wheel. But that pile effect comes into play with a double order (20) where the spokes are covered with the extra wings. "It makes a huge difference," Clark insists.

There are at least eight different sauce styles and a gradation of heat levels to rival Duff's: mild, medium, medium hot, hot, extra hot, and suicidal (for $1 more). They do honey dijon, zesty honey pepper, teriyaki, Cajun (add 50¢), honey butter BBQ, hot and spicy BBQ, spicy Asian, and Sicilian wings with long strands of Parmesan shavings applied liberally.

It's always tempting to want to split an order into two flavors at places that do so many, and Bar Bill is reasonable about letting you do so. They just charge an extra dollar. It's almost always worth doing. After a while in Buffalo, you're not surprised to come across requests to give your server special instructions in anticipation of wing proclivities and first-time interactions with their wing-iosyncrasies. At Bar Bill, if you like your wings extra saucy you should speak up.

If you want to speak up about special preparations, do so when you first arrive. No matter what happens, though, your mouth is going to be busy soon with a plate of delicious wings. Bar Bill's most popular sauce is medium. Their second most popular sauce is the honey butter BBQ, which is sweet and spicy but not hot. I also opted for a Cajun honey BBQ recommended by the waiter. "You'd be the first person to say they didn't enjoy these." It's a touch sweet, though not cloying, and features a rub that adds an extra dimension of flavor and a sprinkle of extra texture to the wing.

I prefer the non-sweet wing. And there *does* seem to be a bit more crunch to these than most of the city's other crispier wings. It extends throughout the drumsticks and all over the skin on the paddles. And you wonder if there may be something about how the sauce is applied that affects the heat. They're the kind of medium that gets you saying, "Medium is not hot," right before a pleasant burn kicks in.

"I would describe our medium as an out-of-

town hot, so not overly hot, but you know you're eating a chicken wing," Clark explains. "There's a significant jump between our medium and our hot. Our hot is *hot*. So you need to be a person that enjoys hot things. Now if you are, our hot is hot, but it's also very flavorful."

Clark was open about Bar Bill technique, especially where they stand on using Frank's RedHot Sauce. "Our feeling is that if you're a Buffalo purist, then your sauce is based on Frank's," he told me. "And if it's not Frank's, it's not a Buffalo wing, in our opinion. But there's certainly a lot of ingredients that go into the Bar Bill magic." But I couldn't get him on the record about using real butter. "I will not say what we use, but just generically, the Teressa and Frank's recipe is butter and Frank's."

It's a mystery worth trying to solve by returning over and over to this busy, cash-only spot on Buffalo's outskirts, where their beef on weck (served daily until 10 PM) is also regarded as among the city's best, and where they use the meat and skin from actual fried Buffalo wings to make their Buffalo wing pizza. Nice touch. Just remember, they don't take credit cards or reservations and there's not always a hostess on duty.

So seat yourself. Get comfortable. Settle in and

maybe take Clark up on a little Bar Bill Tavern tradition. "There's a little game we like to say we perfected that we call Wing Roulette, that some of our hardy fans like to participate in, where we'll disguise a Suicide wing in their order."

Duck, duck, hot!

#3 Gabriel's Gate

145 Allen Street, Allentown, 14201 | 716-886-0602
gabrielsgate.page.tl | Sun–Wed 11:30 AM–12 AM,
Thu 11:30 AM–1 AM, Fri–Sat 11:30 AM–2 AM

Gabriel's Gate is a well-worn fixture in this Bohemian hood, one that two of the city's other most famous bars, Nietzsche's and The Pink, also call home. For as much of a staple as it's been though, there's actually not much that's been written about its origins over the years. The late David Forness (a former teacher turned restaurateur) bought it in the mid-'80s, but the bar is thought to go back to 1969. The building it's in is touted as "one of the original Tift row houses," which means as much as I can tell it's likely one of the 74 brick-facade houses built in 1863 or 1864 by George Washington Tifft, a capitalist pioneer who made his fortunes in milling, rail, and banking.

Which is all to say that this is old-school Buffalo, something you don't need a history lesson to know intuitively when you climb upstairs inside this creaky joint. There's a wooden cigar store American Indian at the top of the steps along with an aquarium and a dining room filled with tin ceilings, lots of log-legged cushy chairs, faux wood, and Formica. The booths don't match any of the other décor and feel as though they might be church pews. With the way Gabriel's Gate's wings are exalted, they may as well be. Past the front dining room there's a mirror-lined wall behind the bar and hanging a from tall, vaulted ceiling, a huge electric chandelier that looks like something out of a '70s sci-fi movie where they go back in time to the Dark Ages. There's a buffalo (of course) and various other mounted animal heads on the surrounding walls, which according to the menu, were purchased from a science museum in Pennsylvania because the owners "feel it is educationally beneficial to view these rare animals." And who knows, at this point, we may be entering an era so far past saving endangered species for such a politically incorrect statement to actually be true.

Gabriel's Gate's wings are known for being a

little meatier than most. Orders come in just two sizes: single (10, $11.95) and double (20, $17.95). Don't be confused by the menu, those are the prices for mild, medium, and hot wings—heat levels so de rigueur to be assumed. For an additional $1 per single and $2 per double order, your other sauce options are Cajun-style, BBQ, suicide, Sriracha, and Italian.

Wings take a good 15 minutes to arrive—a good sign. Every table is taken, there's a Sabres game on the TVs above the bar, and the folks who have scouted out places in front of the bar's two fireplaces have staked out some of the most coveted bar real estate in the city during winter.

The waitress drops off five napkins before the wings arrive, which seems to be a signature move at places that don't have dispensers. Wings arrive tortoise-style, piled on top of celery sticks on a plate completely covered by a wooden bowl. They're clean, fresh-looking celery sticks, and to anyone who might snigger about the state of celery, the respect given condiments says just as much about a restaurant's dedication to its wings as anything else. The wings are both crispy and plump, though not as crispy on the wings' broad sides. Medium is spicy and tangy. There's a mild linger, though maybe just a tad less hot than a Duff's medium.

#2 Elmo's Bar & Restaurant

2349 Millersport Highway, Getzville, 14068
716-688-7237 | elmosonline.com
Mon–Fri 11:30 am–12 am, Sat 12–close, Closed Sun

When it comes to wings, Elmo's seems like it's been a bit ahead of the curve since not long after it opened in 1985, and it might just be the way of the future for two reasons: price model and wing style.

Elmo's was first owned and operated by Danny Scepkowski, one of the owners of Mighty Taco who is said to have happened to catch the name on a magazine. Some say it was *Time*, others *Newsweek*. But the only Elmo on the cover of either in 1985 was an April *Newsweek* issue featuring mystery author "Elmore Leonard." (Coincidentally, that year happens to be the first that the character appeared on Sesame Street with that name.)

But according to general manager Adam Blake, who started in 1991, it wasn't a big wing spot until Adrienne Meredith took over in the early '90s. "This was an old softball bar that was turned into an after-game bar," explains Drew Cerza, founder of The National Buffalo Wing Festival, who tells me he's on a diet but agrees to meet with me to talk wings. "Then with the college, it became an alumni bar. It's straight-up Frank's and butter. Fry, sauce, grill, sauce, double-dip."

National Buffalo Wing Festival founder "Wing King" Drew Cerza at Elmo's, one of his go-to spots.

Elmo's is next to a little Vietnamese restaurant in a strip mall on Millersport Highway (263) on the outskirts of the city in a hamlet called Getzville. It's a 20-minute drive northeast of downtown and just three minutes from the University at Buffalo, not even enough time to warm your car up. Let's put it this way: if you graduated from University at Buffalo without spending more time at eating wings than you should have, *you* didn't do it right and *they* shouldn't have given you your piece of paper saying you did. I don't care what your GPA was.

Unlike most places (which sell a number of wings by the order), until recently, Elmo's sold by the pound. A single order would net you 1½ pounds of wings and a double, 2½ pounds. No matter what the price of wings were, you were getting consistent poundage. The number of wings just varied. But the fluctuation in wing prices ended the practice two years ago. Now, they don't even put wing prices on the menu. "It's almost like a market price for wings," Blake tells me.

The sauce menu is deceptive in its simplicity. Don't let mild, medium, hot, Cajun, BBQ, and honey mustard fool you. Elmo's is one of the places in town that has embraced, and even suggests that you "Double Dip" your wings and mix two different sauces to create new flavors, like Cajun BBQ and Cajun hot! Double-dipping only costs 50¢ extra, and while it doesn't turn Elmo's into a Disneyland of wings like at Dwyer's, curiosity does make multiple orders a must. And the processes that go into the Cajun wings and double-dipped Cajun-BBQ wings are a little mind-bending. Elmo's Cajun wings go back to

the early '90s, when then-cook Adam Blake was messing around and trying to create a "blackened" wing. They're actually a fried-grilled affair. If you're confused, take this away: Doubling up on cooking techniques is something you see in classic French cuisine. Think of that roast you've sautéed and then roasted. Or that pan-seared duck thrown into the oven. Grilling wings that have already been fried adds extra flavor dimensions: bitterness, caramelization, crunch, crispiness. And when that double-cooking technique is liberated from the barbecue sauce that typically accompanies it in Buffalo, the beauty of it is obvious very quickly.

"Grilling is the way of the future," Cerza confides as our wings are set down with Lincoln Log celery and Ken's blue cheese dressing. "You get the marks and the caramelization."

You can see the internal battle raging inside the man as he surveys the wings set down: Double-dipped BBQ Cajun and Buffalo hot and honey mustard style. His eyes widen, there's a barely noticeable quiver, and suddenly he straightens up letting out a defiant, "Oh, fuck it!" as he reaches for a wing, snatches it back to his mouth like Gollum with "Precious," and bites into it like an addict who's been castaway on Cottage Cheese Island.

You can immediately *see* a difference in these wings before you even taste them, and you can tell they're going to be good. There aren't just char marks on Elmo's barbecued wings, there's *char,* but a sticky-everywhere-char that you only find at backyard grill-outs where the weekend warrior manning it has a beer in hand, a cooler filled with more at his foot, and a dedication to flipping the meat and repeatedly brushing more sauce on all sides throughout the cooking. But as I make my way through the wings, I understand even more why Elmo's wings would be kryptonite to any wing lover looking to shed a few pounds. They're just fantastic: tender, juicy, with a deep dark bouquet of hot sugar, crunch, and salt. The honey mustard are just as tantalizing: tangy and sweet with that crusty char along the sides and on the edges.

Elmo's: "Classic French Chicken Wings" et Les Ailes de Poulet "Triple Trempé"

General manager Adam Blake seems to have some pretty convincing details that maybe he and Elmo's originated Cajun and double-dipping. And if that's not convincing enough, an off-menu Elmo's wing you've probably never heard of may just be all you need to believe this is the only wing place for you.

Cajun wings—how did they start?

I started the Cajun sauce on a slow Monday night. Everything was Cajun-style back then, so we were like, "Let's try it with wings." We came up with a couple of different styles, but ultimately it came down to using Frank's RedHot Sauce as a base, adding some cayenne, black pepper, and a few other ingredients that we keep secret. Then we started grilling the wings and blackening them, and it took off like you wouldn't believe. They put Elmo's on the map.

How did the double-dip come about?

We made an order of Cajun wings and someone said, "Oh, I didn't want Cajun. I wanted barbecue." So we just took them back and put barbecue sauce on them, shook them up, and gave them back. They went off the charts. A mistake wing turned into, "Well, let's try them with honey mustard now. Let's try them with hot sauce, or medium sauce." So, it was grilled to become a dry wing. All of a sudden it looked like a dry rub. And then you put another sauce on top of it, and usually you could do Cajun, or Cajun again with the wet sauce on it, or Cajun with the barbecue sauce on it, and it brings it back to that original Buffalo-style wing, or the wet wing. People went nuts.

When was this that the double-dip was invented?

That was right around the University Games. So 1993.

So were you sneaking a mistake order back out to a customer?

It was two employees, Carl Young and Ryan Stitt. Carl was actually the one who said, "Oh, just give it to him like this." We told him what we were doing. It wasn't like we were trying to be facetious. And they loved it. And then they started passing them around the bar and people were going crazy.

Where'd it go from there?

That whole weekend we started doing it with other wings and people were making up their own wings. Then a couple of the more well-known UB football players, like Khalil Mack, Branden Oliver, and Joe Licata, started naming them. That got really neat. So, Joe Licata would say, "Give me the goat wings," those were the honey mustard Cajun wings. Khalil Mack, we would just call him the Cajun, and he liked medium on top of them, so, we'd do Cajun medium and call them the Mack wings. Stuff like that.

Just to be clear on technique—the Cajun wings—first, they're fried, then they're tossed in the vinegar and reinforced Frank's RedHot with black pepper, mustard, garlic, cayenne, and horseradish, and then those are grilled?

That's right.

And for the double-dipped?

It's fry, sauce, grill, and then off the grill, into a sauce.

And the Cajun-barbecue wings?

You throw the wings in the fryer, get them crispy, shake them in Cajun sauce, grill them to make them blackened, then you take them off the grill, literally from the grill, with two spatulas, lift up the wings, put them in the honey, or put them in the barbecue sauce in a bowl, shake them and plate them.

What's the weirdest or most complicated combination anybody's ever asked for?

Triple-dipped. We kind of shy away from it, because it involves a lot of sauce and the cost of it, but we do it once in a while. We'll do it for our regulars. Ryan has this one sauce he makes, a barbecue Cajun hot wing, and it is phenomenal, but it's really hot. It's very saucy and it's sweet—it's got barbecue sauce in it too—it's an unbelievable wing. He does it with honey mustard too. It's like hot honey mustard, Cajun or hot, barbecue, and Cajun. Those are probably the most elaborate ones we do, and they take a little time. We don't do them on a regular basis, especially when it's busy, but when it's slower, and we've got some regulars in, we'll let them order it like that.

So, that's off the menu? You have to know about it?

Correct.

And how is that made?

It goes in the fryer, and then it's done Cajun. Then he puts his barbecue sauce on, grills that. Then, after that it's grilled Cajun, it's grilled barbecue, and then he takes his extra hot sauce that he makes himself, and puts that on as the final coating. Then it comes from the bowl of the extra-hot onto the plate.

Does the cooking time change for that?

He pulls the wing up a little short of a normal cooking time, because it's grilled twice. It's probably not in the fryer long, but it's on the grill longer.

#1 The Nine-Eleven Tavern

11 Bloomfield Avenue, 14220 | 716-825-9939

www.facebook.com/TheNineElevenTavern

Tue–Sat 4:30 PM–1 AM, Closed Sun–Mon

Let's get a few things out of the way. First, The Nine-Eleven Tavern was founded in 1981 and named for its address; it has nothing to do with what happened *on* 9/11. Second, these are the most beautifully presented wings in Buffalo. And third, while an owner in the kitchen doesn't always mean the food is going to be great, it sure says something about a level of commitment. In this case, it means Mark Gress is making his homemade sauce, working the fryer in his tiny kitchen, and that if it's busy, which it usually is, it may take up to 40 minutes. Forty minutes for wings. That's right. And they're worth it.

The Nine-Eleven Tavern is a quick on and off I-190 or the Buffalo Skyway along the lake. It's a little pillbox of a bar just off Southside Parkway about a 12-minute drive south of downtown on a stretch of auto service shops, empty lots, hardware shops, and stores like Family Dollar that looks ripe for development. There's just a brick facade, a low green awning with the name of the

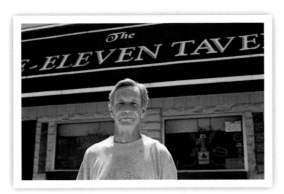

bar and four tiny, impervious windows. It's the kind of place that from the outside even intimidates locals. Food blogger Donnie Burtless, who has been documenting his eating adventures around the city for *Buffalo Eats* since 2009, almost balked on his first visit. "I'm not going to lie, I looked at the exterior and almost chickened out. It's not that I didn't want to eat there because it looked like a 'dive,' but I was afraid it was going to be a 'regulars only' type of establishment. Basically, I was afraid we were going to walk in and get 'who are you' looks for our entire visit. That was not the case at all."

Inside, it's actually a pretty friendly, even playful place. There's an outdoor patio for warmer months, a bar and to its side, a dining room filled with 10 tables and an open doorway at the back to the kitchen (which closes at 11 PM) where you can hear wings bubbling away. There are tin ceilings, wood paneling and boxes of Flutie Flakes on the wall. A sign above the ladies room says "Buffalo" where the "B" is a drumstick and the "l" is a celery stick. On the menus (it's cash only), the "11" in Nine-Eleven are portrayed as wings, each going a different way.

I know. You still don't get the name. "But it's 11 Bloomfield," you're saying, right? Look at the front of the building. See the two doors? Almost like it was one building that used to be split into two addresses at some point? Like 9-11 Bloomfield Avenue. Ironically, as Gress tells me, "We opened on the ninth day of the 11th month… November 9th, 1981."

The space had already been a bar called Ann's Inn, named for its owner Ann Zantac. Before her, Mark says the place was called Mueller's and the

Bloomfield Inn. A customer who found an old directory in his grandmother's attic and brought it in to show Mark discovered that in 1932, near Prohibition's end, it had been a place called Salty's Soda Shop.

When Gress took over, Buffalo was still a big steel town. He said he would open at 11 AM and cash $3,000 in payroll checks on a Thursday. But as more manufacturing jobs disappeared, Mark, who'd kicked around restaurants and bars in Saranac Lake, Lake Placid, Denver, and Aspen, started making wings. "Ann really didn't have a menu, you know? She had a couple of tabletop electric fryers and a stove. There wasn't really much going on as far as food goes. As time went on, the necessity to get into the food end drove me more and more to perfecting the wing sauce."

These days, he's also known for making a mean burger, a crave-worthy corned beef, and his dark, hand-cut "Finn fries." But there's not *that* much more equipment in the kitchen. "It's a shoe-box back there. I've got two fryers, a charbroiler, a stove, and that's it," Gress says. "I clean, I sweep, I mop, I do all the ordering, and I'm the only one in the kitchen that cooks. There's two days a year that I have a helper. He's my bartender. He's been here for, like, 26 years. He'll come and help me during St. Patrick's Day week."

The Nine-Eleven Tavern is all about the basics—wings come mild, medium, and hot, and are served with celery and Ken's blue cheese dressing (or, controversially, ranch) in orders of 10 ($9.45), 20 ($18.45), 30 ($27.35) or 50 ($44.75). Gress notes that his medium might be hotter than other places and says that's what's most popular. "It depends on the night. We had a lot of

hot orders last night. Who knows what tonight's going to bring. I think it's all personal taste. Quite honestly. But I don't buy into, you know, suicidal, blah, blah, blah. Alright, this is our hot, you want them a little hotter, okay, I can maybe do that for you, but if you're expectations are going to be you want smoke coming out of your ears, that ain't happening."

The sauce at this local legend is the subject of speculation and something of a mystery. It's almost always identified as being homemade and usually described as a bit hotter than average and sweeter. Feta, Parmesan, malt vinegar, and cider vinegar have all been suggested as ingredients. Gress won't spill on spice specifics, but he does have pretty strong opinions about how wings should be made.

"I make all my sauce hot, alright?" Gress says matter-of-factly. "So if you buy a jar of sauce here, you're not going to get medium or mild, you're just going to get hot, and I'll tell you how to cut that to make it medium or mild."

The key to that is using clarified butter, which Gress says he also does for flavor.

"A number of years ago I was talking to a guy who owned a place in Cleveland. You know, wings, blah, blah, blah, and he's saying, 'You throw some Frank's in there, you throw some Oleo, you're fine.' Oleo! Oh, my God, it's the worst thing on the planet. It's like Cheese Whiz. You know, it's the Cheese Whiz of butter, you know? So anyway, no, I use clarified butter. It's a little more expensive, but the flavor difference is obvious. I clarify my own butter. In other words, I just melt pounds of salted butter as needed."

As for how his wings get their heat, Gress demurs. "I think everybody starts with the basics. And in my particular case, yeah, I start with the basics, but then I . . . let's just say I've made it my own."

So there's real butter, there's Frank's and then there's a whole bunch of spices in there that you won't go into? "You can interpret it any way you want," he says.

Ha! Fair enough.

Whatever Gress is doing is working. These are the best wings I've ever had. They look just lightly crispy, but both the flats and bats are evenly fried everywhere and there's a really good crispy crunch. The wings are completely dressed, not dripping but glistening and coated on all sides, with at least a teaspoon of sauce under each one. The real butter taste definitely comes through and there's that classic Louisiana hot sauce flavor. While I didn't find medium to be particularly spicy, it *is* tangy.

But before you dive in, you're immediately struck by the presentation. The wings are arranged on a circular plate around a cup of blue cheese with a sprig of celery leaves standing upright in it. There's a celery stick between every two wings and a smattering of sauce drizzled over the wings and dotting some edges of the plate. I've heard Gress' presentation described as resembling a sundial. I can see that, but it looks more to me like a straight-up clock or a wheel, its celery starfish radiating out like a chicken wing flux capacitor that's about to start spinning or pulsing to send me back in time safe and sound now, back to that fateful night Teressa Bellissimo invented them in good old 1964. Double and triple orders are even more impressive. Other layers of wings are stacked on each other in the same formation. It starts to look like some kind of crazy game of chicken wing Jenga, or a toddler

"Well, I went to school at Paul Smith's College, alright? And as part of our schooling we had to work in the Hotel Saranac. I went there for hotel restaurant management. So when I was working in the kitchen I remember the one chef, he said to me one night, he said, 'Mark, you can serve them shit on a shingle but if you make it look good, they'll love it.' So ever since then, everything I've ever done I've always tried to make it look nice. It took me a while to figure this one out, you know, over the years. I tried it different ways but this one, when I started doing it this way, this one stuck you know? I'm, like, 'Man, this looks good.'"   —Mark Gress chef's brilliant architectural innovation assembled with Tinkertoys made out of flats and bats. This is the kind of presentation it would be worth visiting the tavern with a few friends just to be able to see the 50 wings balanced that way, or to turn them into a drinking game. Nobody plates wings like this. No wonder it can take some time. And how on earth did Gress come up with the idea?

The question is, does he plate them that way for himself when he eats them? "Quite honestly, I don't eat wings," Gress says with a little smirk. "I might have … well, I don't know, maybe two wings a year."

RANKING BUFFALO'S BEST WINGS

1.	The Nine-Eleven Tavern	8.	Duff's	15.	McPartlan's
2.	Elmo's	9.	Lenox Grill	16.	Gene McCarthy's
3.	Gabriel's Gate	10.	Kelly's Korner	17.	Doc Sullivan's
4.	Bar Bill Tavern	11.	Mammoser's	18.	Bases Loaded
5.	Judi's Lounge	12.	The Place	19.	Wiechec's
6.	Lovejoy	13.	Bocce	20.	Anchor
7.	La Nova	14.	Dwyer's Irish Pub		

Wings Worth the Road Trip

You could spend weeks eating wings around New York State, finding hidden gems and funky sauces being made by hothead geniuses and barfolk in it for nothing other than the glory of getting a tip of the cap from regulars who know a good thing when they see them. In fact, that's just what director Matt Reynolds did while filming his epic search for the best wings in the world, *The Great Chicken Wing Hunt*, hitting more than 70 places. If you plan on watching the documentary and don't want any spoilers, stop reading now. By the end of his journey, Matt and his merry band of wing-seekers crowned Abigail's the king of all wings. It's a restaurant on US 20 about two hours east of Buffalo in the town of Waterloo (a little less than an hour further east and you hit Syracuse). There's some controversy in the film and a debate about whether you can technically call Abigail's wings "Buffalo" wings because of the special way that they're made, but eventually it's decided that they are. Because they're not *in* Buffalo, I'm obviously not going to list them along with the top

20 wings in Buffalo, but there was no way I was going to miss them, and based on how good they are, if you're even half as serious about wings as you think you are, you wouldn't think of missing them either. If Abigail's was *in* Buffalo, it's hard to believe they wouldn't routinely be considered near the top of every best of list.

Abigail's

1978 US 20, Waterloo, NY 13165
315-539-9300 | abigailsrestaurant.com
Lunch: Mon–Fri 11:30 am–2 pm,
Dinner: Mon–Sat 5 pm– 9 pm, Sun 4 pm–8 pm

"Sometimes I forget about winning, but it doesn't go too long before people come in and congratulate me again," Abigail's chef Columbus 'Marshall' Grady told me. Grady has been cooking for more than 35 years. This former security guard tells me he's cooked elsewhere but seeing him move from one end of the kitchen to the other during service, it's hard to conceive of the place existing before him. His "Bleu Bayou Chicken Wings," made with a sauce that *combines* traditional wing condiments—celery, Frank's Red-Hot, and blue cheese—glisten with a brilliance

that smacks of Teressa Bellissimo's eureka moment.

A plaque on the wall by the door says Abigail's was founded in 1984. It doesn't look like the kind of place you'd expect to be known for wings, from the road or once inside. It's announced by a red and white sign with a rose and the white trim building is set back from the road in a huge parking lot on the outskirts of the small town (population 5,171) that's otherwise famous for the federal government declaring it the birthplace of Memorial Day. Abigail's looks like it could have been an old school, a funeral home, or even a town hall and the cavernous, wood-paneled, yellow dining room filled with linen-covered tables says "Steak," or small-town early-bird special.

Grady invented the recipe for his "Bleu Bayou Chicken Wings" 15 years ago, but netted his 15 seconds in 2014 (his recipe was even published in the *Wall Street Journal*). "My manager wanted to have wings on the buffet," he explains to me. "She asked, 'Can you do a different kind of wings every day?' I said, 'Sure.' So we did some 105 days of different wings."

The idea for Bleu Bayou was all about building a better mousetrap. "I was just thinking, there's gotta be a better way to do this because of the

condiments," Grady told me. "People like to dip, but if you were to mix everything together, you'd get all the flavors and not have to worry about dipping in the blue cheese because it would just be in the sauce. You don't have to worry about the celery because it's in the sauce."

You can buy the sauce at the restaurant (a bottle costs $9 for shipping and handling) where Grady makes two versions, mild and hot, by the gallon. "Celery and blue cheese and the Frank's RedHot Sauce, that's as far as I go," Grady tells me when I pry into how he actually makes the sauce at Abigail's. "I use at least 16 ounces of Frank's RedHot per gallon. The sauce doesn't get cooked. It goes right on. When we bottle it up it has to be prepared a little differently. It has to be cooked."

Bleu Bayou Chicken Wings come 12 to an order ($9.99) either mild, medium, or hot (the menu also always features a honey barbecue sauce, though how you'd be able to resist ordering the Bleu Bayou every time, I wouldn't know). The wings arrive on a big blue plate and are easily more sauced than any others I've ever seen. The sauce is thick, nappant, almost as thick as a cheese soup. "We usually use 2 ounces of sauce per dozen," Grady says. "You don't want them to be really dry. You want to keep the taste of the chicken there." There are tiny flecks of celery in the sauce and if you run a finger through it, it takes about 30 seconds to reconnect. There could be three

tablespoons of sauce on each wing and about another half a cup of sauce under the wings on the bottom of the plate too. Somehow, the wings are still crispy on the sides and crunchy at the edges. The sauce has a subdued funk from the blue cheese ("We use Sysco brand blue cheese dressing," Grady says) and that iconic vinegary tang of the Frank's. Medium has a consistent pleasant burn and wings with the hot Bleu Bayou leave my glasses steamed after I finish eating. I can feel my scalp sweating and beads forming on my cheeks. This is a six-napkin plate of wings. You get the distinct impression you could mix the sauce with queso and make more friends than you could ever want.

I finish the plate with the same rare sense of satisfaction I've found from time to time—a culinary pilgrimage that lives up to the hype, a food discovery not heralded by the mainstream food press, a culinary life-changing tasting menu—Grady's Bleu Bayou wings are truly special. Perhaps the best wings I've ever had. The irony?

There's a side of blue cheese and celery served with them even though the idea was to mix both into the sauce to save folks the trouble of dipping! Why? "People ask for it!" Grady says, chuckling.

An ingenious sauce isn't Grady's only trick. He also employs a cooking technique not used by most. "I bake my wings for 35 to 45 minutes at 350°F, then I fry 'em another seven to eight minutes until they're crispy at 325°F," he tells me, adding that he seasons the wings with a little salt and pepper first. "We use a vegetable oil, but peanut oil would be great if you're making them at home."

Then, of course, that ingenious sauce, which Grady notes the waitstaff can't help but come into the kitchen looking for to pour themselves a ramekin for dipping potato chips and tortilla chips. "People think it's just for the wings," Grady says. "It's for fish, for steak, for pork . . ."

A hundred and five days of different wing sauces. You wonder what other gems Grady has in his recipe box.

The Delicious Dozen

There's a green chile cheeseburger trail in New Mexico. Frank Pepe, Sally's, Modern, BAR, and Zuppardi's comprise the quintet that is pizza Mecca in New Haven, Connecticut. Lockhart, Texas has its big brisket trio (Kreuz Market, Smitty's Market, and Black's Barbecue). You can pursue trails of barbecue (North Carolina and Texas) and bourbon (Kentucky), and get lost for days visiting California's vineyards in Napa and Sonoma. How on earth is it

THE WING TRAIL

The Bar Bill Tavern, 185 Main Street

Mammoser's Tavern, 16 S Buffalo Street

Doc Sullivan's, 474 Abbott Road

Blackthorn Restaurant & Pub,
2134 Seneca Street

Gene McCarthy's, 73 Hamburg Street

Anchor Bar, 1047 Main Street

Gabriel's Gate, 145 Allen Street

Lenox Grill, 140 North Street

Cole's, 1104 Elmwood Avenue

Duff's, 550 Dick Road

Elmo's, 2349 Millersport Highway

Glen Park Tavern, 5507 Main Street

that Buffalo hasn't had an "official" list of spots for wing nuts to make pilgrimages to?

In 2017, Erie County's tourism promotion agency, Visit Buffalo Niagara, started developing a trail with the help of "Wing King" Drew Cerza, founder of the National Buffalo Wing Festival, and soliciting suggestions from the public. Scheduled to launch in spring 2018, the trail features a shortlist of special places in the city picked for their historic, culinary, and wing-style significance, "the kind of corner tav-erns that have disappeared in many parts of the country."

If you're interested in completing "America's Tastiest Drive" in the city that wings were named after, check out www.buffalowingtrail.com and the unranked list opposite. It's ordered as a suggested road trip that starts on the open highways south of Buffalo from the Southtowns to the Northtowns. It starts in East Aurora, proceeds through the city, and ends in Williamsville, but you can obviously wing things however you like.

Rule the Roost Yourself

If you're not so into folks telling you what to do and are looking to do *your own* wing quest, here's a list of the city's other most well-regarded spots to start with (minus Gordon's, Papa Jake's, Century Grill, The Original Honey's, and Big Nick Cafora's, which have since closed). Call this your very own Queen City Buffalo wing trail!

Amherst Ale House, Getzville, 55 Crosspoint Parkway, 716-625-7100

Blasdell Pizza & Wings, Blasdell, 3904 South Park Avenue, 716-822-1138

Brennan's Bowery Bar, Williamsville, 4401 Transit Road, 716-633-9630

Buffalo Brew Pub, Williamsville, 6861 Main Street, 716-632-0552

Buzzy's, Niagara Falls, 7617 Niagara Falls Boulevard, 716-283-5333

Conlon's, South Buffalo, 382 Abbott Road, 716-725-6072

Mister B's Restaurant and Tavern, Niagara Falls, 2201 Hyde Park Boulevard, 716-298-4028

Pasquale's, West Seneca, 3720 Seneca Street, 716-674-0123

Rodney's, Hamburg, 4179 Lakeshore Road, 716-627-5166

Swannie House, Perry, 170 Ohio Street, 716-847-2898

Wellington Pub, North Buffalo, 1541 Hertel Avenue, 716-833-9899

CHAPTER TWO

BUFFALO: AMERICA'S MOST UNDERRATED PIZZA CITY?

"Buffalo-style pizza is a medium thick pizza with a sweet purée sauce. More mozzarella cheese than you need, and if you're smart, it's a hand-cut pepperoni."

—*Larry Santora*

Co-owner of Santora's Pizza

"There's nothing like a slice of pizza with that cup-and-char, the burnt-up edges, and a little fat that accumulates within the pepperoni itself. It's priceless."

—*Anthony Kulik*

Co-owner of Lovejoy Pizza

I've eaten pizza at many of the most well-respected pizzerias in America. For starters, Di Fara in Brooklyn, Pizzeria Bianco in Phoenix, Frank Pepe in New Haven, Pizzeria Beddia in Philadelphia, and Great Lake in Chicago before it closed. They and so many other great places have their merits. But I'm going out on the line and putting a decade of pizza cred built by writing about and visiting hundreds of pizzerias in New York City and across America to say that Buffalo-style pizza is America's most underappreciated regional style.

There, I said it. I'm in love. Buffalo serves some awesome pizza.

Let's be clear: you can, to a lesser degree, get New York-style pizza in Buffalo. The Neapolitan-style wave has landed in the city, too. Pizzaiolo Jay Langfelder's pizza-truck-turned brick-and-mortar restaurant, Jay's Artisan Pizzeria, could be put up against well-regarded masters of the genre in America's other great pizza cities. Roost, chef Martin Danilowic's restaurant in the Crescendo building on Niagara Street on the West Side, serves a tidy menu of pizzas that would cause as much of a stir in New York City as some of its trendier new places, where they plate their pizza in one of the most unique ways I've ever seen. They and a handful of other non-Buffalo-style pizzerias are worth checking out, but you *can* get those *styles* of pizza elsewhere.

You *can't* really find Buffalo-style pizza in other cities. The dough has the lightness of a focaccia, there's always lots of cheese, and while the sauce does happen to be slightly sweet, that ends up being a nice contrast to the spicy oil pooled in the copious charred, meaty pepperoni.

Buffalo-style pizza has been described as a hybrid of Chicago deep-dish and New York, or somewhere between Detroit's airy, high-lipped cheesy crust and New York City's traditionally thin-crust pies. It's also been compared to a circular version of Sicilian-style pizza, but there's less structure to the undercarriage of Buffalo-style pizza and its signature sweet sauce is nothing like what you get at places that make the best Sicilian slices.

I'd flip the description. Buffalo-style pizza is typically a cup-and-char pepperoni pizza, one with a slim, sometimes non-existent crust coastline with ingredients out to, and sometimes even over the edges, a thick, airy undercarriage with little to no structural integrity that's topped by a sweet sauce and enough cheese to nearly always guarantee a cheese pull. If you were going to use other regional styles to describe it, I'd say it's a Detroit amount of cheese with a Motor City trim, a Maine undercarriage (think Portland's Micucci's or Slab), and a New York City soul.

One of my favorite pizza experts, a *Buffalonian* pizza expert who has anonymously reviewed about 100 of the city's pizzas (he's shooting to have reviewed 150 by the end of 2018), and who goes by the handle SexySlices, defines Buffalo-style pizza thusly:

"It has to have cup-and-char pepperoni with grease in the center of each cup and blackening on the top along the rim. A hefty portion of cheese with good browning (some places make it super-dark). Buffalo-style is traditionally an overdone pie, and ordering 'well-done' on top of that is common. The sauce is rich, ladled generously, and a little sweet. It has a thick dough that fluffs up consistently to the edge of a crispy, buttery crust that's typically charred and caked in excess with a super intense, oven-dried sauce."

Buffalonians love their pizza as much as Ange-

lenos love doughnuts (have you seen how many doughnut shops they have?). "You're naturally eating pizza at least once a week," SexySlices told me. "You're not even counting. Pizza and wings—there's no such thing as just getting pizza."

According to The *Buffalo News*, the number of pizzerias went from 62 in 1969 to 274 by 1989 to 360 in 1998. Keep in mind that over that period of time, according to the census, the population went from 462,768 to 292,819. Today? There are fewer people (256,902). But, at least according to Buffalo's local tourism agency Visit Buffalo Niagara, at last count there were more than 600 pizzerias in Buffalo and its immediate surrounding urban area. That means if we're conservative and say just 600, there's at least one pizzeria for every 428 people in the Nickel City. Compare that to New York City, whose some estimated 1,600 pizzerias serve 8.538 million people. That's right, New York City, which has 33 times the number of people as Buffalo, per capita, has less than four times the number of pizzerias. And you thought *you* loved pizza.

And no, they're not national chains. Sure, you'll see a few here and there. I counted 13 Pizza Huts, six each of Domino's and Little Caesar's,

and one Papa John's and Jet's. For the most part, the 600 seem to be independently owned pizzerias. That leaves some 573 independently owned and operated pizzerias. "I was a nervous wreck when Domino's was going to open 27 units," Bocce Club owner Jim Pacciotti told me. "The ones they opened didn't really take off. People are used to what they're used to."

For the pizza-lover uninitiated in the Nickel City, Buffalo should be a pizza destination, though because of a pizza culture largely based on *takeout*, it's one of the country's great cities for pizza while eating it straight from the box in the parking lot on the hood of your car, or with the box warming your lap with the smell of hot cardboard, melted cheese, and cup-and-char pepperoni on a cold winter day. And that is the move for pizza nerds, because the truth is that Buffalo pizza isn't a style that I'd say improves as it sits. There's something about the excess of cheese, pepperoni grease, and cup-and-char that really exists at its peak perfection when it's fresh from the oven.

America's pizza culture is generally traced back to Lombardi's in New York City in 1905. Buffalo's pizza culture goes all the way back to 1927, when Fioravanti Santora started selling pizza by the slice out of his homemade ice cream shop. That means Buffalo's oldest pizzeria preceded New York City icons like Patsy's (1933) and John's of Bleecker Street (1929). Frank Pepe of New Haven, generally regarded as one of America's best pizzerias, was founded just two years before Santora's, in 1925.

Outside Buffalo, the city's probably most well-known as being represented by Bocce Club Pizza. But articles written by folks who sweep

in and out of town after a few days get an incomplete picture of the pizza scene. Bocce Club is a great pie, and it's a great Buffalo-style pizza, but Buffalo-style pizza is not Bocce Club Pizza. Sure, it has cup-and-char, a thick but airy crust, and a sweet sauce, but if you look at it side by side with some of the city's other pizzas, you'll see the difference. Nobody else does toppings that go out *past* the crust. And in Buffalo, the distinction of best-known pizza is shared with La Nova. Wherever you go in Buffalo, prepare yourself for some of the cheesiest, most pepperoni-topped, and indulgent pies you've ever had. This is hibernation pizza. Prepare for a pie that isn't a gut-bomb, but that probably doubles or triples the caloric intake enjoyed in a New York City slice. You probably *could* go outside and shovel, but wouldn't it be more fun to just stay inside and have a few drinks?

Right about now, some of my fellow Manhattan pizza-loving friends are shaking their heads in disbelief. "You think *this* is good pizza?" I'm Long Island born (Queens, actually), so my hyper-regional style is technically geographically the grandma pie if we're talking anything beyond New York thin-crust style. And when it comes to that, I'm generally a fan of the thinnest thin crust New York City slices I can find. I've had flashes where I see the merits of Chicago deep-dish and will even call that casserole a pizza on days that I'm feeling generous. So believe me, I get the skepticism. In addition, I've heard the frustration from Buffalo expats who have bemoaned to me their inability to persuade friends and significant others on the merits of Buffalo pizza, heard locals talk about the snobby Long Island kids who attend Buffalo's universities and say, "that's not pizza."

But I've also heard the local pizza pride. Sitting in Duff's and waiting for an order of wings, I overheard the kids at the next table discussing one of the most recent online lists put out by *Travel + Leisure*, "These Are the Cities With America's Favorite Pizza." Buffalo, it seems, much to some people's surprise, is at number three on the list just below Detroit, and somewhat dubiously, Phoenix (Does one amazing spot make it the best city for pizza in America)? "I was in Miami and they didn't have charred pepperoni, you had to ask for it as extra," one kid says. "It makes you realize how spoiled we are for good pizza."

Pepperoni as a baseline? I can get behind that. And I'd argue that in an era where pizza lovers are falling in love again with America's regional styles—the Emmy Squareds of the world popularizing Detroit-style pizza, Speedy Romeo drawing attention to aspects of St. Louis-style, Slice pizza blogger turned pizzaiolo Adam Kuban demonstrating the appeal of bar pizza—Buffalo pizza could be the next big thing. In fact, I'd argue we're already eating it: Domino's and Papa John's sweet sauces and lack of structural integrity have more in common with Buffalo-style pizza than a slice at Joe's. And while I'm doing a disservice to Buffalo pizza by mentioning both of those national chains, my point is to draw a line of comparison to the financial and nationwide success those qualities have already exhibited.

Before we get back to all the great places in Buffalo, I'll go one step further. There's a slice shop in New York City's NoLita neighborhood called Prince Street Pizza that replaced the original Ray's Pizza. Before it opens, there's usually a line out the door for the Spicy Spring square slice, a light, airy pock-bottomed crust weighed down with a copious cheese coating and a healthy ladling of fra diavolo sauce. There's little structural integrity and the slice is known for being topped with so many small curled up slices of spicy-oil-filled, black-edged pepperoni that they spill off the sides onto the plate. Sure, it's a square and yes that sauce is a little spicy, but that Instagram darling, that super popular Spicy Spring slice, *that's* pretty much Buffalo pizza.

The slice at Prince Street Pizza, the most Instagrammed slice in New York City, is as close to Buffalo-style in Manhattan as you can get.

The Ingredients: What Goes Into Making Buffalo-Style "Buffalo-Style?"

It's hard to pinpoint exactly whose sweet tooth started the trend of a sweet pizza sauce in Buffalo. But after talking with several pizzaiolos and pizzeria owners, it became clear *where* the sweetness was coming from: tomato purée.

One local Buffalo pizza industry expert I spoke with on background (let's call him Deep Pizza) had his own theory, pointing out that while the quality of canned tomatoes has improved, "it used to be really God-awful." A modest amount would benefit the tomato sauce in some instances, especially if it's not hot. And then it's just like anything else—a well-known operator makes a sweeter sauce, it becomes identified with the style, then copy-catted, then even when the quality of the tomatoes improved, it was part of the tradition.

Cans of sauce and bags of flour at Bocce Club Pizza carry the pizzeria's labels. "The sauce is the secret," says one of Bocce's head pizza guys, Mark Daniels, who won't divulge the spices they add. "It's the same recipe we've been using for 60 years. It's sweeter than the typical pizza sauce."

Larry Santora, co-owner of the Santora's in West Seneca, told me he uses six cans of purée to two cans of water ("It's not that thin. Years ago it used to be four cans to two cans of water!"). You get the feeling that there's even more sugar added to the already naturally sweet tomato purée. Lockport, a town about 45 minutes north,

is known for having an *even* sweeter sauce than the ones at pizzerias in the city. The rumor about one place called Pizza Oven is that the sauce even contains Hawaiian Punch!

But the sugar doesn't stop there. "There's sugar in the sauce, there's sugar in the dough," Larry Santora tells me. Why? "Color, it will color. Sugar will burn, so you get sugar in all of them. Almost all the dough products."

And it's not *just* sugar. I could speak at length and in depth about my feelings about the declining quality of the average slice in New York City, but will stop myself short by saying that I found that after eating at dozens of pizzerias in Buffalo, that there's more *flavor* in the average crust *there* than at your run-of-the-mill slice joints in Manhattan. I'm not saying it's better. And we're not talking about Manhattan pizza *icons* or quality stalwarts. But it's different. Something else is going into the dough.

"The majority of pizzerias are doing same-day fermentations," Deep Pizza told me. "But some of them have adopted cold fermentation, 24 hours, 48 hours. And actually, a lot of them are adding shortening. In my opinion, I think a lot of the sweetness comes from the addition of shortening in the dough. A lot of New York-style doughs are very, very lean doughs. The fat addition would be a 2 percent olive oil. I think a lot of them, just my opinion, I think that a lot of the operators here use shortening in their dough. Maybe 40 percent."

Among other pizzeria owners, Lovejoy's co-owner Anthony Kulik confirmed Deep Pizza's thoughts on fermentation, "We're on a one-and-a-half day cycle. If I had the luxury I would like to go a little bit longer to get a better quality dough, but in our business, it's so difficult to have that luxury and allow that dough to have that much time. Just because of inability to keep up with supply."

"Make it today, use it tomorrow," said Santora, who also confirmed that his pizzeria uses shortening. "Shortening is also used on the pan instead of oil, cornmeal, semolina, etc., which results in the pliable crust," Deep Pizza added. "Sugar aids in fermentation and browning, especially if you are observing shorter fermentation times. Shortening is what provides softer texture. Some use oil, but shortening gives the best Buffalo-style effect."

My New York City pizza friends with cred at some of the city's most O.G. places (and I don't mean "One Goal" here) are quick to point out that sugar and shortening aren't Buffalo inventions. Tom DeGrezia, co-owner of Sofia Pizza Shoppe and owner of Sofia Wine Bar, whose pizza pedigree is linked to one of Brooklyn's longstanding, unheralded neighborhood pizza institutions, Bensonhurst's J&V Pizzeria, balked at the idea Buffalonians may have invented using shortening in pizza when I told him about places that said they used shortening in their dough. He said that was something New York pizzerias did decades ago.

"Back then no one asked you how you made your dough. No one cared. As long as the slice was great, that's all that mattered. As we've become more of a health-conscious society, people proudly state the ingredients they use and more importantly what they *don't* use in their dough. Few to no one is using shortening anymore. Or at least they won't publicly say it."

But it does seem that at least, in Buffalo, it's a tradition that's more pervasively enduring.

Pizza expert, restaurateur, acrobat (!), and author Tony Gemignani isn't from Buffalo. Don't hold it against him—he's friendly with the Todaro family, which still owns and operates La Nova—but he's perhaps America's pizza maker most known for his expertise in regional American pizza genres. His book *The Pizza Bible* features recipes for more styles than you've probably ever heard of (his restaurant, Pizza Rock may serve even more).

"The low hydration, shortening, dense dough, and specific ingredients used such as the thick tomato paste-based sauce and hand-cut pepperoni makes this style a special one," Tony said. "Shortening has been used for decades as a common ingredient in doughs and at bakeries, especially with pan pizzas where applying it to the pan helps with sticking. It makes the dough a bit softer and easier to use. I've had many people tell me this including Joey Todaro. As for the important role it plays in texture and flavor profile, it's not cheating or a bad thing. It's just like using lard."

Shortening or not, almost *every* pizzeria in Buffalo docks their pies to help prevent air bubbles. Lift up a slice and look at the undercarriage and 99 percent of the time, you'll see at least one, usually two, concave dimples a little lighter than

the cooked crust all around it. On some of Buffalo's thinner pies there will even be a dozen or so impressions left behind by a dough roller docker like you'll find on a New Jersey bar pie.

At least at Santora's, shortening is not the only unexpected ingredient that goes into Buffalo-style pizza. "I think the difference in our dough is powdered milk," Larry tells me. We put powdered milk in our dough. It just fluffs it up. Makes it lighter, but it holds. Other than that, it's flour, water, salt, sugar, and yeast."

Galbani, produced locally in South Buffalo, is the big player in the pizza cheese business for the area, SexySlices tells me. "Practically everybody uses some blend of mozzarella and provolone. Up to fifty-fifty."

At Bocce Club Pizza, they use Galbani's 100 percent whole milk mozzarella, but they, like many Buffalonian pizzeria-owners still call it by the name for which it has been known some 70 years around these parts, Sorrento. Louis Russo, who immigrated to the U.S. from Sorrento, Italy, founded Sorrento in Buffalo in 1947, even though Lactalis, which bought it in the '90s, rebranded it under the Galbani name a few years ago. Hey, local pride.

And then, of course, there's the famous cup-and-char pepperoni. What's the best product to get that iconic effect? "Battistoni is the local brand, and I personally believe it to be the best," SexySlices tells me. "However, some places use Margherita as well."

Bocce's Jim Pacciotti said he uses natural casing sausage. "When you don't get natural casing, you don't get the same great effect," he said. "We use Margherita pepperoni. We've been using it for 60 years."

"We started cutting our own stuff," Larry

"To you guys less is more, for us more ain't enough. It's crazy man, I'm not even kidding. We laugh all the time because it's like you can't give people enough, man. A large pizza in my place gets on average 12 ounces of mozzarella. In New York, you guys would laugh. But for a lot of pies in Buffalo, that's nothing man. There's a guy here who is putting a couple pounds of cheese at a minimum on a large pie, which is crazy. But that's what people in Buffalo want. They love cheese, man. I don't know what they do in Wisconsin, but I'm not kidding. I'll put Buffalo people up against Wisconsin all day. All you have to do is just walk around and look. People in Buffalo, they love to eat, they just love to eat."   —Anthony Kulik, Lovejoy Pizza

Santora told me, noting that he too uses Margherita pepperoni. "We went back to the old way of doing it.

No matter where you eat pizza in Buffalo, and however pizzerias' ingredients differ, one thing is consistent: a heavy hand. Some places even suggest double-pepperoni as a topping. In Buffalo, more is more.

A Slice of Buffalo Pizza History: Santora's, Bocce, and La Nova

Santora's: Buffalo's Oldest Pizzeria

Bocce, La Nova, Imperial, Lovejoy, Mister Pizza, whichever place you call your favorite pizzeria, you have to first pay homage to Buffalo's oldest: Santora's. Santora's may also be one of America's oldest pizzerias. If you discount Lombardi's, which opened in 1905 but closed for a decade before reopening in a different location, by my research, Santora's is the sixth-oldest pizzeria in America.

The white-pockmarked crust undercarriage is poofier than most Buffalo-style pizzas, but well-browned, its edge crust lined with a blackened edge and a slight "trim" attached where the cheese had melted and turned dark and crusty. The sauce was sweet, the pepperoni was *significantly* charred, extending inward about a quarter-inch, there was a crispy-crackly bite and a hot melted string of cheese that stretches cartoon-like as you bite. There's an impressive drag of grease across the plate left behind from the bottom of the slice. And while it looks less like the thin round pies of yesteryear that can be seen in grainy black and white photos on Santo-

ra's website, and more like the Bocce Club Pizza style that has become incredibly popular in Buffalo since that restaurant opened in 1946, one thing is clear: this is a great Buffalo pizza. Strike that. This is great pizza.

So why doesn't Santora's get the love? That's the question I had to ask after biting into a mind-bendingly good slice at the Santora's location on Transit Road in Depew, about a 20-minute drive from downtown Buffalo. And why is it that every-time I mentioned the pizzeria that preceded all others in the city, as one of the best pizzas in Buffalo, was I getting blank stares?

It becomes clear after talking with folks around town that I may have lucked out on two fronts: first, I've landed at the oldest of the five remaining Santora's pizzerias. It was founded in 1970. And while its owner, Larry Santora, later tells me his cousin Paul is killing it at the huge Santora's north of his on Transit Road, he also tells me that all the Santora's make their pizzas differently, "Different dough, different sauce, I couldn't tell you how," he says, "It's definitely different, yeah." So it may be that this Santora's is better than the other three locations. Second, being from out of town, I'm lucky enough to not know any better than to ignore local prejudice.

"My grandfather Fioravanti Santora started the pizza business in 1927," Larry Santora tells me in a booth at his Transit Road location in Depew.

Fioravanti arrived in Buffalo in 1915 from Naples, Italy, and initially worked on the docks.

Fioravanti's first pizzeria was located downtown at 259 Seneca Street just down the street from where two of Buffalo's most famous

Larry Santora

Italian restaurants, Chef's and DiTondo's are still today. "Santora's Pizza Restaurant in Napoli Town, they called it," Santora says, though one old photo I came across declared "Santora's Pizzeria Napolitana Restaurant" along with "Wine–Beer–Liquor DANCING," which sounds like the kind of pizza party I can get down with.

Fioravanti supposedly started selling pizza by the slice out of his homemade ice cream shop. Larry says that family lore has it that there were lines out the door every day with people vying

"Previous to that he worked on the loading docks, and at that time, Italians were persecuted. He couldn't take the humiliation, so he said, 'That's it. I'm never going to work for somebody else.' Next thing, he started selling, making candy and stuff like that, and ice cream in the cooler weather. And, then pizza came along. He started making pizza. Pizza at that time was just dough, sauce, anchovies, grated cheese. That was it. A fish product. It was something to eat for your stomach, rather than just a piece of bread. Pizza dough with some oil, baked in the oven, some anchovies, pour on a little bit of grated cheese, fresh grated cheese, and that's what it was. My grandmother Maria and him would make the pizza and the boys would put the stuff on wagons. They would go to the door (knock), 'Want to buy a pizza?'"

for pizza. Fioravanti had eight sons and three daughters and as they got older and pizza became increasingly popular, the family business grew. At one point, Santora tells me, there were 21 Santora's in town.

The next thing Santora tells me may be the key to the lack of resonance the city's pizza diehards seem to have with it. Through the 1950s, they couldn't buy tomato sauce ("You had to grind the tomatoes"), could only get stick pepperoni, and could only get mozzarella in a cube. Everything was homemade. As Santora tells it, as the pizza business took off, the key ingredients started being canned and mass-produced. Santora explained, "I said, 'We're going to go with that. It saves the labor and you can hardly tell the difference.' But the quality was different then, in terms of a lot of the canned goods or food products for a certain period of time. It changed. Until 1990-something, you looked for the least expensive stuff to cut the labor, to cut the cost and sell pizza at a lower price. But we didn't like it. We were selling it. We were open. We were still in business, but the quality wasn't there. We don't even like the pizza we're making! What are we doing here!"

It was 1995 and Santora said they were known in town for making some of the cheapest pizza around. They knew they were going to lose a lot of business, but they decided to change things up. "We started buying the best sauce, the best cheese, we started cutting our own stuff. We went back to the old way of doing it."

The way he tells it, chasing away the folks who were looking for cheap pizza meant the shop took a nosedive for a few years, a reputation that the pizzeria may still be fighting. But let me tell you, Santora's is back.

Bocce Club Pizza: Buffalo's Most Famous Pizza

"Funny story," Larry Santora says, "when Santora's was on Seneca Street, behind us was the Bocce Club where they used to throw the bocce balls and the guys would go there and smoke cigars. And my grandfather's sons would go around the corner and knock, 'You want to buy a pizza?' And the Bocce Club would buy pizza. Well, the guy who owned Bocce pizza, they used to buy pizza. Then they started their own thing. That's how Bocce started. You look on Bocce's box, you see the Bocce Club. You see the bocce ball on there."

Hickory Street, where the original Bocce Club was downtown, is only about three blocks away from 259 Seneca. "We had a location on Hickory years ago, but people were skipping out on mass for pizza and liquor and the priest wasn't happy about it," Bocce's owner Jim Pacciotti tells me. "So we moved to Bailey in 1959."

There are two Bocce Club Pizza locations in Amherst, one on Bailey and one on Hopkins. I

meet Pacciotti at the Bailey Avenue spot, which they chose because of its proximity to the University at Buffalo south campus. It's in the northeastern quadrant of the city just a few minutes past The Buffalo Zoo, on Bailey Avenue, one of the north-south arteries that cuts across the city. From the outside, the building's yellow and white arches make it look like it's going to be a pizza palace filled with folks sitting at tables. But all of that space is used up for the ovens. There's a standing-only area up front by the take-out counter with a few places to stand with a slice while you look at the Bocce timeline on the walls along with years of press ("Apple May Keep 'Doc' Away, But Pizza Is Better").

Pacciotti tells me they'll be returning downtown with a new location in the fall and then goes on to recount the Bocce origin story a little differently from Santora, and unsurprisingly, without any mention of the other pizzeria.

Bocce's pizza is like a New York slice on steroids. "Thicker dough, sweeter sauce, slices of pepperoni, no crust, ingredients out to the edges," 17-year Bocce vet Mark Daniels says when I ask him for the definition of Bocce Club pizza. "We're known for

Bocce's owner Jim Pacciotti

big hearty pizza: 18 inches. You know when you're getting it what you're getting yourself into."

"The idea of having the cheese go out to the edge of the dough was just to be something different," Pacciotti tells me. "My father believed that you should have a bite of cheese with every bite of your pizza, even at the end of the slice."

Jim says all the portioning is done by eye and that they hand-stretch their dough. "A couple of my big competitors are starting to buy their dough. I don't want a stamped out frozen pizza dough."

Standing in the waiting area in front of the counter gives you a great view of the cavernous open kitchen behind it where the wall of the pizzeria is lined with double-stacked ovens. "I put a conveyor oven in years ago," Jim explains. "We tried it. I had it taken out within seven months. It just wasn't the same."

The current operation is truly something to behold, the young, confident pizzaiolos walking back and forth, opening and crashing shut the

Blodgett deck ovens' doors, sliding peels under the pizzas to lift them up and check the char on the undercarriage, knowing when to lift them out of their pans and onto the decks where they're finished. "The pizza is cooked on a pan until the cheese melts and then you deck it," Jim explains, noting that while they try to keep them all at 550°F, the ovens are all different.

"Sauce, cheese, then toppings," Daniels tells me. "Ten minutes cooked at 650°F."

Jim tells me that his pizzaiolos really have to know the temperatures of each oven and their temperaments. "I had some ovens in here that were 30 years old. But they all work differently. It's a real skill to be able to use them. To know how they all behave and know when and how to move the pizzas inside them. We have to replace them as they go. They're not built like they used to be."

La Nova: La Cosa Pizza? Basta! What We *Actually* Know about La Nova Pizza

Let's level right away: La Nova is known for three things. The first two are tremendously great pizza and famously good wings. The last is the rumor about why the business was originally started:

it was supposedly a family business created to launder the *family* business. *"The family was part of the mafia and they started a pizzeria to launder their money!"* everyone will tell you. *"But then the pizza and wings were so good that they made so many millions and got out of the Mob!"* Whether because it's true and they *have* to remain quiet, or because it's not but they want to maintain the mystique and reputation the rumors give it, La Nova remains quiet on the subject.

Here's what's actually been reported:

"Papa" Joseph E. Todaro, a former construction laborer, founded La Nova north of Buffalo in the city of Tonawanda on 43 South Niagara Street in 1957. In 1967, Todaro and 35 other men were arrested at a stag party for his son Joe

("Big Joe") at a lounge called Panaro's where Todaro was charged with "consorting with known criminals," a charge that was later dismissed. In 1974, Stefano Magaddino, who was one of the most powerful mob bosses in America, passed away. It's speculated that then Papa Joe Todaro took over as Buffalo's don. Todaro was acquitted of federal tax evasion charges in 1985, then he and his son were named as the leaders of Buffalo's Mafia family in 1989. A 1996 Justice Department report listed them with other organized crime figures, but they've always denied the claims, and nobody has ever successfully made any charges stick against Papa Joe, or his son.

Papa Joe passed away in 2012, but he declined to comment on the FBI claims in 2004, telling the *Buffalo News* he didn't want to dignify the allegations. And for his part, Big Joe has politely declined to comment on any aspect of organized crime to the *Buffalo News* over the years. "All I can tell you is, I'm here working at my restaurant seven days a week, just as my father did, just as my family did, just as I have since I was 12 years old," he told the *News*. "I'm not going to comment on organized crime questions, but if you

want a great recipe for cheese and pepperoni, I'll tell you."

So let's talk cheese and pepperoni.

La Nova was founded north of the city, but Todaro moved his restaurant twice, once in 1971, to the intersection of Delaware and Tacoma in North Buffalo (the same year they introduced their white pizza and steak-and-cheese subs) and then in 1973 to their now iconic, West Side location at West Ferry and Hampshire Street topped with the bright red awning. (Another La Nova opened in 2001, in Williamsville.) If you could look down on it from above, La Nova's always-packed parking lot sits at the tip of a pizza slice-shaped intersection whose crust would be Grant Street. It's a gruff little area near the West Side Bazaar and just a few blocks away from a roundabout that takes you into the beautiful tree-lined Parkway System—folks waiting in their cars for take-out orders, the occasional panhandler—but inside, it's a clean, well-lit, well-staffed pizza performance machine.

There's a long counter stacked with glass cases and a marble countertop with the most recent pies just out of the oven available to be purchased by the slice. There's a guy whose sole

job seems to be to do reheats in the beautiful, fire-filled oven behind him, something that tells you how serious La Nova is about their pizza. So you can usually get a slice here that's almost as good as if it came from a pie baked just for you, like still hot enough to have long thin threads of cheese pulling away from the slice as the guy picks it up to put it back into the oven to warm it. This is a busy operation. There's also a guy dedicated to taking orders, another guy who seems to be helping them both, and *another* guy in the alcove across the counter from them behind you surrounded by three stacks of boxes. His job is to keep folding to make sure they don't run out for take-out orders. And that says nothing about the huge operation in the kitchen emitting sizzles and clangs whose view is mostly obscured.

Unlike many well-loved Buffalo pizzerias, there *is* a dining room at La Nova. It's filled with marble pillars, sconces, no fewer than nine TVs going with music, and wall-to-wall photo collages of locals, little leagues, sports celebrities (there's Joe Montana eating wings!), and founder Joseph Todaro with one of his signature cigars. This is the kind of place where you can get a pie in 15 minutes even when a party of 18 walks in after a Sabres game, and they won't even take over a full third of the dining room.

The menu is a diner-long epic. There are so many things on it besides wings and pizza—appetizers, calzones, tacos, wraps, subs, burgers, salads (including the wonderfully bizarre meatball salad), and dinners that include fried chicken and baby back ribs—that it would literally take two years of eating there every day to try everything. But you're really here for the pizza, and they do it a

few different ways besides by the slice: by the pie, as sheet pizzas, New York-style, and in 30-inch super-sized pies you have to order in advance and that they call "The Big Joe."

There are at least 21 toppings to choose from and 19 set specialty pies. Besides their founder's favorite, the "Papa Joe" (spinach, ricotta, and special sauce), and their famous white pizza—a sauceless pie with grated cheese, fresh-cut tomatoes, garlic, onion, herbs, and (recommended) anchovies—there are other Buffalo classics like the chicken finger, breakfast, and steak pies. There's a taco pizza with taco meat, sour cream, tomatoes, black olives, cheddar, and lettuce; a deep-dish pepperoni pie ("Deli Old World Style"); and two other interesting riffs on pizzeria classics. Consider a Greek pizza that comes topped with feta, diced tomatoes, cheddar, chicken, and homemade Greek dressing, and if that doesn't surprise you, the Hawaiian pizza with mozzarella, ham, pineapple, and some maraschino cherries (!), which would be enough to stop you in your tracks before tripping over its other rare topping: almonds.

But one of the unheralded, most unappreciated features at La Nova is the ability to customize your crust for free with sesame seeds, onion, garlic, Cajun spice, or Parmigiano-Reggiano. In an age of dieting and gluten-free, when too many times I see grease-stained paper plates filled with pizza bones (leftover crusts), when national chains have added sides of ranch dressing, tomato sauce, cheddar, and garlic butter as a flavorful solution for the otherwise crust agnostic, I'm perpetually stunned that more pizzerias don't do flavored crusts the way La Nova does. And La Nova does them well.

La Nova has been described by Pizza Marketplace as the world's busiest pizzeria, and the business has been reported to have annual gross sales of $5 million, which, at the time was nearly 10 times the per-store average! The company claims it's the largest independent pizzeria in America and says on its website that the wholesale wing business they launched in 1993, now supplies pre-cooked, heat-and-serve wings to other restaurants in all 50 states. And while I personally wouldn't endorse eating pizza in stadiums because it's generally not going to be as good as at a dedicated shop, La Nova is the official pizza of all of Buffalo's major sports teams (the Bills since 2011, the Bisons since 2014, and the Sabres since 2015). And it's easy to see why—biting into a fresh cheesy-pepperoni slice with sesame seeds, it's enough to make you only ever want to eat the crust that way again.

That Time "Big Joe" Todaro Asked Where I Live

After talking with area writers and foodies, and doing plenty of research, it became clear that these days, two of the hardest print interviews to get in town are Anchor Bar and La Nova. They've both been approached so many times over the decades, and because of their fame, they just don't need the press. Despite several efforts, I never did hear back from Anchor Bar, but after multiple visits, a few missed connections, and an interview of *me* to *get* the interview, I finally did one day get a call from La Nova owner "Big Joe" Todaro and his manager Dave Alessi.

When did you start doing wings?

In 1970, we started the wings. We started the white pizza, and we started the barbecue wings.

Did you guys invent the pit-roasting wings?

Yes. I was fooling around with ribs one day. We threw some wings on. The rest is history. My ribs were selling so much, I decided to open up a rib place. That's another story. If you want to start talking about all the businesses I was in, you've got a couple hours to kill, maybe we could talk.

How did La Nova arrive at its original pizza recipe?

That's the reason my father started in 1957. He liked to cook. One day, he went by a place. He seen it, and he seen pizza was a novelty item at that time. He jumped in.

He just decided he could make as good a pizza as anybody else?

Goddamn right, he did. And he did. We were awarded the number one independent pizzeria in the country. That's right on the front page of the trade magazine.

Buffalo-style pizza is a little bit thicker than what you guys do—how would you describe the Buffalo-style pizza that La Nova does?

Just a medium thickness. When my father first started in '57, pizza was thin. Gradually, over the years, it went thicker, and thicker, and thicker. Now it seems to be coming back to a little thinner. That's why we have a New York-style pizza that we also offer.

Why did they get thicker? Who started that trend?

You're asking me a 60-year question.

What kind of ovens do you guys use?

Blodgett. You understand if I don't swear at you, it's because we're not real good friends yet. If we were good friends, I'd swear more.

I'd like to be friends. What kind of cheese do you guys use? Is it a mixture?

Whole-milk mozzarella. There's no mixture here. The neighborhood might be a mixture, but not the pizzas. We use Sorrento cheese.

How did La Nova pick the location on West Ferry?

I grew up in the neighborhood. This was an all-Italian neighborhood.

Many places in Buffalo tell me that they use a purée-based sauce. Do you?

Yeah. But we put our own ingredients in it.

Did your dad have a philosophy in terms of the ratio of cheese to sauce to dough?

You've got to weigh the dough. Your sauce, you just put on the scoops. And the cheese, we load everything up. We get our price, but we load up. We use the finest ingredients. That's why we're La Nova. That's why we're 61 years in business.

Which pepperoni do you use?

Margherita.

What's the most popular topping besides cup and char?

We sell a lot of specialty pies. Out of specialties, our white pizza is one of the most famous we're noted for. Now, all of a sudden everybody else is trying, but no one could duplicate it, because what we put on it, food cost is high.

How did the white pizza come about?

In the old days, my grandmother made white pizza completely different. As times go on, and my father started with a white pizza, one day we started fooling around. I added tomatoes. From tomatoes to the grated cheese and everything. You walked in, I grabbed a piece of pizza, and I put it right in your mouth physically, and said, "How do you like it?" No, I'm kidding you.

Many pizzerias tell me they put shortening in their dough. Do you guys?

A little.

Your dough, is that a same-day fermentation?

Rise one day, then we use it the next day. It needs to rise. Where are you from, Art?

Long Island, originally.

Rhode Island.

Long Island.

You don't understand my jokes? I'm close. It was an island anyway.

The Hawaiian pie has ham, pineapple, maraschino cherries, and almonds. I've never heard of a Hawaiian pizza with almonds. How did that come about?

How do I know? I put it on. It tasted good. I had some extra almonds around. I tried them, and it worked. We get a lot of Canadian business because we're real close to the border, and they're the ones that really like the Hawaiian pizza with the ham and everything.

Joe, when did you guys start doing Buffalo chicken pizza?

Joe (asking Dave): You think we did?
Dave: I don't know.
Joe: I can't remember when exactly. I don't remember anybody else with it. You're talking to me over 50, 60 years. We don't put dates down or anything—maybe 15, 20, 25 years ago.

It's reported you have annual gross sales of $5 million a year. Do you care to update that figure?

It's more than you could estimate. Can I say about 250 a week? We sell minimum, minimum we sell 250,000 to 300,000 pounds a week.

Why don't more places do customized crusts like La Nova?

Too lazy.

You dedicate significant manpower to reheat slices. That's not something many places do.

Three guys. When it gets dry, we throw them away. We only give the freshest ingredients. That's why I'm there seven days a week and my manager Dave is on call seven days a week. That's why some places drive Chevys and other people drive better cars. Excuse me, but you're from Long Island, you'll understand: Fuck that.

So now we're becoming better friends.

Yeah, maybe next year we become closer. I'll let you come and baptize my goldfish. We're becoming closer friends, Art. Soon, I'll be calling you Artooch.

I have never heard that one before. Some places are proud to say they use Frank's RedHot Sauce on their wings. Do you?

We're from the West Side of Buffalo. We don't give out no secrets. We're sworn to secrecy.

How about butter? Can you tell me if you use that?

Butter, yeah, we like to butter people up.

Is there a story you could tell me about your dad that people should know?

My father worked every single day of his life until he got sick. He died at 89. He worked seven days a week right alongside me since I've been 12 years old. That's the truth. When you have a father that's your hero. You have to say that. Thank God I had my dad. Otherwise, I might be shining brown shoes with black polish. I might be your shine guy. Now what?

Joe, all these rumors about the pizzeria being linked to the mafia, anything you want to tell me about that?

Would you please tell me where you live?

That's okay. I'd rather not. You're funny, Joe.

Yeah, I'm going to make you fucking laugh pretty soon. You know what, Art. This place here, we rough it up. We kid around, because that's what life's all about. So if I offended you, I probably meant it, but I didn't mean it. That's the way we talk. I'm kidding with you all the time, but how much information could you really give out when we've been doing business all these years. It's family operated. When you say, "When did you do this? When did you do that?" As you get old like me, I've got mad cow. I forget a lot of things. Next time you come to Buffalo, we'd love to see you.

Buffalo-Style Pizza Timeline

1915 Santora's founder Fioravanti Santora arrives in Buffalo in from Naples, Italy.

1927 Santora starts selling pizza by the slice out of his homemade ice cream shop.

1946 Dino Pacciotti buys a local bocce ball court and uses an old oven found in the basement to serve thick, generously-topped, crispy pizza with toppings edging out over the crust.

1947 Louis Russo, an immigrant from Sorrento, Italy, founds the company Sorrento Cheese, since renamed Galbani, a worldwide brand owned by Groupe Lactalis.

1957 Joe Todaro (Papa Joe) opens La Nova Pizzeria on 43 South Niagara Street in Tonawanda with his 12-year-old son Joe ("Big Joe").

1959 Bocce Club Pizza moves from its original Hickory Street location downtown to Bailey Avenue.

1967 Joe Todaro and 35 other men are arrested at a stag party. Todaro is charged with "consorting with known criminals," which is later dismissed.

1969 There are 62 pizzerias in Buffalo (population 462,768).

1970 The current oldest location of Santora's pizzeria is opened on 3440 Transit Road in Depew, and according to owner Larry Santora starts serving wings too, which could make it the first pizzeria to do so.

1971 Papa Joe moves La Nova to the intersection of Delaware and Tacoma in North Buffalo and the pizzeria introduces a white pizza, steak-and-cheese subs, and Bar-B-Que wings.

1972 Ettore Leonardi, his brother Luigi, sister Anne, and wife Argia found Leonardi's Pizzeria.

1973 La Nova moves to their now-iconic West Side location at West Ferry and Hampshire.

1979 Franco Kroese founds Franco's Pizza.

1980 Calvin Trillin is on his way to check out the wings at Santora's when he meets John Young, who claims to have invented Buffalo chicken wings.

1989 There are 274 pizzerias in Buffalo (population 313,570).

1992 Robert Cordova starts his Pizza Logs business behind a grocery store in Niagara Falls.

1992 David Powers and partner Jim Bouris open Imperial Pizza.

1993 La Nova launches its wholesale wing business.

1995 The Transit Road Santora's changes its pizza recipe to go back to the old ways of doing things and refocuses on quality.

1996 In what appears to be the earliest reference to "Buffalo chicken pizza," the Saint Paul Pioneer Press reports on the pie being served at a restaurant called Table of Contents in St. Paul and Minneapolis.

1998 There are 360 pizzerias in Buffalo (population 292,819).

1998 Anthony Kulik and John Skotarczak found Lovejoy Pizza in the east Buffalo neighborhood for which it was named.

2002 Little Caesar's is selling a Buffalo chicken pizza with celery and blue cheese dressing.

2002 Chuck Maciejewski opens Macy's Place Pizzeria.

2004 Pizza Hut introduces their version of Buffalo chicken pizza nationwide.

2009 Domino's launches a Buffalo Chicken pizza as part of their American Legends specialty pizzas.

2011 La Nova becomes the official pizza of the Buffalo Bills.

2012 Papa Joe Todaro passes away.

2014 La Nova becomes the official pizza of the Buffalo Bisons.

2015 Anonymous pizza reviewer SexySlices launches and completes his quest to review 52 of Buffalo's favorite pizzerias.

2015 La Nova becomes the official pizza of the Buffalo Sabres.

2017 *Travel + Leisure* ranks Buffalo number three on a list of cities with America's favorite pizza behind Detroit and Phoenix. New York City lands at number six.

2017 According to sources, there are more than 600 pizzerias in Buffalo and a population of 256,902.

2017 After experiencing success with his food truck O.G. Wood Fire, Jay Langfelder opens his modern Neapolitan spot Jay's Artisan Pizzeria.

Why is (Almost) Every Pizzeria in Buffalo a Takeout Joint?

Each time I asked that question I saw the same sequence of facial expressions: quizzical, recognition, and bemusement. "You mean it's not like this everywhere?" the last one seemed to ask. Um, no. There *are* exceptions—most notably La Nova on West Ferry and Bob & John's La Hacienda on Hertel—but aside from a small counter, the average pizzeria in Buffalo is a takeout joint.

Even before delivery became de rigueur in Buffalo, the *Buffalo News*'s former restaurant critic Janice Okun recalls going to great lengths to get it. "When I was in high school, people were ordering Bocce pizza," she said. "Bocce pizza at that time was in the wealthy neighborhood on the East Side. We used to have it sent by taxi. We were so young we couldn't drive, but we had to get it somehow."

My undercover pizza industry expert Deep Pizza told me that these days, "If you're running a popular pizzeria, it's almost 60/40 delivery and takeout as opposed to dine-in." Bocce's Mark Daniels told me, "Fifteen percent of our business is delivery. A majority of people just like coming in to pick up their pizzas." But why?

Larry Santora attributes the pizza's popularity to the fact that you can take a family of four out and feed them for $30 and said that his business is 80 percent takeout. "You'll fill the tables once, and then the rest of the day it's two parties, three

Bob + John's La Hacienda on Hertel Avenue is one of the rare pizzerias with an extended dining room.

Santora's in Depew on 3440 Transit Road.

A tailgating sign at Imperial Pizza.

parties, four parties, two parties, three parties, empty, two parties, empty. Meanwhile, the take-out and the delivery is through the roof."

In Buffalo, pizza is just mostly a takeout or order-out item. SexySlices explained:

"A lot of it has to do with infrastructure and culture. We're a winter sports town for most the year. When we're out of work, we wanna get the hell home, get out of the cold, put on a Sabres game, and spend some time with our loved ones. This city is coming up strong with a thriving urban culture, but don't kid yourself. We're still at our core a blue-collar city, meaning bigger families, large, comfortable, relatively cheap living accommodations and an urban entertainment center, that although growing, is still relatively dead mid-winter on a weekday. All that spells 'eat at home.'"

But doesn't the quality of the pizza suffer while steaming in a box on the way home?

"Unless somebody piled up the highway, no matter where you are, you're probably going to get home from the pizzeria in under 15 minutes after, and that's conservative. My family's favorite spots and most of mine today are within walking distance. We have hundreds of pizzerias that serve big pies that stay hot and fresh longer, and typically see less than 15 minutes of travel time. You don't lose quality. Wings on the other hand justify going out for. Ten minutes in a steamy box kills wings."

Janice Okun seconded weather as a primary factor, but added that women spending more time as part of the workforce played a role:

"When women started to work second jobs, when it started to be okay to not cook at home, stopping and picking something up on the way home became the way to put a fast meal on the table. You couldn't take the whole family to eat at McDonald's because it was too cold out. Dad or mom picked something up on the way home from work. It became so prevalent that shops then became only take-out shops, because there wasn't a need to have a dining room and a wait staff and all that overhead."

One side-effect of being a takeout-centric business in Buffalo is that like some of America's best slice shops—take Joe's in the West Village in Manhattan—there's high slice turnover. And that means that at most places in Buffalo you have a good chance at finding a really fresh slice (a plain cheese slice ranges from about $2.15 to $3). And because that's the business, there's a lot less attitude given if you decide to just wait for one from a new pie. In the rare event they do cop any, leave. It's a sign they're one of the few who don't get it.

Buffalo-Pizza Obsession: An Interview with SexySlices

Most Americans love pizza. Then there are those of us who take that love to an unhealthy obsession. Without diminishing the seriousness of the word, let's go ahead and call it pizza stalking. When it comes to Buffalo-style pizza, it's hard to imagine a man more obsessed than an anonymous Instagram pizza reviewer whose *nom de plum* is SexySlices. Aside from a few well-intentioned reviews of pizzerias outside Buffalo that start pizza box half full but seem to end with him looking forward to settling into the real thing back home in the Nickel City, SexySlices' focus is local. At last count SexySlices (it never gets old, especially in person) had reviewed and ranked (on a letter grade scale) somewhere between a third and a half of all the pizzerias in Buffalo since launching his account in July, 2015—more than a hundred.

Until a point in his reviewing and only by accident because he was caught *in flagrante delicto* posting a review, even SexySlices' girlfriend didn't know what he was up to. Why all the secrecy?

"Because it's a little abnormal and I don't want my coworkers to figure it out," he told me, laughing. "Also because I never want anything I say about pizza to be influenced by anything but the pizza itself. I don't want to be recognized and get free pizza, or have people treat me or the product differently when I order, or have friends be bummed when I hate their favorite. There's not a crazy amount of money in the small-time pizzeria game. These families deserve my money and they all deserve to be judged on a level playing field."

Fair enough. If you're in town and looking for the latest in pizza news, SexySlices is the account to check out. In addition to fighting Buffalo's neighborhood pizza provincialism (he says folks are often reluctant to branch out beyond their go-tos), his confident, funny reviews are filled with cheese pulls, breakfast pies, Buffalo chicken pizza topped with more hot sauce than you'll find applied to an order of wings, and photos of pepperoni fields that seem to go on forever. I'll go ahead and credit him for teaching me the term "pepperoni lotus" (when a slice is served with multiple pepperoni slices cradled inside each other) and somewhat shamefully admit that I never thought of ordering a pie with double pepperoni before I met him.

You're Buffalo born and bred, right?

A hundred percent. Outside of a small stint in Ohio for college (a pizza desert) I've lived in Buffalo and the greater Buffalo area my whole life. Go Bills.

Which Buffalo pizzeria did you grow up on?

Certainly not ones I love today. I grew up an outsider in a family of sweet sauce-lovers. I was unanimously outvoted my entire life and forced to eat excellent pizza from places like Frankie's and Pizza Oven that was ruined by the addition of a local delicacy: sweet sauce. It's a plight I've shared with many in the area. It's probably why I was so passionate to find other pizzerias around Buffalo. Whenever I had the chance to house-sit alone, I would order Lock City, a pizza notorious for its crazy herby, acidic sauce, intensely salty and greasy cheese, and crusty chewy dough. Everything my family hated. I still get a personal Lock City pie when I'm in town to this day. Very Kevin McCallister-y.

Can you talk a little about pizza balkanization in Buffalo? Most people have their spot and stick to their spot, right?

To both good and bad effect. It's great to see the tradition Buffalo pizza culture is steeped in. It's a matter of fact that there are people now ordering from the same pizzerias that their great-grandfathers patronized. I remember sleeping over at my friends' houses and being floored to find out which place was their family's pizzeria. These are mostly mom-and-pop places, and it's a testament to the quality of the pie and the loyalty of this population to see how long some of them have stuck around.

But?

The barrier to entry is steep. Every year, dozens more places pop up and fail, and sometimes it's not necessarily due to market saturation or a lack of quality. People don't like to stray from the beaten path. Trying a new place is hard when you know you've got ol' reliable in your back pocket that you hold dear as your favorite meal of the week or month. You don't wanna risk blowing that, even if we eat it much more frequently than most of the country. But I encourage everyone to try it. Some will suck. Big time. However, you might find, like me, that some of your favorite places will fall off your top 10. Or maybe you find the grass isn't greener and you can now brag about how dope your lifelong spot is. Just get your slice on at lunch, Buffalo! Please! Some of these places are putting out INCREDIBLE quality, and they might be getting overlooked because you don't want to question the status quo.

What made you start venturing out to the city's many different pizzerias?

I got my first full-time job in South Buffalo, I didn't know much about the area, let alone the pizza scene. I decided to try the three closest to my work and the circle just expanded and expanded until it became the once-a-week, 52-in-a-year project that I completed in 2015.

What are the three pizzerias that most represent Buffalo's pizza as a style?

Bocce (you can't talk Buffalo Pizza without mentioning it), Imperial, and Leonardi's. The holy trinity of the "Buffalo Style." If you were doing a pizza tour and wanted to taste the most legendary regional slices, that's where you'd go. All three tick every box of the Buffalo pizza definition.

What are your top five pizzerias right now?

#1 Lock City: *My childhood favorite is not even close to "Buffalo Style," but has a crunchy, chewy, sloppy, salty, acidic style all its own that's truly one of a kind.*

#2 Picasso's: *All the good from the Buffalo style and none of the bad with thick-cut crispy pepperoni, loads of cheese, a crispy char, but a thinned dough and a heartburn-inducing acidic, herby sauce.*

#3 Mister Pizza: *A crapshoot that 75 percent of the time will score you the greatest garlic-crusted crunchy-bottomed gooey*

A rare cornmeal-dusted undercarriage on the outskirts of Buffalo at Lock City Pizza.

mess of a pizza in your life that delivers late, and the other 25 percent of the time will be a messy disaster that one-time-buyers will hate you for loving.

#4 Carbone's: Hunger-killing heft crafted with care and consistency, baked with love and no bullshit frills from the city's industrial heart: South Buffalo.

#5 Gino & Joe's (this spot is on my constant rotation): King of Buffalo's New York-style slice shops. If you're tired of the Buffalo-style life and want to throw your lunchbreak a curveball with an eggplant Parmesan slice that you don't have to eat in your car, look no further.

Do you have any sleeper picks for Buffalo pizzerias that you think should be getting more attention?

Artone's. They're doing the classic Buffalo-style as good (if not better) as anyone. It's hard though. How do you get people to try a different shop when Imperial (which with all due respect makes an excellent pie) is a stone's throw away? They're competing on the doorstep of a giant with a similar recipe. Another must-mention is one I've only just tried recently: Favorite's in Lewiston. They're slinging some of the most truly creative, affordable, and delicious slices I've ever seen out of a shop that's connected to a hidden suburban apartment complex. Both their classic cheese-and-pep and their "Honey Stung" (BBQ Chicken, bacon, sesame seeds, and scallions) blew me away. They're putting everything they have into that shop and it shows. I just hope everyone starts to notice. Lastly, shout out to Matayo's doing my second favorite New York-style slice in the McKinley Mall. If you're into that and want to look like a deep-cut pizza badass, impress your friends and head there.

Are there any non-pizza sides at any particular pizzerias that you've come across that are worth shouting out?

Wow. Excellent question. All shops sling a bunch of crazy menu items on the side that admittedly, I don't often enough consider. Outside of the wing-sub-taco realm that everyone seems to compete in, Molinaro's has an incredible stuffed pepper roll. That's about all I've got. Now I feel like checking this out.

Have you noticed anything about the sub-genres of pizza style within Buffalo's pizza style?

A fascinating one are the New York-style places. I don't know anyone who orders whole pies from them to take home. Just thinking about it seems funny to me for some reason. Probably because my favorites are in malls! They're really just considered slice shops, but a few are really damn good. So much so that I would be happy to eat a whole pie, but my mind can't wrap around the idea of going to Gino's, or Joe's, or Gino & Joe's (yes, all three different shops entirely) and getting anything but a slice. Transplants from New York City often reach out to me for the best New York City style, but I don't think we have anything that fully scratches that itch. There's still a little "Buffalo" in one aspect or another in all of them.

Buffalo chicken pizza is a thing across the country. What are your thoughts about it as a topping? How do most Buffalonians view it?

As long as you're not a sadist and putting red sauce on it, I'm all for it. I can't think of a single more heart-attack inducing item on a pizzeria's menu, but it's incredible stuff. Specialty pizzas in general are a vast landscape out here that I actually don't see many people, myself included, stepping foot into all that often. Again, they go for a premium and you don't wanna screw up a good thing. That being said, if you're going outside of the "normal" boundary, more often than not you're ordering Buffalo chicken. After all, if it's going to kick ass anywhere, it should be here. Most times, that's true.

Let's talk about breakfast pizza culture in Buffalo ... what's breakfast pizza? Who makes it? Who makes it the best?

It's polarizing. A lot of people I recently found out hate breakfast pizza. I get down on the breakfast pizza, big-time. It's a delicacy if you can find it, because not a lot of places open early enough to sell it, and a lot of them don't advertise it. Places that do it best in my opinion are Daddio's, Tops (actually a local grocery chain), and Leo's.

Is there a Toronto pizza scene?

Absolutely not. There is no pizza culture over the border. They come here to eat our pizza. I don't know anybody doing it the other way around.

To ranch or not to ranch?

Let your ranch flag fly.

To blot or not to blot?

No blotting. You're eating pizza for Christ's sake. Do some sit-ups.

How many toppings are too many toppings on Buffalo-style pizza?

More than three, and one should be a veggie. It won't cook properly.

Anchovies?

Best insurance against people stealing your pizza. Learn to embrace them as a weapon.

Pineapple?

Never touch the stuff.

Is there any other topping that shouldn't be put on a pizza?

There are plenty that shouldn't be on my pizza, but I don't believe there are any that shouldn't be on a pizza. As long as you like it.

Is a reheat an inferior or superior slice?

Inarguably inferior.

How to Read a Buffalo Pizza Menu: Sides, Toppings, Crusts, Cuts, Half-Bakes, and Special Pies

La Nova isn't the only Buffalo pizzeria with a diner-long menu. Traditional Italian-American dishes like stuffed shells, lasagna, veal Parm and the like make appearances on most menus at Nickel City pizzerias along with too many other items from nonna's *piatti preferiti* to note. In addition to classic pizzeria entrées, chicken fingers, fish-fries, and tacos make frequent appearances, and subs make up a pretty good portion of most pizzeria menus. It should go without saying that you're better off looking for the city's best tacos at lloyd Taco Factory on Hertel or one of the other legit taco places that have sprung up, and for fish-fries at its most storied homes. On the other hand, pizzeria subs are tremendous. They frequently even share toppings (and names) with places' specialty pies. But we'll get to Buffalo's sandwich culture later. It's important to note recurring toppings, specialty pies, and sides that are iconic to the city's pizzerias, some of which you won't frequently find elsewhere.

Sides: Just In Case You're Worried About Being Hungry . . .

As every Buffalonian knows, almost every pizzeria makes wings (Buffalo-style, pit-roasted, and boneless), most do wing-and-pizza specials, and many make better wings than Americans will eat at places dedicated to wings in their own hometown. But we've talked about those already. You see a laundry list of all the classic bar apps—mozzarella sticks, fried zucchini, onion rings, calamari, potato skins, fried mushrooms, tater tots, jalapeño poppers, toasted raviolis, bread sticks, fried shrimp—as well as sides like chili, pickle chips, fried broccoli-cheese bites, deep-fried cauliflower, coleslaw, and potato salad, which you might not expect to see at a pizzeria.

They have their merits. But you can find them anywhere. Buffalo pizzerias' takes on garlic bread technically fall into the same category, but their cheese, spinach, and garlic smothered, butter-and-oil-griddled variations deserve, at least, a mention. Similarly, french fries, which depending on the place come in combinations of straight-up, wedge-style, waffle, curly, shoe-string, steak-cut, and beer-battered (beer-battered?!) get a shout-out because Buffalo's proximity to Canada means the latter's poutine treatment often sneaks onto menus. Fries smothered Italian-style (mozzarella and pepperoni), taco fries (cheddar, chives, taco meat, sour cream, and salsa), and garlic sauce and Parmesan frequently show up with dipping sauces like BBQ and ranch and toppings like blue cheese, nacho cheese, bacon, jalapeños, gravy, and of course, gravy and cheese curds. What a town.

You'll see calzones plainly listed on many pizzeria menus, but there are a handful of places that give them their own names, or slightly tweak their ingredients or shape. For instance, Pizza Plant serves "pods" that are essentially crimped-closed football-shaped calzones. La Nova makes what they call "super stuffed calzones," which they trick out with garlic, sesame, hot pepper, onion, of Cajun dough. And Deniro's makes what they call Lunas, exaggerated crescent-shaped calzones filled with the same topping combinations on their specialty pies.

But there are three sides that most pizzerias have, that every Buffalonian knows, two of which, out-of-towners might need explained, and one that's a requirement to eat before leaving town: stuffed hot peppers, Pizza Logs, and Buffalo Crunch Rolls. Stuffed hot peppers are a truly amazingly delicious dish. Variations abound, but they're usually stuffed with a combination of cheeses, breadcrumbs, sautéed and served with sauce. They're a must, but they deserve their own shout-out so check out the chapter on Buffalo's Italian specialties.

Buffalo Chicken Crunch rolls are a more recent local invention along similar lines to Pizza Logs (rolled cheese, sauce, and pepperoni in a crispy wrapper) but with two non-pizza related flavors, Buffalo chicken and stuffed peppers. The Crunch Roll Factory was founded in 2016, and set up a new factory just south of Buffalo in Westfield. They're quickly becoming just as prevalent as Pizza Logs. In the Buffalo Chicken Crunch Roll, white chicken meat gets cooked in a spicy sauce, mixed with a cheese blend, and wrapped in a coating of what looks like a deep-fried marriage of panko and corn flakes. Then you're supposed to dip in either blue cheese or ranch dressing. The Banana Pepper Crunch Roll is a mixture of sliced Hungarian banana peppers with a four-cheese blend, chopped garlic, and spices wrapped in that same crunchy shell. It's meant to be paired with marinara.

Given the success of these two wholesale products that are also available in the city's groceries, one could easily imagine restaurant menus solely stocked by its frozen food aisles. Be forewarned, and this is not to disparage either invention, but if you don't feel like you should eat a salad after a first bite of either, God bless either your fine-tuned metabolism or your ability at self-deception.

Another Pizza Log in Buffalo's Snack Food Wall

Out-of-towners ask, "Pizza Logs?" But to Buffalonians, these cheesy fried pepperoni sticks are just part of the furniture on appetizer menus in the city's bars and pizzerias. It's almost hard to believe that they haven't *always* been there. The Original Pizza Logs' founder, Robert Cordova, passed away in 2013, but in the intervening 21 years, he made eating a pizza appetizer a completely logical thing to whet your appetite with before sitting down to a full pie.

The Original Pizza Logs is veteran-owned and -operated. Since a year before Mr. Cordova passed away, his son Jason Cordova, a former Army Captain with the 5th Special Forces Group, has worked to further his father's legacy, spreading the gospel of what you could argue is a fusion of Italian and Chinese-American food, well beyond Buffalo's borders. Here, Jason talks about how the company started, how his Dad turned it into a Buffalo snack icon, and his favorite way to eat them.

How did you serve?

I was an Army Captain with the 5th Special Forces Group. I was the Communications Detachment Commander.

What is a Pizza Log?

It is a gourmet pizza egg roll. That is the best way to describe it. A gourmet pizza egg roll that contains cheese, sauce, and pepperoni.

Wrapped in a wonton wrapper of some kind?

Exactly.

And at least some local products go into Pizza Logs?

Absolutely. I source locally whenever possible because local people are supporting me, so I do my best to support them.

Pizza Logs are fried but can be oven-baked at home, right?

We make two versions. One is for the fryer and one is for the oven. The retail version is for the oven.

You have one iconic flavor, right?

There are new ones coming out. There's no way I can tell you what I've got coming but there will absolutely be new products. The thing you can mention is that I built a new factory in 2016 and we're SQF Level 2. That's a big deal in the food industry.

What does that mean to you?

We're small but mighty.

So how did Pizza Logs come to be?

The Original Pizza Logs, just for full disclosure, started off as Pizza Fingers in 1986. It was with some other guy back in the day. The guy that had the original Pizza Fingers, had the idea, it just didn't work out. It evolved. Original Pizza Logs evolved from original Pizza Fingers. I think that's the best way to say it and not offend any of the guys that were involved in Pizza Fingers. I don't think that was a very good breakup.

There's an origin story online about your father rolling cheese sauce and pepperoni in a crispy wrapper to invent the Original Pizza Logs behind a grocery store in Niagara Falls.

I saw that article that you're talking about, it was on a race track, and my dad was so private, I can assure you, he never had that conversation. Whoever wrote that article . . . My dad was very private. It started behind a convenience store in Niagara Falls, Original Pizza Logs. I don't think it's certain my dad invented . . . it evolved. Pizza Fingers were invented by somebody else. I think you know, to give them proper credit, but they didn't last, we lasted. They deserve credit for having a product but they didn't have the staying power that we have, obviously. I'm an honest guy and I want to make sure that my dad gets the credit for having built this company behind a very decrepit Wilson Farms convenience store. He built it with will and hard work and I took over in 2012. We've been making them in Niagara Falls, New York, ever since. Twenty-five years in business and we are now the official finger food of the Buffalo Bills, the Buffalo Sabres, and the Buffalo Bisons. Second generation now and stuff's going great.

Pizza Logs are everywhere in Buffalo. Everyone knows them. How did that happen?

A lot of door-to-door. My dad just muscled through it, man. He would tell you he went to the school of hard knocks and he just built it one account at a time. But I think the thing to really highlight, the reason it keeps proliferating was because of his attention to detail and quality. He never compromised quality. The same product my dad made, I make still. We've made no changes, I keep it just like my dad made. We focus on quality.

You've started to expand outside of western New York too . . .

We absolutely are. PNC Park, we're now at PPG Paints Arena, home of the Stanley Cup champion Pittsburgh Penguins. We're also at Wells Fargo Center in Philadelphia. We've been served at MetLife Stadium. They bring us in from time to time at Universal Studios in Orlando. We've expanded, just working really hard. That's the motto: the harder you work, the more you're lucky.

Where else are you?

We're in New York City, we're just not in a lot of retail in New York City. We're in Stew Leonard's in Connecticut, so we're not in a lot of places, but we're in a lot of restaurants. We're in Wegmans. We go as far west as Las Vegas, Florida, Texas, Northern Wisconsin, and Boston. We're expanding.

When people see Pizza Logs outside of Buffalo, do they realize where they're from?

That's how I sell the product and we say on our website that they're from Buffalo, which is arguably the capital of finger foods.

It says you recommend eating them with straight-up marinara, blue cheese, and hot sauce. Is that right? Any tips for how to best enjoy Pizza Logs?

Yeah, I would say if you want to know how to eat them the way the owner likes, it's Buffalo style. You bake the product, you let it stand for two minutes—don't touch it. The cheese melts all the way through and then you brush wing sauce on and then dip it in ranch or blue cheese and it will change your life.

Toppings: It's Chicken Finger Lickin' Good

You'll find many of America's most familiar pizza toppings in Buffalo. But there are several toppings that are surprises and a few that demand double-takes.

Let's agree on and put aside conventional toppings: mushrooms, onions, green onions, red and green peppers, tomatoes, black olives, pepperoni, sausage, bacon, feta, grilled chicken, ham, bacon, anchovies, pineapple, meatballs, broccoli, spinach, and roasted sweet peppers. And we'll consider banana peppers, hamburger, taco beef, jalapeños, hot cherry peppers, as perhaps a bit rarer across America, but not beyond the pale. All of the above are, give or take, pretty prevalent at most Buffalo pizzerias.

Toppings like Canadian bacon, artichokes, chopped garlic, cappocola, ricotta, eggplant, zucchini, and shrimp can be found, but are outliers in Buffalo. Less frequently seen outside Buffalo, but also pretty common in the city are green olives, blue cheese, cheddar, hot cherry peppers, and sirloin steak. If you're shrugging your shoulders, consider the pizzerias that offer chicken fingers, slices of Buffalo's signature stuffed hot peppers, dandelions, and almonds. As any self-respecting Buffalonian will tell you, the first is a key component in one of the city's favorite pies. Count dandelions (at Mister Pizza, an old-school sub component that's largely been replaced by spinach elsewhere) and almonds (featured at La Nova) among rare toppings even in the Nickel City.

Special Crusts: For No Extra Charge

While far from de rigueur, a few pizzerias in Buffalo take very seriously their mission to establishing a no-pizza-bones zone. One way to make sure we leave no crust behind is to flavor it. Four places I came across in Buffalo all offered special crusts: La Nova, Lovejoy, Mister Pizza, and Sugo's. All of them offer sesame, garlic, onion, and Cajun crusts. Lovejoy, Mister Pizza, and Sugo's also do hot pepper. But Sugo's and Mister Pizza go next level. Each have their own variations on honey crusts (honey BBQ, honey garlic, and honey sesame), Sugo's does a lemon pepper crust, and in addition to also doing poppy seeds, Mister Pizza offers to mix and match any of its 9 crust offerings to your delight. And at least at all four of these gems, when it's offered, it's at no extra charge.

Cuts

If you need further evidence for Buffalonians' pizza obsession, just take a look at the menus from some of its most popular places. The detailed columns, sizes, slice counts, cut specifications, and sometimes even diagrams, should be convincing.

In Buffalo, pizzas are by default round. Beyond the slice, pies usually come in five sizes: personal (ranging from 8"×8" to 12"×12" wide), small (around 9"×9" to 13"×13"), medium (about 12"×12" to 15"×15"), large (about 16"×16" to 17"×17"), and by the sheet (also known as a party tray, party pizza, and a tray).

Sheet pizzas are the largest pies you'll find, popular for offices, sporting events, parties, slumber parties, any occasion really, including a random weeknight when you're feeling adventurously hungry. "Pizza keeps so well that you never feel like an idiot for getting a tray," SexySlices told me. "You can feed off it like a wild animal for days." Their sizes are inconsistent—16"×21" at Franco's, 17"×25" at Deniro's, 24"×18" at Just Pizza, 30"×30" for "The Big Joe" at La Nova—but the most prevalent tray size is probably 18"×26".

When it comes to cuts (how a pizza is sliced), for the most part, Buffalo pizzerias default to the isosceles slices characteristic to the "pie cut." Personal pies are usually cut in four slices while small and medium pizzas have anywhere from six to 12 slices. When it comes to the standard large-sized pizza, Buffalonians default to the traditional eight-to-a-pie New York City-style "pie cut."

But they're also sometimes cut into 12 slices and there are places in town that go rogue (seemingly without any rhyme or reason), doing tavern-style slices, long *rectangular* slices, and trapezoids. There are even places that do uneven slices that look like double-cut and triple-cut pies, a style that results in super pointy slices. And mysteriously, many places cut round pies into squares. "Please specify if cut in squares," Imperial's menu notes. "All Pizza Cut in Squares. Slices Available Upon Request," Mister Pizza's declares.

For all the difference a few inches might seem to make between trays at different pizzerias, you actually do see a difference in how Buffalo's mightiest pizzas are sliced, coming in 24, 30, 32, and sometimes 48 slices. Party pizzas almost always get the square cut treatment known as party cut or tavern cut, but there are places that do the isosceles slices instead.

Think I'm making a big deal out of nothing? Some places give you more than one square-cut option. Just Pizza offers its jumbo pie (their tray) in 24 or 30 square cuts, and they even do square-to-slice conversions—a large pie breaks down to being 16 square cuts or 12 slices.

"People get livid if it's not a party pizza and it's cut into squares," SexySlices told me. "I personally like it. I'm a middle piece man all the way and my girlfriend is nuts over crust. So it's a win-win. It's like flats and drumsticks for wings in that way."

Specialty Pies

Given the thickness that characterizes Buffalo-style pizza, it shouldn't be a surprise that there's little in the way of Sicilian in the city. And while there is *bakery pizza*—places like Guercio & Sons and Gino's Italian Bakery do rectangular slices cooked in trays and plenty of menus call out certain pies for being made "the way grandma" did—there's little actual grandma pizza. But there *are* plenty of specialty pies.

Spinach artichoke makes cameos, but the much-maligned yet omnipresent Hawaiian pizza is practically everywhere in Buffalo (they serve it, mysteriously, with almonds at La Nova and with bacon at Santora's), and "Greek" pizzas show up with basil pesto, feta, black olives, onions, tomatoes, and sometimes spinach. Perhaps to hold up to all the cheese and cup-and-char, a few places in town do "double dough" pies (name-check: Blasdell and Bob & John's La Hacienda). BBQ chicken ranch pies can also be found with frequency. And cheeseburger pizzas occasionally prevail—John's does two, a bacon cheddar burger pizza and one they call "Bob's Big Mac," which if you're old enough to remember, to paraphrase the commercial, features all-beef burger, sauce (Thousand Island dressing), lettuce, cheese (mozzarella, American, and Swiss), pickles, onions on a sesame seed crust.

There are interesting one-offs around town: the French bread pizza (something you see more in homes and frozen food aisles) at Artone's, blue cheese pizza at Bob & John's La Hacienda; Franco's Philly cheesesteak pie; Deniro's bacon, lettuce, and tomato pizza; Judi's "sub-style" move that essentially turns any pizza into a tricked-out salad pie by adding chilled lettuce, tomato, and onion; and Sugo's does a "Polish Pie" with a caraway-seasoned cream sauce topped with mushrooms, onions, mozzarella, kraut, Polish sausage, and bacon. Pizza Plant does Buffalo's take on deep dish with stuffed pizza, a high-walled crust (plain, sesame, spinach, or garlic) stuffed standard with cheese and sauce, and jammed with a host of other toppings

But if you're looking for a very *Buffalo* Buffalo-style pizza beyond the cup-and-char baseline, you're going to want to try one of these nine local standbys.

Beef on Weck Pizza: Buffalo's signature sandwich has made the transition to pizza style around the city, though it's not as available as you might think. Typically, this pie involves a creamy horseradish base, roast beef, and a salt-and-caraway kummelweck crust. The cheese choice is where pizzerias show their personality. Brick Oven Bistro does one with Swiss; Chick-N-Pizza Works goes with straight mozz; John's Pizza & Subs goes garlic butter, cheddar, and mozzarella; Good Guys blends Swiss, American, and mozzarella; and Mister Pizza goes mozz, provolone, and cheddar.

Breakfast Pizza: With the proliferation of egg porn, runny yolks have been making more appearances on pizzas across America. But in Buffalo, breakfast pizza means much more than just tossing an egg on. It's entirely its own genre. Per SexySlices, "Breakfast pizza has a scrambled egg base, some sort of cheese blend that should include cheddar, bacon, sausage, or both. Beats the hell out of a bowl of Chex." While persuasive menu notes like Just Pizza's "Want to improve your business morning? Pre-order and have breakfast pizza delivered" and Imperial's 11 AM cutoff indicate, this is a pie that's more associated with the sunrise. But while early morning is the time of day you're going to be able to sample these egg-based pies by the slice, Buffalo's an eat-breakfast-for-dinner-if-you-want kinda town—you can order a full breakfast pie at most pizzerias well into the night.

If you're into potato, you're going to want to visit Just Pizza for the Giambotta, just one of their six breakfast options, a pie with eggs, sweet or hot peppers, onion, thick-sliced potatoes, mozzarella and Romano, and your choice of Virginia ham, Italian sausage, pepperoni or meatballs (it's the rare breakfast pizza also advertised as available with marinara) or Franco's, where all breakfast pies come standard with American cheese, mozzarella, and hash browns. For a kitchen-sink breakfast pie though, you're probably going to want to head to La Nova, where their sauceless pizza is topped with scrambled eggs, Romano, light taco cheese, light cheddar, mozzarella, oil, salt, pepper, garlic salt, garlic, ham, sausage, *and* bacon.

Buffalo Chicken Pizza: If inventing Buffalo *wings* was a stroke of genius, whoever decided it was a good idea to take that flavor profile, marry it with one of America's most favorite comfort foods, pizza, aced the culinary Mensa test. The only problem is, the inventor seems to be somewhat hard to track down. Buffalo chicken pizza has become a staple at many pizzerias across America, but the city's iconic chicken *finger* pizza is more popular *in* the city. When you do find Buffalo chicken pizza *in* Buffalo, pizzerias usually swap out the traditional marinara for a blue cheese or hot sauce base (hot, medium, or mild). Cheeses typically include cheddar and mozzarella, with fontinella, blue cheese, and Romano making appearances. Deniro's does a hot sauce base but includes a side of blue cheese dressing for dipping and Mister Pizza uses a blue cheese dressing base with chicken that's been cooked in hot sauce to your preferred heat level then tops their pie with celery, carrots, and onions (the last is up to you). The celery is a rare but thorough touch, one executed with even more finesse at Just Pizza where pies are topped with crisp diced celery after baking.

Chicken Finger Pizza: Instead of Buffalo chicken pizza, perhaps food detectives ought to be seeking out whoever invented this dirty little pizza secret that Buffalo's been keeping from the rest of America. If chicken finger pizza sounds beyond the pale to you, good. You're probably sane (deprived, but sane). Still, when it's done right, chicken finger pizza is enough to make you aspire to being fat. The key ingredient, of course, is the breaded chicken, which gets fried first, then diced or chunked. Hot, medium, or mild sauce is the go-to when it comes to flavoring, but there are pizzerias including Good Guys, Imperial, Lovejoy, Macy's, Ricota's, and Santora's that offer the option of adding a sour-sweet dimension to this pie via BBQ sauce (what!?). Mozzarella is the most prevalent cheese, but cheddar, fontinella, Romano, and American do make appearances. And while blue cheese is the most prevalent base, there *are* pizzerias that opt for a dough *lined* with hot sauce. That *does* mean that red sauce is an outlier on this pie, but places like Blasdell, Leonardi's, Ricota's, and Santora's *do* stand against the tide. Among more idiosyncratic versions, Mister Pizza tops their chicken finger pizza with whole tomatoes, Judi's adds a spread of garlic, and Deniro's goes the salad slice route, topping theirs with lettuce and tomato after baking.

Steak or Chicken in the Grass: It's no surprise that this staple of Buffalo's sandwich menu has made its way to some pizzerias around the city, it's only perplexing that it hasn't become more prevalent. Steak seems to be the default, but you typically get the choice between that or chicken (and sometimes even shrimp), and the pies are usually covered with mozzarella, with spinach substituting for the one-time star of the show: dandelions. At Santora's and Picasso's they add a drizzle of olive oil and a scattering of Romano and spices along with hot peppers. Mister Pizza's pie (*so* close to "Mister Pizza Pie!"—now how about that as the name of a pizzeria, eh?) Popeye's out with spinach, but they are one of the rarer spots in town that stocks dandelions,

so if you're into authenticity and you're nice, it's hard to believe they wouldn't go all out for you if you asked.

Steak Pizza: Not to be confused with steak in the grass, steak pizza always gets onions, the question is whether they'll be cooked first and how. Fried? Caramelized? The pie also almost always gets peppers (though whether they're sweet, green, or hot depends on the pizzeria and customer preference) and sometimes, garlic. Mozzarella is the standard on a steak pizza but you'll see Swiss and American cheese playing "me-too" (here's looking at you, John's Pizza & Subs). Of course, those are just the standard toppings. Places sometimes like to trick out this pie too. Franco's and John's add mushrooms (roasted at Franco's) and Good Guys sees the mushrooms and raises banana peppers.

Stinger Pizza: "I take it back," my Buffalo pizza friend SexySlices said when I asked him about the Stinger. "*This* is the single most heart-attack inducing item on a Buffalo pizzeria's menu." The stinger is its own animal. "It's a very low-key regional specialty," SexySlices explains. "Even a deeper cut than the beef on weck. It's like the roast pork in Philly. Every pizza place does it, but it's not very well-known. It's absolutely regarded as the fattest thing you can do. It's incredible though. If you're absolutely famished and you just need to eat the most filling thing on the menu, you almost have to. It's the light at the end of the tunnel in a city where the bars close at 4 AM, and the pizzerias are open until 5 AM." Expect chicken fingers (fried, obviously) ordered with whatever sauce you prefer (hot, medium, mild, or BBQ) and chopped steak covered in mozzarella (usually, and as at John's Pizza & Subs, sometimes provolone too) and served on a sauce that follows in the footsteps of its cousin the "Buffalo chicken" pizza. Most places use a mix of Frank's RedHot and blue cheese, but some places tempt derision for purists by using red sauce.

Taco Pie: Buffalo doesn't claim to have invented it (that distinction is said to go to a place called Happy Joe's in Iowa), but this is a city that loves it some taco pizza. In the Nickel City that almost *always* means "taco" or "enchilada" sauce, seasoned ground beef, and cheddar and mozzarella, topped, after baking, with fresh chopped tomatoes and (usually) lettuce. Hot, medium, and mild sauces are frequently offered, occasionally Monterey Jack makes an appearance, and sometimes there are black olives, diced onions, and sour cream on the side. Good Guys tries to take things to the next level by taking their tomato, onion, and lettuce and topping it with tortilla strips, but it's hard to outdo Artone's, which channels Taco Bell, adding a small bag of Doritos.

White Pizza: Gauge the popularity of this pizza archetype by the fact that Bocce's menu features *nine* versions of it. You can easily trace Buffalo's white pizza back to 1971, when La Nova says they first put it on their menu. Whether or not that means they're responsible for inventing the Nickel City's version of a pie that's also been offered in pizzerias in New York City and elsewhere around the country for decades, is impossible to tell. Unlike those white pies, how-

ever, Buffalo's white pizza doesn't rely on ricotta. Why? "Ricotta was not an item we could use in a lot of our pies, so I just never invested in it," Franco's Pizza owner Franco Kroese explained.

Per the name, this is a sauceless pie. In sauce's stead, that means salt, pepper, garlic, herbs, lots of olive oil, mozzarella, and a grated cheese (Romano or Parmesan), with fontinella making cameos. There are almost always tomatoes and onions, which provide the moisture that going sauceless requires for making a good slice pleasant to chew. Santora's supreme adds Italian sausage and hot banana peppers and among the nine versions of white pizza at Bocce, black olives, steak, zucchini, yellow squash, cheddar, spinach, artichoke, and sautéed peppers. Interestingly, the white pizza at La Nova comes with a recommended topping: anchovies. It's a move you'll see at several other pizzerias, including Artone's, Deniro's, and Mister Pizza. It's been theorized that white pizza's popularity and origin in Buffalo may be tied to Lent—the idea being that on Fridays, families needed something other than ol' reliable: cup-and-char pepperoni.

Franco Kroese said that white pies were one of the first gourmet pizzas to really resonate in Buffalo. "It was either California Pizza Kitchen or it was somewhere out of town that I first saw that. We started selling it, not that I was the first guy to bring it here, but it just kind of took off."

And consider this: The pizza that Larry Santora said his grandfather Fioravanti Santora peddled door-to-door likely wasn't a saucy pie. The "sauce" Larry cited was likely to be the thick, relatively sparse spread of baked tomato characteristic of a transportable, easily divisible pizza.

So maybe it's just as likely that *in* Buffalo, at least, given the through-thread of the anchovies, that this genre came into being out of the humble origins of the city's purported *first* pizza.

Who Invented Buffalo Chicken Pizza?!

Whether you agree with Buffalo chicken as a pizza topping from a culinary or philosophical perspective or throw it in with pineapple and ham as a controversial bastardization, you'd be hard-pressed to deny its popularity on pizzerias menus across America. And while Teressa Bellissimo is credited with inventing wings at Anchor Bar in 1964, credit for the *pizza* topping is hard to pin down. When did wings move out of the side dish and *onto* the pie?

I asked everywhere in Buffalo, and nothing. I reached out to national chains, pizza publications, and America's *foremost* pizza experts. Nobody, I mean *nobody*, knew. That's funny considering that as history of toppings goes, we know Sam Panopoulos invented the Hawaiian pizza at Satellite Restaurant in Chatham, Ontario. And that happened in 1962!

A search begins in 1964 at Anchor. From there, consider La Nova is accepted as Buffalo's first pizzeria (in 1971) to serve wings (Santora's says it started in 1970). Either could be a starting point. La Nova serves a chicken finger pizza, but its origins are hazy. "I don't remember anybody else with it," Joe Todaro Sr. told me. "We don't put dates down or anything—maybe 15, 20, 25 years ago."

Domino's started serving wings with pizza in the Buffalo area in 1992. So proximity of wings as a pizza flavor made by local shops and chains is 1971 to 1992. Domino's said its Buffalo Chicken pizza was created for their American Legends pizzas in 2009, many of which used geography as muse, and that the style was inspired by a limited-time product called "Buffalo Stampede pizza," a test in small markets, but no one knows *when.* They're not the only chain in this game. Pizza Hut introduced theirs nationwide in 2004. And Little Caesar's was making one with celery and blue-cheese dressing in 2002.

But this seems late in the game.

Does the secret rest with Ed LaDou, the first pizza chef at Wolfgang Puck's Spago? LaDou was famous for outlandish toppings and was a developer of California Pizza Kitchen's menu in Beverly Hills in 1985. LaDou passed away in 2007, so unless CPK's founders Rick Rosenfield and Larry Flax know, we won't.

In 1997, monthly women's magazine *McCall's* (defunct since 2002) announced their 1996 Recipe Contest Winner was Buffalo Wing Pizza: shredded chicken seasoned with Mrs. Dash and scattered on a prefab crust with Monterey Jack, chopped celery and blue cheese or ranch. But the first reference to "Buffalo chicken pizza" I found was in the *Saint Paul Pioneer Press* on February 14, 1996 at Table of Contents (closed, 2000) in St. Paul and Minneapolis by chef Kristine Szczech.

Szczech left behind life on the line, but I found her at an electrical contractor, NEI Electric in St. Paul. She described TOC as an early farm-to-table restaurant opened by two Macalester College grads, Sam Ernst and Jim Dunn, who later became screenwriters. The former chef said they did two six- to eight-inch wafer-thin pizzas nightly, cooked on a stone in a conventional kitchen oven. She couldn't remember doing the pizza (Szczech said she wouldn't even order such a pie unless she was *in* Buffalo), but said they would've made everything scratch.

"Now Philip, I can imagine doing that," Szczech said. "It wouldn't have fallen within the scope of my flavor profile."

But Szczech's former longtime sous-chef Philip Dorwart, now owner and executive chef of Create Catering in Minneapolis, remembered. "We changed our menu every two weeks and Buffalo chicken was a favorite (it wasn't the thing it is now, obviously)," Dorwart said. "I worked at the World University Games in Buffalo in the summer of 1993. My brother-in-law is from Buffalo and took me to Anchor Bar to have them for the first time and I was smitten."

While Dorwart is sure he'd never heard of anyone doing it at the time they did, he's fuzzy on the genesis. "We used, what at that time were exotic ingredients on pizza—pears, blue cheese, sriracha, caramelized onions, balsamic vinegar, fresh herbs, prosciutto, duck confit—and the Buffalo idea just seemed to make sense. It would have been a round robin with a bunch of cooks talking about ideas at a menu meeting and someone saying, 'Why can't we do Buffalo pizza?' This is what we were about—pushing junk food and comfort food into haute cuisine, long before the kitsch of it."

Maybe it *was* a combination of Szczech, Dorwart, and a few cooks. Maybe Dorwart invented it! It does seem far from wings' origin though. And while 1996 feels closer to a logical birthday, it's hard to believe Buffalo chicken pizza didn't happen earlier. (Interestingly, 1997 is when B Dubs' founders moved their Ohio-based company to Minneapolis!)

It's circuitous, but let's finish back in Buffalo, where many say Tonawanda's John's Pizza & Subs is the inventor of the chicken finger *sub*. Putting aside who invented the chicken finger—the restaurant Puritan Backroom in Manchester, New Hampshire, claims *it* did in 1974, but some credit Cornell University professor Robert C. Baker in 1963—John's co-owner Gene Mongan said that in 1982, the "chicken finger was new in the area and we just decided to put it on a sub."

John's sandwich is topped with fingers shaken in hot sauce, topped with lettuce, tomato, and provolone, then smothered with blue cheese. Chicken finger subs are a story we'll get into—suffice it to say, Mongan said it was something he made for himself to eat while working in kitchens in 1977. He and his partners put it on the menu at John's in 1982. But . . . John's *also* sells what they *claim* to be "The Original Chicken Finger Pizza," topped with "tender Tyson chicken fingers, creamy blue cheese, celery, hot sauce, and mozzarella." Like wings, both sub and pizza can be ordered mild, medium, or hot.

Is the original Buffalo chicken pizza John's "Original Chicken *Finger* Pizza"?

"I believe that we were the first ones to do chicken finger pizza," Gene says, adding he can't prove it, but that they first sold them in 1997 (some 1955, *Back to the Future*–year confluence).

So maybe, this hot-sauce drenched fried chicken pizza is the original Buffalo chicken pizza. After all, you don't order a Greek salad in Greece, right? Maybe Buffalo's chicken finger pizza inspired copycats that spread Buffalo chicken pizza everywhere. Maybe co-owners Mongan and Raepple deserve the credit!

Except Mongan says that they were inspired by Wegmans, a supermarket chain out of Rochester. "They had a chicken wing pizza, and everybody was talking about it," Gene said. "It was pulled off the bone. We kind of looked at it, and went, 'Well, that's really good, but I bet it would be even better if we did it with chicken fingers.'"

Michele Mehaffy, Wegmans' Buffalo Consumer Affairs Manager told me that while Buffalo chicken pizza was one of their core recipes, they developed it in Buffalo in 1999. (Sigh.)

What can I tell you? If this is what it takes to trace the origin of *one* Buffalo-flavored dish, a timeline of all the others might be lost to history. Why did the Buffalo chicken wing cross the, er . . . how did the Buffalo chicken wing get on a pizza? That's my prima facie theory. Know the *true* story? Hit me up. I'm dying to know.

In Search of Buffalo's Best Pizza

Ranking pizza is serious business. I've done it for years as a national pizza writer for websites like the *Daily Meal*, *First We Feast*, and in New York City for the same publications along

with *TimeOut New York*. Burgers, fries, the country's best restaurants—these are subjects that have been known to spawn knife fights in online comment threads. But because of Americans' love of it and its accessibility, pizza may be the most contentious food to rank of all. So expect the works when it comes to ranking the best pizzas in cities known for it—everyone's an expert. Given Buffalonian pie passion, an uninformed ranking of the city's best pizzas could get you run out of town by a mob wielding pizza cutters.

If it was a full-time job, it would take a year to eat at Buffalo's 600 pizzerias to definitively claim one king of them all. It would be God's work, and

I'd be happy to volunteer for the position of chief pizza critic for the *Buffalo News*. Hey, like they say (and as Mister Pizza's menu notes), seven days without pizza makes one weak! As it was, I spent a month asking for recs and eating around the City of Good Neighbors' pizzerias in search of its best pies. The pizzerias most frequently recommended won't surprise locals. Even then, the picture would be incomplete. The same way Buffalonians will visit one pizzeria to pick up their pie and another place to get wings, they'll visit certain pizzerias for cup-and-char, but others for steak in the grass, chicken finger, stinger, and white pies. Still, over and over, Bocce Club, La Nova, Lovejoy, Imperial, and Bob & John's rounded out the top five places I was asked if I'd been.

Instead of visiting 600 places, I cross-referenced recent lists of Buffalo's best pizzerias, then added experts' and locals' recommendations to establish a shortlist of 40 places to review. From there, I eliminated pizzerias that weren't known for Buffalo-style pizza like Gino & Joe's, Joe's, and Gino's. They may be well regarded, but they're New York City pizzas, and don't belong on a list of standard-bearers for the city's style. Because places like Roost and O.G. Wood Fire *are* special, they deserve mention as destinations, but also shouldn't be included on a list of Buffalo's best pizza that ranks pizzerias for execution of its signature style. All told, I visited 27 places, which I narrowed to a list of 15.

The Criteria

In pizza circles, "You always have to establish a baseline" is the mantra of any expert worth his or her sauce. Usually, that means visiting a pizzeria and ordering a plain cheese pie along with the following: a sausage pizza, the restaurant's signature pizza, or pepperoni pizza. Given Buffalo's predisposition to cup-and-char, pepperoni pizza *is* the baseline. So that, along with signature pies, breakfast pizzas, stingers, chicken finger pies, and Buffalo chicken pizza, are what a ranking of the city's best should entail.

Establishing that, pizzas were judged based on the following:

- ★ Appearance of the slice
- ★ Quality and flavor of cheese, sauce, and dough
- ★ Application of pepperoni and quality of cup-and-char
- ★ Ratio of cheese to sauce to dough to pepperoni

Because the ratio of crust and toppings can change considerably from personal pies to sheet pizzas, I tried to judge only one: large. And because you're usually not going to get the best experience from a sitting slice pie, as much as possible I tried to give pizzerias their best shot, a *fresh* slice from a large pie.

Locals are bound to miss some personal favorites, and the omission of at least one or two standbys may be controversial. Bob and John's La Hacienda, a favorite for many, was one of my least favorite slices. I did have a slice from their display and not a fresh pie, but given it was dinner and the dining room was well-populated, it should have been as good a time as any for representational quality. Pizza Oven was cold and too sweet not to be listed as a dessert, and Blasdell was a congealed, greasy (in a bad way) disappointment. It could be they all were having bad days, and that a few lesser known places had good ones, but that's the way the crust crunches.

When it comes to a golden, pillowy undercarriage, more cheese than anyone should have business eating on a slice, and the cup-and-char pools of spicy oil dreams are made of, you can't beat these 15 pizzerias.

Buffalo's 15 Best Pizzerias

#15 Franco's Pizza (Multiple)

1924 Eggert Road, Amherst Street, 14226

716-835-7100 | francospizza.com

Sun–Thu 9 AM–11 PM, Fri–Sat 9 AM–12 AM

"We don't cut corners!" Franco's slogan proclaims. And its five locations keep Tonawanda, North Tonawanda, Wheatfield, Amherst, Kenmore, and North Buffalo supplied with a rare pizza animal in the Nickel City: the non-sheet tray square Buffalo pie.

Franco's was founded by Franco Kroese in 1979 (he owns it with his brother Mario), who made the leap to owner after working as a manager at one of the cafeterias at the University at Buffalo and being exposed to the pizza business through his then girlfriend who worked at a pizzeria, and a good friend, whose family owned one.

The first Franco's, now closed, was on Delavan Avenue on Buffalo's East Side. It moved north to Tonawanda, which is currently the

The Kroese crew at Franco's Pizza in 1979. From left to right: Mario (brother), Stella (Mom), Franco (owner), and Frans (Dad). CREDIT FRANCO KROESE

oldest location, but its locations are fairly central to the city. Like lots of places around town, Franco's used to use deck ovens and do circular pies, but they moved to conveyor ovens in 1984 when they started seeing national chains switching to achieve consistency. That's when they switched to square pies too. Pizzas come personal (8″×8″, four slices), medium (12″×12″, 12 slices), large (16″×21″, 18 slices), and party-pie sized (18″×26″, 32 slices).

COURTESY WALT SMIETANA/FRANCO KROESE, FRANCO'S PIZZA

"My original thought came from just giving the customer more, the idea being that we don't cut the corners," Kroese said, explaining that their round pizza was three-quarters the size of their rectangular large pie. "We give you the corners basically for free."

They also used to be much more careful about cheese and sauce application. "Years ago, we'd tell the kids not to sauce beyond the width of your thumb around the edge," Franco explained.

"We wanted to have that clean crust line. Things change. I would go out and try different pizzas and I really discovered that when you let the sauce fall off the edge of the pie, or you get a little sloppy with the cheese, it creates flavor. So we eliminated that whole thing. Now, we sauce and cheese right to the edge. If it goes over, God bless."

Buffalo pizza sometimes gets tossed into a category in between Chicago and New York City. That's really not a good fit, because Buffalo's crust is nothing like the buttery one so signature to deep-dish. You're better off filing it between Detroit-style and New York City. And there may be no standard large pie in Buffalo that leans more closely towards Michigan. While there

may not be the crusty, cheesy side of the crust signature to Detroit pies, there *is* a slight crispness along the finish that cantilevers out.

Still, this is very much a Buffalo pizza. "We're basically a General Motors pizzeria," Franco likes to say. "We're selling to the middle of the crowd." Their pizza has one of the softest undercarriages in the entire city, bordering on too soft, like eating an oil-brushed pizza pillow. Slices get six to eight slices of pepperoni. There's a slight cupping with edges that have just begun to char. The sauce, which Franco says isn't purée-based, is one of the least sweet and well-seasoned in town, and runs in thick rivulets underneath a thick blanket of 100 percent whole milk mozzarella that's thoroughly freckled and extends out to the edge.

Beyond cup-and-char, there are 21 specialty pies and three breakfast pizzas. They've only been making breakfast pizza since 2017, but already offer more variety than most places. They each come standard with egg, American cheese, mozzarella, and hash browns. The Italiano takes pepperoni; the traditional ham, bacon, or sausage; and the Western gets sausage, grilled onions, and peppers. There's no sauce to speak of,

but the scattered shreds of potato are both soft and crispy with a big peppery presence.

The only pizza you won't find is beef on weck. Besides that, Franco's makes a few tweaks to the classics. Their taco pie is topped with roasted sweet peppers and black olives. Fontinella makes appearances. Their stinger gets American cheese. And both their chicken barbecue and Hawaiian pies get bacon. There are also chicken bacon ranch and cacciatore pies you won't find much elsewhere.

#14 La Pizza Club

1511 Hertel Avenue, Buffalo, 14216 | 716-837-3838
lapizzaclub.com | Sun 12 pm–9 pm, Mon–Thu
10 am–10 pm, Fri 10 am–11 pm, Sat 12 pm–11 pm

With lloyd Taco Factory next door, and both Bob & John's La Hacienda (one of Buffalo's more well-known pizza spots) and Craving (one of its more well-regarded restaurants) a block away, this stretch of Hertel is ripe for a food crawl.

This family-owned and operated wood-paneled pizza hut has been going since the bicentennial. Its goofy logo, a curly-haired pizza chef in full stride, pie held above his head, looks more like a gymnast in mid-split. A blank pie dots the "i" on the Pepsi-branded sign announcing the Club as dine-in, but in warmer weather you'll be more comfortable at one of the red umbrella-shaded tables on the curb out front than in the tiny booths inside.

La Pizza Club has all the classic sides, salads, and apps (they've even snuck in a chimichanga), and makes 13 specialty pies and serves by the slice, 7-inch minis, small, large, and by the sheet. They do the standards: Mexican, white,

chicken bacon ranch, Hawaiian, and stuffed hot pepper pies ("This can be a hot one!!"). Noteworthy tweaks include the Club's chicken finger pie, which gets a blue cheese base, mozzarella, and both Monterey Jack and cheddar; a barbecue pie that gets mozz, cheddar, and bacon (and onions on request); and the "bruschetta pizza," which has an Italian dressing base, chopped bacon, diced tomatoes, spinach, mozzarella, and Asiago. There are two crust upgrades (sesame and garlic Parmesan) and they're one of the few places to offer eggplant. Besides that, the only extraordinary topping? Cold cuts.

La Pizza Club's cup-and-char slice gets about eight roni slices, each with a classic black rim and a third filled with spicy pepperoni oil—you're almost tempted to grab one, lift a pinky, and sip. It's a thinner than average Buffalo slice with a visible sauceline at the cornicione, lots of brown cheese freckles, and a sauce more acidic than most. La Pizza may be overshadowed by Bocce as the most famous pie club in town, but as at Buffalo's preeminent pizzeria, an open membership means everyone gets treated to one of the most satisfying slices around.

#13 Gino's Pizza Place

351 Fries Road, Tonawanda, 14150 | 716-836-8020
ginospizzaplace.com | Sun–Tue 10 am–9 pm,
Wed–Sat 10 am–10 pm

If University at Buffalo students can pride themselves on having Elmo's, one of the city's best wing joints, as their go-to just off campus to the east, they can thank their good fortune for Gino's Pizza Place a stone's throw to the west.

Gino's Pizza Place (not to be confused with Gino's & Joe's, Gino's NY Pizza, or Gino's Italian Bakery) sits on the corner of Fries Road and Brighton Road in a little pale yellow brick building with red trim across the street from Kenmore East Senior High School. It was founded in 1983 by Gino Pinzone. A simple red and white sign announces its name and phone number with a guy wearing glasses looking at a steaming pizza in wide-eyed excitement. With its barred window and screen door, it looks more like a cross between an old West prison cell and the backyard entrance to grandma's kitchen than pizzeria. Inside, there are three tables and a décor dominated by civic awards. It's just Gino at work when I visit and he has a soccer match on the TV in the kitchen. "Send Gino to Italy for vacation not forever," the note on a collection jar says on the counter.

This is one of the city's simplest pizza menus: cheese, cheese and pepperoni, Gino's "Famous White Pizza" (sliced tomatoes, fresh onions, garlic, Romano, breadcrumbs, and spices), rib-eye steak pizza, chicken finger pizza, "Sicilian thick pizza" (extra thick dough), and an "Old World pizza," which features "lots of sauce," olive oil, Romano, and spices. Standard pizza toppings are rounded out by capicola, bacon, and ham.

Gino's cuts wide slices, almost like their slice pie is a small, but it's big on flavor. One triangle features nine well-charred pepperoni slices. Sauce is a major player, thinner than others but still pretty thick, its presence made visible by cheese distribution that's draped over the top and over the sides. It almost looks like the tentacles of some cheese octopus reaching up and over the high, puffy crust out from under its gently golden-fried undercarriage. The inch-thick cornicione is just as notable for being covered with cheese, a third of it with bubbles that look like American cheese in the toaster under the broiler, as for being one of the crunchiest in town.

#12 Lovejoy Pizza

1244 E. Lovejoy Street, Buffalo, 14206
716-891-9233 | lovejoypizza.com
Mon - Thu 11 AM–10 PM, Fri–Sat 11 AM–10:30 PM,
Sun 3 PM–9:30 PM (open at noon during Bills' season)

900 Main Street, Buffalo, 14202 | 716-883-2323
Mon–Thu 11 AM–9:30 PM,
Fri–Sat 11 AM–10 PM, Sun 12 PM–9 PM

Walk into co-owner Anthony Kulik's downtown location, and if he's behind the counter (he likely will be), even if it's your first time, you'll be greeted with a "Good to see you, bro" and be offered a few free wings from the display carousel while you wait for your order. It's a nice touch, and maybe just a little déjà vu because after you taste the pizza, there's little doubt but that you'll return. In fact, in recent years, there's been a call out by the *Buffalo News* that it should be named

to the city's list of pizza icons. The downtown spot is Lovejoy's second location, opened in 2012. It's as equally tiny as the original, which Kulik opened with John Skotarczak in 1998 in the east Buffalo neighborhood for which it was named.

Lovejoy does a day-and-a-half dough ferment. For the sauce, they add basic seasonings (salt and pepper, garlic, oregano, onion powder) to a sugar-sweetened tomato purée, and they top their pies with Margherita pepperoni. Kulik prefers a dark finish, which he achieves in Blodgett and Baker's Pride ovens. There's actually a little restraint when it comes to cheese and pep, about nine rounds of cup-and-char with a black, pronounced rim and more cheese than a New York slice, but not so much more that it doesn't leave bare the puffy under-crust and complete saucing when a slice is pulled away from the pie. There's a bit of a gumline and not tons of color on the undercarriage, but unlike many Buffalo-style pies, there's a little crunch to it.

Lovejoy's free crust upgrades—garlic, sesame, onion, poppy, hot pepper, Cajun seasoning, and deluxe (everything)—put it in a tier of places that go that extra step. They do a great chicken finger pizza with blue cheese and mozzarella, and some of the best stuffed hot peppers you'll ever have (a blend of six cheeses, herbs, and spices sautéed with olive oil and fresh garlic and served with a sliced, oil-gridded Constanzo's roll that you wish could just replace nearly every bread basket you've ever had), which they slice and put on Big John's "World Famous" Stuffed Hot Pepper Pizza. Those hot peppers get tucked with chicken fingers under a heavy blanket of baked mozzarella on their Lovejoy St. sub, which

has been singled out as one Buffalo's star sandwiches, and is just one of several menu winners.

Funnily enough, Kulik was most proud of the work that goes into their Ultimate Veggie Pizza, topped with spinach, broccoli, tomatoes, and mushrooms he said they buy from the market daily and simmer for four hours in butter, garlic, salt, pepper, and olive oil.

"Be careful, bro," Kulik says as you walk away from the counter with a slice fresh from the display, because what you're holding may be the hottest slice of pie you've ever seen. "I'd wait a few minutes for that to cool off, bro. Give him a knife and fork. That's how they eat it in Italy, bro, with a fork and knife."

#11 Ricota's Pizza & Subs

2405 William Street, Cheektowaga, 14206
716-893-0408 | ricotaspizza.com | Mon–Thu 3 pm–10 pm,
Fri–Sat 3 pm–11 pm, Sun 3 pm–9 pm

206 Elk Street, South Buffalo, 14210 | 716-823-7636
Mon–Sat 9 am–11 pm, Sun 9 am–10 pm

"Have you had this pizza before?" the gentleman behind the counter asks. "Nope."

He nods and smiles proudly. And you're not sure *what* to expect. Outside, near the well-lit, but somewhat sketchy corner, the only place that has much light on this quiet, otherwise deserted stretch of William Street in South Buffalo lined with vacant lots, bikers rev engines as they peel away from the curb and a bunch of kids with freestyle bikes ask customers for money. Inside, if you've arrived looking for a pizzeria, the bare deli shelves make it feel like an understocked gro-

cery. Are you in the right place? If you're looking for great Buffalo-style pizza, then yes.

The Ricota's I visited is one of two locations, purchased in 1988, by Simon Khoury and his brothers from the original owner, who Simon said opened it in 1932. "In the beginning, it was just a store and a butcher shop," Simon said. "It's an old neighborhood and Mr. Ricota catered to it. He had a butcher shop, he had frozen foods, he had a supermarket in there. Later on they started a pizzeria inside the supermarket."

Simon owns the Cheektowaga location outright and co-owns the Elk Street location with his brother Samir. Ricota's may not look like much, but it's one of Buffalo's most underrated pizzerias. It's known as a favorite of former Sabres players who've since left Buffalo, and has become a go-to pizzeria for visiting NHL teams for postgame feasts delivered to the KeyBank Center—fitting given that the Khoury brothers, who moved to Cheektowaga from Lebanon in 1974 as kids, grew up playing hockey in the neighborhood streets.

The menu's more extensive than the sparse shelves would lead you to believe. There are cold subs and hot hoagies, wings, sides, salads, tacos, and fish fry. The pizza menu includes the classics: taco pizza, chicken finger pizza, and pies with steak and Buffalo chicken.

Ricota's standard cup-and-char is one of the less pepperonied pizzas you'll find, just six little concaves, but each one glistening and upturned with that perfectly executed fraction of an inch of crispy black rim. The sauce is salty-tangy and there's a thinner than normal but super-pillowy undercarriage. A poofy cornicione billows up, having thrown off its cheese and all but a trace of light sauce like a spent lover on a Sunday morning.

Yeah, Khoury's got a reason to smile. *This* is a pie to be proud of.

#10 Artone's Pizza & Subs

1882 Seneca Street, Buffalo, 14210 | 716-822-2311
artonesbuffalo.com | Sun–Wed 11 AM–9 PM,
Thu–Sat 11 AM–10 PM

Artone's is just a sliver of a place on Seneca Street in South Buffalo with a yellow sign out front, but the inside bleeds red, white, and blue with a series of patriotic signs that say things like, THIS IS AMERICA. WE PLAY IN THE SNOW . . . WE EAT CHICKEN WINGS AND PIZZA. WE LOVE FOOTBALL. It's enough to

make you want to order both and start a pickup game, but you'll settle for a slice.

There's not much to it besides the black-curtained windows, the spic-and-span counter surrounding the register, and the Frank's Red-Hot sauce by every napkin dispenser. And don't expect to see any of the spatula-scratching flat-top action you can hear going on behind it. Hey, a little mystery always makes things a little more interesting, right?

All the Buffalo classics make the rotation: white, Greek, steak, chicken finger, and taco pizzas along with the more elusive stuffed hot pepper pie. They're joined by the Dargavel (pepperoni, bacon, meatballs, and sausage, named for the owner), and pies named for Congressman Brian Higgins (cheese, onions, and hot cherry peppers suggested as best on a thin crust pie), controversial real estate developer Carl Paladino (Italian sausage and hot cherry peppers—unshockingly enough), and his wife Mary Catherine Hannon's family name (their white pie with sautéed spinach and grilled chicken).

The sauce has a sweet bent. Pepperoni is perfect cup-and-char. You can see the tomato seeds in the sauce. The cornicione has a ¼-inch brown lip that is crispy, thin. There's a lighter brown strip about the same size, a bit thicker, that joins the edge to the rest of the crust. And the sauce coastline starts before the cheese. Whatever your politics, it's one of the best Buffalo slices you'll have.

#9 Imperial Pizza

1035 Abbott Road, Buffalo, 14220 | 716-825-3636
imperialpizzabuffalo.com | Mon–Sun 11 AM–11:30 PM

Which pizzeria do you take Lord Stanley's cup to when you win the Stanley Cup Finals? If you're a good South Buffalo kid like Patrick Kane? Imperial Pizza. The Imperial visit was in 2013, a few months after Kane led the Chicago Blackhawks to a second Cup and won the Conn Smythe trophy as playoff MVP. Of course, he went on to win a third, and obviously, pictures of his cup visit are on the walls inside this pizzeria on the far edge of South Buffalo that feels like it's barely bigger than a hockey crease.

Imperial may be small, but it's mighty, powering the surrounding neighborhoods of Hamburg, West Seneca, Orchard Park, Blasdell, Lackawanna, and Downtown Buffalo with delivery. It's a white, squat red-roofed building on the corner of Eden Street and Abbott Road with a year-round message to tailgate-inclined Bills fans: "Open 9 AM all home games."

Pizza Success, Pizza Perfect, Skyway Pizza, Southtown Pizza, Paradise Pizza—these are all the names David Powers wrote on a scrap of

paper his wife Janice framed for him that Imperial Pizza could have gone by. Dave, who Janice said had always wanted to own a pizzeria, picked Imperial at random and, of course, now it seems it could never have been otherwise.

Powers and his partner Jim Bouris opened Imperial in 1992. And if you see a similarity to Bocce, like the fact that they serve portions of a full 18-inch pizza as their "sizes" (a quarter pie, a half pie, or a full 18-inch pie), there's a reason. Janice said they both worked at Bocce and that the building once used to *be* a Bocce as well.

They turn all the Buffalo pizzeria tricks: wings, fingers, subs, burgers, tacos, loaded fries, salads, and dinners (fish fry is Friday only, a promising sign), and do just 10 specialty pies—nine after 11 AM when they stop making their breakfast pizza (eggs with your choice of sausage, bacon, ham, or Canadian bacon). Toppings are city standard, so too the classic Buffalo combinations— steak, white, stinger, taco, chicken finger, and Hawaiian pies get full marks for attendance.

As for the baseline cup-and-char, it's on the cheesier end of the spectrum with slice pies (and ones to-go from the look of photos online) that can go light on the char. That slightly burnt crunchy

'roni edge really adds nuance to a slice and on top of that, haphazard distribution doesn't guarantee spicy meatiness in every bite, but somehow, the sheer number of Margherita slices (a dozen) carrying several pepp' leaflets still comes together. Lifting up the cheese blanket reveals a thick layer of sauce. There's a poofy, inch-deep incline to the crusty-edged cornicione with a deep-red dried-out sauce on the crust that leaves behind a concentrated sweetness like the memory of a crest of a summer wave.

Imperial may only have one location, but with a pie like this, its empire of South Buffalo and the surrounding area is safe from all comers.

#8 Mister Pizza

1065 Elmwood Avenue, Buffalo, 14222
716-882-6500 | misterpizzaelmwood.com
Sun–Thu 10 AM–12 AM, Fri–Sat 10 AM–1 AM

I'd been warned about Mister Pizza being inconsistent. But in a town where Bocce, the most iconic pizzeria, is known for a biblical topping tsunami that crashes over its crust, what should "sloppy" lead you to expect?

Certainly not Mister Pizza's fastidious logo:

a very fancy "Mister" with a well-kept mustache holding a pizza with one hand while wearing a tux with a white dinner jacket and a top hat. But besides its logo being silhouetted and backlit to a dramatic nighttime effect, that's pretty much where the fanciness ends. Founded by Anthony Colicchia in 1996, Mister Pizza is a well-lit takeout spot on the corner of Elmwood and Bird around the corner from the city's iconic Frank Lloyd Wright building, the William Heath House. During warmer months, there are tables and chairs outside. There are a few chairs inside, but you'll be lucky if they're not covered with takeout cases.

There are nearly 60 subs, almost 20 wing sauces (it's one of a handful of places that does wings with Chiavetta's), tacos, wraps, garlic bread (one with anchovies), poppers, calzones,

salads, and dinners. And this is Buffalo's Rosetta stone of pizza menus. When it comes to pie variety, if you're looking for it, they have it. There are some 40 pizzas (double La Nova) on a menu dominated by pies with a white base. Pulled pork, shrimp scampi, and potatoes stand out as ingredients you won't find at most other area joints. About 30 feature Mister Pizza's blend of olive oil, garlic, black pepper, and Romano as a base instead of traditional sauce. In addition to standard toppings, Mister Pizza offers Greek olives, zucchini, and eggplant (infrequent in Buffalo) and it's one of the rare pizzerias to feature dandelions as an a la carte ingredient. You can order cup-and-char by the slice and pies come medium (15 inches), large (17 inches), or by the sheet. You can even have any of their pies "New York-style" (Buffalo's take on thin crust, which is still typically thicker than New York City pies).

The first difference you notice about the slice at Mister Pizza is the cheese. There's just more of it, and in a cheese-loving town, *that* says something. Cheese seeps over the side and will quickly spread a quarter-inch away from the slice if you wait a few seconds. The siren call of the glisten-

ing 17 pepperoni slices should prevent that from happening though. That generous cheese coverage hides the fact that this isn't a very thick pie, one with a secret: an undercarriage with all kinds of flat and crunchy browned spots of various geometric shapes that provide a nice textural contrast to the otherwise pliant crust. There's a thin layer of a well-spiced, deep-red acidic sauce that's not as thick as most places. This pizza is a chewy, cheese indulgent slice, and if that's your jam, Mister Pizza's an all-star.

#7 Macy's Place Pizzeria

3348 Genesee Street, Cheektowaga, 14225

716-565-6229 | macysplacepizzeria.com

Mon–Thu 11 AM–10 PM, Fri–Sat 11 AM–10:30 PM,
Sun 12 PM–9 PM

Macy's Place Pizzeria is a tiny spot with a good deal of personality on a quiet stretch of Genesee Street next to a sign for a 24-hour snowplowing service. The squat little building's white-brick facade and baby-blue trim would be easy to drive right by if it weren't for the statue, perched on the edge of the roof of a pizza chef with a bright white toque leaning back over his head, sipping a spoonful of sauce.

Inside, there's a Captain Buffalo comic on the wall, a snow shovel-wielding, sunglasses-wearing superhero races toward you in a yellow leotard and orange boots, a bison on his chest (Green Lightning, The Polish Falcon, the Maid of the Mist, and The Griffin on the left). "Meet the crime-fighting king of the Queen City!" it proclaims.

Father-and-son team John and Nick Argy took over Macy's in 2009. The original owner,

Chuck Maciejewski, opened it in 2002. "He just turned that into Macy's," Nick explained. "And we kept the name. We liked the name, we didn't really want to change it."

Macy's is one of the few spots that offers seating. There are two small tables and a blue counter with three stools where you can eat a slice and

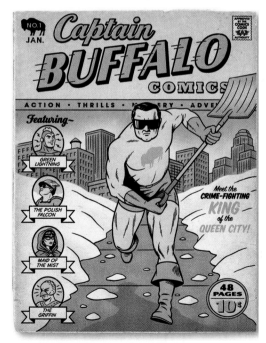

CREDIT: MICHAEL GELEN, INKWELLSTUDIOS.COM

look out on Genesee Street. Pizza fries or an order loaded with bacon and cheddar round out standard apps that also include Buffalo shrimp, fried pickle chips, and cinnamon churros. There's also a tidy number of calzones, subs, and salads. You can order by the slice or go with personal (four slices), small (six slices, 12-inches wide), large (eight slices, 17-inches wide), half-sheet (12 slices, 17-inches wide), and sheet (24 slices) pies. Their 16 specialty pies include stinger, chicken finger, taco, and classic white pies, two steak pies (one "Philly-style" with a garlic base, mozz, mushrooms, onions, and hot or sweet peppers, and a three-cheese steak with garlic, mozzarella, provolone, and cheddar), and a rare spinach and feta pie. Macy's "Sicilian white" gets pepperoni and sausage and their white supreme gets green peppers, grilled chicken, and, also (a rare move in Buffalo) ricotta.

The classic features a modest 9 to 10 cup-and-char Margherita pepperoni rounds per slice, a third of them with browned edges, but all fully cupped. There's a light film of zesty orange grease across the top of the cheese, which seeps over both edges of the slice a good quarter-inch. Cheese is the prevailing focus—Macy's goes light

on the salt and on the sauce (what there is of it there's more the farther from the tip you get). The one-day fermented dough is a little sweeter, with visible docking pockmarking the undercarriage more than the two dimples found on the typical Buffalo slice. Nick says they don't use shortening in the dough but they do use it to grease their pans.

"Most pizzerias large pies have an 18-inch pizza," Nick says. "We actually keep it at 16 inches to make sure the pizza you get still is going to be a thicker crust. Not thick to the point where it's deep-dish. But we definitely keep it as a smaller large pizza where it's going to be a very chewy, thicker crust so you can really taste the dough when you're getting into it."

That's a nice touch. There's a pleasing crunch-crack to the cornicione. The tidy triangle looks like a little magic pizza carpet, a concentrated version of Buffalo-style pie worth a ride to Cheektowaga, where they even make sure to poke a hole in the top of the Styrofoam to-go container so it doesn't steam away the crunch.

#6 Leonardi's Pizzeria

614 Grover Cleveland Highway, Amherst Street, 14226
716-835-8700 | leonardispizzeriainc.biz
Mon–Thu 3 pm–10 pm, Fri–Sat 3 pm–11 pm,
Sun 3 pm–9 pm

Leonardi's has crept northward over the years since it was founded by Ettore Leonardi with his brother Luigi, sister Anne, and wife Argia in 1972, starting on the corner of Bailey Avenue and Manhart Street on Buffalo's East Side before moving a few blocks north in 1975, and to its cur-

rent location in Amherst in 1992. But there's been a constant: its tradition of family. "Myself, my dad, my aunt, my aunt's husband, Julian, my mother, Claudia, as well as my brothers, Tony and Nick continue to run the business after 45 years," owner Silvio Leonardi explained. "We operate only one location as it allows our family to oversee operations. At least one family member, if not all of us are at our store seven days a week."

Leonardi's has a fairly restrained menu. There are just three hot subs and six straightforward cold ones, fries, wings, and fingers. That focus may have something to do with the high quality of their pies. There are just five specialty pizzas—the deluxe, chicken finger, Hawaiian,

"Quattro Stagioni" (a Venn diagram of pepperoni, sausage, mushrooms, and peppers)—but they're probably best known for their *white* pie. The *Buffalo News*'s food editor Andrew Galarneau named it to a list of his favorite pizzas in 2015, noting a quilt of thin-sliced onion and tomato over a creamy sauce that exudes garlic and Romano (anchovies by request).

This small brick pizzeria shares billing with Bob White Insurance, About Hair Salon, and Coke logos. It sits in a dark asphalt parking lot behind a huge grass apron at a six-way intersection just a stone's throw from Bocce Club Pizza and, like Bocce, Leonardi's sauce creeps over the crust to near the edge, but uncheesed. A scattering of herbs tops the cheese, the cornicione is slightly puffy and in some places narrower with a crisp edge, and there are oily patches of gold and brown on the undercarriage, which darken along ridges. Someone at Leonardi's definitely got the memo about cup-and-char. There's more pepperoni—15 rounds on each trapezoid, some overturned and with blackened edges making it look like you're about to play pizza Connect 4—than some people will have ever seen on a slice. All that crisp-edged meat must have overturned some spicy oil because the thick, sweet sauce has a definite, and welcome, bite.

Leonardi's has gotten some love here and there, but not as much as it should. It wasn't considered in *Buffalo Spree*'s 2010 pizza showdown. If Bocce and La Nova are two of the city's best pizzerias, Leonardi's cup-and-char baseline isn't far behind. Amherst natives have to know that they're damn lucky to be sitting on one of the city's longstanding, underrated takeout spots.

#5 Santora's

3440 Transit Road, Depew, 14043 | 716-668-3355
santoraspizza.com | Sun–Thu 11 AM–10 PM,
Fri 11 AM–11:30 PM

"WOW." That's what I wrote after taking *one* bite of Santora's pizza. "Top three, I think." And that was after already being 10 pies into my quest. A few subsequent pizzas leapfrogged that pie pole position, but it was still one of the top five I tasted.

I can't speak to the quality at all locations—even Larry Santora admitted the various locations go their own way with recipes. But given the skepticism I experienced from locals when I mentioned it, all I can say is you need to go to the old, squat, brick-and-red paneled barn-looking Santora's with its name in yellow lettering on the side in the huge lot on Transit Road in West Seneca. Look for the big pizza pie sign and the double-sided marquee featuring pizza-related dad jokes, which change depending on the time of year ("This is no sham. Our pizza rocks," and "Our pizza will shamrock your sox off," each side said in February, followed by "Get it").

The walkway outside is lined with flower pots

and kitschy statues, the tall windows are tinted, and the outside feels Pizza Hut–esque circa the '80s. Inside across from the register and the kitchen behind it, there's a leather couch where you can sit and look at framed pictures of servicemen in the Air Force and the Navy or the spotlit paintings of family members while waiting for takeout. Santora's has a cozy dining room—Muzak, hanging lamps lighting tidy booths made for people who have bellies that don't get filled with lots of pizza. There are worn Formica faux wood tables, red Coke glasses, and a Buffalo statue up on the wall with pies painted on it that, if not life-size, at least makes a run at it.

Santora's has one of those we-do-everything menus too long to go into, but a few things deserve mention. Their stuffed hot peppers are like three docked canoes split open and so overflowing that they look like they've been submerged in a Lake Erie of cheese.

Their freshly baked rolls come with famous homemade garlic butter and mozzarella. Santora's "Famous Mozzarella Garlic Bread" comes three ways (standard, topped with spinach and sausage, or everything they can find in the kitchen).

And their loaded fries come four ways besides plain, each with blue cheese. Loaded steak fries come with mozzarella, bacon, and jalapeños and are served with barbecue sauce and ranch dressing (?!). Barbecue fries are topped with sweet and tangy sauce. Italian garlic steak fries get a sprinkling of Romano and pizza fries feature mozzarella and pepperoni and get served with blue cheese and ranch.

You can order pizza by the slice in sizes medium (six slices), large (12 slices), and party (32 slices). Overall, there's slightly more structural integrity at Santora's than you'll find with the average Buffalo-style slice, due to the undercarriage being more uniformly browned and less docked. The pizzerias on this list are ranked on their execution of classic cup-and-char pies, but we've expounded on its merits so it bears noting that they carry 14 specialty pies, including barbecue chicken ranch, steak in the grass, chicken finger, Hawaiian, chicken wing, stuffed hot pepper, and their classic white pizza, which sandwiches a layer of tomatoes and diced onions between layers of mozzarella.

I generally prefer a saucier pie, but the stinger pizza is almost too good for words. The edge is a uniformly just-blackened frico cheese cracker that creates a crispy-crackly crust and undercarriage. There's a blue cheese and wing sauce base covered with magma-hot and mottled brown provolone and mozzarella that still pulls three bites in. There are fried onions, huge chunks of juicy steak and craggy, breaded fried chicken boulders that rise up nearly an inch above the crust covered with melty cheese slopes that are tan, deep-brown, and black on peaks and in crevices. Spicy, tangy, slightly sweet and completely over-the-top, this is a pie made for a beer or a Coke if there ever was one.

It's a sign of excess perhaps only overshadowed by another specialty pie, the spaghetti and meatball pizza Parmesan, a garlic butter, Parmesan, and garlic laden crust topped with sauce, cooked spaghetti, chopped meatballs, and mozzarella. Parm pizza? Only in Buffalo.

#4 Lock City Pizza

379 Davison Road, Lockport, 14094 | 716-433-3413
Sun–Thu 4 PM–12 AM, Fri–Sat 4 PM–2 AM

If Mister Pizza is a sloppy cheese pizza lover's all-star, consider Lock City Pizza a Hall-of-Famer. Nothing about this pie should appeal to a pizza purist who holds balance, nuance, and structural integrity dear—there's not even proper cup-and-char pepperoni and it's distributed wildly, inconsistently, and with abandon. And yet... Like the proverbial bad boy or girl, there's something magnetic about a pizza from Lock City that lights the fire of insatiable desire.

Lock City Pizza is about a 45-minute drive

north of downtown Buffalo and sits on the out-skirts of Lockport (so named for its Erie Canal locks) across the street from the Niagara County Golf Course. This is the kind of place where your heart slows and during the summer you smell cut grass and pizza in the parking lot.

"Love it or hate it" is a cliché, but the messy swirl of a cheesy soup vortex that forms in the pie's center inspires those reactions. And the renowned brusque service is enough to turn some around and back out the door before fin-ishing their order. Lock City is owned by Carol Little, and was supposedly preceded by a pizze-ria that went by the name of Pontillo's. Details are hard to pin down though. "Well, I'll give her the message," says Tom, the friendly enough, if matter-of-fact pizzaiolo on duty when I called, "if she gets back to you, great. If she doesn't . . . well, that's just the way the world works."

True, Tom. So true. Lock City's a cash-only joint where pulling out a debit or credit card will garner the same reaction as trying to pay with Bitcoin. Reviews range from bewilderment and hate to nostalgia and near desire for pizza shinjū (Japanese lovers' double-suicide).

Lock City Pizza's menu is on the wall by the

counter—with makeshift amendments and big enough to see from across the room, where it's safe to evaluate without fear of reprisal—and it's one of the simplest around. They do small and large pizzas, with your choice of green or black olives, hot or banana peppers, double cheese, onions, sausage, anchovies, mushrooms, and pepperoni. They have just one specialty, a white pie, and the only other things on the menu are wings, fingers, and about a dozen subs.

Consider this a Buffalo-based amalgam of a few styles. There's some Bocce trim where the cheese, sauce, and pepperoni extends over the crust, there's a coal oven-esque dry crust in spots, and a cornmeal-dusted bottom and a scat-tering on top. There has to be twice, maybe even three times as much cheese as there is under-carriage and as much sauce as dough. Somehow there's still a chew-pull to the undercarriage, which resists every bite with a distinct tug. The sauce is ridiculous (sweet, acidic, spicy) and pepperoni distribution is like the last grasp of matter trying to escape a pizza black hole: one triangle will have four pieces and others will have 12, four of which on closer inspection are pepperoni leaflets, stacks of four, five, or seven

slices (SexySlices calls this a pepperoni lotus). The result is nearly a salt bomb, a pungent pie with lots of chew, but it's really, really good.

Here's the move: order your pie and head over to The DRI (no, not DUI, The Davison Road Inn) at the back of the parking lot for a drink at the bar inside or on the patio out back—there's a whole party going on back there after work that you can't see from outside. You'll have just enough time for a quick one to inure yourself against a curt transaction. Then if it's warm enough (this works even if it's not) put the pie on your hood, flip the lid, and dig in.

Some say pizza's like sex—that even bad pizza is still, well, pizza. "And pizza's never bad," right? Maybe. It makes me suspicious that whoever first said that actually hadn't had very much sex, very good sex, or, for that matter, good pizza. But if we stick to that analogy, let's just say that Lock City Pizza is the illicit tryst you know you should regret, but can't help risking everything for.

#3 Deniro's Pizzeria

2251 George Urban Boulevard, Depew, 14043
716-681-5555 | denirospizzeria.com
Sun–Thu 11 AM–9 PM, Fri–Sat 11 AM–11 PM

Deniro's was a dark horse rec, word-of-mouth, friend of a friend. I couldn't find anything about it online or in the *Buffalo News*'s archives before visiting except a wedding announcement for one of its drivers. But the recommendation was promising ("Rumor has it this place is legit," I was told) and the source was credible. Legit it was.

Deniro's is a tiny pizzeria with a yellow awning

on the far-right corner of a small strip mall on a quiet stretch of George Urban Boulevard, just around the corner from the Duff's on Dick Road in Depew. It's pure takeout in a part of town where the grass aprons are as wide as a highway lane. Just a 10-minute drive to the airport—Deniro's and the nearby Macy's Place would make terrific last bites of pizza on the way out of town.

"Small place, big menu," the takeout flier proclaims. And while this could be used to describe many a Buffalo pizzeria, it's certainly true at Deniro's. You'll find your Buffalo standard appetizers, salads, burritos, fingers, and wings. Deep-fried stuffed peppers are wrapped in dough first and come Buffalo-style with chicken, hot sauce, blue cheese, cheddar, and gorgonzola, or with sausage and cream cheese. There are more than

30 different kinds of subs and you can turn any of their specialty pies into subs.

A la carte toppings are standard for Buffalo and there are 21 specialty pies. They carry no beef on weck or breakfast pizzas but you'll find all the other Nickel City classics. Parm and bacon cheeseburger pizzas both make appearances and there are two pies fairly unique to Deniro's in the city. A Mardi Gras pizza features spicy-Cajun chicken, sausage, cherry peppers, and onions under mozz and cheddar, and a bacon, lettuce, and tomato pie is topped with mayo and lettuce. Pizzas come mini (9 inches, four slices), medium (12 inches, six slices), large (17 inches, eight slices), and by the sheet (17″×25″, 24 slices).

As for the classic cup-and-char, it's a lion of a pie. The first thing you notice is the pepp distribution. Many slices even have cup-and-char perched on the crest of the cornicione. Most slices don't have less than 12 rounds of pepperoni and several have more than 20. You could give a few demerits for that kind of discrepancy if you could stop eating to mark them down; but regardless, you get a burst of spicy pepper flavor and roni edge crackle with almost every bite. Heck, every bite. There's a cheese pull on bites midway through the slice, ample cheese coverage, but also exposed ridges where you can see the sauce is thoroughly, though not swimmingly, applied. Grease drips down underneath over the edge of your bite to the bottom of the crust. It's a very bendy slice with a very soft undercarriage and little crunch or crisp except along the cornicione, which is crisp and dark at the very edge and tastes golden brown and delicious.

Unless you have someone you really, really love that you need to get back to with food, this is quintessential parking lot pizza: place on passenger seat, flip open, eat, repeat.

#2 La Nova

371 West Ferry Street, West Side, 14213
716-881-3303 | lanova-pizza.com
Sun–Thu 10 AM–11 AM, Fri–Sat 10 AM–12 AM

5151 Main Street, Williamsville, 14222
716-634-5151 | Sun–Wed 10 AM–10 PM,
Thu 10 AM–11 PM, Fri–Sat 10 AM–12 AM

The large pie at La Nova is a thinner, crispier pie. Cheese and pepperoni sneak out in places toward the edge like a man hungry for second base who knows the pitcher has a notoriously slow move to first. But there's almost always an actual exposed crust. It's almost like the La Nova pizza is a cousin of Bocce Club's style, but one whose parents were transplanted from New York City.

Craters of sauce peek through the cheese and out from under uneven slices of charred pepperoni, some of which are shallow red life rafts of

grease. The pepperoni is generously, if unevenly scattered. If there wasn't so much of it, the uneven distribution might lead to a fight over the most 'ronied triangles—some slices get seven rounds, others twice that. The sauce is sweet but not *so* sweet; there's a faint shimmer of grease on the crust and an oil-scarred edge to the cornicione. It's significantly cheesier than the average slice in America, but there's not as much cheese as at Bocce. It's a thinner pie and has a thinner, though very flavorful crust. Still, you're pretty full after two slices.

The crusts on a fresh La Nova pie are a revelation, particularly the sesame, which they're not cheap on. There's enough to make it look like you ordered semolina bread pizza! And it's obviously been applied *after* all the other ingredients because it's scattered out nearly an inch-and-a-half from the edge of the crust and over the toppings. The seeds toast in the oils from the cheese and pepperoni in the oven for a wonderfully nutty, slightly crunchy effect.

#1 Bocce Club Pizza

4174 North Bailey Avenue, Amherst Street, 14226

716-833-1344 | bocceclubpizza.com

Sun–Thu 10 AM–11 PM, Fri–Sat 10 AM–12 AM

1614 Hopkins Road, East Amherst Street, 14221

716-689-2345 | Mon–Thu 10 AM–10 PM,

Fri–Sun 10 AM–12 AM

Imagine a New York slice with a softer crust and a sfincione or focaccia undercarriage. There are bites toward the end of the slice where you get a crunch, surprising because of the softness of so much cheese and sauce, but there's absolutely no structural integrity to this pizza. There's double to triple the cheese and twice the sauce of a New York City slice. You need all the fingers of one hand to hold it up or you have to eat it with two hands, or a bite at a time from the edge of a plate you lift to your mouth. Fresh from the oven and sliced on a wood block with a two-handled blade, there are shallow pools of grease and a scattering of herbs on the surface of this 18-inch pie. Thick rounds of pepperoni with pronounced ridges are thoroughly charred and you get a cheese pull with every bite.

But this pizza has little visible cornicione. The cheese, sauce, and even sometimes the pepperoni go out and over the edge of the "crust," where some kind of pizza alchemy happens. The "trim" as Bocce's Mark Daniels calls it, ends up tasting like a burnt sweet cheese. One of the several young pizzaiolos working the pizzeria's many ovens (they can cook 36 pies at a time) chimes in over his shoulder, smiling mischievously, "That's called a 'Bocce cookie.'" I can't tell whether he's messing with me, but Mark deadpans, "Some people ask for that stuff, the trim to be saved and put on top of the pizza or to take with them in an extra box."

RANKING BUFFALO'S BEST PIZZA

1.	Bocce Club Pizza	**6.**	Leonardi's Pizzeria	**11.**	Ricota's Pizza & Subs
2.	La Nova	**7.**	Macy's Place Pizzeria	**12.**	Lovejoy
3.	Deniro's	**8.**	Mister Pizza	**13.**	Gino's Pizza Place
4.	Lock City Pizza	**9.**	Imperial Pizza	**14.**	La Pizza Club
5.	Santora's	**10.**	Artone's	**15.**	Franco's Pizza

Beyond Buffalo-Style Pizza

Just because Buffalo loves cup-and-char doesn't mean other styles aren't available. There are bar pizzas, bakery pizzas made by places that specialize in cookies and desserts, artisanal pizzas, New York City-style pizzas, and Neapolitan pies too. And while they don't belong on a ranked list of Buffalo-style pizza, it'd be remiss to overlook them.

Elm Street Bakery

72 Elm Street, East Aurora, 14052 | 716-652-4720

Tue–Fri 7 AM–9 PM, Sat 8 AM–9 PM, Sun 9 AM–2 PM, Closed Mon

These are thin-crust pizzas with charred, poofy-crunchy corniciones. Elm Street serves a handful of 6-inch and 12-inch sized pizzas from 11 AM to 9 PM, with a lunch menu limited to the classic, a nod to local taste (Parmesan and pepperoni), and the Margherita. Dinner and special pies have a seasonal, farm-to-table bent. For example, the white pie takes sausage, radicchio, and pepperoncini, a scape pie gets bacon, goat cheese, and confit tomatoes, and a corn pizza features nduja, cherry tomato, pesto. Extra toppings include Calabrian chili honey, farm egg, ricotta, and arugula. Unlike many places that serve pizza in Buffalo, this is a full sit-down, dinner situation. Just be aware that they occasionally suspend take-out to maintain quality control.

Gino's Italian Bakery

1104 Kenmore Avenue, North Buffalo, 14216

716-874-2315 | ginositalianbakery.com

Tue–Fri 8 am–5 am, Sat 8 am–3 pm, Sun 9 am–1 pm

Gino's Italian Bakery has been a Kenmore Avenue staple for more than 30 years, but it's been under the care of Pamela DiPalma since she took it over in 2010. Ms. DiPalma may have blood boosted by a bread starter and sweetened with confectioner's sugar running through her veins—both of her paternal grandparents worked in panetterias in Naples, Italy before coming to America. And she's probably more well-known for her Italian cookies especially the cuccidati (a Sicilian fig-stuffed Christmas cookie) and giugiulena (sesame seed cookies), but they do bake an old-school, Italian tomato pie baked in a rectangular sheet tray every morning. You have to enter through the door in the parking lot in back—the front door is locked and barred by a baking rack. It's a soft, rectangular sheet pizza that's heavy on a sauce that tastes like tomato paste ($2 per slice, $20 per sheet). There's a healthy scattering of grated Parmesan and a drizzle of olive oil. Pillowy and thick with

not even a little crisp at the edge. It folds and sags, it's soft and sweet, with little rivulets that form in the paste when you pick it up. The soft undercarriage is uniformly blond, olive oil-blond. This is a slice almost totally without *any* crispiness, like a Buffaloized focaccia.

Jay's Artisan Pizzeria

2872 Delaware Avenue, Kenmore, 14217

716-322-1704 | jaysartisan.com

Wed–Sat 4 pm–9 pm or out of dough

Jay Langfelder made his name in the Queen City with his food truck O.G. Wood Fire, which he drove around with a 2,000-pound oven in it, attracting lines like the pied piper of pizza. Langfelder may be the original gangster of Neapolitan pizza in Buffalo, but he always said that the "O.G." stood for "one goal," making the *best* modern American Neapolitan pizza. That goal used to be something he was trying to do on the run, and while he garnered acclaim, Langenfelder never seemed satisfied—the truck meant limitations on consistency. With his Kenmore brick-and-mortar opened in late 2017, in a former Chrusciki Bakery, he may finally have the setup he needs to meet his own expectations (it's allowed him, at least, to leave behind the O.G. in favor of a new name). At the time of writing, Jay was serving nine 12-inch pies made with imported Italian mozzarella and cooked in a 900-degree wood-fired oven. There's the obligatory marinara and Margherita pies. The quattro formaggio and Amanda (fontal, gorgonzola, chile flakes, and chile honey), named for his girlfriend and assistant pizzaiolo Amanda Jones, are holdover favorites from the truck. Other pies include the diavola, amatriciana, speck, and a ricotta and arugula pizza with citrus preserves. These aren't strict Neapolitan pizzas—Jay uses ingredients like California tomatoes instead of San Marzanos—but if you're looking to trade cup-and-char for leopard-spotting, you won't find anything more legit.

Judi's Lounge

2057 Military Road, Niagara Falls, 14304
716-297-5759 | judisbarandgrill.com
Mon–Sun 11 AM–2 AM

As we've already noted, Judi's wings are top notch. But even its flats-and-bats devotees might not know how good its pizzas are. Don't expect a great representation of Buffalo pizza however. This pizza is its own thing. Bar pies, by definition, are very thin-crusted, crisp, well-done (to near-burned) pies that are large enough to share but small enough for one person to eat. At Judi's, it's almost as if a Buffalo pizza effect—a cheesiness and poofiness—has melded with that style. Let's call it a Buffalo bar pie. Judi's makes a small personal-sized pie (nine inches wide) with a cornicione that's an inch tall, with puff halfway in from an edge that bevels down to the peel it's

served on. They offer three specialty pies—steak and cheese, Greek chicken pizza (with pepperoncini, feta, and Greek dressing), Buffalo chicken finger pizza—all featuring a garlic spread (no pies come standard with marinara, but red sauce can be subbed in). You can choose from 20 toppings and you can make any pizza "sub style," which means adding lettuce, tomato, and onion, for 75¢. The Buffalo chicken finger pie is amazing. There are two to three chunks of chicken that are super crispy and blackened by the bake after already being fried. There's a light scattering of cornmeal and a Buffalo-esque amount of cheese. It's served with blue cheese dressing for dipping and tastes like junk food—fluffy-crust chicken finger pizza junk food—in the best way. You'll be surprised by how much you like it.

Roost

1502 Niagara Street, West Side, 14213
716-259-9306 | roostbuffalo.com
Wed–Sat 11 AM–10 PM,
Sun 11 AM–3 PM, Closed Mon–Tue

If every loft building in New York City had this kind of restaurant, rents would be even worse. Roost is the latest act of chef Martin Danilowicz, who wanted to open a larger restaurant after only being able to cook for 18 people at a time at his previous restaurant, Martin Cooks. Danilowicz opened Roost in late 2016, in The Crescendo building on the Tesla Heritage Corridor. And while that may be going places, it's largely still a stretch of in-between so busy it can be hard to cross. Roost isn't a pizzeria per se, with a menu that includes dishes like strawberry gaz-

cornicione has pockets that shatter and there's a tangy, light, well-seasoned sauce. Roost features about seven pies, and doesn't even bother nodding to cup-and-char—there are plenty of places for that. Instead you'll find pies topped with combinations like eggplant and lentils, roasted mushrooms and smoked blue cheese, bacon and leeks, and fennel sausage with giardiniera. The meatball pie with Hungarian hot pepper ricotta and bell peppers is a masterpiece, light, juicy, and pleasantly spicy meatballs, but all the pies are dramatically plated in one of the most interesting ways you'll ever see pizza presented in America. Eight-inch long slices are served completely detached and balanced on their edges, cornicione-to-cornicione, tips out, four rows deep like a carefully built house of pizza cards. You wonder how the toppings will hold, but they do, and the chefs insist it keeps the crust from steaming. It's hard to argue with an empty plate.

pacho, smoked eel, ramen, sweet bread tacos, and chicken liver pâté, but pies *are* highlighted. And it *is* the kind of place you'll want a reservation for. There's a loud, long open space well-lit by walls of windows on either side and an open kitchen surrounded by a long shiny bar. As the sun sets, the golden light illuminates plants swaying in front of the windows and the beautiful people at the bar. The pizza is really good, lighter than it looks and very thin toward the center and crispy. The

Knead Your Own Little Slice of Heaven?

Don't take my word for it, whether it means trying a place outside your go-to or having your first slice of cup-and-char, venture out. Do your own pizza-spelunking. See if you don't find yourself falling in love with a new joint, or spreading the gospel of Buffalo-style pizza. Here's a list of the city's other most well-regarded spots to start with (not all strictly Buffalo-style). Call it your very own Nickel City Buffalo pizza parade.

A slice at Mister Pizza.

Bella Pizza, Lackawanna, 3330 South Park Avenue, 716-822-6242

Blasdell, Blasdell, 3904 South Park Avenue, 716-822-1138

Bob & John's La Hacienda, Hertel Avenue, 1545 Hertel Avenue, 716-836-5411

Buzzy's, Niagara Falls, 7617 Niagara Falls Boulevard, 716-283-5333

Casa di Pizza, Downtown Buffalo, 11 E. Mohawk Street, 716-883-8200

Carbone's, South Buffalo, South Park Avenue, 716-855-1749

Good Guys, North Tonawanda, 1248 Ruie Road, 716-695-1592

John's Pizza & Subs, Tonawanda, 1436 Niagara Falls Boulevard, 716-832-4343

Just Pizza, Downtown Buffalo, 300 Elmwood Avenue, 716-883-5650

Molinaro's, Lockport, 90 Walnut Street, 716-438-0631

Picasso's, Williamsville, 6812 Transit Road, 716-631-0222

Pizza Oven, Lockport, 54 Vine Street, 716-433-4390

Pizza Plant, Canalside, 125 Main Street #110, 716-626-5566

Romeo and Juliet, Hertel Avenue, 1292 Hertel Avenue, 716-873-5730

Siena Trattoria, Snyder, 4516 Main Street, 716-839-3108

Sugo's, Cheektowaga, 2501 Harlem Road, 716-895-7846

CHAPTER THREE

BEEF ON WECK

New York's (and America's)
Best Unknown Sandwich?

America has some great cities for beef sandwiches. Chicago has Italian beef with spicy giardiniera. Boston's got its roast beef sandwich smothered with mayo, cheese, and barbecue sauce (barbecue sauce? Can you get more Yankee?). Los Angeles is the home of the original french dip (Philippe the Original or Cole's, depending on who you want to believe). Philadelphia has its world-famous cheesesteaks ("whiz wit"). Even New York City has roast beef meccas: Brennan & Carr, Roll-n-Roaster, and Defonte's. But Buffalo's just as, if not more passionate about their rare, thinly sliced, juicy, and deliciously salty beef on weck. Few cities have a signature sandwich this good and fewer still have a food icon that's stayed this local and that flies this under the radar.

"Beef on wha?" Weck. Not "beef on wickie" per John Madden circa 1996, not "a beef on a weck" per fallen-from-grace chef Mario Batali and well-meaning *Tonight Show* host Jimmy Fallon in 2016, but *beef on weck*. Beef on weck is a sandwich that's said to have its origins with German immigrants in the early twentieth century. "Weck" is short for kummelweck with "kümmel" being the German word for caraway and weck meaning "roll." Beef on weck, for the uninitiated is, a slow-roasted beef, served on an old-fashioned caraway- and pretzel salt–studded kummelweck roll, usually served with a kosher dill pickle and fresh horseradish. It's been said that beef on weck is the original chicken wing, a salty Buffalo bar food supposedly invented to inspire patrons to order a few more rounds to quench their thirst.

Recent studies show that eating more salt makes you less thirsty but somehow hungrier, putting the eternal wisdom behind this practice in doubt, but science aside, for all its simplicity, this is a delicious sandwich. You bite into the soft, squishy bun and get hit by fruity caraway and the abrasive sharpness of pretzel salt that seems like it's going to be too much until a fraction of a second later when the thin, still rare layers of beef flood your mouth with bronzed, unsweetened, underseasoned, caramel notes, coming together, the bottom of the bun holding true just long enough for you to get through the sandwich, the sharp bite of horseradish flaring your nostrils and your brain looking for pleasant-unpleasant safe harbor. Think beef on weck as a lesson in sandwich masochism.

This is a two-handed sandwich with its own internal timer. Unlike a great Italian sub, where a little extra time just allows the flavors to meld and the dressing to soften a crusty bread your teeth were going to have to tear at, beef on weck doesn't improve as time goes on. In fact, at least one of the light, squishy halves of kummelweck usually gets an au jus dunk, and it's not bread that can stand up to moisture long. Given how much beef is usually layered on, that means you're racing a little against the clock, or in this case, against picking up pieces of beef that fall onto your plate. But given how delicious it is, you're not likely to want to put it down until you're finished anyway.

Once Upon a Weck ... Joseph Gohn, William Wahr, and the Origins of Beef on Weck

Unsurprisingly, as with wings and Buffalo chicken wing pizza, details surrounding the origin of beef on weck are hazy—and given the mysteries surrounding wings, mercifully so. We don't have to look much further than Steve Cichon's reporting in the *Buffalo News* for the most reliable story. It takes into account origin lore shared in some two dozen articles written between 1943 and 1980.

Enter Joseph M. Gohn. Gohn owned three taverns on Delaware Avenue, his first called Delaware House at 2070 Delaware Ave. (at Amherst Street, just north of Delaware Park). As the *Buffalo News* explains, Gohn's customers were mostly folks traveling between Buffalo and Tonawanda until a few years before the Pan-American Exposition of 1901. In 1898, a *Buffalo News* article credits him with netting a tidy sum for selling his property to make way for the exposition, or more specifically, for one of its entrances. Gohn opened a new tavern-hotel at 1401 Delaware Ave., at West Delavan Street (near the park's southwestern edge).

"It would have been from this location just a few streetcar stops south of the Pan-Am that Gohn would have plied hungry tourists with roasted beef on kimmelweck rolls—mostly in an effort to make them thirst for more of the Phoenix Beer his tavern served," the *Buffalo News* notes.

Gohn and his family operated their business through Prohibition (getting busted a few times as a speakeasy), and he and his son Charles eventually moved their business again, this time next door to 1389 Delaware Ave. When they finally sold in 1943, it was Buffalo lore that "Gohn's Place" was where beef on weck was made famous. It's unclear whether Gohn's first beef on weck was served at the Delaware House before 1901 or at the corner of Delaware and Delavan avenues as the Pan-American Exposition started, so take your pick as to which of these intersections being the one where it was *actually* born.

According to the *News*, Joe Gohn's obituary doesn't mention the sandwich, but his son Charles' in 1943, states that *he* "continued the glorification of the roast beef sandwich begun by his father in Pan-American year." And apparently, inventing the sandwich that proliferated throughout the city's taverns was a distinction the senior Gohn *did* embrace. Around the 1943 sale, Joe Gohn explained to the *Buffalo Courier-Express* that there wasn't much of a secret to his beef on weck: "I never had any particular recipe, but always made certain it was good, lean beef."

The origins of kummelweck are generally attributed to William Wahr, a German immigrant said to be from somewhere near the Schwarzwald (the Black Forest) a forested mountain range in the state of Baden-Württemberg in southwest Germany. Wahr, a baker, who supposedly worked in the tavern, though it's unclear when, is said to have patterned his pretzel salt and caraway bread after the rolls of his youth. But by all indications, Wahr was successful in his own right, passing away in 1924, having operated a bakery on the East Side of Buffalo on Herman Street near Broadway in 1891.

A Brief History: Schwabl's, Eckl's, and Charlie the Butcher

Joe Gohn and William Wahr may be the two men credited with inventing beef on weck, or at least popularizing it, but unlike the Bellissimos and Anchor Bar, Gohn and Wahr are names largely lost to most Buffalonians, even many of the ones who carry on the city's tradition of beef on weck. But *everyone* knows the names of three of the city's most famous practitioners: Schwabl's, Eckl's, and Charlie the Butcher. All three have histories just as deep and synonymous with beef on weck, and the origins of two of these icons go back to the early nineteenth century.

The building that houses Eckl's is supposedly constructed in 1816! Its first owner was Wilhelm Willink, a wealthy Amsterdam merchant who was one of 13 investors in the Holland Land Co., a company formed with the goal of profiting off of buying large tracts of land in Western New York. The building is said to have been a saloon, feed store, and place of worship. It was bought in 1906, by Luis Schroeder who operated it as a tavern-restaurant then taken over by Emma Schroeder in 1926. The Eckl name entered the picture in 1934, when Emma's daughter Martha

took over with her husband Jack Eckl. Dale and Shirley Eckl moved the restaurant to its current location, reopening and expanding in 1964, after New York State required Eckl's original location to widen South Buffalo Road. After more than 50 years, the Eckls retired, selling the business to its current owners, Ted Smith and Jim Cornell in 2016.

Sebastian Schwabl opened his place on Broadway in 1837, followed by his sons, who opened their own places (there was also said to have been a Schwabl's at the Pan-Am Exposition, the same one Joe Gohn made that profit from). Schwabl's has moved around Buffalo over time, first to Bailey Avenue, then to Humboldt Parkway and East Ferry Street. In 1942, Ray Schwabl Jr. moved it to its current location in West Seneca on Route 15 near Union Road. Current owners Cheryl and Gene Staychock bought Schwabl's in 2004 from Ray Schwabl Jr.'s son—Cheryl started at the restaurant as a waitress in 1989. Carrying on the Schwabl's tradition means dealing with a busy dining room, but it hasn't been without its trials. In 2013, after 176 years of continued service, the restaurant was shaken when an SUV driven by an octogenarian crashed into the west wall near the carving station while trying to avoid hitting another car. The accident closed Schwabl's for nine months and led to $200,000 in damages. But reopen it did in 2014, with its grand register, its old-school "Ladies" and "Gents" lights announcing the bathrooms, white waitress dresses, and the discovery during renovation that wood used to build the original came from old boxcars.

Charlie the Butcher actually started out as a wholesale outdoor meat market in 1914, launched by Charles E. Roesch (rhymes with "fresh"), the grandfather of *today's* well-known Charlie. The facility Charlie has with customers and the press today seems to run in the family—the original Charlie went on to become mayor of Buffalo from 1930 to 1934. He left politics and opened a butcher shop in the Broadway Market in 1936, passing away that same year supposedly due to an infection suffered after banging his leg on a butcher's block. His son Charles J. took over the business through 1987. The Charlie the Butcher personality that's iconic in Buffalo today is a marketing strategy begun by Charles J.'s *son* Charlie W., who opened a restaurant kiosk in 1984, where he started wearing the now

well-known "Charlie the Butcher"-embroidered apron. He and his wife took over in 1987, and can be credited for the Charlie the Butcher packaged roast beef available in grocery stores, and the seven expanded locations, including the one on Wehrle Drive.

All three of these classic weck places are in pretty much a line on a straight shot just off Union Road. You could easily do a beef on weck crawl starting with Charlie the Butcher near the airport—there's just about 45 minutes between them all. You just may want a designated driver. "Cold beer with a beef on weck—you're missing out on the full experience without the beer," Brian Hayden, Visit Buffalo Niagara's communications manager explained to me when I began my research. "The beer complements the caraway and salt."

That may be true, but as easily as the sandwich goes down, the beer (or the second that follows), beware. The combination may anchor you to the seat.

Medium-Rare and Thin on a Fresh Roll with Horseradish

Great beef on weck is something that isn't easy to pull off, which is probably why you haven't seen it take off across America. To do it right, you need to cook a large hunk of beef slowly, cut it extremely thin (tracing paper thin), and you need a fresh, salt-and-caraway studded roll, a roll that defies transportation as a finished product because pre-applied salt is thought to dry out the roll en route. If you don't have a market that's going to demand the core components at peak perfection, and you can't transport them in a lucrative way to create the market, well, you end up with Western New York as the only way to truly appreciate the art form. And it is an art form, but despite these complications, one whose ingredients and variations are mercifully uncomplicated.

Typically, the same cut is used by most restaurants. "We use top round," Charlie the Butcher, perhaps Buffalo's most well-known food personality, locally and nationwide, tells me. "It's the single leanest muscle, but we tenderize and age it overnight. We serve four to five ounces of meat per sandwich."

And it's a beautiful thing to listen to the tap-tap-tap of fork-to-knife as that five ounces of meat is sliced by the dedicated carver behind the counter at Charlie the Butcher as you wait to order. But we're getting ahead of ourselves. That top round gets slow-roasted to medium-rare, then sliced thin and dipped in savory au jus to warm and juice it up before layering a huge pile of it inside the untoasted weck whose top is dipped in au jus before covering the beef.

That's pretty much it. With the rare exception

of places that make their own kummelweck, restaurants in Buffalo tend to use Costanzo's rolls that they then apply salt and caraway seeds to with an egg or cornstarch wash. Variations in the amount of salt and caraway occur between restaurants—some seem like they may be salting in anticipation of Lake Effect snow—but even at some restaurants, salt levels can vary depending on who is on shift doing the salting.

There are places that seem to pride themselves on seeing how thin they can slice their medium-rare beef without turning it into shreds. And some like to see how high they can stack layers. The five ounces of meat at Charlie the Butcher is nearly doubled at Schwabl's, where they serve a half pound of hand-carved beef.

Several places will throw you a pickle, offer a plain kaiser roll (what's wrong with you?), maybe toss in some fries or chips, and name the horseradish that they're serving if it isn't freshly grated by the staff. You can double up on the Buffalo icons and get a deal on a small order of wings with your beef on weck at both Cole's and Gene McCarthy's. But beyond that, there are just two major variations—cheese and gravy.

Anderson's, the local custard-and-everything roadside stop with several locations offers sliced provolone, American cheese, cheddar, hot peppers, feta, or blue cheese dressing, but that's about as tricked out as it gets. Eckl's serves their beef on weck with gravy, served open-faced on Texas toast, or as a dinner with

COURTESY OF NICHOLAS CHRISTOU

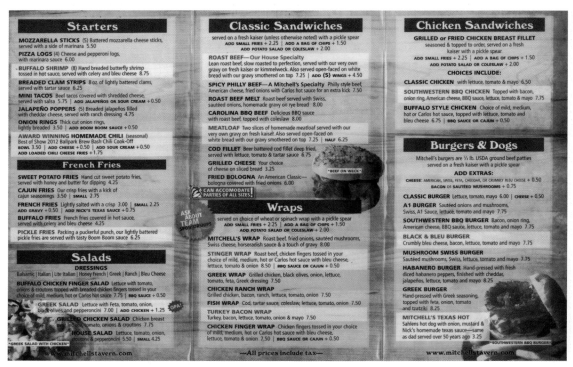

Starters

MOZZARELLA STICKS (5) Battered mozzarella cheese sticks, served with a side of marinara 5.50

PIZZA LOGS (4) Cheese and pepperoni logs, with marinara sauce 6.00

BUFFALO SHRIMP (8) Hand breaded butterfly shrimp tossed in hot sauce, served with celery and bleu cheese 8.75

BREADED CLAM STRIPS 8oz. of lightly battered clams, served with tartar sauce 6.25

MINI TACOS Beef tacos covered with shredded cheese, served with salsa 5.75 | ADD JALAPEÑOS OR SOUR CREAM + 0.50

JALAPEÑO POPPERS (5) Breaded jalapeños filled with cheddar cheese, served with ranch dressing 4.75

ONION RINGS Thick cut onion rings, lightly breaded 3.50 | ADD BOOM BOOM SAUCE + 0.50

AWARD WINNING HOMEMADE CHILI (seasonal) Best of Show 2012 Ballpark Brew Bash Chili Cook-Off
BOWL 3.50 | ADD CHEESE + 0.50 | ADD SOUR CREAM + 0.50
ADD LOADED CHILI CHEESE FRIES + 1.75

French Fries

SWEET POTATO FRIES Hand cut sweet potato fries, served with honey and butter for dipping 4.25

CAJUN FRIES Our crisp fries with a kick of cajun seasonings 3.50 | SMALL 2.75

FRENCH FRIES Lightly salted with a crisp 3.00 | SMALL 2.25
ADD GRAVY + 0.50 | ADD NICK's TEXAS SAUCE + 0.75

BUFFALO FRIES French fries covered in hot sauce, served with celery and bleu cheese 4.25

PICKLE FRIES Packing a puckerful punch, our lightly battered pickle fries are served with tasty Boom Boom sauce 6.25

Salads

DRESSINGS
Balsamic | Italian | Lite Italian | Honey French | Greek | Ranch | Bleu Cheese

BUFFALO CHICKEN FINGER SALAD Lettuce with tomato, onions & croutons topped with breaded chicken fingers tossed in your choice of mild, medium, hot or Carlos hot sauce 7.75 | BBQ SAUCE + 0.50

GREEK SALAD Lettuce with feta, tomato, onion, black olives and pepperoncini 7.00 | ADD CHICKEN + 1.25

GRILLED CHICKEN SALAD Chicken breast lettuce, tomato, onions & croutons 7.75

HOUSE SALAD Lettuce, tomato, onion, croutons & pepperoncini 5.50 | SMALL 4.25

GREEK SALAD WITH CHICKEN

www.mitchellstavern.com

Classic Sandwiches

served on a fresh kaiser (unless otherwise noted) with a pickle spear
ADD SMALL FRIES + 2.25 | ADD A BAG OF CHIPS + 1.50
ADD POTATO SALAD OR COLESLAW + 2.00

ROAST BEEF—Our House Specialty
Lean roast beef, slow roasted to perfection, served with our very own gravy on fresh kaiser or kimmelweck. Also served open-faced on white bread with our gravy smothered on top 7.25 | ADD (5) WINGS + 4.50

SPICY PHILLY BEEF—A Mitchell's Specialty Philly style beef, American cheese, fried onions with Carlos hot sauce for an extra kick 7.50

ROAST BEEF MELT Roast beef served with Swiss, sautéed onions, homemade gravy on rye bread 8.00

CAROLINA BBQ BEEF Delicious BBQ sauce with roast beef, topped with coleslaw 8.00

MEATLOAF Two slices of homemade meatloaf served with our very own gravy on fresh kaiser. Also served open-faced on white bread with our gravy smothered on top 7.25 | HALF 6.25

COD FILLET Beer battered cod fillet deep fried, served with lettuce, tomato & tartar sauce 6.75

GRILLED CHEESE Your choice of cheese on sliced bread 3.25

FRIED BOLOGNA An American Classic— bologna covered with fried onions 6.00

"BEEF ON WECK"

CAN ACCOMMODATE PARTIES OF ALL SIZES!

Wraps

served on choice of wheat or spinach wrap with a pickle spear
ADD SMALL FRIES + 2.25 | ADD A BAG OF CHIPS + 1.50
ADD POTATO SALAD OR COLESLAW + 2.00

MITCHELL'S WRAP Roast beef, fried onions, sautéed mushrooms, Swiss cheese, horseradish sauce & a touch of gravy 8.00

STINGER WRAP Roast beef, chicken fingers tossed in your choice of mild, medium, hot or Carlos hot sauce with bleu cheese, lettuce, tomato & onion 8.50 | BBQ SAUCE OR CAJUN + 0.50

GREEK WRAP Grilled chicken, black olives, onion, lettuce, tomato, feta, Greek dressing 7.50

CHICKEN RANCH WRAP Grilled chicken, bacon, ranch, lettuce, tomato, onion 7.50

FISH WRAP Cod, tartar sauce, coleslaw, lettuce, tomato, onion 7.50

TURKEY BACON WRAP Turkey, bacon, lettuce, tomato, onion & mayo 7.50

CHICKEN FINGER WRAP Chicken fingers tossed in your choice of mild, medium, hot or Carlos hot sauce with bleu cheese, lettuce, tomato & onion 7.50 | BBQ SAUCE OR CAJUN + 0.50

—All prices include tax—

Chicken Sandwiches

GRILLED or FRIED CHICKEN BREAST FILLET seasoned & topped to order, served on a fresh kaiser with a pickle spear.
ADD SMALL FRIES + 2.25 | ADD A BAG OF CHIPS + 1.50
ADD POTATO SALAD OR COLESLAW + 2.00

CHOICES INCLUDE:

CLASSIC CHICKEN with lettuce, tomato & mayo 6.50

SOUTHWESTERN BBQ CHICKEN Topped with bacon, onion ring, American cheese, BBQ sauce, lettuce, tomato & mayo 7.75

BUFFALO STYLE CHICKEN Choice of mild, medium, hot or Carlos hot sauce, topped with lettuce, tomato and bleu cheese 6.75 | BBQ SAUCE OR CAJUN + 0.50

Burgers & Dogs

Mitchell's burgers are ⅓ lb. USDA ground beef patties served on a fresh kaiser with a pickle spear

ADD EXTRAS:
CHEESE: AMERICAN, SWISS, FETA, CHEDDAR, OR CRUMBLY BLEU CHEESE + 0.50
BACON OR SAUTÉED MUSHROOMS + 0.75

CLASSIC BURGER Lettuce, tomato, mayo 6.00 | CHEESE + 0.50

A1 BURGER Sautéed onions and mushrooms, Swiss, A1 Sauce, lettuce and tomato 7.75

SOUTHWESTERN BBQ BURGER Bacon, onion ring, American cheese, BBQ sauce, lettuce, tomato and mayo 7.75

BLACK & BLEU BURGER Crumbly bleu cheese, bacon, lettuce, tomato and mayo 7.75

MUSHROOM SWISS BURGER Sautéed mushrooms, Swiss, lettuce, tomato and mayo 7.75

HABANERO BURGER Hand-pressed with fresh diced habanero peppers, finished with cheddar, jalapeños, lettuce, tomato and mayo 8.25

GREEK BURGER Hand-pressed with Greek seasoning, topped with feta, onion, tomato and tzatziki 8.25

MITCHELL'S TEXAS HOT Sahlens hot dog with onion, mustard & Nick's homemade texas sauce—same as dad served over 50 years ago 3.25

SOUTHWESTERN BBQ BURGER

www.mitchellstavern.com

COURTESY OF NICHOLAS CHRISTOU

potato salad, a relish tray, and bread and butter. Gabriel's Gate calls their beef on weck a "Cottage Street" and serves it with horseradish sauce. Mitchell's Tavern Beef & Beers serves theirs dripping with gravy (they also do a roast beef melt, a "Carolina barbecue beef," spicy Philly beef with American cheese, fried onions, and hot sauce). Gene McCarthy's toasts their kimmelweck and gives you the option to add New York State cheddar or a "crumbled bleu" (mon dieu!) and Swiston's serves theirs with french fries and the option of cheese or gravy. And at Wiechec's Lounge, you can add gravy or turn their "famous roast beef" on weck into a French dip with fried onions and cheese with a side of au jus.

Beef on Weck Timeline

1816 The building that houses Eckl's, first owned by wealthy businessman Wilhelm Willink, is constructed.

1837 Sebastian Schwabl opens his place on Broadway.

1891 A German immigrant named William Wahr from somewhere near the Schwarzwald opens a bakery. He'll go on to be credited for having invented, or originated kummelweck in Buffalo.

1898 Joseph Gohn nets a tidy sum for selling his property to make way for the Pan-American Exposition.

1901 The year of the Pan-American Exposition, the date that Joe Gohn's son Charles' obituary says his father began serving his roast beef sandwich.

1914 Charles E. Roesch starts a wholesale outdoor meat market. Decades later, his grandson Charlie W. Roesch will turn this family business into the business known as Charlie the Butcher.

1934 The Eckl name enters the restaurant landscape when Jack Eckl and his wife Martha take over the business from her mother Emma Schroeder.

1936 After a stint as Buffalo's mayor, Charles E. Roesch leaves politics and opens a butcher shop in the Broadway Market.

1942 Ray Schwabl Jr. moves Schwabl's to its current location in West Seneca on Route 15 near Union Road.

1964 Dale and Shirley Eckl move Eckl's to its current location.

1943 "Gohn's Place" is sold. At that time, it was Buffalo lore that this was the place where beef on weck was made famous.

1949 Joseph Gohn, the man who is said to have made beef on weck famous, passes away.

1987 Charles W. takes over the family business from his father Charles J.

2004 Cheryl and Gene Staychock take over Schwabl's.

2013 After 176 years of continued service, Schwabl's closes after an SUV crashes into it.

2014 Schwabl's reopens after being closed for nine months and suffering $200,000 in damages.

Kimmel-, Kummel-, Kuemmel, Kümmel, Which Weck is Wick(ch)?

After you look for beef on weck on just a few menus in Buffalo, you'll quickly notice that it's spelled in a variety of different ways: kimmelweck, kummelweck, kuemmelweck, kümmelweck, and even kummel weck. So which is it!? Is it just a typo? And if not, why the different spellings and which one is correct?

We've already noted that *kümmel* is the German word for "caraway" and that *weck* means "roll" but if you dig around, it seems like *weck* means "roll" in the southwestern German dialects of the regions of Saarland, Swabia, and the surrounding areas—not everywhere. In northern Germany, or at least in formal textbooks, "roll" is generally *brötchen*. That could back up the idea that the original baker was from somewhere in southwestern Germany. (Are you hav-

ing visions of William Wahr following a trail of kummelweck crumbs left behind in the Schwarzwald by Hansel and Gretel or is that just me?) To boot, the roll used in the Buffalo sandwich tends to be softer and fluffier than a standard German *kümmelbrötchen* or *kümmelweck*!

Buffalo's 5 Best Places for Beef on Weck

There are too many places to count that serve this sandwich in Buffalo. Sometimes it seems as though every place that does wings *also* does a beef on weck. But if this is your first time, don't mess around. Do not pass Go, do not collect $200 dollars, and *do not* go to Anderson's. Nothing

against Anderson's, good custard, and folks will recommend their weck (they've been offering it since the '60s), but theirs is a fast-food version that will make you wonder what the big deal is.

Wherever you seek out great weck, the beef should be super thin, medium-rare, piled high

The carving station in the dining room at Eckl's.

and the weck should be soft, squishy, and covered with about a teaspoon of caraway seeds. The roll should be studded with enough salt that you worry about your blood pressure but not about a heart attack. Beyond that, there are three truths that generally hold. First, if they have a dedicated carving station in full view of your table, you're likely in the right place. Second, give the place another point if you're asked what level of doneness you prefer (I'm taking all your points away if you say well done, boo!). And last, if they don't bring the horseradish, they're not serious.

#5 Bar Bill Tavern

185 Main Street, East Aurora, 14052 | 716-652-7959
barbill.com | Sun 12 PM–2 AM, Mon–Sat 8 AM–2 AM

As you know from already reading about Bar Bill's meticulous wings, owner Clark Crook believes Buffalonians appreciate their traditions. And the dedicated slicing station sure is a tradition practiced at some of the city's most well-regarded beef on weckers. But it's a rare and reassuring sight at a bar.

When I first posited the slicing station the-ory to him, Bar Bill's owner Clark Crook told me, "You're onto something there. If you've got beef sitting in au jus, it's cooking. And so the longer it's cooking, the more well-done or overdone it's getting. Our beef isn't sitting anywhere very long. It comes out of the oven and it goes into your mouth. So it's a level of freshness that our success affords us, because there's enough people in the place to get enough of the stuff so that nothing's sitting around."

Bar Bill is many folks' pick for the best beef on weck in town. It's also generally regarded as the best place to get wings *and* beef on weck that are *both* excellently done, making it an ideal stop if you're in town without a ton of time. (They only serve beef on weck until 10 PM, so don't procrastinate.) Crook wouldn't share his recipe with me, but he said that the same scientific method his wife's uncle Joe applied to improving and standardizing Bar Bill's wings was used to perfect a consistently delicious beef on weck.

Fortunately for adventure eaters who may have already made several stops before arriving (or folks who have filled up on wings but still want that one last great bite), Bar Bill is one of the few places in town that offers beef on weck

in different sizes: mini, small, and regular (they all come with a pickle and a plain roll is available, but if you order that, consider yourself dead to me).

Bar Bill toasts their kummelweck, which makes it stand up to the au jus soak better than most places. It's a boon to slow eaters and those who like to put down their sandwich in between bites. The beef is tender and juicy, piled high, nearly too high, but it's thin enough to quickly disappear. There's something about the proportions of beef to toasted roll and the moisture in the bread that makes the regular sized beef on weck the best move, but if you only have room for the mini, you won't be disappointed. Remember: cash only.

#4 Kelly's Korner

2526 Delaware Avenue, 14216 | 716-877-9466

Sun-Thu 10 AM-2 AM, Fri-Sat 10 AM-3 AM

There's no carving station sitting out in this small corner bar, making it one of the rare places on this list to make a killer beef on weck without one. But despite that, like Bar Bill Tavern,

it's *also* one of the best places in town to get eye-rolling good wings *and* beef on weck.

Head cook and sometimes bartender Lite Finocchiaro is the man behind the weck at Kelly's Korner. He said he starts with a really lean top round that he trims all the fat from then cooks in a roasting pan with a false bottom filled with water at 275°F, letting it come down until it reaches a range between 130°F to 145°F. His secret? "Then you season it with Lawry's Seasoned Salt, regular salt, and black pepper. We put a little bit of the Chef Tournade's Kitchen Bouquet Browning & Seasoning Sauce."

Whatever he's doing, it works. The beef on weck is almost as big as the small plate it's served on and has to be 3 inches tall. With its wrinkles and poof, the roll at Kelly's Korner—lightly-salted and even more lightly flecked with caraway seeds—looks a little more kaiser than kummel, but it's *fresh* and piled high with dead-on medium-rare beef that hangs over the sides and the long pickle spear accompanying it.

But it doesn't just look great. The very pink, wet beef is deeply flavorful, and juicy enough to wet both sides of the bun without making it a complete mess.

#3 Eckl's

4936 Ellicott Road, Orchard Park, 141271

716-662-22621 | eckls.com | Mon-Fri 4 PM-10 PM, Sat 12 PM-10 PM, Sun 12 PM-9 PM

"I don't know where we're all going to go." That was what folks were saying near the end of 2015, when the Eckl family, which had owned it for decades, announced they were getting out of the

business. Fortunately, new owners Ted Smith and Jim Cornell are all about carrying on this great Southtowns tradition.

And there's some considerable tradition here considering the building celebrated 200 years in 2016. Except for the large parking lot out front, pulling up to Eckl's feels more like arriving at some well-off relative's home during the holidays. And given the central role the restaurant plays in this area of town, it may as well be. Inside, a muted TV above the bar shows the most relevant sporting affair. The rest of the homey dining room is quiet but not hushed. There are blinking lights up front well past Christmas, dark walls and beams, white ceilings, and candles flickering on tables dressed in creased din-

ner whites with small bowls of whipped butter packets. But the centerpiece of the dining room is the six-foot long station with steam rising from it where they carve their slow-roasted cap-off Certified Black Angus Top Round.

The rest of the menu is French onion soup, fish fry, French-fried dinners, burgers, and on the weekend, prime rib. But you're here for beef on weck. It comes on kummelweck or with gravy, or as a special with coleslaw, a vegetable, and potato. Medium is de rigueur, the waiter says, but unlike at many places, Eckl's does ask how you want yours. It arrives with one pickle spear and a shiny ramekin of horseradish. The well-salted kummelweck has pronounced crescent ridges—imagine a saggy umbrella on a day when the snow is wet. It's well-filled but nowhere near the half pound at Schwabl's. Maybe the bottom got a dunk, but there's no dip in au jus visible on the underside of the top half. It makes you second-guess the wisdom of such a dip as this thin beef is juicy enough as it is—this is as close as medium can get to rare and still be medium—though it definitely benefits from the weck's seasoning.

Watch out for the horseradish, as the stuff here is potent!

#2 Charlie the Butcher
(Multiple locations)

1065 Wehrle Drive, Williamsville, 14221

716-633-8330 | charliethebutcher.com

Mon–Sat 10 AM–10 PM, Sun 11 AM–9 PM;

Winter Hours (Jan 1–April 1): Mon–Sun 11 AM–9 PM

Dorothy? Aunt Em? Yes, you're in Buffalo, but something about Charlie the Butcher's Kitchen

on Wehrle Drive makes it feel like you're sitting down to a meal in a Kansas country kitchen. The white tiled walls with beige and baby blue stripes, the floral print tables, it's all just downright American. There's a tousled newspaper on a table by the door ready for you to read as you eat, but first, the line.

Charlie's Kitchen is literally across the street from Buffalo Niagara International Airport, making it the easiest, and first or last, Buffalo food icon to visit in town. "Let me cook for you tonight!" the LED display shouts from a tall red pole topped by Charlie's hard-hatted head, which you half expect to tilt back to eject some PEZ. As soon as you enter through the door closest to Cayuga Road, the idea of cooking anything yourself falls into the realm of the absurd. *Tap, chink, tap, chink . . . Tap, chink, tap, chink*—that's the sound of the carver tapping and slicing with his fork and knife behind the big counter at a cutting board that's so well-loved it dips in the center. The carver moves the thinly sliced medium rare beef around, slicing and piling it high on the roll. He places the top on and weighs each sandwich on a small scale behind the counter under a heat lamp, adjusts the amount as

needed, then dips the underside of the top in the au jus. "Next?"

That would be you, friend. Know what you want? Order in front, pay inside at the register by the Formica bar. They do a different sandwich special daily that ranges from baked ham and meatloaf to prime rib. This is also one place in town where you can get central southern New York's most famous food: the chicken spiedie. And they have a catchy way of selling their fried bologna sandwich, that makes you want to order it: "Grilled like a steak, priced like bologna, and served with onions and peppers". But if this is your first time, you're getting beef on weck, slow-roasted and served on old-fashioned kummelweck with a kosher dill pickle and horseradish from Broadway Market, the city's famed bastion of Polish foods (for a dollar less you can get a "mini," but, you're not going to do me like that, right?). Care for some German potato salad? Charlie will suggest you might. It's warm, sweet, and smoky with little bits of bacon.

Take your red tray, sit down at a booth, or sidle into one of the seven old-school barstools at the counter so you can watch the kitchen action. See how all the male servers wear ties? The Charlie the Butcher T-shirts they sell have ties on them too. But hey, your sandwich is getting cold. Let's go! Look at that kummelweck: super light and speckled with small translucent salt crystals and just *a pinch* of caraway seeds. The beef is cooked medium-rare to just-done and is sliced *super* thin. These really are the simple principles of a great beef on weck. Juicy . . . mmm! The rolls just become a vehicle and a seasoning accent—present enough to get the beef to your mouth, flavorful enough to accentuate and season, but airy and light. And there are diminishing returns the longer you wait to take another bite, because it gets soggy from the dip in the au jus.

So spoon as much of that horseradish on as your nasal passages can afford and dig in!

#1 Schwabl's Restaurant

789 Center Road, West Seneca, 14224
716-675-2333 | schwabls.com | Mon–Thu 11 AM–9 PM, Fri–Sat 11 AM–10 PM, Sun 1 PM–8:30 PM

Sitting in the always-full dining room (Tom & Jerry in hand), beef on weck on the way, and the winter wind whipping the flags outside, you're filled with a feeling that's half satisfaction, half anticipation. Then, the thought comes to mind that there could hardly be a better moment imaginable or anywhere you'd rather be. Now consider that Schwabl's (rhymes with "wobbles") is a restaurant that has been at this since 1837!

Like Eckl's, Schwabl's is just off Union Road (only 15 minutes separates them). It's a narrow white building set just off the intersection with Center Road a few blocks south of the Aurora Expressway. It's a railroad dining room with two entrances, one in front and one on the side. Inside up front is the bar with a magnificent, picture-worthy register behind it and a mirror frosted with the restaurant's name and date of birth framed by pine garland and white Christmas lights in mid-February. "If you're drinking to forget, please pay first," the sign above the bar says. But if you're going to drink yourself unconscious

here you'd have to sleep standing up. There are no stools at this bar. That's okay, because standing gives you a better view of the slicing station at the end of the bar anyway. That's where a gentleman wearing a white smock never seems to stop slicing Schwabl's famous beef on weck with that comforting *tap, tip, tap* sound of the blade and the carving fork. If a Tom & Jerry wasn't enough to put you to sleep, the tap-tipping could be.

You can upgrade your roast beef to surf-and-turf with yellow pike, and Schwabl's does do more than just beef on weck. "Step back in time for real traditional Buffalo food," they promise. And you can see glimmers of that history. There are boneless sardines, Bavarian pretzel sticks with homemade beer cheese, hot ham, roast turkey, and a special Hungarian goulash and dumplings dish they serve only on Saturday. But they also serve chili fries and several types of poutine, including "Schwabl's Poutine," which is basically a beef on weck version with slivered beef, homemade beef gravy, coarse salt, and caraway seeds.

Beef on weck falls under the menu's "Specials" category, where it notes you can have it on

kummelweck or with bread and gravy. It comes with french fries, coleslaw, or plate of pickled beets, but they'll let you substitute mashed potato, sweet potato fries, or their German potato salad for the fries. Like any good steakhouse, they ask how well you want your beef done. "Medium is standard," the waitress says, "or medium rare, but you can get it done however much you want."

Schwabl's aligns itself with more recent restaurant customs; its menu pleads with customers to keep cell phone use to a minimum. There's also a warning that they reserve the right to move you along when you're done if they're busy (unless you plan on continuing to order Tom & Jerrys, which would be tempting), and a note that "good food takes time to prepare," so thank you for your patience. The sentiment is, "It may take a while to get the food to you and once you get it we may need you to move along," but waiting for your food gives you time to read the considerable history told on the menu and the sandwich is satisfying enough to take any edge off.

Beef on weck arrives with a pickle and a jar of super-smooth horseradish. There's a domed roll that's toothsome and more structured than poofy, topped with a thin scattering of small salt crystals and two dozen caraway seeds. There's an eight-ounce portion of meat here and they slice it a little more thickly, but it's juicy with a robust beef flavor—truly a delicious sandwich, and when it comes to Buffalo, quite arguably, the definitive one.

RANKING BUFFALO'S BEST BEEF ON WECK

1. Schwabl's
2. Charlie the Butcher
3. Eckl's
4. Kelly's Korner
5. Bar Bill Tavern

What's Your Beef?

You can't go wrong at any of the five places we've covered—each serves a life-changing beef on weck. But folks have been known to swear by the other places below. Where's the beef? Right here. Set out on your own search for Buffalo's best beef on weck.

Anderson's, Multiple locations

Bases Loaded, Blasdell, 3355 Lakeshore Road, 716-823-0158

Blackthorn Restaurant & Pub, South Buffalo, 2134 Seneca Street, 716-825-9327

Buffalo Brew Pub, Williamsville, 6861 Main Street, 716-632-0552

Cole's, Elmwood, 1104 Elmwood Avenue, 716-886-1449

Eddie Brady's Tavern, Downtown, 97 Genesee Street, 716-854-7017

Gabriel's Gate, Allentown, 145 Allen Street, 716-886-0602

Gene McCarthy's, First Ward, 73 Hamburg Street, 716-855-8948

McPartlan's Corner, Amherst, 669 Wehrle Drive, 716-632-9896

Mitchell's Tavern Beef & Beer, Tonawanda, 734 Sheridan Drive, 716-874-8907

Steve's Pig and Ox Roast, Lackawanna, 951 Ridge Road, 716-824-8601

Swiston's, Tonawanda, 101 Young Street, 716-692-9723

The Public House on the Lake, Hamburg, 4914 Lakeshore Road, 716-627-5551

Ulrich's, 1868 Tavern, Downtown, 674 Ellicott Street, 716-989-1868

Vizzi's, Kenmore, 967 Kenmore Avenue, 716-871-1965

Wiechec's Lounge, Kaisertown, 1748 Clinton Street, 716-823-2828

CHAPTER FOUR

⦾━━━━◆━━━━⦾

BUFFALO IS JUST
ONE BIG FISH FRY

Buffalo may not have invented fish fry, but as popular as it is, it may as well have. It's everywhere! You're just as likely to see it offered at sandwich shops, pizzerias, and bars as places known to specialize in fish. Visit Chiavetta's on a Friday from October through Lent, and you'll find a dining room filled with as many folks eating fish fry as their famous chicken.

Buffalo's own food cognoscenti look elsewhere for the origins of the city's love for fried fish. To the church who embraced it as a way to go meatless on Friday and Sunday to honor Jesus' sacrifice. To the working class and poor, who could bait a line even if they didn't have anything else to eat. To Prohibition when bar owners used it as a way to get folks in the door. And to the South, where the culinary practices of slaves from West Africa and the Caribbean became part of food tradition.

These days, you can eat fish fry in many Buffalo restaurants just about any day of the week. But Lent means there's absolutely no escape.

It also marks the onset of fish fry *season*: the community fish fries served at the VFW, listed in church bulletins, and announced locally in print, online, and on TV. If you're into authenticity, this is it—fish fry that some might argue is also the best. Just Google "best church fish fry in Buffalo" and look for the most recent list.

Old-timers say that once upon a time, the fish fry fish of choice was yellow pike (walleye), a freshwater fish native to Canada and the Northern United States. These days, you're likely to find haddock, and somewhat less often, cod. Typically, the fish is either coated in a light flour dredge or beer-battered and fried. Frequently, you can also have it broiled, blackened, or steamed. And some places add their own unique flare to the dish: Joe's, for example, does a broiled haddock "Florentine" with sautéed spinach, garlic, tomatoes, Asiago, and lemon. Sides tend to be fries, coleslaw, and macaroni or potato salad (sometimes German), and, of course, there's tartar sauce and lemon wedges.

The Criteria

The keys to a great fish fry are really pretty simple and should go without saying: fresh fish, a beer batter or dredge that's well seasoned, an exterior crispness that adds textural contrast, a fry that's not overly oily or grease-sodden, crispy fries, plenty of tartar sauce, and sides given as much attention as the main event. And, oh yeah, you should never have to ask for a bottle of malt vinegar. It should be automatic.

Buffalo's Best Fish Fry

Not all fish fry is created equal. Given its popularity in Buffalo, there are plenty of places serving under-seasoned fish and frozen French fries from a bag to fill out a line on their menu every day. That can make it tempting, after experiencing the Friday crowds at Gene McCarthy's, to draw a potentially controversial conclusion. Could it be that the places that don't cook their fish fry daily do it better on days they do cook it than other places that do it all the time? There are always exceptions. Take Joe's Deli, a sandwich shop that's beloved for its fish fry—made daily, and from scratch, including all of its accompaniments—and restaurants like Parker's and Bailey, which specialize in fish and fish fry and offer it daily. Still, you could make the case it's a good rule of thumb that if you're going to eat fish fry at a bar, pizzeria, or other spot not obviously tied to fish, that the days they dedicate themselves to it, they're going to do it with love (they may even pause making wings to free up their fryers).

#5 Curry's Restaurant and Pub

864 Kenmore Avenue, North Park, 14216
716-447-0502 | curryspub.com
Mon–Tue 11:30 am–10 pm, Wed–Sat 11:30 am–11 pm,
Sun 4 pm–9 pm

Like some of Buffalo's many other gems, Curry's is the proverbial diamond in the rough, a cozy neighborhood bar in a strip mall. Curry's is known for two things. The first is the "Dibble," their stuffed banana pepper and melted mozzarella sandwich, which can be outfitted with any one of six cheeses, and protein-upgraded with everything from meatballs and sausages to fried bologna or New York strip. The second, and perhaps even more popular, is their fish fry.

Curry's Restaurant and Pub was founded by Pat Curry in 1994, and was taken over in 2013 by Shannon Rhonemus, who started working with Pat a decade earlier. She's continued the Curry tradition of a crispy fish fry made with beer-battered haddock that's known to stretch over both sides of the plate by nearly two inches. The one Friday-only fish fry tradition is the German potato salad, otherwise Curry's serves it daily (you can also order it breaded or broiled) with coleslaw, macaroni salad, rye bread, and either French fries, rice, or baked potato.

#4 Bailey Seafood

3316 Bailey Avenue, LaSalle, 14215 | 716-833-1973
baileyseafood.com | Mon–Thu 11 am–8 pm,
Fri 9 am–9 pm, Sat 11 am–8 pm, Closed Sun

You can buy raw fish to take home to cook. They sell lobster tails, clams, and crab legs. They don't carry sushi. The prices are online. And there aren't any tables. That takes care of the answers to the most popular questions asked of Bailey Seafood since George Kontras founded it in 1985. So now we can talk about the fish fry being served inside the big blue building on the corner of Bailey and LaSalle, and why it's routinely noted among Buffalo's best.

Bailey is purely a takeout spot, the kind of place you order from and eat in the car or take home (the former if you want to experience that prime fry), and they do an old-school, thorough but light breading that turns golden brown with the fry. (They do also serve their fish baked or steamed.) One thing that truly sets them apart are the sheer number of fish options at your perusal: haddock, whiting, tilapia, catfish, porgie, smelts, perch, yellow pike, butterfish, and salmon.

The shellfish section of their menu notes they have "everything under the sea," a claim that's hard to argue with, and there's an appetizer menu longer than the alphabet that includes frog legs, chicken gumbo, hush puppies, and mac and cheese. If you haven't filled up on that, three Bailey signatures should do the trick. The "Super Sandwich" is your choice of fried haddock, perch, whiting, Cajun catfish, or tilapia piled onto a roll with fries, coleslaw, tartar sauce, and cheese. The "Belly Buster" includes a pound of fried fish "tid bits," 10 fried shrimp, five chicken fingers, five hush puppies, and fries. And then there's the homemade sweet potato pie they make from scratch.

If that all sounds like something you're going to need to make several trips to try, order online. Bailey gives a 15 percent discount on your first online order and 10 percent off every order afterwards for life.

#3 Gene McCarthy's

73 Hamburg Street, Buffalo, NY 14204
716-855-8948 | genemccarthys.com
Mon–Fri 11 AM–12 AM, Sat 11 AM–1 AM, Sun 11 AM–12 AM

Gene McCarthy's only serves their fish fry on Wednesdays and Fridays, and only after 5 PM. They're so popular, in fact, that owner Bill Metzger said two of his managers had been angling to do something seemingly unthinkable: do away with *wings* on Friday because they slow the fish fry down too much! "We're like, no! You're not doing away with wings!"

Gene McCarthy's fish fry includes a 14-ounce piece of beer-battered haddock that's made with Irish red ale, a malty red beer. The crust is impeccable—that thin crispy crackle that seems impervious until it's shattered, revealing the steaming flakes of fish inside. It's served with macaroni, potato salad, coleslaw, and, of course, tartar sauce, over a bed of fries. Anyone who has been eating wings all day will be heartened to know that half portions are available.

#2 Parker's Proper Fish & Chips

1216 South Park Avenue, South Buffalo, 14220
716-292-2012 | parkersbritishinstitution.com
Tue–Thu 11 AM–6 PM, Fri 11 AM–7 PM,
Sat 11 AM–6 PM, Closed Sun–Mon

There's *fish fry* and then there's *fish and chips*. What's the difference? Kind of like all bourbon is whiskey, but not all whiskey is bourbon; fish and chips can be fish fry, but not all fish fry is fish and chips. Buffalo's fish fry is only sometimes beer-battered but always served with sides and crispy fries (if they're being made right), and fish and chips are *always* beer-battered and fried, then accompanied with soft fries (usually enough for two people) to be doused in malt vinegar. Husband-and-wife team Vicky and Damian Parker serve the latter, and as the name of their chippy suggests, they make a *proper* fish and chips that's also arguably Buffalo's best fish *fry*.

The chippy (opened in 2014) is just one part of the empire the Parkers have been building in South Buffalo since they launched their English Pork Pie Company (since renamed Parker's) in Vermont in 2008, and relocated to the Nickel City. Buffalo's own Little Britain includes kitchenware, bakery, a butcher (the *Wall Street Journal* said Parker's may be the best bangers in America), cake shop, and they're working on creating their own "proper High Street" where they'll sell everything else British from West Yorkshire textiles to bath spa cosmetics.

The fish selections are simple: an 8- to 10-ounce portion of flaky battered Icelandic cod, battered cod and chips made with King Edward potatoes, battered cod sandwich and chips, or the kid portion of battered cod and chips. For those less fish-inclined there's a chip butty (chips on buttered white bread), cheesy chips with gravy, battered sausages, pies, Cornish pasties, sausage rolls, and mushy peas.

#1 Joe's Deli

1322 Hertel Avenue, Hertel Avenue, 14216
716-875-5637 | Mon–Sat 11 AM–9 PM, Closed Sun

There's a whole philosophy behind the fish fry (served daily) at Joe's Deli, a place primarily known, ironically, for its sandwiches. "There ought to be a delicious beer batter—not too salty and not too sweet," as I've learned the thinking goes. "It can't be too doughy when it's cooked, or soggy in any way. The perfect fish fry is crisp and crunchy through and through. This requires a homemade beer batter made with local beer cooked to perfection. If you cook the fish too long, it's hard as a rock. If you cook it too slow, then the whole thing is going to fall apart and the batter slides off everywhere."

If all of this sounds about right, it's something CIA-trained chef and owner Joe Lyons should know something about, being Buffalo born and bred. He's also one for holding up Buffalo tradition. He opened the first Joe's Deli in 2006 on the corner that, until 2005, had housed Mastman's Delicatessen, an institution that had been serving kosher sandwiches, homemade pickles, and sauerkraut since just after World War II. (The corner's history as a deli goes back even further, to 1936, when it was known as Zarin's Delicatessen.)

Joe's uses haddock for their fish fry, serving it with fresh-cut fries, a from-scratch, crispy coleslaw that's crunchy with carrots and cabbage, tartar sauce, lemon wedges, and bread and butter. And while you can order it Cajun-style, lemon-pepper broiled, or Florentine, after the explanation above, are you really going to do me like that?

Go Fish

Do you have great fries? Yes? Thanks, I'll take those. How about some good sides? Mmm. Nice. How about a great batter? Wow. What luck! And fresh haddock, pike, or cod? Yes? *Schooling* everyone here.

Is there another great fish fry place that wasn't mentioned in this group of the best? Hey, just playing the cards we were dealt. You're welcome to try some of the other places routinely noted as having some of the best versions of this classic Buffalo dish. Go fish . . .

Gabriel's Gate, Allentown, 145 Allen Street, 716-886-0602

Hamlin House, Allentown, 432 Franklin Street, 716-885-8084

Happy Swallow Restaurant, East Side, 1349 Sycamore Street, 716-894-4854

Hayes Seafood House, Williamsville, 8900 Main Street, 716-632-1772

Hoak's Lakeshore Restaurant, Hamburg, 4100 Lake Shore Road, 716-627-4570

Pearl Street Grill & Brewery, Downtown, 76 Pearl Street, 716-856.2337

Scharf's German Restaurant & Bar, West Seneca, 2683 Clinton Street, 716-895-7249

Squire's Tap Room, Tonawanda, 127 Niagara Street, 716-692-2093

Wellington Pub, Hertel Avenue, 1541 Hertel Avenue, 716-833-9899

Wiechec's Lounge, Kaisertown, 1748 Clinton Street, 716-823-2828

Vizzi's, Kenmore, 967 Kenmore Avenue, 716-871-1965

CHAPTER FIVE

❖

WIENER WINNER
HOT DOG DINNER

With all the attention wings, weck, and the pizza from Bocce and LaNova get, it sometimes means that Buffalo's love of hot dogs gets glossed over by the national media. But trust me, Buffalo's hot dogs are worth your attention. Today, that means Sahlen's, founded by Joseph Sahlen in 1869. It means Ted's iconic charcoal-broiled dogs. It means Louie's Texas Red Hots and its Greek-style sauce. And it means Buffalo's summer hot dog stands. But there are a few other quirks and details surrounding Buffalo's hot dog history worth noting.

Beyond Sahlen's: Wardynski, Shelly, and Malecki's

Sahlen's smoky, pork-and-beef, natural-casing dogs are king. But there were, and still are, some other big Buffalo hot dog brands, many of which arose out of the stockyards of Buffalo's East Side. Polish émigré Frank Wardynski started producing his recipe for Polish sausage not long after arriving in 1919, and eventually went wholesale in 1954.

Then there's Polish-born Anthony Szelagowski, who went wholesale in 1914. His Shelly Brand of Sausage and Smoked Meats, which included "Extra Polish" Polish sausage were popular enough that when it went out of business in the '90s, Wardynski Meats took it over.

Then there's Malecki's Meats, founded by Polish-born Joseph Malecki. Malecki opened a smokehouse and wholesale operation in 1915. According to the *Polonia Trail*, a site dedicated to documenting prominent sites in the Polish community of Western New York, Malecki's went on to become the hot dog of choice of Ted's in 1965, before closing its doors in the '90s.

In a Pickle: Did Buffalo Invent the Chicago-Style Hot Dog?

Anyone who *loves* hot dogs knows that in Chicago, they come steamed and "dragged through the garden" (though nobody *from* Chicago ever says that) in a soft and squishy poppy seed bun and topped with yellow mustard, neon green relish, onions, tomato wedges, sport peppers, a dash of celery salt, and a pickle slice or spear. The style is said to have solidified somewhere between 1920 and 1950.

But as any Buffalo hot dog enthusiast will tell you, that pickle-on-a-dog thing is quintessential Ted's. Ted's president, Thecly Liaros Ortolani, finds it interesting that anyone would question who invented the practice of pairing hot dog and pickle spear *in* a bun. "To me, I know nothing else," she said, noting that her grandfather Theodore Spiro Liaros, was doing that since the "very beginning" in 1927.

Certainly, both hot dogs and Jewish sour pickles have rich traditions as pushcart foods, so it's not hard to imagine vendors rubbing elbows and the practice of piling them together in a bun happening on a street corner. But which one? In which city? It's hard to believe it was New York City where there seems to be little evidence today of the tradition at its most famous stands or dirty water carts.

Chicago? Hey, nobody there has been able to prove (including Abe Drexler of Fluky's) that they invented the practice. I'm not saying Buffalo *did* invent it. But they're both Great Lake cities, and they're only separated by a little over 500 miles. Maybe someone got a taste of it at Ted Liaros' shop under the Peace Bridge in the late '20s. I'm just leaving the door open—he *might* have, no?

1901 Pan-American Exposition

According to the 1901 Pan-American Exposition history site *Doing the Pan*, there were frankfurters served at the Pan-Am Exposition. This is the same huge event visited by 8 million people over six months that year that beef-on-weck inventor Joe Gohn made money off by selling his restaurant, where Joe Fowler sold chocolates, and where Schwabl's had their stand too. In fact, according to *Doing the Pan*'s Susan Eck, they weren't *exactly* cheap eats.

"The charges varied widely, but most agree that the two most expensive places to eat on the ground were the Electric Tower restaurant (the higher of the two restaurants charged the higher prices) and Alt Nürnberg, a Buffalo concession that brought in famed New York restaurateur August Lüchow (of Lüchow's) to manage the restaurant," Eck writes. "A frankfurter at Alt Nürnberg cost 45¢ ($9.00 in today's money); whether a bun was included is not known!

The whole bun thing gets hazy, and Buffalo doesn't stake a claim to any of it. Or does it?

Some say German baker Charles Feltman sold the sausages at his first Coney Island hot dog stand in a milk roll in 1871. The National Hot Dog and Sausage Council notes that hot dog historian and author of *Hot Dog: A Global History*, Bruce Kraig, PhD, argues Germans always ate these kinds of sausages with bread.

Others point to the 1904 World's Fair in St.

Louis (also known as the Louisiana Purchase Exposition), credited for popularizing the ice cream cone, peanut butter, and the hamburger. Supposedly, Bavarian concessionaire Anton Feuchtwanger was lending white gloves to his customers to prevent their hands getting dirty while they were eating his sausages. Only they kept walking off with the gloves. So he asked his brother-in-law, a baker, to make some soft rolls to serve the same purpose.

The New York Public Library has a copy of a May 24th menu from Lüchow's Pan American Restaurant *at* the 1901 Pan-Am Exposition. Lüchow's was a restaurant just off Union Square on East 14th Street in Manhattan's East Village from 1882 to 1983. And Eck's right, there's "Imported Frankfurter with Sauerkraut or Potato Salad" listed along with "Nuernberger Bratwurst, Bayrische Kraut," Bavarian sausage and kraut. Only here's the thing, nestled in the "Kalte Speisen" (cold plates) under "Strassburger Ganseleber Pastete" (pâté de foie gras) and just above "Caviar with Toast" is, "Liver Sausage, Dill Pickle" listed for 40¢. And later, under the Sandwiches section are "Liver Sausage" 15¢ and "Cervelat."

A sausage . . . with a pickle? Could this be the missing link? (Rimshot). You could argue that liver sausage likely could have been liverwurst, which isn't a frankfurter, but maybe not. And cervelat, a natural casing sausage made in Switzerland, France, and parts of Germany *is* similar to that of a frankfurter, just smokier. Pickle? Bread? Bun? All the components are there.

The Great Wiener Menace and The Mayor Who Hated Hot Dogs

"There was a Buffalo mayor who was mad about all the hot dog stands, and he wanted to start a Prohibition of new hot dog stands," Ted's President, Thecly Liaros Ortolani tells me.

She's right. According to eighth-generation Buffalonian, former radio news man, historian, and author Steve Cichon of Buffalo Stories, that would be Mayor Frank X. Schwab (1922–1929). In 1922, Schwab, the city's brewer mayor (convicted of violating Prohibition laws while in office) "fought for and won the right to license and regulate the city's growing number of hot dog stands with the notion to close them down, threatening to 'arrest any hot dog merchant who held forth in the streets.'"

Okay, so Cichon notes that it wasn't hot dogs that Mayor Schwab hated per se, but the willful disregard many vendors exhibited toward sanitation and keeping their surroundings tidy. Still, he goes on to explain that Buffalo's roadside hot dog stands *were* declared "a menace to public health" by state leaders, and the state health department called them "an institution which must be brought under special state control."

Hey, he wasn't alone. In the following decade, mindful of public-health risks, New York City Mayor Fiorello La Guardia moved vendors into indoor markets. Buffalo: street food trendsetter in the '20s.

A History of Ted's Hog Dogs with Ted's President, Thecly Liaros Ortolani

Standing on line at Ted's, listening to the *hiss*, *tap*, *tap* of the dogs being moved around on the charcoal, listening to other customers give their customized orders, and taking one of the coupons they often pass back, one to another, it's hard to believe how fast food spots like McDonald's and Burger King exist. You get your food in just about the same amount of time, maybe a little longer since it's not coming off a shoot or sitting under a heat lamp, and it's just so much . . . better. Walking into Ted's and smelling the dogs cooking and the charcoal burning, it's a simple thing that warms the heart and reminds you there's still some good in the world. That's a tradition Ted's President, Thecly Liaros Ortolani, said she's committed to continuing.

How did Ted's get started?

My grandfather, Theodore Spiro Liaros, came over from Greece in 1912. He was 20 years old. He was just your typical American dream: coming here not speaking the language, taking a boat for like 25 bucks, crossing the ocean, and not having a job. He started out with popcorn and peanuts, selling them from around his neck. And then he had a lunch wagon that went around to feed the farmers. Back then, a lot of people were opening hot dog stands. And in 1927, when the Peace Bridge was completed, my grandfather bought the construction shack nearby for $100, and that's when he started selling hot dogs. We opened up with exactly what we had now: mustard, ketchup. The hot sauce, we make it ourselves, and it's a secret recipe.

Have you always cooked over charcoal?

Back then, the hot dogs were not cooked on charcoal. My grandfather cooked the hot dogs on a flat grill. Put some oil on there, put the hot dogs on the flat grill, put the rolls under the grill to warm them up. No dining room, just sold them just like that, right out of the window. That store was there until 1969. It closed only when they were constructing new access ramps for the Peace Bridge. They needed to close down my grandfather. Kind of a bittersweet story. A month after they closed that little store, my grandfather passed away. It's like he kind of . . . that store went, and he went with the store.

How did you make the move to charcoal?

The next store was on Shirley Drive. It opened in 1948, also with the hot dogs being cooked on a flat grill. My father, who was a young whippersnapper, told my grandfather, "Dad, the guys down the street are cooking on charcoal grill. I think we ought to do that too." Somewhere around 1950, they switched to a charcoal grill. And it's ironic, because that's what differentiates us now, everything cooked over charcoal.

What's the key to cooking a Ted's hot dog?

We shoot for 15 minutes. But, it always depends. The fire can vary. You can move the food around a lot on the grill, to hot spots wherever the charcoal is. The best way to cook hot dogs, as far as I'm concerned, the way I like mine is well-done but not burned. You cook them slow over the back, not over the hot part of the fire, and you let them sit there until the steam bursts through that skin and opens it up, and then you roll it over the fire a little bit to give them some color.

But you *do* pierce them?

You give them couple of pierces. The piercing is to control where the split happens and to also keep the hot dog straight, so you can roll it.

How many locations do you have now?

We have nine locally in Buffalo, and the food truck.

And one downtown...

We are so excited to be part of the resurgence of this city. It broke my heart, that after we closed the location on Porter Avenue years ago, there's been a few stores that have closed because of lease problems and stuff, and that was one of them. So, for 17 years, we weren't in the city of Buffalo, and yet we always talk about ourselves as being a Buffalo tradition, but we weren't even in Buffalo. So, this is our 90th anniversary. Lieutenant Governor Kathy Hochul gave us an award here this year, just for celebrating out 90th year and being a part of Buffalo. And it was really so special because we're just so happy to be back in Buffalo where my grandfather started. And to be part of this very, very exciting renaissance in the city.

And one in Tempe, Arizona. Why Arizona?

It's right near ASU. My father retired out there. And we are buying a piece of property in Chandler, Arizona, to open a second location.

Would you ever open in New York City?

My son lives in Brooklyn. He'd love us to have a spot there. One of the places that we admire is Shake Shack. Maybe we could possibly do some franchising down the line.

How did your secret sauce come about?

The folklore, and it makes sense to me, is one of my grandfather's vendors had a wife who made what my grandfather used to call "chili"—hot chili sauce. So we think that's where he got the recipe.

There's some kind of hot pepper, and then onions in there, maybe, some pickle...

Uh-huh.

And then when one of the employees asked if I wanted ketchup and sauce and I asked for everything, he said, "There's already ketchup in the sauce." So . . .

Oh well, that's easy.

Folks looked on the back of the bottle and theorize about what goes into the sauce and how to make it at home. What are some of the keys to your sauce?

Good luck if you look on the back of the bottle. I have the recipe at home, locked up. All the sauce that's served in the store, we make ourselves in the store. The sauce that's sold in the grocery, we have to have a bottler make that because it has to be shelf stable. I will warn you that the longer the hot sauce sits in the fridge, it gets hotter, and hotter, and hotter. I really can't tell you more than that.

Last question: Can you get good wings outside the Nickel City?

Never order wings outside of Buffalo.

This interview has been edited and condensed for clarity.

Buffalo's 5 Best Hot Dog Spots

It may seem obvious, but you'd be surprised by how many hot dog places across the country (outside Chicago) get this wrong: to make a great hot dog, you need a soft, fresh bun, preferably steamed. For all their fame, that's one of the reasons New York City's dirty water dogs don't rise to the level of quality of ones you'll find in the Windy City, along the Connecticut hot dog trail, and even in New Jersey. You're also looking for a well-spiced but not overly seasoned dog made with a thin casing. And while there are arguably merits to steaming, you're hoping for a cooking method (flat top or grill) that's going to add some more texture and flavor elicited from the

caramelization and light burning of the meat. There's the rare breed of place where they make their own dogs and condiments. That's a beautiful thing. But really, what you're looking for is a place that doesn't use processed toppings warmed in their plastic bags in a hotel tray of water to mask the taste of their dogs, or failing that places that do, but know how to apply them in a way that makes you feel good about having been so obviously bad. And for the love of God, please, whatever you do, unless you're twelve, don't call it a tube steak.

#5 Louie's Texas Red Hots (Multiple locations)

1098 Elmwood Avenue, Elmwood, 14222

716-882-4687 | louiestexasredhots.com

Sun–Mon 8 AM–1 AM, Tue–Thu 8 AM–5 AM, Fri–Sat 24 Hours

Louie's may not have quite the pedigree as Ted's, but even half of that kind of longevity is impressive. Like Ted's founder Theodore "Ted" Liaros, Louie's founder, Louie Galanes is also originally from Greece. He opened shop on Bailey and Delevan Avenue in 1967, when he's proud of telling

folks, there were some 20 other hot dog stands in town. Now, there are seven Louie's locations and the chain and its sign, with "It's all about the sauce!" in the splatter of the "O," is a Buffalo institution. Not bad at all.

The menu options have multiplied at least as often as the locations. There's an all-day breakfast along with burgers, soups, salads, Buffalo classics (fried bologna etc.) and specialty items like souvlaki and gyro. But it's really all about getting an old-fashioned milkshake (simply vanilla, chocolate, strawberry) and a Texas Red Hot: a Sahlen's hot dog grilled on a flat top, served on a steamed roll with mustard, silver onions, and topped with Louie's spicy beef sauce.

#4 Abbott Texas Red Hots

1291 Abbott Road, Lackawanna, 14218

716-825-3025 | Mon–Sat 6:30 AM–9 PM,
Sun 6:30 AM–7 PM

It doesn't have the polish of a Ted's or even a Louie's, but Abbott Texas Red Hots, just a few blocks
south of Imperial on Abbott, does serve their own
mighty fine version of a Texas Red Hot. The tiny
little brick building and its electric blue shingle
roof seem like they're straight out of early '80s
central casting, which just about jives with when
the business owned by Vasiliadis Konstantinos
was established, 1985.

It's the same inside: just a few tables, and a
short little counter with fixed stools where you
can order eggs, omelets, sandwiches, and a few
simple dinners (souvlaki, liver with bacon and
onions). There's a Friday-only haddock fish fry
too. But like the neon sign in the window indi-
cates, Abbott specializes in "Texas Red Hots."
The dog is warmed on the griddle, but not
browned, then nestled inside of the steamed bun
already lined with mustard and chopped onions.
It all gets completely covered with a very thin,
very fresh ground black peppery chili sauce.

#3 Taffy's Hot Dog Stand

3261 Orchard Park Road, Orchard Park, 14127

716-675-0264 | facebook.com/TaffysRedHots

Daily 11 AM–10 PM (April 1–Oct 31)

Taffy's is not Buffalo's only summer hot dog
stand, but it may very well be their king. It's been
around since 1949, opened by Lebanese émigré
Toufic "Taffy" Eliah. Taffy worked the stand
until he was 90, using the same grill he bought
when he first leased the ramshackle place on
what was then nearly void of anything else. It's
now run by Taffy's son, Richard, who if he follows in his folks' footsteps, should be in health
for years to come. His mother Nellie was still
working at Taffy's, washing trays through 2016,
at age 100. Today, lots of traffic passes Taffy's
at its five-way intersection, but, a good portion
stop when they see the red neon Taffy's sign and
green-trimmed roof.

The real move is to score one of the rocking
booths surrounding the stand while a representative for your party waits to place the order (you
order, give your name, and pay when they call out
that your food's ready). It's a good thing the line
is long, as there will undoubtedly be some time

needed looking at the menu. There are some 130 milkshake flavors to choose from, divided up among Fruit "Moos," Chocolate Moos, Coffee Moos, and Silly Moos. Shakes can arrive a bit thin, but you can order them extra-thick (as well as with malt and by the quart). With flavors like Bubbleberry (strawberry, raspberry, and blueberry) and Fruit Loop (lemon, orange, and cherry) under the fruit section, they don't seem any less silly, but it's all in good fun.

So are the fries, straight, sweet potato, and curly, all hand-cut daily. They even made news in 2010, when two co-workers encountered a 34-inch French fry from a pile of curly fries, gaining the two fame for having the longest French

fry in the world. These aren't the curly fair fries you're used to—they're big, airy, bracelet-sized open circles and you should ask for them dusted with Cajun spice. Sahlen's dogs and foot-long dogs come charred with a pickle spear and your choice of chili or cheese. "The works" here means mustard, relish, and chopped onions, but there's an extras section that enables you to add fried peppers and onions, mushrooms, sauerkraut, sour cream, and bacon too.

#2 Frank's Gourmet Hot Dogs

617 Main Street #200, Downtown, 14203
findfranknow.com | Mon–Fri 10 AM–9 PM,
Sat 11 AM–8 PM, Closed Sun

Frustrated by the lack of quality hot dogs and the ketchup-and-mustard limitations usually served with them, wiener fiend Frank Tripi persuaded his brother Paul to join him in launching a hot dog stand that used "only the good stuff" as a food truck in 2013.

There are now two trucks. You'll want to check Twitter (@FindFrankNow) or their online schedules to find their locations, but they can frequently be found at Buffalo State College and

at the Key Bank Center. There's also a brick-and-mortar spot inside the Expo Market (expo buffalo.com), and a new location in Tonawanda on the way in 2018. Since opening, their "Honest food cultivated with respect" has garnered them awards for best food truck, and best hot dog and fries from *Buffalo Spree*.

These aren't your run-of-the-mill wieners. Frank said they partnered with The Piggery, a family-owned butcher shop in Ithaca in 2015, to create their original frank, a hot dog free of nitrates, preservatives, and artificial ingredients. Other specialty links are sourced from boutique meat shops throughout America. But it's not just the dogs. Practically everything that these guys do is from scratch. I'm told they make 5 gallons of mayo from scratch every day for the sauces for their French fries. "I don't know a lot of people going to that extreme for 'junk' food," Buffalo food writer Christa Glennie Seychew told me.

You choose your link: original (local New York pork and beef), classic (100 percent grass-fed beef), or vegetarian (lentil, brown rice, and vegetables). Then pick your style: standard (ketchup, mustard, onion, and pickle), "Holy Moly" (guacamole, sriracha, fried jalapenos, and cilantro), and chili dog (all-beef chili, mustard, onion). Or go with their homage to former *New York Times* restaurant critic and current Op-Ed writer Frank Bruni (spicy mustard and sauerkraut). You can also add jalapeños, cheddar, and cilantro. Or order from one of the six special dogs (including a "Modern Chicago" dog and a riff on a banh mi), all named with a wink and topped with ingredients like onion crunch and blueberry barbecue sauce.

#1 Ted's Hot Dogs (Multiple Locations)

2312 Sheridan Drive, Tonawanda, 14150
716-834-6287 | tedshotdogs.com
Daily 10:30 AM–11 PM

Everything at Ted's is cooked to order in front of you while you listen to the snap and crackle of the dogs over the coals. And that time it takes to cook your dog affords a moment to consider Ted's saying, "Everything tastes better cooked over charcoal," and wonder: How much longer does it really take to charcoal-grill than it does to make the fast food churned out by America's most famous chains? And why would you go anywhere else for a hot dog or any fast food joint if you had Ted's nearby?

Dogs come regular, foot-long, all-beef jumbo, and "kid's" (a skinless dog). You can also order from the "Awesome Dogs" section, where they're topped with bacon and cheese, bacon and mac and cheese, chili and cheese, and mac and cheese and onion rings. There are grilled chicken sandwiches, a "sea dog" (fish fry on a bun), salads, and thin burgers, which come on fluffy, fresh buns and taste like a summer cookout or an idealized McDonald's burger (maybe the way those used

to taste). But Ted's keeps things pretty wiener-centric, which is good.

The order: Charcoal-grilled dog with everything. That means minced onions, neon yellow mustard, and Ted's secret hot sauce. The Sahlen's dogs are blackened and poked, coddled and turned until they're browned in most places. The bun is fresh, the dog is moist inside but almost boudin-like, and there's the tang of that mildly hot sauce. And if you're looking to do the pro-move, do like many on line ahead of you and ask for your dogs to be burned. As one older gentleman noted one winter day. "What's the point

in having them charcoal-grilled if you can't taste the charcoal?" Sounds like a refrain a few other businesses should listen to.

Who's Top Dog?

A hot dog quest around Buffalo, especially one during the summer when the seasonal stands are open, is a tour of outdoor eating accompanied by all the magic of summer months: fireflies, picnic tables by the water, milkshakes, and lots of onion rings and fries. If you're not sure you're on board with this ranking, go ahead, find some other wieners.

Connor's Hot Dog Stand (Seasonal), Angola, 8905 Lake Shore Road, 716-549-1257

George's Hot Dogs (Seasonal), Hamburg, 5808 Herman Hill Road, 716-648-0320

Lucky's Texas Red Hots, Kaisertown, 1903 Clinton Street, 716-826-6873

Mississippi Mudds (Seasonal), Tonawanda, 313 Niagara Street, 716-694-0787

Old Man River (Seasonal), 375 Niagara Street, Tonawanda, 716-693-5558

Red Top Hot Dogs (Seasonal), Hamburg, 3360 Big Tree Road, 716-627-5163

Sullivan's Hot Dogs (Seasonal), Niagara Falls, 501 Cayuga Drive, 716-236-4119

The Silo (Seasonal), Lewiston, 115 N Water Street, 716-754-9680

Zorba's Texas Hots, Depew, 5 Lee Street, 716-685-4948

CHAPTER SIX

SUB-CULTURE

Buffalo's Best Sandwiches

What to Call a Sandwich in Buffalo

Beef on weck *is* Buffalo's most iconic sandwich. You could also argue it's the best. But it *would* be an argument—the city has *at least* four and maybe seven other sandwiches that join its roster of stalwarts. Buffalonians know these sandwiches so well that many of the folks I talked with don't even seem to ask where they came from and how they started. They just . . . are. And while perhaps they wouldn't single them out this way, I'd argue there's a holy sextet of Buffalo sandwiches and subs: fried bologna, steak or chicken "in the grass," chicken fingers, stingers, cheeseburger (cheeseburger subs, not straight-up cheeseburgers), and the royal. At least two of them are uniquely Buffalo sandwiches.

I say "sandwiches and subs" but Buffalo's sandwich menus get more complicated, even to its food experts and restaurateurs. America's foodies and food media enjoy the occasional debate about whether hot dogs, burgers, wraps, and tacos are "sandwiches," but wherever you fall with those (my take: no, eh, no, and no), when it comes to the long split rolls we love to stuff with combinations of meats and cheese, we typically keep to the regional terms we grew up calling them by, be that blimpie, grinder, torpedo, wedge, Garibaldi, zeppelin, bomber, sub, hoagie, hero, spuckie, or spiedie.

Not Buffalo. The 716 is not content with having just one classification of sub. Sure, you can see dividing menus between hot and cold subs (which they often do). But in Buffalo, you'll see subs, hoagies, bombers, and sandwiches listed separately, and sometimes three out of four on the same menu!

Take a look at some of Buffalo's beloved sandwich shops and it gets dizzying. Café 59 serves sandwiches and bombers. John & Mary's separates their menu into subs and hoagies. Shy's Subs serves hot and cold subs, and sandwiches (where they list burgers). Joe's Deli serves "hot" and "cold sandwiches" under which you can find sandwiches made with both sliced bread *and* split rolls. Lovejoy just goes with hot and cold subs. Jim's serves hoagies, hot subs, and cold subs (chicken finger subs get their own category) and will let you choose whether their "famous hoagies" are made on 8-inch bomber rolls or 12-inch sub rolls! You just may get punched for asking at The Pink, where they're just bologna and steak sandwiches (even though the steak sandwich is served on a short sub roll). Thankfully, Viola's just serves subs, which is a relief considering it calls itself a "Submarine House."

And that's just a sampling.

Listen, most of us can agree on Merriam-Webster's definition that a sandwich is two or more slices of bread or a split roll having a filling in between. We can agree to disagree about hot dogs and hamburgers being sandwiches. We can even accept and understand *states* like New Jersey, where in different parts of the *state*, different terms are used for the same thing. But what on earth is the difference between a sub, a hoagie, and a bomber in the same *city*?

"When the meat is chopped up and grilled and served in a tinfoil shell, in my mind that's hoagie status," Buffalo pizzeria expert SexySlices told me. "Like a 'steak sub' qualifies as a hoagie. Also, subs come on full-length Costanzo's rolls. I feel like hoagies are shorter and on a different roll."

Mister Pizza has a "Subs and Hoagies" section on their menu divided into hot subs, cold subs, hoagies, and bombers. And before you get excited about seeing "all hoagies are served on eight-inch rolls—they say the same thing about bombers. "It's like pornography," *Buffalo Eats'* Donnie Burtless told me. "I don't know if I can explain a hoagie but I know it if I see it."

What about straight-up sandwich makers? "A hoagie is a hot sub," one of the John & Mary's locations offers, then confusing the matter further by lobbing this culinary grenade, "(like a bomber)."

Gene Mongan, co-owner of John's Pizza & Subs, credited for inventing Buffalo's chicken finger sub, explains, "Our understanding is that a hoagie has no lettuce and tomato, *and* that a hoagie has fried onions, mushrooms, and peppers, usually with steak, and in our case steak or sausage."

Guy Macon, Jim's SteakOut's Director of Operations agreed that the hoagie-sub-grinder-hero debate is usually more of a regional thing, then explained, "For us, the difference is that we call any chopped meat item a hoagie and flat items subs. Also, we cut the hinge on the roll for subs and leave the hinge intact on the hoagie."

Whatever they're called, wherever you go while hitting up Buffalo's most storied sandwich spots…they're really good subs, er, hoagies… forget it. They're really good.

"On A Fresh Costanzo's Roll"

Those are words seen on countless menus in Buffalo. Costanzo's isn't the only bakery that Buffalo has ever been in love with. There were more wholesale bakeries years ago, including the Burczynski Bakery (which supplied the city for 80 years before closing in 1983), and companies like Di Camillo Bakery in Niagara Falls still provide Buffalo with old-school Italian bread. But these days, if you're eating a great

hamburger, hot dog, sandwich, sub, or even beef on weck (restaurants "weck" Costanzo's kaiser rolls) in the Nickel City, it's likely Costanzo's made 'em. I'd guess after talking with restaurants and food experts that the number is somewhere around 70 percent.

Along with their hard rolls, kaiser rolls, dinner rolls (used for sliders), and hot dog rolls, Costanzo's makes some 50 roll variations, including the 12-inch sub rolls, 8-inch sub rolls, and hoagie rolls that many of the city's great sandwich shops use. Local sub shop John & Mary's claims that it was its founder, John Guida, who asked Angelo Constanzo to make his rolls thinner and 12 inches long, calling them "submarines." *Bon Appétit* points to the OED's first printed record of "submarine sandwich" in a 1940 phone book for a restaurant in Wilmington, Delaware, which torpedos (nyuk, nyuk) the idea he may have originated the term, but Guida could have been responsible for the bread length! Legends aside, how did Costanzo's get started?

According to the company, Costanzo's has been one of the city's bakeries of choice since 1933. Its founder, Angelo Costanzo, started in a small bakery near the Niagara River called Costanzo's Bread. It was from that shop that Angelo "delivered Italian breads to mom-and-pop grocery stores throughout Buffalo." From there to supermarkets, and in the '70s, they focused on servicing restaurants, pizzerias, and sub shops. Angelo Jr. and his brother took over the bakery in 1977, and moved into a new location, then Angelo groomed *his* sons to take over in 2000.

And why is Costanzo's so good?

"That's a bakery that runs 24 hours a day,"

John's co-owner Gene Mongan said. He noted that John's has been using the rolls for 44 years. "They come to us in the morning, to our back door in a poly bag. Sometimes they're so warm they couldn't put them in the poly. They're baked that morning, and you're eating them that afternoon. That makes a very big difference."

Okay, so freshness. But it isn't just that.

"It's the standard in this town for rolls when you're doing sandwiches," The Pink's bartender Rob Fatta said. "Some places are making their own artisan rolls. Those are good too, but day in, day out, Costanzo's. If it's toasted right on the outside, it's nice. It's got that little bit of crunch to it then."

Costanzo's rolls are also kind of squishy, in a good way. They're very soft and airy, and while they have good flavor, that squishiness means the bread condenses, and in the same way that as a kid, you may have torn off the crusts of your favorite white bread and balled the center up to enjoy, sweet and thick, you get that effect; but as the vehicle for all the great ingredients Buffalo's restaurants stack between the rolls. They also make for great scarpetta. You can mop up lots of great sauce with this bread.

You can press 'em, toast 'em, griddle 'em, and fill 'em, and they present a fresh, slightly-sweet and airy canvas. Just as there's something to be said for a crusty baguette, there's something to be said about squish factor. And while you've got to give credit to the places making the sandwiches, similarly, they have to know that there's some truth to the company's slogan, "The roll makes the sandwich when Costanzo's makes the roll."

Not everyone in Buffalo knows this, but Costanzo's also operates a sandwich shop. And if you're all about the bread, well, it doesn't get any fresher.

Costanzo's Sandwich Shop

30 Innsbruck Drive, Cheektowaga, 14227
716-656-9093, ext. 2 | costanzosbakery.com
Mon–Fri 6:30 AM–6:30 PM, Sat–Sun 6:30 AM–3 PM

The Holy Sextet

Remove the tuna sandwiches, turkey clubs, and occasional Parms (only really ubiquitous in Buffalo at pizzerias) from most menus, and you could argue that many of the sandwiches listed on the city's top joints become a pretty unique collection not seen in other cities. Sure, you can find places in cities beyond Philadelphia that do Philly cheesesteaks, but those shops usually *specialize* in them. In Buffalo, you'll find cheesesteaks next to Pittsburgh-Primanti–style sandwiches (with the fries *on* them) and fish fillets, with those next to sandwiches topped with sausages, meatballs, souvlaki, and for lack of another term, what we'll go on to call the holy sextet: fried bologna, steak in the grass, the stinger, the chicken finger sub, the cheeseburger sub, and the royal. This isn't to say there *aren't* other Buffalo sandwich archetypes, just that these are essentials.

I'm a man with a big appetite, and I ate my way through the first four, but I'll cop to having run out of room to explore the nuances of the last two, which while they should be considered part of the canon, seem, perhaps, to be less heralded players. Still, the cheeseburger sub is typically a two-patty affair, always topped with cheese, lettuce, and tomato, sometimes onions and the house secret sauce. As for the royal, before you go channeling your inner Jules Winnfield from *Pulp Fiction*, this isn't a Quarter Pounder in France, but a hot Italian sausage patty topped with capicola and melted provolone.

Let's dig into the essentials.

My Bologna Has a First Name, It's BUF-F-A-L-O

Bologna. It's cheap, accessible, has a long shelf-life, and is frequently associated with German immigration. Is it any surprise then with its blue-collar dynamic and strong German and Polish communities, that Buffalo developed a strong bologna tradition? And while yes, it has a rep as prison food and wears the stink of bad school lunches, it's actually undergone a resurgence, garnering attention from chefs like David Chang of New York City–based Momofuku, who have rediscovered its potential and old-school appeal. If you've had it thick and hot, you know the indulgent greatness it can be. If you haven't, you poor, poor thing, read on.

It's nice that bologna is doing its best to fight the Dangerfield ("I don't get no respect"), but in Buffalo, it never went anywhere. You'll find it on the menu at most sandwich shops and pizzerias (which essentially double as some of Buffalo's best sandwicheries). Sure, cold with cheese, lettuce, and tomato, but usually also hot, fried in fact, topped with sautéed or grilled onions and/or peppers and melted white American cheese (ask why white, and folks will tell you it's just . . . better, and melty-er). Better yet, go double cheese (what's that noise Homer Simp-

son makes when he sees great food? *Graaa*). A few half-inch thick slices, griddled on a flat top where the surface gets caramelized and the edges get crispy, or charred on the grill, draped with melted cheese and soft, sweet onions tucked into a soft, squishy roll? The bologna gets soft and warm inside and melts into the cheese—sweet and salty . . . when done properly, the way many places do around Buffalo, it's a transformational sandwich.

Buffalo's Best Bologna Sandwiches

With so many places doing great fried bologna, where to go for the best? There are three top-tier spots most would agree on (even chef James Roberts, who makes one of the best, pointed to one of the others on this list), but experts added a few more for good measure (or a bologna quest). "Fried bologna is as Buffalo Polish as you can get and Wiechec's is the go-to for old-school Polish Buffalo," Donnie Burtless of *Buffalo Eats* told me. Then there's Pete &

Toutant's late-night bologna sandwich is an upscale version whose flavor and texture is hauntingly good.

Paul's, which SexySlices noted, comes in a pita pocket with peppers and onions, making it pretty unique in town.

Here are three places where you're guaranteed to find Buffalo bologna royalty.

#3 Sophia's Restaurant

749 Military Road, Black Rock, 14216 | 716-447-9661
Tue–Sat 7 AM–3 PM, Sun 7 AM–2 PM, Closed Mon

In a city where you can find a beef on weck stacked nearly a half a foot high (Vizzi's), it would seem only right for there to be a bologna equivalent. At Sophia's, there are usually about five quarter-inch slices of bologna stacked inside their fresh, seeded roll. No surprise then that Guy Fieri of *Diners, Drive-Ins and Dives* found it of note when he visited. But it's not just the height that's eye-catching. Christa Glennie Seychew singled out Sophia's because of its awesome char, sweet onions, and the thick slathering of hot mustard.

#2 The Old Pink

223 Allen Street, Allentown, 14201 | 716-884-4338
Daily 11 AM–4 PM

The steak is more famous, but the grilled bologna at The Pink is epic in its own right. "We don't use the local bologna," bartender Rob Fatta says. "Not for any specific reason other than just that our purveyor sends us bologna from their people. Sometimes it's Kretschmar, and sometimes it might even be a German one."

Three half-inch thick slices of bologna are tossed on the same grill behind the bar with the steaks, and cooked until each side is covered with a thin char. Then they get stacked, covered with about three-quarters of an inch of peppers and onions, and dressed with three slices of provolone. The whole thing gets pressed a little, and the barely-toasted kaiser roll gets a little condensed, then sliced in half and served in a little red basket soon destined to be empty. Don't choose. Steak for dinner. Bologna for dessert.

#1 Toutant

437 Ellicott Street, Downtown, 14203 | 716-342-2901
toutantbuffalo.com | Thu 5 PM–12 AM,
Fri–Sat 5 PM–2 AM, Sun Brunch 11:30 AM–2:30 PM,
Sun 5 PM–12 AM, Closed Tues–Wed

Chef James Roberts is the undisputed king of Buffalo bologna, but you'll never *actually* see it *on* the menu. It's a feature of the restaurant's late-night lineup that rotates in and out of the spot at the bottom of the menu, labeled "The One." They use the bread they bake for their burger, and spend two days making the bologna, a process the chef explains in the accompanying interview. There are two three-quarter inch thick slices of bologna covered with sautéed onions that have been marinated in Genesee and at least three slices of gooey, melty white American cheese. It doesn't get more Buffalo than that. It's one of the best sandwiches I've ever had and should be as sought after as any of the late-night "secret" burgers that regularly get national attention. And in the event that "The One" isn't bologna, order it anyway. The man's a genius.

Full of Bologna: Fried Bologna

The late-night menu at Toutant was inspired by Manhattan chefs' favorite longtime post-dinner shift spot Blue Ribbon Brasserie in the West Village, where you can order from an extended menu until 4 AM. From the moment chef and owner James Roberts walked in one night at 3 AM, and had a full-service meal complete with cocktails, hors d'oeuvres, wine, salad, and appetizers, he knew that one day when he had his own place, he'd do something similar.

So at Toutant, which is open until 2 AM on Friday and Saturday, along with cracklings, corn dogs, popcorn shrimp, and a boneless fried chicken basket (they went boneless because before that the chef said, "at the end of the night, there'd be chicken bones everywhere"), at the bottom of the menu there's always the heading, "The One," with the explanation, "This is it! Daily late-night feature." And according to Roberts, that usually means one thing, "Bologna's our bae, for sure. If we're actually taking it off to go to something else, it better be a real humdinger."

Where'd you learn how to make a homemade bologna this amazing?

I was working with Craig Deihl in Charleston, South Carolina, who had been with a restaurant called Cypress for a long time as a young chef. They were doing a lot of charcuterie. He's regarded as one of the most proficient charcuterie masters in America, and he's got some interesting techniques for cold temperature-aging meats. We were talking about how much we love Leberkäse and olive loaf, then how much we love bologna. He gave me his formula for country bologna and I got to tinkering with it while I was working at Park Country Club here in Buffalo.

You started making it at a *country club*?

I started making it for the guys in the members' locker room. After golf, these guys would come in, and I'd serve them this thick-cut, all-beef bologna sandwich. It blew their minds. Country club life is about tenderloin, lobster tail, caviar, and fresh fish, and here are these guys in the locker room annihilating bologna sandwiches! Word got out and they asked me to put it on the menu. At one point, I roasted the whole bologna log and had it out there on a carving station in the dining room of the country club. It was funny, but deep down, I knew it was just delicious.

What goes into it?

Depending on the size of the batch, there might be half a brisket, a full top round, a quarter of the ribeye, the front end of the chuck, and the short rib. We find a good ratio of marbling. It's probably 70/30. Maybe 60/40. It's not hamburger lean, but it's pretty lean. We mix it with a spice blend that's got some coriander, curing salt, white pepper, a lot of brown sugar, some garlic, and a little bit of mace to give it that bologna flavor.

How's it made?

We grind it a couple times with a coarse grind and stuff it—the double grind gives it a little bit of emulsification. It's a traditional bologna collagen casing that's basically five inches in diameter. Then we fill it with 7 or 8 pounds, twist it up, cure it, and smoke it in the hot smoker over oak and hickory for five or six hours at 225°F, and ice it overnight. It's a two-day process and about an 8-pound log.

Steak (or Chicken) "In The Grass"

There's very little easily discoverable documentation of the tradition around something as ubiquitous as both steak and chicken in the grass subs that are on menus at pizzerias and sandwich shops in Buffalo. The story you will hear goes something like this. Back in the day—we're talking early twentieth century through maybe the '70s—foraging for their key ingredient was not an uncommon sight. "You used to see it," former *Buffalo News* restaurant critic Janice Okun told me, "but not anymore. You never see it anymore. These old guys on the side of the road in the spring digging up dandelions."

Side of the road, railroad tracks—locations vary. But the foraged dandelions were cleaned, boiled, and sautéed in olive oil with garlic, maybe some onions and crushed red pepper flakes, then served with steak. It's hard to imagine that those who could afford steak would be foraging for dandelions, but it's unclear which cut was traditionally used (or if there even was just one). Maybe it started as a marginal cut that was supplemented by free greens.

Eating sautéed dandelion greens *is* an Italian (and Greek) tradition. One of the most popular Italian cookbooks, *The Silver Spoon*, notes it's a dish eaten especially in southern Italy, and that while it doesn't have great nutritional properties, "thanks to the bitter substances it contains it acts as a diuretic and is thought to help purify the system, protect the liver, and act as a tonic." In addition to suggesting they be picked young, the book also advises, ironically, that the dandelion greens should be sourced, "well away from the roadside." So much for that!

"At Buffalo's Italian festival, you'll see a lot of people eating actual dandelions, but really only then," Christa Glennie Seychew explains. "People eat that stuff for reminiscent purposes.

It's a very twice-a-year thing. It's not on your regular menu."

The bitterness is an acquired taste, so it's not surprising that as the foragers have disappeared, the traditional dandelion greens have turned into spinach. Or that given the higher cost of steak, that chicken became an accompaniment somewhere along the way. But if you do get the chance to taste one, there's a delicious argument to be made for the real thing. The new way, using spinach, really is nothing like the old dish. One has a pronounced bitterness that's softened a bit by cooking, but still strong enough to create a contrast that almost seems to draw out the sweetness and juiciness of the steak, and the other's . . . well, just spinach.

Three Places You'll Actually *Want* to Get "In The Weeds"

Spinach, steak (or chicken and even sometimes sausage), and cheese—those are the three major components of steak in the grass. From there, the variations. Often, the steak is chopped. Less frequently, you get a grilled filet. Sometimes you get onions, sometimes the roll gets turned into garlic bread. The cheese? It can vary—mozzarella at some places, provolone at others. Sometimes, the ingredients are listed and the "in the grass" gets left by the side of the road.

Those who would make the case that Molinaro's in Lockport makes one of Buffalo's best pies, will also point to the specialty section of the "sottomarino" menu for the city's best steak in the grass. They actually just say, "In the Grass" and give you the option of steak, chicken, or sausage, which they pile onto garlic toast with spinach, onions, and provolone.

#3 Mike's Subs

2862 Delaware Avenue, Kenmore, 14217

716-877-6000 | mikes-subs.com

Sun–Thu 8 AM–12 AM, Fri–Sat 8 AM–1 AM

Mike's has been a Delaware Avenue institution in Kenmore since about 1956. It was started by Mike Davis and passed on to a Kenmore policeman in the late '60s before being sold to the current owners in 1981. It's gone through name changes—Mike's Submarines to Hoagie Brothers, then back to Mike's Subs in 1994. And the shop's menu has been an evolution, starting with just cold-cut subs dressed with Mike's special oil (no mayo, no toaster) and dramatically expanding its menu in 1984 with the addition of a grill and a fryer. That all being said, what's important to know is that locals, and by that I mean Kenmore residents, are adamant about the superiority of its steak and spinach sub, made with fresh spinach, garlic, thin-cut, chopped sirloin, onions, mushrooms, and peppers topped with melted provolone.

#2 Jim's SteakOut (Multiple Locations)

194 Allen Street, Allentown, 14201 | 716-886-2222

jimssteakout.com | Mon–Thu 10:30 AM–5 AM,

Fri–Sat 10:30 AM–6 AM

One way or another, you're going to Jim's Steak-Out. You just *have* to (preferably *after* several drinks at The Pink across the street after already eating one of their sandwiches). Otherwise you're not doing Buffalo right. Jim's started in 1981, and has gone on to become a successful local chain that makes sandwiches in 4-inch, 6-inch, 8-inch, and 12-inch lengths. If that kind of sandwich specification doesn't indicate the passion for subs in Buffalo, doubtless nothing will.

The Steak in the Grass shouldn't be the *only* sub you have at Jim's. If you're only going to have one, it should probably be the Stinger (more, momentarily) or the pizza steak hero (steak and pepperoni chopped on the grill, mixed with marinara, and topped with mozzarella and grated Parmesan), but it does do one of the most well-regarded versions of steak in the grass. Steak is chopped on the grill and topped with melted provolone, sautéed spinach, and Jim's secret sauce. It isn't bitter, but it's tasty.

Jim Is a Real Guy from the West Side of Buffalo

There are 11 locations of Jim's SteakOut around Buffalo, but there's not a ton written about how the local chain got started. Jim's current director of operations, Macon, shared this history:

"Back in the late '70's, James Incorvaia was working various jobs in and out of the restaurant business. He was intrigued with the Philly cheesesteak which was being introduced at a local restaurant and wanted to bring it to Elmwood Village. Before he would open his first restaurant, Jim wanted to develop his own steak sauce. It was long process of trial and error that took place in his West Side apartment kitchen. His wife was slightly irritated because for weeks on end, he used every glass container in the apartment, constantly changing and improving the sauce until he was satisfied.

"In 1981, he was ready to open the first Jim's SteakOut at 938 Elmwood Avenue between Delavan and Bidwell. He focused on serving all the night owls on Elmwood with high-quality food, his new steak sauce, the unheard-of chicken finger sub, and good service. His pregnant wife worked the day shift and he took the nights. Jim started the business with very little and worked tirelessly to build his restaurant.

"He grew that store in a short time to 10-plus very dedicated and hard-working employees. Some of the original employees were Marc Coppola, who went on to be a member of the New York State Senate, Rudy Alloy Jr. (owner of Just Pizza), and Marco Scorintino of Marcos Deli's and the spokesperson for Galbani. Dave Muscoreil began working for Jim several months after opening the first restaurant. He had the same drive for quality food and good service and was instrumental in expanding Jim's SteakOut. Dave is still with Jim and operates the locations on Chippewa Street and Main Street.

"On Sundays after Bills games when the team would visit the next door No Name Bar, it was common to have Bruce Smith or Jim Kelly come in. One night after a Jim Kelly golf tournament he had Jim Kelly, Dan Marino, and John Elway all in the store at the same time.

"Jim is no longer working behind the counter but he is involved in the business and says that as long as his name is on the building, the best ingredients are used and employees make the hoagies the way he did over 35 years ago.

"Jim is very proud to say that Jim's SteakOut was born in Buffalo and remains a Buffalo run business."

#1 Dandelions Restaurant

1340 N Forest Road, Williamsville, 14221

716-688-0203 | Mon–Thu 11 AM–1 AM,

Fri–Sat 11 AM–3 AM, Sun 12 PM–10 PM

Dandelions Restaurant is a pretty nondescript roadside tavern and restaurant with bold block green letters spelling out the name. But inside, the horseshoe bar has the homey feeling of a place that's been around since 1982, the year it was founded. The steak in the grass here could not possibly be more well-seasoned. The steak is fabulously juicy and topped with a portion of Parmesan-dusted mildly bitter dandelion greens about half the thickness of the steak. It's all served on a toasted hamburger roll that's somehow both hard and squishy. This is one of those perfect examples of dishes where all you need are the basic ingredients, salt, and pepper. It could very well be one of Buffalo's most underrated sandwiches.

Chicken Finger Subs

There are other places across America with chicken finger sandwich tradition. Anyone who has rooted for the Scarlet Knights will quickly point to the "fat sandwiches" served on Rutgers' College Avenue Campus by its famous grease trucks.

The original fat sandwich invented in 1979, the Fat Cat, featured a double cheeseburger, French fries, and fixings. While two of the three other early fat sandwiches contained chicken, the Fat Sam (a cheesesteak and chicken combo) gets discounted because the cutlet was grilled. And the Fat Moon, whose toppings beyond chicken fingers—bacon, eggs, fries, and fixings— are nothing like a Buffalo chicken finger sub, doesn't get the Buffalo hot sauce and blue cheese treatment, and seems likely to have originated at least a few years after Buffalo's. Fat Darrell fans know his trademarked chicken finger sub with mozzarella sticks and fries was invented much later (in 1997).

If we're going to play a game of Darwin's finches with chicken fingers (Darwin's fingers? finchers?), Robert Baker, the inventor of the nugget might just as easily be Johnny Appleseed. No, Buffalo seems to have just as much if not more likelihood of having invented the genre, and in the 716, "chicken finger sub"

means pretty much the same thing to everyone: a fried finger sub with a very specific, set list of ingredients. You could argue it's a much more well-established sandwich, one that through fast-food chains, whether they want to call them the Buffalo Ranch McChicken or the Crispy Buffalo Chicken Melt (Burger King), has been eaten coast to coast for years.

Most chicken fingers are somewhat rounded in shape and not uniformly shaped or sized, making them far from the ideal sandwich ingredient from the POV of stacking and protein distribution. (To say nothing of the merits of frozen breaded tenders from a bag.) Sure, shredded lettuce fills into the space left for it, but it and blue cheese dressing contribute more messiness, and nothing to stabilize the layering for onions and tomatoes. The thin layer of cheese helps if it's melted, but that doesn't always happen. In short, everything about this sandwich *shouldn't* be. And yet, if the cheese is layered on heavy, the whole thing is smushed together a bit, and it's not put down once picked up . . . the crunch of the fried chicken coating, the hot tang of the sauce, that blue funk and the crispness of iceberg, all come together to create something really good that those folks who built the food pyramid would *not* be happy you're eating.

The Chicken Finger Sub Was Born at John's Pizza & Subs. You Are Welcome.

"The year was 1983. I came to work at John's Pizza & Subs, I took off my Members Only jacket and turned on the Ms. Pac-Man machine. It was a heady time. Darth Vader was Luke's father, my girlfriend had just broken up with me. ("Like, oh my God, I just need my space!") But I was doing what I do best: cooking. And then, inspiration. Like a lightning bolt hitting a clock tower. Chicken

> "I got involved with the guys at John's Pizza & Subs, and they were serving chicken planks shaken in hot sauce with blue cheese on the side, and I actually, at the time, I thought it was kind of weird, like, where's the coleslaw? And, it turned out to just be a really, really, really popular item, chicken fingers, shaken in hot sauce, medium, mild, or barbecue, just like chicken wings. And so we just started putting that on sub rolls, with blue cheese, and hot sauce." —Gene Mongan

fingers, Costanzo's roll, John's hot sauce, lettuce, tomato, blue cheese dressing: the chicken finger sub was born at John's Pizza & Subs. You are welcome."

At least, that's the stylized radio commercial version of the story.

John's Pizza & Subs was founded in 1977 by John Schmitter who operated it through 1982. That's when a group of five guys, Gene Mongan, Kurt Raepple, Mark Raepple, Jay Raepple, and Paul Miller took it over. When I called to talk with Gene, he said he was wearing an apron and making a chicken finger sub.

Mongan said that the invention of the sandwich was an evolution. He first started playing around with it as a teenager in high school, while working at a pizzeria in Grand Island called St. Angelo's, where they were called "chicken planks," served with coleslaw and French fries, and used as a substitute for fish fry. Bored with having eaten all the subs on the menu, he said he and a few other workers started making chicken Parmesan and other subs in 1977, just for themselves to eat, none of which became menu items there.

In 1982, within the first year of operating John's, they put it "on the menu," which meant writing up the sandwich on a paper plate taped near the order window. "People would come up and be like, 'What's the chicken finger sub?' and we would explain it to them, but usually by the time we were done explaining, they'd have already ordered it."

Gene and his partner Kurt (Mark, Jay, and Paul are retired) said that they've sold millions of chicken finger subs and that at one point, they calculated the sandwich made up 10 percent of sales. Now, every pizzeria in Buffalo makes a chicken finger sub. You can also find them nearby in Rochester, and Erie, Pennsylvania. Then in 1997, they turned their famous sub into a pizza too.

Mongan and Kurt Raepple guard John's reputation as the originators of the chicken finger sub carefully. There have been those from time to time who make claims, some serious, others that seem intended just to drum up business temporarily.

The sandwich even makes it into the Jim's SteakOut origin story though without outright claiming to have invented it. "In 1981, he [Jim] was ready to open the first Jim's SteakOut at 938 Elmwood Avenue between Delavan and Bidwell," said its director of operations, Guy Macon. "He focused on serving all the night owls on Elmwood with high-quality food, his new steak sauce, the unheard-of chicken finger sub, and good service."

"I have all the proof I ever need to disprove all other claims," Kurt told me.

Mongan and Raepple are both fairly humble about the two creations you could argue they were responsible for rippling across America's culinary landscape. "Just another day at the job, I guess," Mongan said, laughing. "It's funny. I was going to be a certified executive chef and I ended up in the pizza business. I went to the CIA in Poughkeepsie. I was a dropout."

But Mongan said he's happy as a businessman and glad he *didn't* become a certified chef, adding, "Blue cheese and hot sauce, put those two things together—you can make a cake and put frosting on it, and people would eat it. It's just a great combination."

Best Chicken Finger Subs? Look No Feather . . .

No question: a true chicken finger sub pilgrimage should take you to John's. But if you dig this sandwich, you really shouldn't end the quest there. Given how much the sub has traveled around town and the passion for it that people have, it should be no surprise that in the years since 1982, there have been riffs that have become destination-worthy in their own right.

#3 John's Pizza & Subs (Multiple Locations)

1436 Niagara Falls Boulevard, Tonawanda, 14150

716-832-4343 | johnspizzaandsubs.com

Mon–Thu 10 AM–10:30 PM, Fri 10 AM–12 AM,

Sat 11 AM–12 AM, Sun 11 AM–10:30 PM

The chicken finger sub at John's is made with fried Tyson's chicken shaken in Frank's Red-Hot Sauce then stacked with lettuce, tomato, and Sorrento provolone, and smothered with Kraft's extra heavy blue cheese. It's all layered inside a Costanzo's roll, which John's has used for 44 years. This chicken finger sub can veer toward the taller end of the spectrum, a daring tactic considering the average structural integrity of a sandwich like this. But they seem to compensate by using pretty flat chicken fingers.

#2 Café 59

62 Allen Street, Allentown, 14202 | 716-883-1880

cafe59.com | Mon–Wed 11 AM–10 PM,

Thu 11 AM–11 PM, Fri–Sat 11 AM–12 AM,

Sun 11 AM–8 PM

The rest of the menu features some fancier fare—a ratatouille tart, salmon Niçoise, Puerto Rican vegetable stew—but there's still that distinctive Buffalo flare. It's just all a little more from scratch, which is a nice take on the sub. There are field greens instead of shredded lettuce and instead of going the conventional Costanzo's roll route, they use a sesame seed roll. *Buffalo News* food editor Andrew Galarneau notes that these chicken tenders are crumbed and fried to order. They're also wide and thin, which makes for great distribution through every bite, and they're absolutely saturated (but still crispy) with hot sauce and drenched with homemade blue cheese dressing. And if that all sounds a bit too indulgent, hey, they do a salad version with romaine, crumbled blue cheese, carrots, celery, and onions. Because nothing says healthy like a salad with chicken fingers!

#1 Lovejoy Pizza

1244 E. Lovejoy Street, Buffalo, 14206

716-891-9233 | lovejoypizza.com | Mon–Thu 11 AM–10 PM, Fri–Sat 11 AM–10:30 PM, Sun 3 PM–9:30 PM (open at noon during Bills' season)

900 Main Street, Buffalo, 14202 | 716-883-2323

Mon–Thu 11 AM–9:30 PM, Fri–Sat 11 AM–10 PM, Sun 12 PM–9 PM

It should be no surprise that any dish or sub made with chicken has also long since been made into a sub made with fried chicken fingers. So you'll see subs like "The Cordon Blue" where chicken fingers are paired with ham, Swiss, and American cheese, or the Chicken Finger Club with bacon. But it's the addition of about a dozen sliced stuffed hot pepper medallions and a very generous layer of baked mozzarella along with the traditional shredded lettuce and tomato that makes this souped-up version of the chicken finger sub something really special. Andrew Galarneau called it "a gooey, spicy chicken Alfredo effect" when including it among Buffalo's hot sub stars. Need we say more?

The Stinger

Let's get two things out of the way. First, this has nothing to do with honey and chili pizza. It's steak + chicken fingers + sub = the stinger sub ("Ohhh," wink). As in a sub topped with steak and chicken fingers (usually with the choice of mild, medium, or hot sauce, which allows the name to pun) and cheese, then depending on the place, also lettuce, tomato, and sometimes blue cheese dressing. Second, this is a great post-soak sandwich, but even those of us who aspire to being in shape can agree, that it's not just the booze talking, it's a really tasty treat even for the sober.

Stinger subs are everywhere on sandwich menus in Buffalo, though sometimes listed as just "Steak and chicken finger." They've become wraps, tacos, fries, and pizzas. But who invented them? And if trying to determine the origins of something that sounds like junk food seems ridiculous, just stop and consider 1) that for all the energy put behind trying to determine the inventor of a dish like Marea's famous bone marrow and octopus in Manhattan, that dish, for all its glory, has been mimicked far fewer times than the stinger, 2) the big business that wings has become, and 3) one other equation. After all, Buffalo has seen this kind of thing time and again: creativity + simple food = iconic eats copied endlessly.

For all the menus this sandwich is on *in* the Buffalo-Niagara area, there's very little easy to find that seems to have been written about its origins. As far as Buffalo's local publications go, online archives for *ArtVoice*, *Buffalo Spree*, and the *Buffalo News* turn up barely any mention. And area food lovers that I spoke with were largely at a loss to explain where they thought it started.

If you believe self-promotion, word-of-mouth, and a handful of online articles, there are two likely possibilities (neither of which obliged me by going on the record). First, the national food media discovered the stinger in 2011, when the website *Endless Simmer* collected a follow-up list of "America's Top 10 *New* Sandwiches" (emphasis mine) for the Huffington Post, singling out the version at Jim's SteakOut.

Jim's has been happy to run with the acclaim, calling itself the "Home of the Stinger" and the sandwich a "National award-winning sub." And God bless. Why shouldn't they? But did they actually invent it? They don't use the "i" word, and as far as it's possible to tell, while there are drinks, missiles, epoxies, and machine parts with the stinger name nobody has trademarked a *sandwich* of that name with the United States Patent and Trademark Office.

The other possibility? An article by the *Ithaca Voice*, a free online-only news site, reported on its possible origin in Tonawanda on the outskirts of Buffalo as part of trying to establish who invented a sandwich at a local sub shop that had become intensely popular 150 miles east with students at Ithaca College. The originator? Colosso Taco, the site says, founded in the 1960s. Tracy Bennettt, owner of Colosso since 1999, credited its founder: "It was at Colosso Taco that founder Dwight Jeeves invented the stinger sandwich, which consists of chicken tenders, steak, lettuce, tomatoes, and onions, with one's choice of mayonnaise, bleu cheese, or oil, coupled with various types of chicken wing and barbecue sauces."

Only if that's the case, why on earth would Colosso's online menu have "New!" written next to the stinger sub on their menu? Eh, it has said that for years. But from here? The trail? It runneth cold. Think you know better? Hit me up at buffaloeverything@outlook.com.

You're a Tasty One, Mr. Stinger: Sting, Stang, Stung

While Jim's SteakOut and Colosso go back to the '80s and '60s, respectively, as far as anyone can tell, the stinger sub is actually a fairly recent phenomenon—we're talking the past 15 years or so. (That citation of it being a "new" sub in 2011 doesn't make much sense considering chef Ed Forster was quoted in 2012, saying, "Every time I used to come back to Buffalo, I would crave the Stinger Taco at Colossal Taco in Tonawanda.") And Jim's SteakOut's director of operations Guy Macon said they put the sandwich on the menu in 2008. But this all means there's still some real room for anyone with stomach lining strong enough to go questing out an extended list of the city's best renditions.

In the meanwhile, the ones at Imperial (chopped steak and chicken fingers with melted cheese—lettuce and tomato upon request), The Dockside (sliced New York strip steak, buttermilk fried chicken tenders, provolone and sautéed peppers and onions with mayo, blue cheese, or ranch), and Colosso (chicken, steak, cheese, blue cheese, lettuce, and tomato) would kick off a good top 10 list, and a list of three of the best follows.

But first, one pro-tip: you know that late-night rotating sandwich at Toutant? Its unicorn of late-night sandwiches just may be their stinger. It doesn't happen often, just during the holidays while they're already doing smoked prime rib, but even if you just take a look at the photos online, it's easy to see why it would be worth calling after. Chef Roberts said he basically makes Steak-umms out of smoked prime rib that they warm in rendered beef fat, layer into a homemade po'boy roll, and serve it with a horseradish-y Alabama white barbecue sauce and a red-eye gravy made with cayenne and chicory coffee.

#3 Mooney's Bar & Grill (Multiple Locations)

1531 Military Road, Kenmore, 14217 | 716-877-1800 mooneyssportsbarandgrill.com | Sun–Fri 11 AM–4 AM, Sat 11 AM–12 AM

Mooney's is probably *most* well-known for its framed photo of New England Patriot quarterback Tom Brady Photoshopped to have breasts,

its burgers (a peanut butter and jelly burger?!), its mac-and-cheese menu (nearly 20 different kinds, including riffs on Buffalo chicken, stuffed banana peppers, fried bologna, and beef on weck, so of course there's a stinger version too), and the Moses Challenge. The last is a 6-pound sandwich eating challenge topped with ham, turkey, roast beef, coleslaw, lettuce, tomatoes, and fries, which you can walk out without paying for along with a free T-shirt (you might not be able to fit in the one you walked in wearing) if you can eat it within 45 minutes. To date, only two humans and a 240-lb mastiff named Thor have done it despite more than 100 attempts. But Mooney's also makes a damned fine stinger with chicken, steak, lettuce, tomato, and cheese that you can order "Moses-style," topped with coleslaw and fries.

#2 John & Mary's (Multiple Locations)

3513 Harlem Road, Cheektowaga, 14225 716-836-7093 | Daily 11 AM–9 PM

The classics—the A-Bomb and the royal—are your priorities if you've never been to John

#1 Jim's SteakOut (Multiple Locations)

194 Allen Street, Allentown, 14201 | 716-886-2222 | jimssteakout.com | Mon–Thu 10:30 AM–5 AM, Fri–Sat 10:30 AM–6 AM

Here it is, the Buffalo stinger that has gotten more national acclaim than any other in town. Sirloin steak topped with chicken fingers (hot, medium, or mild), with your choice of oil, mayo, or blue cheese. Two pieces of advice. Don't choose between oil, mayo, and blue cheese—get all three for prime solid to moisture ratio; and don't lift up the hood of the car. Just like mom says nothing good happens out after 2 AM, nothing good is going to happen if you lift up the top piece of bread. Just dig in and accept.

& Mary's, but man if they don't make a mean stinger too (see the entry under Essentials for more on this shop). It's under the hoagies section at the top of the menu, and it's one of the simpler versions in town featuring just steak, chicken finger, and cheese in between those classic toasty-squished and cracked roll halves.

Everything's Better With Weber's

Do you even *need* mayo if you have Weber's? No, seriously. Do you? Okay, maybe you always need mayo. But the passion in Buffalo around Weber's Horseradish Mustard kinda makes you wonder. And the advertising campaigns, "A pickle in the middle and Weber's on top" and "Everything's better with Weber's" (c'mon, you know they're catchy), are pretty hard to deny after you get a tiny taste of that intense horseradish-y mustard. It is super smooth and super flavorful. French's? Gulden's? Grey Poupon? Wallflowers, all of you. Where have you been all our lives, Weber's?

Actually, right here in Buffalo since 1922. The ingredients in this carpet-staining, bright yellow mustard are simple enough: mustard seeds, vinegar, water, horseradish, turmeric, red pepper, and salt. But there's a bite that's anything but typical. Heintz & Weber Co., Inc. was founded in the Broadway Market in 1922, by Joseph Weber and John Heintz (no relation to the ketchup folks). Weber bought out Heintz in 1926, and it's been liberally spread on sandwiches to burn strong in Buffalo nasal passages and hearts ever since. If a roll from Costanzo's is a prerequisite for a great

Buffalo sub, Weber's horseradish mustard isn't far behind.

Egg salad, potato salad, deviled eggs, hot dogs, hamburgers, and sandwiches, sure. We know. They'll all be better with Weber's. But they're always all better with any mustard. Somehow though, the promise that baked beans, dips, and bologna will be better too? I don't know. You better get some Weber's. For the record, don't buy it before you go through airport security (or buy it before you head to the airport and put it in your checked bag). The TSA says mustard is a liquid, so they'll confiscate yours, and they sell it after you get through security anyway.

5 More Essential Sandwiches

You could take a Costanzo's roll, butter and oil it, just toss it on the griddle, and stuff it with just about any chopped meat and melted cheese, and frankly, you'd have a great sandwich. And we haven't even started talking about the places making their own bread. That makes singling out some of the city's other greatest sandwiches really difficult. There are a ton of sandwiches deserving of mention. So let's just go on record and say that these five sandwiches will put you ahead of the game in any debate about the city's best.

together for three years. They produce all of their own bread, bagels, and pretzels using a long ferment sourdough process and either King Arthur Flour, or whole grain flour milled in central New York by Farmer Ground Flour. According to Yeah! Buffalo, the $65,000 needed to open their wholesale bakery was raised $1,000 at a time through 40 community members. At last count, there were 65 community members whose investments had been instrumental in Bread-Hive's success, in exchange for a few perks and a small annual return.

BreadHive Bakery & Café

402 Connecticut Street, West Side, 14213

breadhive.coop | 716-980-5623

Tue 8 AM–6 PM, Wed–Sun 8 AM–3 PM, Closed Mon

Emily Stewart, Allison Ewing, and Victoria Kuper founded this bakery cooperative in 2014, after honing their hobby into a craft through Fancy & Delicious, a breadshare they worked on

But you don't have to be an investor to reap returns at the cafe, which opened a mile away from their wholesale operation in 2016. Just order one of the signature sandwiches served on sourdough, rye, or seeded multigrain, all named for pop divas: The Gwen (turkey), Bjork (tempeh bacon and kimchi), Fiona (brie), Stevie (roasted eggplant), Mariah (chicken salad), Robyn (pastrami), Whitney (roast beef), and Dolly (seitan and barbecue sauce). Better yet, order one of the breakfast sandwiches served all day. Bagels are chewy and size appropriate, scaled back from the behemoths they've typically become, the sourdough is soft and tangy with a wonderfully crispy edge, and these may be the best pretzel rolls you'll ever have. Usually, this type of bread is stale with undelivered promise. BreadHive's is light and moist with a crisp yellow-brown edge.

The move: The Aaliyah with house breakfast sausage, scrambled eggs, cheddar, and maple butter. Order it on a pretzel and they brush butter on the inside of the pretzel halves. The gouda stretches out as you tear the halves apart, and each bite is a peppery burst of juicy sausage,

layered with thin folds of egg piled underneath. Wow. "Good Bread, Good Work"? I'll say.

Five Points Bakery & Toast Café

44 Brayton Street, West Side, 14213 | 716-884-8888
fivepointsbakery.com | Mon–Wed 7 AM–3 PM,
Thu 7 AM–6 PM, Friday 7 AM–3 PM, Sat–Sun 9 AM–3 PM

Okay, so technically maybe not a sandwich, not the conventional kind, but toast. Open-faced toast. If you're the kind of person that finds it hard to get excited about toast and right now find yourself saying "I can make that at home," Five Points Bakery may change that. Melissa and Kevin Gardner launched in 2009, and in late 2014 moved to the current location where West Utica, Brayton, and Rhode Island streets converge. The couple makes their whole-grain bread by hand with local grains stone-ground at the bakery, then toast and outfit them with delicious and thoughtful spreads and accoutrements.

There's a sense of disembarking from reality upon visiting Five Points. The brick and light wood facade is set off from the intersection, and you have to walk through a gate along a grass-

lined path and through a courtyard. It's almost as if you've just hiked through a West Side Rubicon in Buffalo and crossed into Vermont. (In an effort to encourage people not to drive, they even give a discount if you walked or biked over.) The inside is just as transporting. Tall ceilings, open beams, and an earthy atmosphere where you can sit at a table or at the counter and see the entire baking and kitchen operation right down to the Blodgett ovens.

There are about a dozen kinds of bread including deli rye, apple cider, and extra sharp cheddar, and about a half-dozen pastries—apple and crumb cakes, cowboy and chocolate chip cookies, scones, brownies, and whole grain cinnamon rolls (whoa)—which are made with free-range

eggs and other local ingredients. The menu features 11 different toasts with toppings that include triple-cream brie, hard-boiled egg and Gruyère, sauerkraut, and raclette.

But it's hard to believe you wouldn't want to order what's essentially Buffalo-ized toast: the extra sharp cheddar bread. The toast triangles arrive saturated with butter, their tears and nooks oozing cheese, and accompanied by pewter cutlery, a schmear of sour cream, and a large melon ball scoop of soft St. Agur Bleu cheese, a little pot of hot sauce, and chopped garlic pickles. The sour cream seeps into the buttered crustiness, you get that creamy funk, a hit of spice, and the tang from the pickles. You only wish you could use all the condiments on one piece of toast. But hey, you've got to save room for the rest of Buffalo.

John & Mary's (Multiple Locations)

3513 Harlem Road, Cheektowaga, 14225
716-836-7093 | Daily 11 AM–9 PM

At last count, there were nine John & Mary's locations in and around Buffalo that are owned by a variety of folks, but that all have a common origin.

"In 1951, John Guida told his sister, Rose, that he was going to open a sandwich shop on Harlem Road in Cheektowaga. When Rose saw where he was going to buy, she asked him if he planned to sell to dead people because the building was across from a cemetery. In 1952, Johnny's opened its doors for the first time with three sandwiches: the regular (capicola), the royal (capicola and sausage), and the sausage. Later, around 1954, the A-Bomb was added, which was sausage and homemade hot sauce."   —John & Mary's

John Guida and his wife Mary, who opened the first one in 1952 in a small rented used car building as Johnny's (a name that supposedly lasted as long as it took for Mary to tell him either her name was added or he could cook everything himself). John opened other locations with family and friends, some closed, others moved, and a few have been sold to trusted operators, but there's still a fourth-generation of Guidas involved in at least one shop.

The menus at the locations differ (the original is still there on Harlem Road complete with Formica booths, Bills and Bisons paraphernalia, and windows looking out on the cemetery), and they're much longer than those aforementioned subs, usually served on toasted white or wheat rolls with lettuce, tomato, provolone, and either oil or mayo (onions on request).

Everything's really good, including John & Mary's stinger and chicken finger subs, but there's something about two of the originals made with Mary's recipes—the royal (even better, the super royal with capicola and double sausage) and the A-Bomb—that are next-level. The A-Bomb comes with two thin, stacked Italian sausage patties topped with fried sweet peppers and onions, and John & Mary's hot sauce. The sausage is flecked with fennel and very peppery, and the top of the soft roll gets all brown and blackened, cracked and flaky before the sandwich is flattened for easy eating.

Like John & Mary's says, "Well, those dead people could eat!"

The Old Pink

223 Allen Street, Allentown, 14201 | 716-884-4338

Daily 11 AM–4 PM

It's been mentioned in passing, but it bears repeating that the steak sandwich at The Old Pink—otherwise known as The Pink—may very well be, even more than beef on weck, Buffalo's most beloved sandwich. At least by students, chefs, writers, restaurateurs, bartenders, and late-night carousers who will all swear it's best experienced post-souse (or *in media res*) after 2 AM.

According to *Buffalo Rising*, the steak sandwich was actually inspired by an unnamed restaurant in New York City that supposedly used the entire loin of strip steak for its steak sandwich. Brothers Dennis and Kevin Brinkworth brought the idea back with them and riffed on it at The Pink, reducing it in size. Today, it's a

12-ounce center-cut New York Strip steak sandwich, covered with provolone, and onions and peppers made in a crock pot at the start of the shift. It's juicy, there's a thin crustiness to the compressed roll, and the onions and peppers send immediate signals to the brain that no matter how much more damage is done that night at the bar, things will be better than they would have been otherwise for eating it.

Little-known fact: if you're looking for a secret ingredient besides the bartenders' knack for nailing a dead-on medium-rare steak while cooking in the dark, at least according to one enterprising reporter for *Buffalo Rising*, it's Guinness.

Viola's

1717 Elmwood Avenue, Niagara Falls, 14301
716-282-7094 | Mon–Sat 11 AM–4:45 PM,
Closed Sun

1539 Military Road, Niagara Falls, 14304
716-297-3550 | Mon–Sat 10 AM–10 PM,
Sun 12 PM–10 PM

Forgotten Buffalo calls Viola's "the grandfather of all Niagara Falls sub shops," tracing its history to 1958, when the Elmwood Avenue Niagara Falls location opened. What was then founded by Luigi Ricciuto, Otto Viola, and Joseph and Rita (Viola) Tardibuono (the second shop opened on Military Road in 1960), is now owned outright by the Tardibuonos today. And locals' passion for it is the stuff of legend.

They'll tell you that you need to go north to Viola's for a steak sandwich. They'll say it's the kind of sandwich that's *so* messy that they have to roll it tight in Saran Wrap. They say it's one of the *best* steak subs in Western New York. They'll tell you the story of Hawaii-resident Robert Stokes, who so loved Viola's that his daughter once flew members of the shop to Oahu to make him their steak sandwiches for his birthday. You can take them all on their word. Look it up. It's true.

Just make sure you listen when they also tell you to ask for double steak. This is a moist and flavorful, thinly sliced rib-eye sandwich with an airy roll, and when ordered with everything (and why would you ever not?), comes with shredded lettuce, diced tomatoes, onions, Italian seasoning, and oil (no mayo, and Miracle Whip only on request), but not quite enough meat until the double is executed. Then it's perfect.

Buffalo's Best Since Sliced Bread

The spots in this chapter are essentials, but also leave out many great sandwiches. You'll hear people sing the praises of Wegmans, and note that every pizza parlor doubles as a great sandwicherie. So check out these other spots, or peruse the menus of some of the parlors mentioned in the pizza chapter, and start your own sandwich quest.

Colosso Taco & Subs, Niagara Falls, 2440 Pine Avenue, 716-284-1498

Costanzo's Sandwich Shop, Cheektowaga, 30 Innsbruck Drive, 716-656-9093, ext. 2

David's Steak Hoagy, Niagara Falls, 8442 Niagara Falls Boulevard, 716-283-3322

Guercio & Sons, West Side, 250 Grant Street, 716-882-7935

Joe's Deli, Hertel Avenue, 1322 Hertel Avenue, 716-875-5637

Jonny C's, East Amherst, 9350 Transit Road, 716-688-8400

La Flor Bakery, Lower West Side, 544 Niagara Street, 716-812-0187

Marco's Italian Deli (Multiple Locations)

CHAPTER SEVEN

WHERE BUFFALONIANS ROAM

20 Essential Old-School Restaurants

Worn wooden bars, tarnished brass, and windows where flickering neon still shines—time has been kind enough to leave standing some of the old-school restaurants that let you step back into Buffalo's bygone eras. These are the places where birthdays, break-ups, proposals, and run-of-the-mill Tuesday nights make up the culinary fabric of a century of hearty eating.

Some serve similar signatures, some stand out for single dishes, and some are important more for the fact of continuing their (and the city's) traditions, but these *are* icons of the restaurant scene—places that lined guidebooks before the internet and still routinely make locals' you-have-to lists. There are, obviously, more than 15 old-school restaurants in Buffalo. If you're from the city, many favorites likely come to mind that you won't find (space is a cruel mistress). And, of course, you could argue Bocce, Schwabl's, Anchor, and other pizza, wing, and weck spots could all be mentioned. But we've covered those elsewhere.

No, this is the list of restaurants where you'll find great pierogi, capicola topped sausage patties, chicken in vinegar marinade, and Buffalo-famous dishes like spaghetti Parm and stuffed hot peppers. And while not *every* dish on these menus is going to be life-changing, these are the places whose signature dishes have been copy-catted or whose names are writ large in local memory.

5 Old-School Italian Restaurants

According to the U.S. Census, there were 26,739 self-described Italian-Americans living in Buffalo. That's nearly 10 percent of the city's population. And it's estimated that in the 1930s, that number reached 80,000. No surprise then that this is a pizza-loving city with lots of red sauce joints. At least at these essential spots, don't go looking for gravy made with heirloom tomatoes. We're talking chicken cacciatore, veal Parmigiana, lasagna, and all the other Italian-American classics. And while farm-fresh vegetables and sustainably sourced proteins are

A meatball bomber at Santasiero's, one of Buffalo's oldest red sauce joints.

the way of the future, there's something to be said for a blanket of crusty, broiled mozzarella and a basket of garlic bread. Just don't leave the city (or dare consider yourself a local) if you haven't tasted its two quintessentially Buffalo Italian-American dishes: spaghetti Parm and stuffed banana peppers.

Chef's Restaurant

291 Seneca Street, Perry, 14204 | 716-856-9187
ilovechefs.com | Mon–Sat 11 AM–9 PM, Closed Sun

Chef's hasn't always been the sprawling bottle-of-red 300-seat spot it is today. It was just one room when founders Gino Silverstrini and Lee Federconi opened it on the corner of Seneca and Chicago in 1923. The expansions, one in 1966 and another in 1969, are credited to Lou Billitier, who started as a dishwasher, working his way through the ranks from busboy to waiter, then restaurant manager. Billitier became co-owner in 1950, took over the restaurant in 1954, and is the man behind Chef's signature dish: spaghetti Parm. It's said to have been invented over lunch in 1962, by Billitier and Dave Thomas, the host of a local children's TV show. Supposedly, Billitier added butter and Thomas added the cheese. "Thomas and Billitier were forever 'melted' together by a cold afternoon in '62," the story goes. Lou passed away in 2000, and his son, Lou Jr., runs Chef's now, and yes, they still bake the bread on premises.

Got all that? Good. Hey, listen, now that the history lesson is over: Those aren't napkins under the knife and spoon! That's an apron to help prevent spaghetti-Parm sauce, cheese, and butter-slurping catastrophes. Wait, "What's spaghetti Parm," you ask? Oh my dear, dear friend. Let's rewind.

Welcome to Chef's. You like the big, bright, clean dining room? Sure you do. Check out the "Sauce Wall" (multiple walls, actually) with celebrities holding bottles of Chef's sauce. That all started with Jerry Springer. He asked to be photographed with the sauce. You can buy it at Wegmans, Tops, and other area groceries (they started to sell it in supermarkets in 1997). It's pretty sweet by the way. But never mind that! Sit down! Spaghetti Parm? Of course! You want it with a meatball? The waitress likes hers with meatball *and* sausage. Listen to her. Want some stuffed banana peppers too? Or Chef's own sweet Palermo peppers stuffed with sausage, pepperoni, salami, and cheese? How about both!

You've probably had Parm-ed veal, chicken, eggplant, and ziti. Maybe you've even had spaghetti covered with melted-crusty mozz that nobody made a big deal about. But *butter-drenched* pasta under a thick blanket of mozzarella that gets all brown and crispy, but still stretches a foot long with the spaghetti when you twirl a fork in and pull it away? Probably not.

"Spag Parm" (available in sizes extra small, small, and large) arrives like some collapsed, brown-speckled big top from the cheese circus, buttery, broiled to the edges of the plate with a browned edge, and bubbling away with a cup of sauce on the side for dipping. Pasta peeks out through the top in a few places, but just barely. And after you've twirled into the dish, and gotten your guaranteed cheese pull, there's that magic orange melted-cheese, butter, and sauce shimmer. You twirl the fork, the cheese wraps up with the spaghetti strands as you turn it, you manage the cheese pull, dip into the side of sauce, hope you put on that apron, and *mangia!*

Listen, there's nothing *fancy* about spaghetti Parm, or really any secret regarding how it's made. In fact, it's a dish, with its let's-smother-it-in-cheese philosophy, that Buffalo's more refined palates may think is anything but "okay." Put aside any culinary pretension! This is pure indulgence! Leave your hoighty-toighty pants at home. You're just going to get sauce on them anyway.

Como

2220 Pine Avenue, Niagara Falls, NY 14301
716-285-9341 | comorestaurant.com
Mon 11:30 AM–3 PM, Tue–Thu 11:30 AM–8 PM,
Fri–Sat 11:30 AM–9 PM, Sun 11:30 AM–8 PM

Restaurant longevity can sometimes result in menus overrun with Dead Sea Scrolls' worth of dishes trying to be too much to too many. That, in turn, can lead to not doing anything right. You might be forgiven for thinking that when opening up the 13-page menu at Como, but as of 2018, this standby for wedding receptions, reunions, retirement parties, and annual award dinners has been at it for 90 years, and hasn't given any indication of slowing down. That may have something to do with the owning family's involvement. Francesco Antonacci opened the Como Restaurant on Pine Avenue in 1927, and since then, five generations have been involved with it. Still, you could be forgiven for taking the entire 40-minute drive north from downtown Buffalo, or at least the seven-minute drive

from Niagara Falls State Park, to decide what to order.

Como notes that it serves traditional dishes from the south of Italy, but this is an Italian-American red sauce joint if there ever was one, serving all your favorites along with the requisite steaks, chops, and lobster tails. This is the kind of place you can build your own pasta entrée by choosing one of nine pastas, eight sauces, and seven toppings after all. But instead, consider one of the Como Classics—the eggplant or tripe Parm, brasciole marinara stuffed with hard-boiled eggs, or ground beef-stuffed peppers topped with mushroom sauce—or, from under sandwich favorites, the sausage a la Siciliano, served open-faced on homemade pizza bread and topped with green peppers, mushrooms, and mozzarella. You'll want some of that pizza bread in any case, made in-house where it's flattened, seasoned, and pan-baked. Just don't fill up on the bread basket.

DiTondo's Tavern

370 Seneca Street, Perry, 14204 | 716-855-8838
ditondos.blogspot.com | Mon–Thu 11 AM–2 PM,
Fri 11 AM–2 PM, 5 PM–9 PM

They only do dinner on Fridays at DiTondo's. Otherwise, it's lunch Monday through Friday, a simple menu. You have your spaghetti, the off-menu sauce choices (meat, mushroom, regular, or you can ask for a sampling), and your option to Parm it, add a sausage link, or a meatball. There are also sandwiches: Italian sausage, meatball, grilled or cold capicola, fried bologna, a well-charred 12-ounce cheeseburger, and Italian sau-

sage patty with cheese. (There's a Friday-only grilled steak sandwich as well.) Dinner on Friday is just as simple: clams casino, stuffed hot peppers, stuffed eggplant Parm, and a dinner salad make up the appetizers, with fresh-baked haddock "Italian-style," linguine with clam sauce, and spaghetti with sauce with your choice of rolled steak, breaded chicken breast, meatballs, sausage links, and Parming it.

DiTondo's spag Parm is less domed and buttery than down the street at Chef's—there's a little less cheese coverage and the sauce thins at the bottom of the bowl. But it does the trick. The thing to get is the sausage patty sandwich, 8-ounce Italian sausage patty with cheese, sautéed hot peppers along with grilled and/or cold capicola and served with a hard-boiled egg. The sausage is juicy, the peppers are slightly spicy and cooked until they're soft and wrinkled; you get that extra savory flavor from the sliced meats—it's tempting to think of it as Buffalo's own muffuletta.

DiTondo Owner Alan Rohloff: "They call me Mr. DiTondo"

DiTondo's is on a quiet stretch of Seneca Street between Downtown and Larkin Square, a brick building with shaded windows under a shingle awning with its name written large in white cursive. It's just a block from Chef's, but Amedeo DiTondo opened it in 1904, so it actually preceded Chef's by nearly 20 years, making it one of the city's oldest Italian restaurants.

Inside, vets sitting along the bar discuss the merits of their service in Vietnam and whether it was a good experience. The owner, Alan Rohloff, stands at the window in the kitchen, arms crossed, looking out at the bar and talking to a customer. "They call me Mr. DiTondo," he tells me. "When someone walks in and says, 'Well, how you doing, Mr. DiTondo?' Then I know they don't know who I am."

Rohloff is the curator of DiTondo's century-old tradition, a retired postal worker, and also the head chef who arrives hours before lunch every morning to prep. He took over in 1985 with his wife after its owner, her father, passed away. "Mr. DiTondo" has been helping one way or another at DiTondo's for decades, opening it for his father-in-law while still working his mail route, an amount of time that from the sound of it may be nearing the end of an era. Along with some of the other tips and tricks about some of DiTondo's signature dishes, in this interview Mr. Rohloff says they may be looking to sell. And while it seems likely the restaurant will live on, Buffalo may be nearing the end of knowing it by its current name.

Why do you only serve lunch?

In its heyday, they were doing nights but as my father-in-law got older, he just did lunch. It was small at first. Guys would come up to the window and order something. You'd come over, pick your order up, and take it back. It was kind of neat. When I started, I became the dishwasher, the busboy, and everything else. I was running back and forth. When my wife and I took over, we had to hire some people because we made the back room bigger. In the '90s, we added to the outside, and then we expanded further to fit about 250 people.

Where do DiTondo's recipes come from?

My mother-in-law, who was born in Italy. She came over, I think, by boat when she was about 14. Then we added some things. The recipes for the meatballs and the sauce are my mother-in-law's. But the sausage patty, and stuff like that, we came up with.

Sausage topped with capicola is something you don't see all the time. How'd that start?

I asked Mineo & Sapio to make the patty bigger—I was always into having a little more meat. We do a hot patty and we do a mild patty, and those are half-pounders. Then we started another thing with Wardynski's Meats with the Polish sausage. I'm Polish. I like the links okay. But on the small Polish sausage, I asked him if he could use a bologna casing. The same way you eat bologna, well, now you'll eat Polish sausage that way. It's cut off maybe half an inch to an inch thick. You cut it, fry it, then you put it on fried onions, then the hot peppers, then you put the cheese on top on a Costanzo's roll.

Spaghetti Parm ...

They're going to say Chef's started it, and of course, Chef's started it. Okay, so Chef's started it? You put spaghetti in the bowl with sauce. Then you put mozzarella on it, or whatever kind of cheese you want, but usually it's mozzarella. Then you bake it. You can put it in a broiler, or put it in the oven. It gets nice and brown. Some people like it burnt. It's not for me. I like cheese, but I don't like cheese on spaghetti like that.

If you're making it at home, you toss the spaghetti in the sauce first, right?

It's better to do it that way. You can put your meatballs on it too. Then put the cheese over the top. Then just bake it so it gets hot. We sell a lot of those.

The Italian Sausage Special with capicola and hot peppers, how did that come about?

You take about six, eight pieces. You fry it up. You put it down ... What they usually want on it, usually it's cheese and hot peppers, or cheese, onion, and hot peppers. Then you put it on a roll, same thing. I've been doing it for years, but there's a lot of other places that have been doing it too. I mean, pizzerias, and places like that.

You keep the menu pretty simple ...

You go to some places, and they've got a menu this long. I don't know how they can get everything so that it's going to be fresh all the time. As you see, we only have four people working in the kitchen. You get anymore, and they'd be killing each other in there because you're banging into each other. And this kitchen is big now, compared to what it used to be.

What are the most popular dishes?

The stuffed hot peppers are good. Everything we have here is pretty good because otherwise I would have taken it off. It depends on what the people want to eat that day.

You and Chef's are right here down the street from each other. You get along?

People try to drum things up in the papers, or whatever. Somebody will say, "Oh, Chef's. Yeah, your spaghetti is better than Chef's." I say, "Yeah, but they make more money than we do." That's all I tell them. Then I'll kid around a lot of times, and somebody will say something and I'll just say, "Yeah, I just ran up the street. I got it from Chef's for you because we ran out."

What kind of role has DiTondo's played in the neighborhood?

Well, this is the Democratic bar. You got to be a Democrat to sit here. The Republicans go over there. But like the mayor, Mayor Griffin, when Griffin was the mayor. He was always in here. My father-in-law knew a lot of them. There were some of the mafia people, the Italians. I shouldn't say mafia, the Italians, they used to come in here. My father-in-law would say, I don't want any part of this. He knew them. He shook their hands. But he wasn't fooling around with that. He didn't want to see his family get hurt. I mean, it's been a good run for us. My father-in-law was the type of guy that, when I first started coming in here, before I married his daughter, he used to throw me the keys. I was a mailman, and he used to work downtown. On Saturday mornings, I would get done with my route real quick, then I would come over here. Because I came in here, he threw me the keys, "Open it up." But I'd still be working. I'm working for the post office. Now, I'm opening up his bar so he could get stuff, or he'd come down, and I'd say, "I've got to get back. I've got to go back and punch out." I'd go back. At that time, the mailman used to drink, and we used to drink. I mean, on Saturday mornings, we'd be in here with a bunch of guys. They'd have steaks cooking, and stuff like that. We'd have something to eat, and never look back.

Is that how you learned to do all the cooking?

My parents used to do a little catering too. They were involved in the catering. When I was in the Army, I was looking to get out of anything, and to get into something real nice. The guy asked me if I wanted to work in the mess hall. Sure, why not. I was a cook for a while. After that, I went back out in the field, and back into the infantry, again.

You don't see the owner also cooking behind the counter in the kitchen all the time.

It's just what I do. Like everybody says, you're only open three hours a day. It's all you work. I says, "No, I don't. I'm here Saturday. I'm here Sunday. I get here at, sometimes, six o'clock in the morning." We do what we have to do. My wife will come in. My wife used to work for the court system. She retired a couple of years early. Then, like I say, she was born upstairs here. I told her, I says, "You know, if we ever decide..." I says, "It's getting close." I'm 70, and she's 70. Could be time now. She says, "Well, no it's up to you whether we retire." I says, "You're the one that's got 71 years here, eh. Seventy-one years in here. How would you feel?" She says, "All things come to an end. It's got to come to an end." I says, "I don't want to drop dead here."

Ristorante Lombardo

1198 Hertel Avenue, Hertel Avenue, 14216

716-873-4291 | ristorantelombardo.com

Mon–Thu 5 PM–10 PM, Fri 11:30 AM–2:30 PM, 5 PM–11 PM, Sat 5 PM–11 PM, Closed Sun

Ristorante Lombardo hasn't been around as long as these other essentials—it was founded in 1975—there's a little less kitsch and a little more polish. Think *new-school* old-school Italian-American.

Thomas J. Lombardo Jr. opened Lombardo's with his father Thomas J. Lombardo Sr., in 1975, when it was a watering hole that served stuffed shells and meatballs. The restaurant started to change in the '90s, with Tom Jr. and his wife Donna bringing back inspiration from trips to Italy. These days, Ristorante Lombardo has the feel and finesse of fine dining: valet parking, white tablecloths, white-collared wait staff, and regional Italian specialties. Tom Jr.'s son Tommy, who graduated with a degree in hotel and restaurant management, and worked at New York City restaurants including L'artusi, Dell'anima, and Anfora with restaurateur Joe Campanale, joined the family business in 2012, and guides the restaurant with executive chef Michael Obarka today.

There are small thin-crust, brick-oven pizzas with refined toppings like fig, gorgonzola, taleggio, and goat ricotta. The antipasti still include fried calamari and stuffed banana peppers (with gorgonzola and anchovy), but they're joined with dishes like grilled octopus and wood-roasted figs. You won't find spag Parm here. The closest you'll get to that is eggplant al forno with fresh mozzarella. Think orecchiette with caramelized cauliflower in brown butter, lobster and mascarpone ravioli, and tagliatelle Bolognese with a veal, pork, and beef ragu. And secondi like grilled veal chop, veal Marsala, and roasted chicken saltimbocca.

And consider this, in 2014, Andrew Galarneau gave it 10 out of 10 plates and called it his most memorable Italian meal in Buffalo, going on to remove any qualifiers and call it "one of the best restaurants in Western New York."

Billy Ogden's Stuffed Banana Peppers

In a city full of signature dishes, stuffed banana peppers may be the one most recently invented. People have been stuffing peppers forever, of course. And the Hungarian dish, *sajtos töltött paprika* (Hungarian peppers stuffed with Parmesan, ricotta or farmer's cheese, eggs, and parsley) sounds remarkably similar to the dish that's proliferated across the city's menus. But as far as things go in Buffalo, credit for their popularity goes to the late chef Andy DiVincenzo.

Before returning to Buffalo and finding success at Billy Ogden's, DiVincenzo, a trumpeter, was road manager for the British rock band Emerson, Lake and Palmer, and also operated restaurants and catering operations in New York City, Shelter Island, and Phoenix. DiVincenzo opened Billy Ogden's Lovejoy Grill, a corner tavern (on William and Ogden streets, thus the name) filled with old-Buffalo memorabilia donated by friends and neighbors from their attics, in the Lovejoy area in 1989. Even the "Lovejoy Grill" part of the name came about because of a donation—the beaten neon sign from the people who ran Lovejoy Tavern just blocks away.

It all immediately gave the place the feeling

Stuffed peppers may not have been invented at The Place, but they make a damn fine version of them.

that it had been there for decades. The space at 1834 William Street had, in fact, been a restaurant previously—Coppola's—which went from being the kind of place where you'd find chicken in a basket and spaghetti and meatballs to a restaurant that served white pizza with dandelions, scallops with Champagne cream sauce, crispy sea bass, homemade seafood sausage, and handmade raviolis.

DiVincenzo became known for a contemporary cuisine with an Italian bent and a blackboard filled with a long list of specials (sometimes five columns long) and creative dishes, among them, his Hungarian stuffed peppers. DiVincenzo created the peppers for the Taste of Buffalo in the summer of 1990, where they won top honors. From there they moved to his specials blackboard, getting singled out in the *Buffalo News* review in 2002, as the paper's favorite dish there. They were even mentioned as DiVincenzo's creation in his 2004 obituary.

Billy Ogden's is no more. It only lasted a few years without its chef. These days, though, you can still find many versions of DiVicenzo's stuffed peppers—if not everywhere, then in enough places that you don't have to go looking for them. They've even become ingredients that routinely top other dishes, namely pizzas and subs, though they're not made according to the original recipe.

Unfortunately, DiVincenzo's obituary says he kept the stuffed pepper recipe secret, and even Christopher Daigler, chef and owner of Falley Allen, who worked for DiVincenzo and cooked them at his side, told *Buffalo Spree* that only Andy and Andy's grandmother had the real recipe. We know from Janice Okun's review that DiVincenzo served four or five peppers per order at Billy Ogden's, that they were seared Hungarian peppers, that they were spicy, and stuffed with an assortment of cheeses.

Many of the recipes for these stuffed peppers that you'll find today call for some combination of ricotta, cream cheese, parsley, Parmesan, and Asiago. Some call for lemon juice, egg, mozzarella, and red pepper flakes, and there's even the occasional call for crumbled sausage or ground pork. But it's anchovy paste that, along with ricotta, cream, cheese, parsley, mozzarella, and

Parmesan, seems to be a running theme as an ingredient. Unlike many online recipes, which call for baking the peppers, the real secret may have been DiVincenzo's technique.

"What Andy did differently was that he didn't bake his peppers in the oven," Daigler told *Buffalo Spree*'s Christa Glennie Seychew. "He used a smoking hot pan to sear the peppers until they were blackened on one side. As soon as the stuffing started to ooze from the pepper, we'd remove them from the pan. Then, using the same oil—because it's got all those delicious browned bits of stuffing—we'd hit the pan with coarsely chopped garlic and parsley and then brown it. Then we'd dump that oil right over the pepper. It's that technique that made them so good."

Falley Allen

204 Allen Street, Allentown, 14201 | 716-464-3903
Sun–Thu 5 PM–11 PM, Fri–Sat, 5 PM–12 AM

If you want to experience Andy DiVincenzo's peppers as close to the original as possible today, your best bet may be to visit Falley Allen, where chef Daigler serves his version of "Billy Ogden's Stuffed Banana Peppers" with rustic toast, garlic oil, and parsley.

Santasiero's Restaurant

1329 Niagara Street, West Side, 14313
716-886-9197 | Mon–Sun 11 AM–10 PM
(cash only, ATM inside)

Who knows why the wide green, white and red painted bands on the restaurant's vinyl siding aren't *vertical* stripes? Just tilt your head to

the left—you'll get the idea. Domenic and Filomena Pace Santasiero had the right idea when they came to Buffalo from Potenza, Italy (about 100 miles east of Naples), and opened their restaurant on Niagara Street in 1921. "During the Depression, when things were bad, they started giving away free pasta with a nickel beer, and they actually built a great reputation on their sauce," their great-grandson John Brands Jr. told *Buffalo Spree* in 2016.

The sauce is one of *two* big draws for the locals at Santasiero's, the other being a bit player on the Buffalo food icon scene, pasta fagioli, listed on the menu as "Pasta Fasoola." And considering Santasiero's history is linked to beer, it's no wonder the bar plays a central role. It's right there when you step inside, with a small dining room sandwiched between it and the open kitchen where they put whole crushed tomatoes, tomato

paste, garlic, onion, and spices in huge pots and let them bubble away for up to five hours before ladling them onto their pastas, bombers, and sandwiches.

If it all looks like it's been there forever, this cash-only joint will be happy to hear that. While they've been here nearly 100 years, a radiator pipe explosion caused them to have to completely renovate in 2015. Look no further for the menu than the large wall in the back of the dining room. While it's not as long as the ones at some red sauce joints, anyone coming in who hasn't been eating there for 60 years is going to have to approach with culinary hermeneutics: What's "Peas and Macaroni?" "Cajun Mushroom Sauce?" "The Only 'Venetian Stew'"?

So many questions. But your ordering philosophy should be simple. You need to order the "Pasta Fasoola." It's a huge heaping bowl of lima beans and garbanzos with ditalini, the short tubular macaroni you usually see in Minestrone. And you should order something with lots of sauce and tons of cheese, like a three-ball meatball bomber, that's so enveloped with cheese you almost think that's what you ordered, topped sided, under and all around. And you need to get a side of sautéed peppers. Zesty, light, and heartening, they change the dynamic of every dish. That's it. Don't stray.

The Feast of St. Joseph

It's a tradition that seems to be fading, like others across America affiliated with religions, but if you're in Buffalo in March, you'll still probably hear *something* about the Feast of St. Joseph. There's *a lot* to know about this annual Sicilian custom that occurs on March 19th. In fact, there are enough dishes affiliated with it to fill a book. Seriously. Chef Mary Ann Giordano published *The Saint Joseph's Day Table Cookbook* in 2015, and it's *full* of menus, stories, lore, and 100 recipes affiliated with the tradition. There are two key dishes to know: *pasta con sarde* and *sfinge*. First, the how and why.

In the Middle Ages, there was supposedly a drought in Sicily and a famine that caused many deaths. Peasants prayed to God for rain, and for insurance, Saint Joseph too. "Please put in a few good words for us with the Big Guy," they pleaded, "and if *he* lets it rain, we promise, you get a special feast in *your* name."

When it rained, crops were planted and harvested, then wealthy landowners threw a feast for the poor in Joseph's name in the town square. It's a tradition upheld annually in Sicilian communities in America today, some of the biggest of which are said to be in Texas, California, Colorado, New Jersey, New York (hello, Buffalo), and Louisiana. It usually involves an altar with a picture of St. Joseph, and three steps representing the Father, the Son, and the Holy Ghost. There are fava beans, there's bread, there's fruit, and

lentils for good luck. Read chef Giordano's book if you want to know more.

In *Buffalo*, the Feast of St. Joseph means many households and churches observe by preparing meatless dishes in observance of Lent, sometimes free for those less fortunate (for the non-Catholics, that means it happens during the 40 days between Ash Wednesday and Easter Sunday, which Jesus spent being tempted by Satan in the desert). During this week, a number of Italian restaurants serve set menus featuring some of the most well-known dishes associated with the tradition, such as *pasta con sarde* and *sfinge*.

In Buffalo, *pasta con sarde* is made with tomato sauce, fennel, golden raisins, sardines, capers, garlic, and parsley then garnished with toasted bread crumbs. Bread crumbs and not grated cheese because cheese was expensive and the crumbs symbolized sacrifice, the poor, and supposedly, sawdust (Joseph being a carpenter and

all). The best versions are made with fresh sardines, and in Sicily, with pignoli nuts; but if you look in Guercio & Sons and any other Italian grocer in Buffalo, you'll find pre-made cans and jars of sarde sauce for sale. If this all sounds dubious, know that when prepared with fresh ingredients (especially fresh sardines), it's a light, flavorful, non-fishy dish that's at turns salty, sweet, and texturally diverse. *Sfinge*? It's an Italian doughnut. Think fancy zeppole and you get the idea.

5 Spots for the Feast of St. Joseph

If you're interested in experiencing the feast of St. Joseph first-hand, consider checking out the special menus made annually on or around the week of March 19th, at these five restaurants.

Como

2220 Pine Avenue, Niagara Falls, 14301
716-285-9341 | comorestaurant.com
Mon–Tue 11:30 AM–8 PM, Wed–Thu 11:30 PM–8 PM,
Fri–Sat 11:30 AM–9 PM, Sun 11:30 AM–8 PM

Gigi's Cucina Povera

981 Kenmore Avenue, 14217 | 716-877-8788
gigiscucinapovera.com | Tue–Thu 4 PM–9:30 PM,
Fri–Sat 4 PM–10:30 PM, Sun 4 PM–9 PM, Closed Mon

Ilio DiPaolo's

3785 South Park Avenue, Blasdell, 14219
716-825-3675 | iliodipaolos.com
Tue–Thu 11:30 AM–2:30 PM, 2:30 PM–9:30 PM;
Fri 2:30 PM–10:30 PM, 11:30 AM–2:30 PM;
Sat 2 PM–10:30 PM; Sun 1 PM–9:30 PM; Closed Mon

Tappo Restaurant

338 Ellicott Street, Downtown, 14203
716-259-8130 | tappoitalian.com
Mon 5 PM–10 PM; Tue–Wed 11:30 AM–2:30 PM,
5 PM–10 PM; Thu 11:30 AM–2:30 PM, 4:30 PM–10 PM;
Fri 11:30 AM–2:30 PM, 4:30 PM–11 PM;
Sat 4:30 PM–11 PM; Sun 3 PM–9 PM

Sinatra's Restaurant

938 Kenmore Avenue, North Park, 14216
716-877-9419 | sinatraswny.com
Mon–Sun 5 PM–10 PM

5 Essential Polish Restaurants

In 1890, the Polish-American population of Buffalo was estimated at 20,000. By 1910, there were 80,000 (about a sixth of its population) and *five* Polish-language newspapers. These days, the greatest concentration of Polish-Americans can likely be found in the city's eastern suburbs (Cheektowaga and Marilla). But they still make up about 10 percent of Buffalo's population and there are lots of places to experience the cuisine, whose most frequently seen and easily identifiable dishes are golabki (aka golombki) and pierogi. Golabki are beef-stuffed cabbage rolls braised in a light tomato broth. And pierogi (actually the plural, but nobody says 'pierog') are dumplings made with unleavened dough and filled with sweet or savory fillings. The latter have easily lent themselves to fusing with many of Buffalo's most famous food icons: beef on weck, wings, and stuffed banana peppers, and been reinterpreted themselves by new businesses, like Ru's Pierogi. Of course, the cuisine

Snag a few Polish dumplings at the Babcias Pierogi Company at the Broadway Market.

goes much further, and these five restaurants while some of the most time-honored and well-known, are just a launch point for kielbasa, bigos (hunter's stew), borscht, sauerkraut, potato pancakes, and so much more.

The Broadway Market

999 Broadway, East Side, 14212 | 716-893-0705
broadwaymarket.org | Mon–Sat 8 AM–5 PM

It isn't what it once was—a bustling market the neighborhood relied on for meat, produce, and the specialties of Eastern Europe many of Buffalo's immigrants left behind—but the Broadway Market is still a custodian of those traditions. It was started by a group of citizens on a city-donated plot in 1888, and expanded to take up a whole block. It's been rebuilt and renovated a few times over the years, most recently in the '80s, and the

fillings include bacon cheeseburger, breakfast scramble, stuffed banana pepper, reuben, and, of course, Buffalo wings.

Just keep in mind that not all vendors are open every day and that hours can vary. It's worth checking the market's vendor page before going.

Gadawski's Restaurant

1445 Falls Street, Niagara Falls, NY 14303
716-282-7246 | gadawskisrestaurant.com
Tue-Thu 11 AM-2 PM, Fri 11 AM-9:30 PM

Opened originally as Jankowski's in 1923, the restaurant was bought by Eddie Gadawski from Anthony and Katherine Jankowski in 1952, and renamed. If the green-painted side of the building doesn't jibe with the name, things clear up inside. Mr. Gadawski was known for being one of America's most ardent Notre Dame fans.

He didn't matriculate. He wasn't Irish. His father just told him it was a good Catholic school for a young man to follow if he wanted to root for a football team. Sadly, Gadawski passed away in December of 2017, but his passion for Notre Dame lives on. He had been to more than 200 games, he once told Joe Montana to "shove it" when the QB refused him an autograph, and he has his initials carved into the cigar of the statue of onetime Notre Dame 3-0 acting head coach Moose Krause.

The food? So said its owner, "Gadawski's is the only place in Western New York where the pierogi, golombki, and Polish sausage from the kitchen are as fresh as the Guinness being poured behind the bar."

high-ceiling space now has a parking garage and some 90,000-square feet, enough room for about two dozen food vendors and cafes, along with a bunch of non-food related businesses. The best (and craziest) time of year to visit is during the two weeks leading up to Easter, when the foods that accompany family traditions tug at folks' heartstrings. Many return from the suburbs to shop, giving the market serious bustle.

If you don't have the time to wander, make a beeline for some rye bread at Mazurek's Bakery and chrusciki from Chrusciki Bakery. This Mazurek's is an outpost of the First Ward institution opened in 1933, by Frank and Jeanne Mazurek. And while there are now three other Chrusciki locations this is the one where Polish immigrants Tadeusz and Hanna Robieniek got their start in the '80s working for E. M. Bakery before taking it over and turning it into the business it is today. Then grab some sinus-clearing condiments at Famous Horseradish (maybe some sauerkraut too), and snag a few Polish dumplings at the Babcias Pierogi Company. Babcias makes traditional pierogi filled with farmer's cheese, kraut, mushrooms, and potato and cheddar. More modern signature

K Sisters Authentic Pierogi

2116 Clinton Street, Cheektowaga, 14206

716-827-4077 | buffalopierogi.com

Tue–Fri 10 AM–4 PM, Sat 10 AM–3 PM

If you're looking for some of Buffalo's best pierogi, you need look no further than K Sisters. Just know that you're going to need a plan for cooking them yourself. K Sisters is just a shop—not a restaurant—the result of one woman, Karen Markiewicz, setting out to make pierogi like her *babcia's* (grandma's) that she couldn't find out there already being made. Karen started the business in 2004, and named it for herself and her sisters Kathy and Karoll. "We all learned how to make handmade delicious pierogi from our grandmother and mother," Karen said. "Our pierogi are the original, old-fashioned ones that people remember from years ago."

There are nearly a dozen pierogi stuffed with traditional fillings (potato, sauerkraut, mushrooms, onions, and cheeses), and an "innovative" group that includes fillings like fruit, chuck roast, "taco," "enchilada," and sweet potato. They're easy enough to make; just sauté the pierogi in 2 tablespoons of butter until brown on both sides, and serve them with sautéed onions (one small onion cooked in 2 tablespoons butter for every four pierogi!).

Polish Villa II

1085 Harlem Road, Cheektowaga, 14227

polishvilla.org | Wed–Fri 11 AM–9 PM, Sat 4 PM–9 PM, Sun 10 AM–8 PM, Closed Mon–Tue

Polish Villa II is the third-generation of Polish restaurants started by Edward and Mildred Kutasi at the Warsaw Inn (now closed) when they came to Buffalo in 1954. Their son Edward and his wife Irene opened the original Polish Villa in 1979, and Polish Villa II was opened by their son Edward and his wife Rose in 1985. Which is all to say that Buffalo has known more than 70 years of Polish restaurants being run by the family.

These days, the Polish Villa on Union is a little rough around the edges. It's a sign of the times, and the demographic, that funeral breakfasts and lunches are enough of a business for Polish Villa II to prominently advertise them at the restaurant. Still, if you're looking for an authentic, stomach-overfull, winter-bracing meal of czarnina (traditional Polish duck soup), beef and kluski noodles, golabki, and kielbasa, things won't get more real. (Note that Sunday's brunch is buffet only.)

R&L Lounge

23 Mills Street, East Side, 14212 | 716-896-5982

Mon–Sat 9 AM–7 PM, Closed Sun

"R&L" stands for Ronnie and Lottie—Ronnie and Lottie Pikuzinski that is, the couple who have

been running this local tavern since 1969, and married since 1957. And it's likely that unless you visit on one of the occasions where the whole neighborhood comes out, you may just be spending the afternoon with Ronnie and Lottie at the bar by yourself and whoever you go with. It's almost like visiting grandma and grandpa.

It's a good idea to call ahead to make sure they're not out of food (and up to making you some). Keep in mind, you can't be in a rush, especially if you'd like a bite to eat. Ronnie and Lottie don't get around quite as quickly anymore. Though they haven't lost a step with a quip. So put your phone away, sit down, and order a drink.

Watch the dying light fade in through the windows. See that string of Christmas pierogi lights above the bar! Maybe queue up a few songs on the jukebox. Some Elvis? The Gin Blossoms? There is, of course, plenty of polka.

The menu is simple: pierogi, "golompki" (golabki), handcut fries, and chicken fingers daily. Fish fry on Friday. That's all, folks. But these are quite possibly going to be the best pierogi you'll ever have. Lottie rolls the dough out extremely thin and doesn't overstuff them. There's just kind of an idea of filling. Then she browns them with butter so they get golden-brown patches and little butter bubbles. They're toothsome but delicate, not like any others in town—completely unchewy—and maybe just two or three times as thick as crepes. The golabki are just as good—delicate and heartwarming in a thin, tomato-y broth.

You'll feel bad about leaving, but happy to have come. This is that kind of real Buffalo, real anywhere for that matter, that you just can't fake or replicate, one of those really special places that you don't know how long will be around, and that you're glad you found.

Chrusciki and Paczki

You'll see lots of baked goods throughout Buffalo, but there are two Polish items that you're likely to stumble across or hear about again and again.

The first are chrusciki (*kroo-she-kee*), a crispy pastry twisted so as to resemble ribbons, butter-

flies, or angel wings (depending on who you're talking with). The Polish word *chrust* means "brushwood," but versions of this pastry are made with different names in France, Hungary, Italy, Ukraine, and Bulgaria, typically with similar ingredients: flour, water, egg yolks, vanilla, and salt. They're shaped, then fried and dusted with confectioner's sugar. Chrusciki are usually served at Polish weddings and during holidays, commonly just before Lent.

The Tuesday before Ash Wednesday (which can be as early as February 4, or as late as March 10) is Paczki Day, which means it's time to throw diets to the wind and gorge on paczki (*pownch-kee*), rich Polish jelly doughnuts that are usually filled with raspberry, lemon, and more traditionally, prune jam, then glazed or sprinkled with confectioner's sugar. Paczki's origins are said to go back to the Middle Ages, spawned from the need to use any remaining sugar, eggs, lard, and fruit in advance of fasting for Lent. Both Chrusciki and Mazurek's make them year-round, Mazurek's on Fridays and Saturdays only. Mazurek's makes them with black raspberry jelly and a rum glaze, but if you're interested in the traditional version, they'll cut and fill one with prune for you (it's said to be too thick for their machine!).

E. M. Chrusciki Bakery

80 West Drullard Avenue, Lancaster, 14086

716-681-9866 | chruscikibakery.com | Mon 8 AM–5 PM, Tue–Fri 7 AM–6 PM, Sat 9 AM–4 PM, Closed Sun

Mazurek's Bakery

543 South Park Avenue, Buffalo, NY 14204

716-853-7833 | mazureksbakery.com

Mon–Fri 8 AM–5:30 PM, Sat 8 AM–3 PM

10 All Around Old-School Favorites

Strictly speaking, you could be forgiven for calling someone crazy for compiling a list of essential old-school spots that doesn't include The Place, Bocce, Chef's, Oliver's, and Anchor Bar. But we've covered them in special categories to celebrate their unique roles in Buffalo's culinary history. Beyond the obvious, after the dust settles, these are neighborhood institutions and Buffalo-famous places that have been

second homes to the city's denizens, most for generations.

Blackthorn Restaurant & Pub

2134 Seneca Street, South Buffalo, 14210

716-825-9327 | blackthornrestaurant.com

Sun–Thu 11:30 AM–10 PM, Fri–Sat 11:30 AM–11 PM

Along with Hoak's and the Broadway Market, Blackthorn Restaurant & Pub was one of the places legendary NBC Sunday morning politics show *Meet the Press* host (and Buffalo native) Tim Russert mentioned as a go-to. Karen Lalley whose husband, Hugger, owns Blackthorn says that it opened in 1976 as Early Times.

Indeed, things have changed a bit over the years since Russert died. Its beef on weck was featured in 2010 on Food Network's *Diners, Drive-Ins and Dives* with Guy Fieri. And the 2017 renovations brought with them a new facade, a two-level steel patio outside, a fireplace inside, and fire pits outside for drinking, er ... waiting around until a table inside frees up. (While the kitchen closes early, the bar stays open until 4 AM.)

But the heart of the place has stayed true to the MO that made this a Russert South Buffalo staple: real food for real people. That means an extensive menu with at least 10 house favorites accompanied by their homemade jalapeño cheddar tots, among them corned beef, shepherd's pie, "The Big Guy's Favorite" (corned beef and turkey on rye), and the Triple D Platter, which has the items Guy ate on the show: beef on weck, crab cake, and Irish beer soup. This is also a place you can score South Buffalo–style wings.

By the way (and if you have to ask, you're from out of town), a "blackthorn" is a thorned walking stick made from a branch of the deciduous tree of the same name, but the bar is named after a men's Irish-heritage social club that holds its monthly meetings at the pub on the last Tuesday of each month. It celebrated its 100th anniversary in 1917, and Russert's dad "Big Russ" was a well-known member.

"There are two display cases upstairs that contain the silver engraved toasting cups they use at their meetings," Karen said. "One case is for current members and the other for deceased members"

Chiavetta's BBQ Takeout

6100 Fisk Road, Lockport, 14094 | 716-625-9503
chiavettascatering.com | Daily 8 AM–6 PM

The post-oak smoked Texas brisket barbeque trend hasn't fully taken flight in Buffalo yet, but the area has a style of chicken 'cue all its own that locals have known for decades. Thomas and Eleanor Chiavetta started as poultry farmers. The Chiavettas learned about barbecuing chicken (low and slow for an hour and a half to two hours over open-air charcoal pits) from the Erie County Farm and Home Center in East Aurora during a farm bureau convention. They started by catering for local fire departments, moved on to weddings and banquets, then expanded to catering in 1957.

That part of their tradition continues. Chiavetta's frequently caters events and fundraisers; you can check out the calendar on their website for upcoming events. These days, they also do ribs, pulled pork, smoked brisket, and fish fry. Not to demean them, but there are other parts of the country perhaps more affiliated with those styles to travel for. At Chiavetta's, the move is the chicken and its signature sauce, which they've been bottling since 1980. It's a watery, mouth-puckeringly vinegar-based marinade made with spices and garlic that's also used as a dipping sauce.

Glen Park Tavern

5507 Main Street, Williamsville, 14221
716-626-9333 | glenparktavern.com
Mon–Thu 11:30 AM–10 PM,
Fri–Sat 11:30 AM–11 PM, Sun 4 PM–9 PM

Vinyl siding, waving flags—there's not much indication from outside Glen Park Tavern that it was constructed in 1887. But that's the story of this welcoming institution with its long, shiny wooden bar, cushioned stools, and carving station for both beef on weck and turkey—"original brick," "hand-hewn beams," "original mahogany bar," and "hardwood floors." And hey, it's said to have operated as a restaurant and pub ever since.

Glen Park calls their beef on weck their signature, serving it "sliced thin and piled high" on a Costanzo's roll with 4, 6, or 8 ounces of beef. But their stuffed hot peppers are just as well-regarded—they get their peppers from fourth generation-run Seabert Farms and stuff them with their garlic, basil, breadcrumbs, and secret three-cheese mix. Outside of that, consider ordering wings, "Nana Grenauer's potato pancakes," fresh-cut tavern fries (with honey butter or gravy), or their fresh-cut chicken fingers.

Hutch's Restaurant

1375 Delaware Avenue, Delaware-West Ferry, 14209
716-885-0074 | hutchsrestaurant.com
Mon–Thu 5 pm–10 pm, Fri–Sat 5 pm–11:30 pm,
Sun 4 pm–9 pm

"In the world of fine dining, Hutch's is the closest Buffalo comes to a sure thing." Those are the words of the *Buffalo News*'s food editor Andrew Galarneau, and if that sounds like Oliver's, no surprise then that one of its former chefs, Mark Hutchinson helms *this* more recent classic. Still, Hutch's has been around since 1995, almost long enough for a generation of Buffalonians to have held both their wedding rehearsal and silver anniversary dinners there.

There's a small enclosed patio, a dark, clubby dining room with brick walls, and a menu that's classic American white tablecloth-fine dining with a parsley scattering on the plate rim.

It's a touch French, a little steakhouse, there's some Italian and Asian fusion, and a little New Orleans flare. This is the kind of place you can find a Caesar or wedge salad, get both the stuffed jalapeños and escargot, and order steak frites, chicken Milanese, or signature jambalaya pasta.

But as much as Hutch's is a restaurant where you can celebrate a special occasion, it's also the kind of place, at least under the skylight-lit bar in the back, where you can dig into a "Pittsburgh" steak sandwich topped Primanti-style with fries and coleslaw, and feel both spoiled and at home.

Mighty Taco (Multiple Locations)

2363 Delaware Avenue, Buffalo, 14216
716-871-8670 | www.mightytaco.com
Dining Room: Daily 10 am–12 am;
Drive-Thru: Sun–Thu: 10 am–1 am, Fri–Sat 10 am–2 am

Founders Dan Scepkowski, Andy Gerovac, Ken Koczur, and Bruce Robertson started Mighty Taco in 1973, on Hertel Avenue (now home to Daddio's Pizza). Scepkowski bought out the other partners, and has some two dozen locations today. The ads and slogans are clever, and

the approach playful (positioning their brick-and-mortars as "stationary food trucks" as that trend continues in popularity).

Mighty Taco is not going to win any authenticity awards from area foodies or Mexican taco aficionados. Those folks now have places like La Divina, lloyd Taco Factory, and Casa Azul. Mighty Taco is essentially Buffalo's homegrown Taco Bell, the place to go for authentic tacos if, as one of the chain's marketing slogans goes, you think about Western New York as "Canada's Tijuana." But really, it doesn't make any pretense about being that kind of food.

This is the place for combinations of beans, cheese, lettuce, tomato, and sour cream with ground beef, ground chicken, pulled pork, and "fajita" steak or chicken from the drive-thru at cheap prices. And while it's not a must-stop, if you do find yourself there late-night after a few too many Genesees, the must-order is the Buffito: Buffalo-style chicken with lettuce and blue cheese wrapped in a tortilla. Of course.

Paula's Donuts: "Buffalo Wakes Up With Us At 5 am Daily!"

For older generations, Freddie's (born 1935) claims Buffalo's nostalgia title. Fred Maier was king until retiring in 1989 (he supposedly held patent on Krispy Kreme's original machines). But in the years since Paula's opened in 1996, it's indisputable: Paula Huber's hand-cut doughnuts baked daily have made her Buffalo's reigning grande(onut) dame. You smell the sugar immediately, greeted by rows of honeydips, twists, fritters, and glazed yeast and cake jelly- and angel cream-filled doughnuts, and can't help but want them all.

Paula and her husband Chuck are former Dunkin' Donut franchisees who went indie, opening on Kenmore Avenue in a former Dickie's Donuts (a Buffalo business reborn as Donut Kraze). "It was like, 'I'm gonna kill myself for everybody else, we might as well just do it for ourselves!'" she recalled.

It was a slog: 19-hour days she spent baking at night and behind the counter daily, making wholesale deliveries in "off" hours until they could afford a night baker. They decided they either needed to sell or grow. There are now three locations — in Tonawanda (where they moved from Kenmore), Williamsville, and Southgate.

Paula's is *nothing* like Dunkin' or Buffalo's other mind-bafflingly prolific doughnut chain Tim Horton's (blame Canada). These are airy, fresh, and delicious old-fashioned doughnuts that stand tall with Round Rock (Round Rock, Texas), Doughnut Vault (Chicago), Holy Donut (Portland, Maine), and America's other great shops. Paula's secret? "Top quality ingredients, we bake fresh every day, and we strip our cases," is all she'd share, though she tipped her cap about wanting to pass on Paula's to daughters Lisa and Christy, and an idea about making *ice cream*-stuffed doughnuts(!).

Among Paula's six categories (glazed, jelly, Bavarian, angel cream, filled, and unfilled), there are more than 50 different doughnuts. Paula's is most known for its peanut stick, a cake doughnut entirely coated in finely chopped peanuts and peanut dust, a Buffalo tradition credited to Freddie's (it also comes round and with chocolate cake). But their cheese doughnuts — glazed soft and stretchy yeast-raised pockets filled with a cheese Danish center that's like a slightly sweet, slightly salty sour cream filling — are also beloved. Their "Texas Donuts" serves six to eight as a frequent birthday cake replacement, and Food Network's Alton Brown said the sour cream old-fashioned ranks with the best he's ever had.

But nobody leaves a doughnut shop without at least a half-dozen. So consider another thing about Paula's is if you ask nicely, they'll usually customize (within reason). Here's your to-do list: a peanut angel cream-stuffed round peanut doughnut, a peanut-cream stuffed chocolate frosted Bavarian, and the ever elusive "cheese-nut 'stick,'" a yeast-raised dough pocket filled with cheese and coated with peanuts.

The Eagle House Restaurant

5578 Main Street, Williamsville, 14221

716-632-7669 | eaglehouseonline.com

Mon–Sat 11 AM–10 PM, Sun 12 PM–9 PM

When you've been around as long as the Eagle House has, folks stop questioning the how and why—it just is and always has been. So it is that even current owners Tricia Brown and her father Bud Hanny don't know how Eagle House got its name.

Legend is it was founded in 1827 by Oziel Smith, who supposedly built it on limestone from his quarry and with lumber from his land, cut at his own sawmill. The latter he must have had to do twice given the property burned down after completion. A parade of owners followed, and its history can be found framed on its walls. It claims to have the longest continuously held liquor license in New York State, and to have been a station on the Underground Railroad.

History aside, The Eagle House is an institution. Depending on the weather or your mood, that means sitting at the wooden horseshoe bar, near the fireplace, or on the patio and digging into starters like French onion soup, stuffed banana peppers, artichokes Montemage (egg-and-cheese battered hearts pan-fried, then baked with butter and herbs). They're one of the infrequent few who do a Welsh rarebit, and one-up by serving its cheddar-and-ale dipping sauce with their order of onion rings (of course, there are also wings). Mains include burgers, fish fry, pastas, and typical grill fare. But the move is either the beef Wellington with wild mushroom pâté wrapped in French puff pastry, or the table-side-prepared chicken potpie.

"Bird, beef, and bottle with a bed for the weary traveler," The Holland Land Company supposedly declared upon coming across Williamsville while surveying nearby. And nearly 200 years after being founded, three out of four ain't bad.

Sophia's Restaurant

749 Military Road, Black Rock, 14216 | 716-447-9661

Tue–Sat 7 AM–3 PM, Sun 7 AM–2 PM, Closed Mon

Sophia is Sophia Ananiadias, the mom to son Sam Doherty, in this Greek-American diner's mother-son tandem. Sam took over in 2004, renovated, opened a few more days a week, and acquired a liquor license in 2012, so that their line-out-the-door brunches can be paired with one of the most well-regarded Bloody Marys in Buffalo. But otherwise, things haven't changed much since Sophia opened in 1981. It's still a no-frills spot for the Greek diner classics you know and love, and a place known for making traditional white bread from scratch and serving it hot and fresh, toasted with lots of butter. The

Spar's European Sausage

405 Amherst Street, Black Rock, 14207

716-876-6607 | sparseuropeansausage.com

Wed–Fri 9 AM–5 PM, Sat 9 AM–3 PM, Closed Sun–Tue

Get ready for some of the best sausages you've ever had. These days, they're made by Joe Kennedy, the former chef de cuisine at Buffalo's Park Lane Restaurant and a local punk musician. He took over the then 20-year-old shop in 2005, from founder Eric Spar after apprenticing with him. If there's an old-world feel to the shop and the fare, that's because Joe continues the tradition Spar learned as a young *metzger* (butcher apprentice) in Augsburg in the south of Germany.

bread was good enough on its own to score a stop from Guy Fieri. Bread!

Befitting a place routinely noted as one of the city's best diners, there are burgers, wraps, salads, fluffy pancakes, French toast made with that scratch bread, and huge omelettes so full that they have to be made with as many fillings as eggs. The "big plates" include skillets, a burrito, items with peameal, carved ham, and grilled kielbasa. But the two musts are the souvlaki featured on Triple D (your choice of chicken, beef, or gyro with eggs, home fries, and toast) and the Giambotta: Italian sausage mixed with home fries, hot and sweet peppers, onion, garlic, eggs, and cheese. Both are delicious and will set you straight for the day.

Spar supplemented the *fleisch- und wurst-waren* (meats and sausages) with the traditional specialties requested by neighborhood customers hailing from Germany, Hungary, Italy, Sweden, Ukraine, and Poland, building a loyal clientele with eclectic expectations. Joe, in turn carried on all of Spar's traditions and developed his own recipes for an even more diverse and delicious international selection including lamb merguez, English bangers, Portuguese linguisa, and hot and sweet Italian sausages. He also reevaluated the shop's sourcing, moving away, when possible, from industrial farms to smaller, local farms. Spar's now sources pork from T-Meadow Farm in nearby Lockport and beef from a collective of mostly grass-fed cows. The result is a butcher who makes about 95 percent of what he sells (they can sometimes smell the meat smoking at nearby Buffalo State).

There's so much to choose from, including various hand-cut chops; ready-to-reheat items like pulled pork, homemade chili, and beef stroganoff; and homemade cold cuts like olive leberkase, liverwurst, bologna, and headcheese. It almost guarantees required multiple visits. Especially since Joe makes all kinds of seasonal sausages too. But you can get a good overview by starting with these three super-popular picks. The "Sexy Brat" is a German bratwurst with tart cherries and apricots, there are cheddar brats seasoned with mustard and ginger, and then there's the "Sweet Potato Surprise," an andouille with sweet potatoes, green onions, and maple syrup.

Yes, you'll have to cook them, but even if you don't have a kitchen it's worth figuring out how to swing it. Either buy some on the way out of town, or go to Wegmans, get some charcoal, and get cooking. Both Front Park and Martin Luther King Jr. Park have picnic areas with grilling stations. It's worth it.

The Swannie House

170 Ohio Street, First Ward, 14203 | 716-847-2898
Mon–Sun 8 AM–4 AM

"Way down upon the . . ."—no, not that Swanee. Swannie House is on the corner of Ohio Street and Michigan Ave, a block between the Seneca Buffalo Creek Casino and the *Buffalo* River, which doesn't sing quite right, until maybe you've had a few inside. And that's easy to do, because this is the type of old place where within

minutes of a night in full swing, you're likely to get a nickname, and before you know it, be buying strangers a round, after they've bought you two.

Old photos show the bar surrounded by other buildings. Today, open lots and roads windswept by Lake Erie make it seem more like a last-standing sentinel to Old Buffalo. The building dates to 1892, and was said to have been opened as the "Swanerski House," a bar run by the Swanerski family, who, according to the guidebook *Buffalo's Waterfront*, changed the name to fly under-the-radar when relations between First Ward Irish and East Europeans weren't so good. In early days, the second floor was used as a boarding house for ship captains, and the third floor

for those of lower rank. These days, it's owned by Tim Wiles, who bought it in 1983, and renovated it.

Wings, weck, peppers, fish fry—all the Buffalo standards and bar classics are here. The food's not bad. Indeed, some dishes and specialties have been noted over the years by local publications. But it's kind of also beside the point. You go to Swannie to know the First Ward, to feel the wind off the lake after a few beers, and to drink in a place that's been drunk in for more than a century. And with all that done, and when the breeze hits you right, wafting across the river from the General Mills plant, it's the place that sends you off smelling like Buffalo.

"My City Smells Like Cheerios"

If you spend any time in Buffalo, you may find yourself walking down a street or driving along an overpass and all of a sudden inhaling a very familiar smell. You inhale again. It's toasty, it immediately makes you feel warm, and (unless you have coal for a heart) it's likely to bring a smile to your face. That's the smell of breakfast, more specifically, of cereal being made by the General Mills plant perched on the edge of Lake Erie.

Not such a surprise considering Buffalo's history as a grain port, right? And Buffalo's General Mills plant has been helping fill cereal bowls since 1941. And not just with Cheerios. They also make Honey Nut Cheerios and Lucky Charms, and in 2016 they announced a $25 million project that added packaging equipment to allow them to also produce Corn Chex and Honey Nut Chex. And while there *are* those who don't like the smell (do you hate puppies too?), there are even "My City

Smells Like Cheerios" T-shirts you can pick up if you so fancy. (To the haters: you would have preferred the Purina dog food factory that used to waft smells out, to have been the plant to stick around?)

So, where can you smell it? And when? That can be tricky. The smell can hit you in different parts of the city at different times depending on production and how the wind is blowing. But the plant is said to be a 24/7 facility. If you see steam coming out the side of the building . . . they're running, and you have a good shot at a sniff. (Rumor has it that the parts of the plant where they puff the cereal and do the sugar coatings are the best smelling areas.) And it's hard to believe you'd have a better chance than as close to the plant as you can get. For that vantage, plot a course for Swannie House across the river from the plant.

General Mills

54 S Michigan Avenue, First Ward, 14203

Ulrich's 1868 Tavern

674 Ellicott Street, Downtown, 14203 | 716-989-1868
ulrichstavern.com | Mon 11 AM–9 PM,
Tue–Sat 11 AM–10 PM, Closed Sun

Grover Cleveland, Babe Ruth, Anthony Bourdain—the list of Ulrich's storied visitors is not without notables. But then, what would you expect from a place said to be Buffalo's oldest bar? Opened in 1868, Ulrich's got its name from one of its owners, Michael Ulrich, who helmed it from 1905 to 1946. But look to the current owner, Salvatore Buscaglia, for making it glisten—he took over and renovated, renaming it Ulrich's 1868 Tavern in a nod to its history.

These days, there's more than just spit shine on this downtown classic. There's a polish to the wood bar and a glint to the stained-glass cabinetry behind it, which was bought by Michael Ulrich from the Iroquois Hotel in 1910. Pressed walls and ceilings lend character, and huge windows on the side dining room bring in reams of light, and vantage a corner view.

Ulrich's is a tavern with a German history, and menu items like schnitzel, warm pretzels, and wurst reflect that. But it also serves classic pub fare: burgers, salads, and sandwiches. Among them, there's a decent beef on weck with a roll with enough salt to keep all the roads in Buffalo free from snow. Okay, at least Ellicott and Virginia streets. There are shout-outs to their chili and hot pepper vodka-steamed Bloody Marys, but you shouldn't leave Ulrich's without ordering their super thin and crispy potato pancakes and a huge stein of beer.

All in all, it's a great pit stop between Founding Fathers and Lovejoy Pizza. Or, given that the bar hours on their website end with a question mark, maybe a good final stop for the night.

CHAPTER EIGHT

EATING OUT IN BUFFALO

Beyond Wings, Weck, and Pizza

Buffalo may be America's comfort food capital, so it's understandable to find yourself revisiting or checklist-eating through its storied wing, weck, and pie spots. But Buffalo's more than wings, weck, and pizza (as much as it pains to admit there's more to life than those three things). From tacos to tasting menus, southern fare to Burmese, there's some great food around town.

New-School Buffalo Cuisine

Perhaps mirroring the development and infusion of investment in the city, Buffalo has been on something of a restaurant tear the past few years. The *Buffalo News*'s food editor Andrew Galarneau went so far as to even cautiously call it "a restaurant gold rush," noting that "from downtown to the suburbs, new places are opening at a pace that industry veterans call unprecedented." Amid the heady froth of new restaurants that have been opened has been born what Galarneau coined in 2015, as "New-School Buffalo cuisine," seeing in it "seeds of uniquely Buffalo greatness in our restaurant community."

Galarneau has described new-school Buffalo cuisine as a wave of chefs opening new restaurants with menus based on the best local ingredients they can find, where you can spend $100 on dinner for four, adding, "They don't have valet parking or decades of polish. Some brainstormed dishes flop. But when the New-School Buffalo crowd nails it, sparks fly. Together, their efforts are redefining Buffalo-style cuisine as something light-years beyond chicken wings." Restaurant scenes can change quickly, but after visiting a few of these places and talking with Buffalo's food experts including *Buffalo Eats'* Donnie Burtless, Andrew Galarneau, former *Buffalo News* critic Janice Okun, and *Buffalo Spree*'s Christa Glennie Seychew, as of writing it's clear that 10 of these new-school Buffalo restaurants make up half of the city's 20 essential restaurants.

Count Carte Blanche, Craving, Dapper Goose, Elm Street Bakery, Lait Cru, Las Puertas, lloyd Taco Factory, Marble + Rye, The Grange, and Toutant are the 10 on this list, but don't be fooled that they're the only game in town. Oliver's, known as one of the city's best special occasion spots, has, in one incarnation or another, been around since 1936. Kuni's has been around since 1996. And Seabar, opened in 2010, is just the latest success for Buffalo chef Mike Andrzejewski, who's routinely credited as the godfather of the city's restaurant scene.

"If All You Know About Buffalo is its Sports Teams, Its Restaurants Will Make You Think Buffalo Can be a Winner After all."

If you live in Buffalo and follow the food scene, you know him. If you don't, allow me to introduce the food editor for the *Buffalo News* of the past seven years. This is Andrew Galarneau, a Western New York native and University of Buffalo alum, and he's a self-described "Buffaholic." What's a Buffaholic?

"Being a Buffaholic means you come from this place and dealing with sort of communal inferiority complex that afflicts people to think that they're living a downtrodden life because they're in a town that has been economically depressed and whose sports teams are known for not winning," Andrew explains. "Another word for not winning is losing. It means looking at the world through that filter. You're prone to overreact to any small sign that your city might be kind of cool, actually. My Buffaholic fever has pretty much broken with my continued exploration, and hopefully championing of some of our great restaurants."

In other words, now *that's* Andrew's favorite team: The restaurants in Buffalo have given him something to cheer for.

Like other influential food writers across America, Andrew has probably responded to more emails from friends, family members, and strangers over the years looking for recs than he would care to ponder counting. So in the interests of giving him a little more time away from his desk, check out his recommendations (at publication) for answering that eternal question, "What and where should I eat tonight?"

Let's get this out of the way: wings?

Where I send people for Buffalo standard wings is Duff's. You're looking for the ambience at Anchor Bar, but I like the wings at Duff's better. They're crispier and, frankly, the last time I talked with the owners about it, which is a couple years ago, they said they use butter in their sauce. Not margarine, like at other places. That was what did it for me.

Straight-up Buffalo-style pizza?

I'm a Bocce on Bailey guy all day long. Obviously, the quality can waiver, but I keep coming back to the overflowing, oozy pepperoni goodness. But if I grew up in the Southtowns I would probably be telling you, Imperial.

Weck?

If you're not hand-cutting your beef I don't even want to talk to you. Glen Park Tavern on Main Street in Williamsville and Schwabl's in Southtowns. You can get more meat on a bun, and if you're a size queen you might want to go someplace else, but if you're asking me my opinion that's my opinion. If you're in town and you need the weck experience and only have time for one, go to Schwabl's.

What about chicken finger subs?

My favorite chicken finger sub is from Café 59 on Allen Street because they are hand dipping their tenders and making their own blue cheese and not using the same old types of factory planks.

Sponge candy?

I'm a Ko-Ed guy. It was recently bought, but the quality, in my opinion, rates the same. But there are savage disagreements about this.

Tom and Jerry?

McPartlan's Corner. They're good and they're like $6. Other places are gonna nick you $12. It's like, "Oh, you did not just do that."

Custard?

I have a new favorite, and it's Churn. That's the lloyd soft serve operation. They use local milk from Ithaca, and they're the only place in town making their own base. Everyone else is using a bulk base and tweaking it. Churn is making their own base, which is a level of commitment that I'm sorry, if you have that stuff you can taste the good milk. It's worth the extra work.

Fried bologna sandwich?

If you're looking for a classic bologna sandwich, you should go taste one at the Swannie House, one of the oldest continuing operating restaurants in Buffalo. It is literally a stone's throw from the canal and the silos.

Fish fry?

Wiechec's in Kaisertown.

Okay, now that we've gotten the icons out of the way, where do you send folks who are looking for something they can get that's good in Buffalo that they can't find elsewhere?

lloyd Taco Factory, which is now in two locations. Polish Villa II for Polish family dining. Lin is the best Burmese restaurant in town. No tablecloths, limited beer and wine, more of a family restaurant, really, but Lin is definitely on that list. The Grange Community Kitchen in Hamburg. Ru's Pierogi. If you thought pierogi were just for dinner, well, think again. And the other one that immediately comes to mind, but I tend to dismiss when I'm talking to people because it's such a humble place, is Niagara Café. It's the city's preeminent Puerto Rican family restaurant. Nothing in there's $12, but what they do is just so freaking consistent. They're slammed out the door pretty much every day.

And what are the places in Buffalo to go for special occasions?

Las Puertas, Black Sheep, Dapper Goose, Marble + Rye, and Craving.

Andrew's readers are his best sources ("They're everywhere," his email signer says, "I'm just one guy typing in an office"). Send him tips on what's new/interesting/delicious in your neighborhood. Follow him @BuffaloFood on Instagram and Twitter for the results.

Where the (Hungry Multicultural) Buffalos Roam

New-School Buffalo cuisine's not all farm-to-table. The 716 features a diverse array of cuisines, much of it thanks to immigration over the past two decades. In fact, according to the census, as with other regions of New York like Syracuse, Dutchess-Putnam, Utica-Rome, Binghamton, and Kingston, the total population count in Buffalo-Niagara Falls, fell from 2010

to 2015, and would have declined more sharply except for the addition of new residents from other countries. Immigrants from Burma, Bhutan, Somalia, and Iraq have brought with them delicious food and have created a demand for it.

Among other foods, you'll find restaurants serving Korean, Szechuan, Vietnamese, Indian, Ethiopian, Thai, Iraqi, and Peruvian cuisines. And if you're looking to go on a culinary adventure, visit the small business, and worldwide cuisine incubator Westside Bazaar. The open-air market, which started at 242 Grant Street in 2011, with business owners from Rwanda, South Sudan, Peru, and Indonesia, has since moved and expanded, usually housing some nine food stalls with Burmese, Mexican, Indian, Pakistani, Thai, Ethiopian, and Chinese among the featured cuisines. Call it Buffalo's culinary zócalo.

Westside Bazaar

25 Grant Street, West Side, 14213 | 716-464-6389
westsidebazaar.com | Tue 11 AM–7 PM, Wed 11 AM–7 PM,
Thu 11 AM–7 PM, Fri 11 AM–8 PM,
Sat 10 AM–8 PM, Closed Sun and Mon

There's a burgeoning taco scene, too. And not just the fusion, food-truck type (as delicious as they are) like lloyd, either. In recent years, fast-food taco Buffalo institution Mighty Taco's Buffalo-style chicken Buffitos have gotten company from much more authentic taquerias, some of which—Casa Azul and La Divina Mexican Store among them—are making their own tortillas.

As with any restaurant scene, Buffalo's is changing, and fast. The 20 essential restaurants this year could be game-changed by five new openings next year. (As of writing, Toutant chef James Roberts was about to open a new restaurant, Dobutsu.) But enough talk. You're hungry, right? Whether you're in town visiting, live in the city, or its surrounding suburbs, here are 20 checklist restaurants you *need* to tuck in at.

Kyar san chat, chicken soup served at the Westside Bazaar with shredded chicken, shrimp dumplings, four kinds of mushrooms, and clear ben noodles.

Buffalo's 20 Essential Restaurants

Bacchus Wine Bar & Restaurant

56 W. Chippewa Street, Downtown, 14202
716-854-9463 | bacchusbuffalo.com
Tue–Sat 5 pm–11 pm, Sun 4:30 pm–9 pm, Closed Mon

Owner and chef Brian Mietus's restaurant opened on the main floor of the renovated Calumet building in 2003, and quickly became known as one of the fancier places in town. The menu is divided into small and large plates. The former includes classics like Caesar salad, tuna tartar, and steamed mussels with white wine and butter. In addition to well-executed standards like roasted chicken, filet mignon, rib eye, salmon, and roasted duck, large plates include raved-over corn and ricotta ravioli, bouillabaisse, and a shrimp-crusted swordfish with romesco and beurre blanc. Bacchus is routinely noted as having one of Buffalo's best wine lists and from June through September they do a summer film series on their back patio with movies shown starting at dusk on a large screen. Just don't miss the signature gnocchi "mac and cheese" with mushrooms, prosciutto, and goat cheese made not far away in East Bethany by First Light Creamery.

Carte Blanche

61 Buffalo Street, Hamburg, 14075 | 716-649-2101
carteblanchehamburg.com | Tue–Thu 4 pm–9 pm,
Fri–Sat 4 pm–10 pm, Sun Brunch 10 am–2 pm

"Carte Blanche" means freedom to act as one wishes. Here, that translates to a tidy menu of homestyle Italian dishes. In addition to arancini and pork and veal meatballs, a broiled butter block toast topped with goat cheese, sautéed mushrooms, and a drizzle of yolk is an early showstopper. The menu is rounded out with homemade pastas, and heavier mains like red-wine braised beef short rib with fresh pasta and mushroom cream. In addition to their signature carafes of Bloody Marys, mimosas, and screwdrivers, Sunday brunch's peppercorn fried chicken and Belgian waffle with ghost pepper maple syrup gets lots of buzz. The rest of your party will have fun deciding between corned beef hash, salted caramel French toast, and popovers stuffed with scrambled egg, bacon, cheese, and brûléed onion.

Casa Azul

128 Genesee Street, Downtown, 14203

716-331-3869 | casaazulbuffalo.com

Mon–Sat 11:30 AM–9 PM

After opening downtown in the former hot dog spot Dog é Style in late 2016, Casa Azul's tacos were quickly called some of Buffalo's most ambitious. How so? Housemade corn tortillas play their part, including one that's beet-infused and another made with spicy chocolate. But perhaps it's also the focus on legit fillings you'll find served out of authentic taco trucks in Los Angeles, and on the edges of Mexico City's great food markets: sweetbreads, braised tongue, trotters, and the like. Only at Casa Azul ('blue house,' for the blue shipping container exterior), Mexican chef Victor Parra Gonzalez and Vincenza "Zina" Lapi (formerly of Mike A's and the Blue Balls Bus arancini truck) add an extra layer of love, infusing the sweetbreads with tequila, wrapping their slow-braised goat in banana leaf, and topping their potato and poblano chile taco with spiced nuts. Wash it all down with horchata, lime and chia, and watermelon agua frescas while watching the cooks work in the open kitchen. And if you're a little less adventurous, you can still find delicious tacos al pastor (shaved pork cut from the vertical broiler called a trompo), carne asada, charcoal-finished chicken leg confit, and either pastor or chicken torta sandwiches. And the place is just a few storefronts down from Marble + Rye and kitty-corner from classic fried bologna and beef on weck sandwiches at Genesee Street stalwart Eddie Brady's Tavern. Who knew?

Craving

1472 Hertel Avenue, Hertel Avenue, 14216

716-883-1675 | cravingbuffalo.com

Mon–Thu 11 AM–3 PM, 5 PM–9 PM; Fri–Sat 11 AM–3 PM, 5 PM–10 PM; Sun 10 AM–3 PM

The menu at chef Adam Goetz's dark, cozy bistro depends on what fresh, farmed, organic, sustainable, and local ingredients that they can get their hands on. Then the philosophy is to "let the ingredients taste for themselves." This can be a challenge during cooler months, but it's just meant that since it opened in 2013, they've developed relationships with the producers named on the menu. In terms of what that means on your plate? Anything from fried chicken and cheddar grits, pork belly with fregola, chicken fried kidneys, to handkerchief pasta with asparagus and mushrooms. You can bet that Goetz, who worked at the Waldorf Astoria in Manhattan, will be making some kind of homemade pastas, likely a ragu, dishes with lamb or duck if he can get them, and a few crunchy thin-crust pizzas that are nothing like the ones found in Buffalo's pizzerias. If you're undecided, take a moment to consider the menu at the small, friendly bar

up front over a glass of one of the organic or bio-dynamic, small production wines they usually carry, or a craft cocktail invented by bar manager Nick O'Brien.

Blogging 900 Restaurants: Buffalo Eats' Donnie Burtless on Buffalo's Dining Scene

If you Google a Buffalo restaurant, chances are Donnie Burtless and his wife Alli have been there and written about it. They're the team behind *Buffalo Eats*, Buffalo's most prolific and consistent food blog. Since launching it in 2009, they wrote about or reviewed more than 900 restaurants in the Buffalo-Niagara area. Since they started *Buffalo Eats*, they've gotten engaged, married, bought a house, and had a daughter. If it's not in this book, you can safely bet you can turn to *Buffalo Eats*.

What are the three biggest changes in Buffalo's dining scene since 2009?

First, the amount of money being put into the restaurant scene. Prior to 2014, new restaurants were fairly modest and had the occasional big buildout, but in the last three years we've seen a ton of money thrown around. It's promising to see people taking these old buildings downtown and putting some life into them. I'm still hoping that it's all worth it in the end. Second, food trucks are everywhere. We started the blog before lloyd, the first local food truck, was on the road. Not only have we seen 60-plus food trucks debut since 2010, but the general attitude has completely warmed to them. At first, they had to fight for every spot. Now, Food Truck Tuesdays bring 5,000 people to Larkinville—they serve food in every work plaza in Western New York (hell, you can even find them in front of Target) and the barrier for entry has seemingly gone down. I was hoping there would be more variety and chef-driven trucks, but that doesn't seem to be the case. Lastly, people are more interested in the newest thing than ever before. It seems the attention span for what's new and cool has become shorter than ever.

What's Buffalo still missing that you think it could really be ready for?

A true barcade would be an answer to my dreams. I'd love to see someone take Buffalo classics and do it right in a cool setting. Kind of like what Parm did to red sauce or Mission Chinese did with Chinese takeout. A talented chef taking Buffalo classics and just tweaking them.

What's the best meal you've had in all your time reviewing?

That's hard. The press-only tasting menu at the now defunct Mike A's in the Hotel Lafayette was truly exceptional in 2012. I was surrounded by people who knew way more about food then myself and they were all freaking out. It seemed like Buffalo was getting ready to take a step forward with our dining scene. That restaurant didn't work out, but it set the tone for what we see today.

What are your top five Buffalo restaurants?

These are my favorites. Not necessarily the best objectively but my favorites. The Grange in Hamburg is the most Instagram-friendly restaurant in Western New York and I love it. I don't know what it is, but chef Brad Rowell's food and my taste buds are just in sync. Toutant is my go-to; I love executive chef and owner James Roberts' execution of southern food staples and the occasional crazy creation from chef de cuisine Joe Fenush. Marble + Rye is my hangout-at-the-bar-and-eat restaurant. They have the best burger in Buffalo and their pastas are criminally underrated. The Black Sheep is my favorite place to just go with no plans, where I like to let the chef take the reins. Chef Steve Gedra is a madman, but I mean that in the best way. Bar Bill Tavern is just a bar with wings and beef on weck, and God, they do both just so damn well.

Top five bars?

I'm not ranking this list but if I did, Founding Fathers is number one because I love everything about it. I don't really care about cocktails but I love Ballyhoo. It's a great place to grab a beer and hang with a mix of General Mills workers and hipsters. Gene McCarthy's is a classic First Ward/Irish bar but updated with some of the best beer brewed in Western New York. I guess a tie of Allen Burger Venture and the Moor Pat because it's as close to the Blue Monk as I can get in 2017 (RIP). And finally, The Pink because it's such a shithole and I lived across the street and there's no better place to crush a steak sandwich and PBRs.

What's your favorite place for the following?

Wings: *Nine-Eleven Tavern. It's still a locals-only wing joint and the sauce is unlike anything I've had.*

Weck: *Bar Bill Tavern serves the most tender beef I've ever had. Watch the show from the bar. It's the best.*

Pizza: *Imperial Pizza is the prototypical Buffalo-style pizza that is great to eat on the hood of a car in the parking lot.*

Sponge Candy: *Watson's because the milk chocolate is better than most. But most of it tastes the same.*

Tom & Jerry: *I hate these, sorry.*

What's your favorite sub and where's it from?

I don't eat a lot of subs, but if we aren't counting the shrimp po'boy at Toutant . . . then the stinger sub at Jim's SteakOut is something special. I know I'm only supposed to eat them at 2 AM but there is some weird magic to those subs that I keep coming back to.

What should out-of-towners know about Buffalo's dining scene that they don't know?

We have really talented chefs that aren't just "Buffalo-talented" but rank with national talent. A lot of chefs have worked elsewhere and brought their skills back to their hometown.

What should more *Buffalonians* know about the city's dining scene that they don't know?

Our ethnic restaurant scene is amazing and you should go outside your comfort zone more often. Also, local restaurants can be way more affordable than chains if you know how to order.

Dapper Goose

491 Amherst Street, Black Rock, 14207

716-551-0716 | thedappergoose.com

Tue–Thu 5 PM–10 PM, Fri–Sat, 5 PM–11 PM,

Sun 11 AM–3 PM, 5 PM–9 PM

In 2016, Peggy Wong, John Beane, and Keith Rai-mondi took over the space that had been Black

Rock Kitchen. Olean native Raimondi made his name in Philadelphia working at Village Whiskey and other Garces Group restaurants, and Beane is a fitness trainer. The reimagined space with silver ceilings and minimalist décor benefits from a dying-light lit bar up front and a back patio that seats an additional 30 seats to the dining room's 60. There are some mean, cleverly named cocktails, and the Dapper Goose's small plates treatment takes vegetables as seriously as the close-your-eyes-and-savor-it beef tartare, crab toast, burrata, and in-house charcuterie. The menu changes with some frequency, but consider interesting pairings and accoutrements like a broccoli dish accompanied with smoked grapes, radicchio dressed with burnt walnut pesto, and the blackened green beans with burnt onion aioli and pepitas that has become a must-order. As for mains, they do one of the city's killer burgers, with a dill pickle aioli and French onion jam. And while ordering Korean fried chicken anywhere not called K-town might concern some, Dapper Goose nails it with an addictive kimchi fried rice you'll probably just want to go ahead and ask for a side order of.

Elm Street Bakery

72 Elm Street, East Aurora, 14052 | 716-652-4720
elmstreetbakery.com | Tue–Fri 7 AM–9 PM,
Sat 8 AM–9 PM, Sun 9 AM–2 PM, Closed Mon

Elm Street Bakery has been oohing and aahing locals since it opened in a former appliance store in 2011. Breakfast is served daily until 11 AM, offering an extensive bakery-forward menu that changes seasonally but includes homemade bialys, muf-fins, granola bars, and breakfast breads. There's a breakfast sandwich served on their artisanal bread with a poached egg, local bacon, and cheddar, and a wood-roasted veggie version with a lightly spiced aioli that's worth skipping the meat for. Elm Street's philosophy is to "let nature take the lead and cook the old-fashioned way, like grandma did, no shortcuts, just real food." As that pertains to pizza, available during lunch (on a more limited scale) and dinner (with more topping combinations), that means making their own dough (an overnight ferment), sauce, and fresh mozzarella, then cooking them in an Alan Scott, 700-degree, wood-fired brick oven, where chicken breast gets that dry heat treatment too.

Kuni's

226 Lexington Avenue, Elmwood, 14222
716-881-3800 | kunisbuffalo.com
Tue–Thu 5 PM–9:45 PM, Fri–Sat 5 PM–10:45 PM,
Closed Sun–Mon

You can find sushi at Wegmans these days, but credit chef Kuni Sato, who opened his little spot in 1996, for giving Buffalonians a taste for it. While there *are* fusion creations like seared Cajun tuna and "sashimi 21" (an assortment of thinly sliced fish with avocado, capers, jalapeño, and yuzu-marinated onions), Kuni's is more traditionally focused. You come here to order some sake and Japanese whisky from the thorough list, and to indulge in the 24 different sushi a la carte options or other traditional Japanese dishes like tonkatsu (fried, panko-encrusted pork) and grilled yellowtail hamachi kama. Just remember, no reservations. *Irasshaimase*!

Four Decades of Restaurant Writing: A Conversation with Janice Okun

Janice Okun was a pioneer in American restaurant writing. Her reviews began appearing in the *Buffalo News* in 1974 (though it was the *Buffalo Evening News* back then), at first every other week. She and her editor Murray Light thought they'd run out of places to review if she wrote them more frequently. "Both of us were wrong," she wrote in her book, *Buffalo Cooks with Janice Okun: Memories and Recipes from a Life in Food*. When she started, Okun notes, we as Americans, knew much less about food. ("Most people didn't even know what cilantro was then . . . they didn't know what a local tomato was, either, come to think about it.") And while she went into semi-retirement in 2009 (she has occasionally contributed reviews since), she celebrates the fact that her time as food editor and restaurant critic gave her a front row seat to watch the changes. In this interview, she shares perspective on her years writing about the dining scene (and wings) in Buffalo.

Forty years as a restaurant editor, starting at a time when women weren't in roles like these . . . what was that like?

And as a working mother.

Did you ever encounter any prejudice for being a woman in this role?

Not really. Two things to remember: We were the first in the area to print this type of review and I was already well-known as the food editor. Readers just took to the idea and most restaurateurs just swallowed hard and accepted it. Of course, they liked the publicity.

Can you give an example of how you noticed things changing?

The woman I replaced, Harriet Cooke, was a nice old thing and she was a good cook, I think, except she was one that didn't season things. She was, I guess, a WASP, and she cooked like a WASP, and she didn't like garlic because she thought it wasn't nice, because it smells. To me, to cook without garlic is, "Thank you very much, I'm not going to bother." Anyway, she called me up one day after I took over from her. She was gracious but she said to me, "Why does every recipe running have garlic in it?" I said, "Because I like garlic."

Were people ready for garlic?

Everybody was still opening cans of Campbell's tomato soup.

But you started to change things.

It changed. It began to change because I didn't like food like that, and I couldn't help but cook the food I liked. I started running around interviewing people, people who were good cooks, farmers, anybody involved with food, and that was the best part. It wasn't making the food that was so great. It was talking to people about food.

Did you enjoy your tenure as restaurant critic?

I loved every minute. I loved it. I loved it. I learned so much. I can go past a field now and say, "Look what's growing in that field. Do you see that?" And I will go into a whole long boring explanation of how you market it and what people can do with it. How would I have known all that? A little girl from North Buffalo who wasn't really used to good food!

Are there any reviews you got wrong or wish you could redo?

I take the Fifth.

Is there any one restaurant that's closed that you wish was still around?

Rue Franklin, which started as a coffeehouse and matured into a beautiful restaurant with a French menu and a beautiful garden. But it was sold to the chef, a fine cook, and it just never was as popular. (Pardon me while I wipe my tears.)

What's one of the biggest challenges you faced as a critic?

It's pretty hard to keep writing about the same crappy hamburger place over and over and over again and say something intelligent.

Are you sick of talking about wings?

No, no, I'm not sick of talking about them, but I wonder what new thing there is we can say!

Do you remember how you first heard about wings in Buffalo?

I think our next-door neighbors told us to try them. We thought, "This is really great." Let's face it. Chicken wings are good. They're not healthy. They're not particularly gourmet, if you want to use that horrible term, but they taste good.

Yours was one of the first wing recipes published. How did it come about?

I visited the Anchor Bar, they wouldn't tell me anything much so I went home and tried to figure it out. Used close to 20 spices and the wings were good but didn't taste the same. I printed it anyway explaining it was my best shot. Then I got a letter from an anonymous person who said he once worked for the Anchor Bar. As you know, the recipe he gave was ultra-simple. And absolutely right on! I printed that one, too. I guess the rest is history.

You wrote about making wings at home: "Don't mess with the recipe. Don't try to gentrify it. Don't try to make it 'healthier.'" Still believe that?

The thing that really is bad about chicken wings is that they started to bake them. Why do they bake them? They bake them because they think they are healthy. Don't tell me about baked chicken wings. I think they're awful.

What about all the newfangled flavors of wings? Are you fine with them?

I wouldn't eat them, but if you want to eat them, eat them.

Do you still go out for wings?

I usually have them delivered. Would I make them at home is the next question? Never!

What are some of the more recent food developments in Buffalo that you've noticed?

For years there was not a decent barbecue restaurant. Mexican. Mexican now is everywhere.

Did you anticipate Buffalo's resurgence? What do you think about its dynamic new restaurant scene?

It amazes me how many new restaurants there are. It just amazes me. It worries me a little bit, too.

Is there too much similarity in Buffalo's restaurant scene today?

There's always been a certain amount of copying with restaurants. It's like television shows. Somebody comes in with a great TV show and everyone else has to do the same thing. For gosh sake, how many of them can you use?

As Buffalo continues its resurgence, you're seeing more chains, especially in the suburbs. Do you see the mom-and-pop places, the community staples that have been such pillars of the restaurant scene being affected?

I worry about it because it takes money. It takes money to stay. It takes money to advertise. Are there enough of the old crowd left so they can keep the doors open? I don't know.

At some point, Buffalo became a flavor and not just a city. Are you happy that wings are so identified with it or do you wish Buffalo was known for more?

What other city in the United States could make this statement! Do you want me to be very honest with you? I'm not going to look down on this at all. I think it was a lucky break. Especially in the old days. There weren't many cities in the United States that had something distinctive like this.

La Divina Mexican Store

2896 Delaware Avenue, Kenmore, 14217
716-447-8989 | Mon–Fri 11 AM–9 PM,
Sat 12 PM–9 PM, Sun 12 PM–8 PM

When it opened in a former Iraqi grocery in 2015, owner Sergio Mucino's La Divina really filled a niche Buffalo had been missing, a legit taqueria complete with a tortilla machine to make fresh corn tortillas, and, in what's frequently a sign of quality and authenticity, a plentiful fixings station with pico de gallo, limes, radishes, peppers, and more salsas than you can try in a standard three-taco basket. The counter also has what any of America's greatest taco spots have: a line. No matter—plenty of time to decide which of 14 different ways you want to fill your tacos or top your tostadas, most of which cost $2.50 and no more than $4. They serve all the Chipotle-popularized classic fillings—barbacoa (brisket), asada (steak), carnitas (pulled pork)—along with greasy-in-a-good way Mexican chorizo; lengua (tongue); tripe; nopales (cactus) with mushrooms, peppers, and onions; and cecina enchilada chile-coated salt-cured steak. For a few dollars more there are also delicious quesadillas, and filing Mexican cemitas sandwiches layered with avocado, housemade chipotle mayo, Oaxaca queso, and your choice of meat on a sesame seed roll.

Lait Cru Brasseri

346 Connecticut Street, West Side, 14213
716-462-4100 | laitcrubrasserie.com
Tue–Wed 9 AM–3 PM, Thu–Sat 9 AM–2:30 PM, 5 PM–9 PM,
Sun 10:30 AM–2:30 PM, Closed Mon

Owner Jill Gedra Forster moved her Nickel City Cheese store into the former Martin Cooks space in the old four-story warehouse turned loft apartment building on Buffalo's West Side in 2016 and raised the game. The *other* side of her gourmet cheese shop now turns out French brasserie fare. The breakfast menu features salads, and sandwiches like their ham and egg with pimento cheese, a triple-crème grilled cheese, over-easy eggs with butter and ham on a croissant, and their playful "Nic Mac": housemade roast beef, American cheese, special sauce, sesame seeds, onion, and pickle, on a toasted roll. And of course, there's always a daily selection of cheese and charcuterie. *Pour diner au soir,* there's a tidy sampling of hors d'oeuvres like a six-minute egg with toast and lemon aioli, savory beignets with Gruyère and Aleppo, and a tomato tart made with housemade mozzarella. *Plats principaux* include classic bistro steak frites with roasted vegetables and horseradish cream, and other high $20 entrées like cast-iron roast chicken with pickled vegetables, roasted quail, and seared scallops.

Las Puertas

385 Rhode Island Street, West Side, 14213

716-807-1141 | laspuertas-buffalo.com

Tue–Sat 5 PM–10 PM, Closed Sun–Mon

Las Puertas is a delicious sliver of a spot billed as "Modern Mexican" that you might not expect to find in a part of town that's on the rise, but still has rough edges. The name literally means "the doors," a nod to the spirit of possibility (not Jim Morrison), that its Acapulco-born chef Victor Parra Gonzalez, his sister Diana, and their mother Olivia Polin feel fortunate to have experienced through the years as the right doors have opened for *them*. The décor and plating are both minimalist and artistic. There's a blond-wood chef's tasting counter in front of a mesmerizing mural by illustrator Carolyn Perillo that feels like both story and transformation as feathers, arrows, and clasped hands highlight its turn from snake to corn to octopus. The dishes that arrive—constructed with classic French techniques—are just as much of a journey. You can start with oysters and one of the well-balanced, creative cocktails made by the chef's mother, and

order a la carte with dishes ranging from $7 for salads, $8 for appetizers, and mains from $14 to $26. But this may be one of the best places in Buffalo to drop some cash and do a tasting menu ($10 per course, with options for five, seven, or 10 courses). Papaya granita, wild bass ceviche, goat broth with cotija and green onions, scallop aquachile with beet and rhubarb ribbons, garam masala New York strip steak…who knows where the night will go? Wherever it does, it will be tasty, it will be beautiful, and it will end with some of pastry chef Jenn Batt's creative desserts. Peach rosemary sorbet with sweet oats? Rhubarb sorbet with pistachio cake and lemon anglaise? Yes, yes, and yes.

Lin Restaurant

927 Tonawanda Street, Riverside, 14207

716-260-2625 | linrestaurantbuffalo.com

Mon–Fri 11 AM–10 PM, Sat–Sun 9 AM–10 PM

Burmese husband-and-wife team Khin Maung Soe and Thain Hla opened Lin Restaurant in 2014, bringing with them authentic Thai and Myanmar cuisine to Riverside, and garnering this complimentary headline in the *Buffalo News*: "A cultural blessing." Strolling through the grocery aisles full of unfamiliar ingredients in the attached Lin Asian Market is a cool way to begin (or end, if you're squeamish), but a meal at Lin is one you *do* need to prioritize. The menu's extensive, so maybe start with *ohn no khao swè* (wheat noodles in a curried chicken and coconut milk broth); *le phet thoat* (the traditional Burmese pickled tea leaf salad) tossed with crispy

Try *le phet thoat* at Lin Restaurant, the traditional Burmese pickled tea leaf salad.

peas, peanut, sesame seeds, garlic, cabbage, onions, and sliced tomatoes; and chicken biryani served with a dome of fragrant rice studded with cashews, golden raisins, and peas. You smell the fish sauce when it's set down and won't want to get up.

lloyd Taco Factory

1503 Hertel Avenue, Hertel Avenue, 14216
716-863-9781 | whereslloyd.com
Mon–Thu 11 AM–11 PM, Fri–Sat 11 AM–2 AM,
Closed Sun ("Go Bills")

5933 Main Street Williamsville, 14216
716-863-9781 | Mon–Thu 11 AM–11 PM,
Fri–Sat 11 AM–12 AM, Closed Sun

Peter Cimino and Chris Dorsaneo made a name for themselves around town with a fleet of four food trucks, and even scored a $250,000 deal while on CNBC's *Restaurant Startup*. But they went brick-and-mortar on their own, taking a

cue from the show that they needed to up their tortilla game. That they did, hiring someone to help them start their own tortilla business (with full on nixtamalization) then opening on Hertel Avenue in 2015 (and a second location in 2017). At lloyd, the menu gets divided between "old school" and "new school." Tacos, burritos, and nachos with your choice of braised beef, grilled chicken, slow-roasted pork, and stewed local black beans. New-school tacos and burritos get filled with crispy wild pollock; buttermilk fried chicken with waffle pieces and bacon aioli (the "Dirty South"); and fried tofu and peanut sauce (the "Skinny Thai"). In another riff on the Big Mac in a town that likes to play this game, the "Big lloyd" is filled with grass-fed ground beef, special sauce, cheddar, pickles, romaine, red onions, sesame seeds. The games don't stop there. There are shrimp tostadas, Mexicali spring rolls, Sonoran hot dogs, Buffalo chicken hot pockets; and a fleet of mezcal and tequila dominated craft cocktails to wash it all down with. Now, who's lloyd, you ask?

The Mystery of lloyd

Start with one part Dos Equis' Most Interesting Man in the World then add one part Fojol Bros. of Merlindia, Washington DC's one-time hit Indian food truck sensation with a wondrous backstory, and you're close to answering the riddle, wrapped in a burrito, inside a chimichanga. Okay, no chimichangas at lloyd, but you get the idea.

Here's what Peter Cimino and Chris Dorsaneo have to say about the man behind the tacos.

"The mystery of lloyd has yet to be fully understood, but there are insights, anecdotes, and fables passed down generation to generation that help us identify the man behind the green truck. It's been said he puts masa in his coffee, stands anywhere from 5 to 7 feet tall, and hasn't gone a day in his life without eating a taco. Yes, that includes the very day on which he was born.

"What we can confirm is that lloyd cares about a lot of things: the quality of the food he creates, bold flavors, fresh ingredients, and Converse sneakers. He understands that making every single item from scratch means countless hours in the kitchen and higher overhead. He has a PhD in Hospitality and is often erroneously (though not undeservedly) credited as the inventor of the margarita.

"Some people believe lloyd is a myth. Is he Bigfoot? Does he own a ranch on Area 52? Is Nessie his pet? These are questions only lloyd can answer, but we're okay with that because isn't the mystery part of what makes lloyd so special?"

Marble + Rye

112 Genesee Street, Downtown, 14203

716-853-1390 | marbleandrye.net

Tue–Thu 5 pm–10 pm, Fri–Sat 5 pm–11 pm

Don't get the wrong impression, Marble + Rye is a 75-top restaurant with good service and a nice dining room, but there's something about the

oven. There are some seriously addicting tangy pickled onion rings, and a nod to the local icons with lemon-brined chicken wings and a *sick* spicy "Bison" dip. There's a great burger, but the menu has Mediterranean range. Depending on the season, you'll find dishes like patatas bravas, falafel, wood-fired octopus with charred onion, and pappardelle with stone fruits.

Oliver's

2095 Delaware Avenue, Park Meadow, 14216
716-877-9662 | oliverscuisine.com
Tue–Thu 5 pm–10 pm, Fri–Sat 5 pm–11 pm,
Sun 4:30 pm–9:30 pm, Closed Mon

Welcome to Oliver's, where leather-backed chairs, half-moon booths, and a lamp-lit horseshoe-shaped bar immediately make you feel like you're stepping back in time. Oliver's *is* quintessential Buffalo fine dining, and has been for decades. Its history goes back to 1936, when it was opened by Frank Oliver. Henry Gorino took it over in 1983, and David Schutte assumed the mantle in 2013, giving the interior an update and makeover. The list of previous chefs—Paul Jenkins, Mark Hutchinson, Brian Mietus, Mike Andrzejewski, Daniel Johengen, and Lennon Lewandowski—reads to many in town like a who's who of Buffalo's well-respected kitchens. The menu has all the marks of old-school, white-tablecloth dining: vichyssoise, Caesar salad, surf, turf, and beef tartare. But old-school at Oliver's also means the classics it's been famous for forever: its eponymous salad with sweet shrimp, sopressata, artichoke hearts, and blue cheese; the chicken Milanese;

bar that's magnetic. You know how food trucks draw crowds? Well, it's almost as if co-owners Christian Willmott and Michael Dimmer somehow transplanted the soul of their former Black Market Food Truck, and that urge to gather, at the bar in the center of their restaurant. The bar opens an hour before the kitchen does daily, and stays open until midnight Tuesday through Thursday and until 2 AM Friday and Saturday, and patrons just seem drawn to it, and not just for craft cocktails, but for eating dinner—solo, couples, heck, parties of four. Marble + Rye is another everything-from-scratch restaurant whose ethos is to use local suppliers and farmers, but one whose technique usually focuses on their cast-iron Mexican plancha and wood-fired and paccheri Bolognese. Then, of course, there's the famed spinach loaf, a split baguette slathered with garlic butter, filled with spinach and cheese, then smothered in more cheese and sliced in sections. But these days, those familiar touches are joined on the menu by a five- or seven-course tasting menu (available Tuesday through Thursday) courtesy of its current executive chef, Ross Warhol.

Peking Quick One

359 Somerville Avenue, Tonawanda, 14150
716-381-8730 | Mon–Sun 11 am–10 pm

Along with China Star and Miss Hot Café, Peking Quick One is generally regarded as one of Buffalo's best places for good Chinese food. It isn't much to look at: a thin yellow "Quick One" sign above a window with some disheveled vertical blinds in a strip mall parking lot on a side street off Brighton Road. Inside, the décor is a combination of fluorescent lights, a few red lanterns, and whatever the latest fashion trend is being worn by the students who typically fill it. So owner Aileen Lin's restaurant isn't a looker. So what? You know those rumors you always hear about secret menus at Chinese restaurants where all the really good, spicy, authentic dishes are? Well, Peking Quick One isn't trying to pull one over on you. Their secret menu is printed and stacked right there next to the one with kung pao on it. The "homestyle menu" is where you'll find stir-fried sliced pork liver or tripe, sweet and sour pork ribs, whole steamed flounder, stir-fried celery with beef, salt and pepper shrimp, and the like. Quick One indeed—quick one on anyone who drives by and doesn't think it's worth stopping inside.

Nickel City Narrator: Christa Glennie Seychew

Christa Glennie Seychew grew up in Seattle, the child of parents who were from farming families in Western New York. Struggling with the cost of living in the suddenly-popular Pacific Northwest, she was drawn by cheap rent and extended family. "I assumed all the snow couldn't be any worse than all the rain to which I was accustomed," she told me. "I was wrong about that, but Buffalo has so many sunny days all winter, it's worth it!"

After attending culinary school, she wrote for a city-based food blog that went on to launch a magazine. She became food editor (and senior editor) at *Buffalo Spree*, which has become the second-largest city and regional magazine in New York State. She's also, along with Andrew Galarneau of the *Buffalo News*, probably one of the most knowledgeable people about the food scene in Buffalo and Western New York. Since founding it in 2009, Christa has also run Nickel City Chef, an Iron-Chef like cooking competition where the secret ingredient is always local—and so are the chefs.

How did Nickel City Chef start?

Out of sheer frustration. Buffalonians were clamoring to buy Rachael Ray measuring cups and lining up to see C-level food celebrities at local bookstores, but no one knew the names of the chefs cooking their asses off in the restaurants down the street. With Nickel City Chef entering its tenth season, that is no longer the case. Some may argue that today, the WNY public knows too much about the restaurant scene and its movers and shakers.

What was the first sign that Buffalo's food scene had really started to change?

In 2010, Steve and Ellen Gedra returned and opened a hole-in-the wall restaurant called Bistro Europa. He served wild proteins, an assortment of flavor profiles, and off-the-beaten path European comfort foods no one in Buffalo had ever tried to sell before. It became so popular that middle-aged suburbanites began frequenting it. By the time the pig head with accouterments hit the menu, I knew that times had changed.

What does Buffalo's food scene need next?

Diversification, people, and restaurants serving Spanish or Filipino cuisine. When it comes to restaurants that are fewer than five years old, we have a lot of sameness as is wont in the era of Instagram. We also need more talent and experience to grow. Today Buffalo is hungry, it has inventors, it has neighborhoods that are still affordable to live or build a restaurant in, but we are short on skilled chefs and talented management, as well as people who both understand the restaurant business and supply services: accountants, interior designers, plumbers, electricians, and construction companies. We also have no legit fine dining to speak of, and though I know it's fading from fashion, every city of our size should have one truly exquisite fine dining option.

Chef Mike Andrzejewski has been one of Buffalo's most influential chefs. Why?

Mike Andrzejewski's passion for Asian fusion was way ahead of the curve, and when he opened his first place, Tsunami, it was clear people could not get enough of his umami-emboldened flavors and fun food presentation. After a terrifying motorcycle accident, the community came together to raise money for his hospital expenses, and it was such a success it made the papers, further cementing his position as the one WNY chef whose name and reputation reached far beyond his restaurant. Since his recovery he's had tremendous success, including several James Beard nominations. But despite this success, it's my belief that his lifelong dedication to training hundreds of bright young cooks combined with the countless hours of charity work he's done is what has earned him his position as Buffalo's most revered chef.

Who else do you think has had a profound influence on the dining scene?

Jon Karel and Cameron Rector brought the craft cocktail to Buffalo at a place called Vera. Chef Bruce Wieszala trained almost every chef in Western New York how to break down whole animals, making way for use of local meat and the creation of housemade charcuterie in a way we would never had accomplished without him. And when chef Andrzejewski opened a very high-end and nearly avant-garde restaurant (Mike A's at Hotel Lafayette in 2012), he hired prodigal son Edward Forster, who had previously worked for David Posey and Graham Elliott in Chicago. Forster subsequently brought on culinary cocktail artisan Tony Rials. The food and drink at that restaurant was the best Buffalo had (and has) ever seen. But it was too far ahead of its time to appeal to the masses. That said, any industry person who ate there was changed by the experience and we see ripples of that to this day. It's my belief it will be a bright point on the map as we look backward in a decade.

Are there any up-and-coming chefs folks should look for big things from?

Joseph Fenush is the chef de cuisine at Toutant, and manages one of the busiest kitchens in Buffalo. Toutant is known for its southern comfort food. But Fenush has a very different culinary point of view and is a bit of a genius. His dishes, which are often featured as specials, are unbelievable. He's easily one of the best chefs to have come out of Buffalo. I can't wait until we have access to a menu of food envisioned solely through his lens. Victor Parra Gonzalez is an Acapulco native who trained in Montreal. Las Puertas has quickly earned favor from food savvy locals. His business model is equally interesting. At Las Puertas all the cooks are servers and all the servers are cooks, so your meal is served by the hands that created it. It's marvelous. Michael Dimmer at Marble + Rye has come into his own. Some might say his strict standards for seasonal, ethical, and local foods once hindered him, but he's turned that over on its head and is creating some of the most reliably delicious food in Buffalo.

What should locals know about the dining scene that maybe they're not aware of yet?

You can enjoy a quick and affordable meal at a "fancy" spot by dining at the bar and sticking to the app menu. Don't save our best restaurants for a special occasion—that's a waste.

What are some of the biggest surprises you encountered conducting your own best-of lists, and what things do national lists always get wrong?

It's safe to say that 50 percent of the hole-in-the-wall mom-and-pop spots are still making things from scratch and are almost always better than their more well-known competition. The other 50 percent are reheating bags of crap from the local warehouse club. It's worth investigating the places you've never heard of, and usually an order of wings or fries will tell you everything you need to know.

I generally disagree with most lists all the time. I don't know what that says about me or the interns working for national media tasked with writing those lists, but I hold the local media responsible for the fact that more accurate info isn't online for interns at national news sites. It shouldn't matter who your advertisers are or where the average Buffalonian thinks the best (fill in the blank) is, because they are often eating from memory and haven't even been to the place in 10 years because they only go when Aunt Sadie and the cousins are in town. Honest and accurate information is hard to find in 2018, it requires bodies and a budget, and until we have more accurate reporting (like Buffalo Everything!), we'll be stuck with crappy lists.

Would you ever open your own restaurant and if so what would it be?

It would have to be with the smartest, most competent partners ever, because I am at an age where I am entirely unwilling to compromise my ethics or standards for quality (in food or people) for anyone! I've always told prospective owners that you can find the opportunity to create success in the restaurant business in one of two ways: dream up the most perfect business cooking what you want to serve in the environment you want to serve it in, and then spend a

few years finding the right building in the right neighborhood with the right demographic to
appreciate it. Or you can find an amazing space, examine the market, look at the neighborhood
and the building's limitations and create the perfect business for that spot. If faced with a future
in the restaurant business, I'd fall into the second category.

What are your icon go-tos—not necessarily Buffalo's "best," but the places you go when you're feeling like a/some:

Craft cocktail: *The Dapper Goose. No question. You will not find more genuine hospitality or balanced cocktails anywhere in town. Killer wine list, too.*

Cheap drink at an old-man bar: *Rohall's, where I go for a gin and tonic, Campari and soda, or any one of their Eastern European beers. I also have a mad crush on McPartlan's, but only get there two or three times a year.*

Tom & Jerry: *I'd rather make them myself!*

Wings: *Kelly's Korner, all day.*

Weck: *Same.*

Pizza: *I eat Neapolitan pizza more than any other kind, and for that I rely on Jay's in Kenmore or Hearth + Press downtown. On occasion, I'm okay with a little Buffalo-style cup-and-char (dipped in blue cheese, I know I'm a heathen) from Imperial in South Buffalo, or Franco's.*

Seabar Sushi

475 Ellicott Street, Downtown, 14202 | 716-332-2928
Mon–Thu 11:30 AM– 2 PM, 5 PM–10:30 PM,
Fri 11:30 AM–2 PM, 5 PM–11:30 PM, Closed Sun

Seabar's chef and owner Mike Andrzejewski wasn't looking to anchor a stretch of downtown with a restaurant that would lead others to follow it. He and his partner (and wife) Sherri were just looking to downsize their living situation after their sons moved out. But a chance meeting with developer and Ellicot Lofts owner Rocco Termini led to the chef and his wife getting a deal on a loft as long as he moved his restaurant downstairs, and now other restaurateurs have followed. With longtime classic Buffalo restaurants like Oliver's and Rue Franklin (now closed) on his resume, Andrzejewski is regarded by many as chef godfather of The 716. At Seabar, that translates on the menu as an upscale sushi bar and restaurant that also serves dim sum, Hudson Valley foie gras, and pork enchiladas. There are crudos and sushi and sashimi tastings, but it's not all sushi; you'll find entrées that include chef Mike's take on ramen (triple pork), fried rice (BLT-style with shrimp, bacon, and

You're not leaving Seabar without trying the beef on weck sushi roll.

full-service restaurant, and in 2013, they opened a "black rice bar," serving sushi on black rice for its purported health benefits. Now, Sun is routinely noted among Buffalo's best Asian restaurants. The pickled tea leaf salad, fish cake salad, *kat kyay kite* (spicy-sweet Burmese flat rice noodles), and stir-fried mustard greens are among the most recommended dishes, but for those intimidated by extensive menus, consider starting with the aforementioned egg noodle and chicken *own no koksware* soup with ginger and turmeric seasoned coconut milk broth, and Sun's spicy chicken (whose "spice" isn't spicy as much as it is fragrant) served with coconut rice and roasted cashews in a clay pot. If you're feeling adventurous (and ask a day in advance), consider trying traditional Chinese bird's nest soup (yes, a real swallow's nest) prepared with rock sugar and served cold, or the "premium version" with Korean ginseng and hearty chicken broth.

tomato), and short ribs (24-hour sous-vided with chive broth and caramelized onion pot stickers). Of course, you're not leaving without trying the beef on weck sushi roll—sushi rice rolled around seared rare beef, draped with beef carpaccio, and seasoned with coarse sea salt, caraway seeds, and of course, horseradish sauce—a late-night creation born out of a few drinks that's gone on to become *a bit* of a signature for the chef.

Sun Restaurant

1989 Niagara Street, Black Rock, 14207

716-447-0202 | suncuisines.com

Mon–Thu 11 am–10 pm, Fri 11 am–10:30 pm, Sat 12 pm–10:30 pm, Sun 12 pm–9:30 pm

Kevin and Stephanie Lin moved to Buffalo in the late nineties and worked in the Wegmans sushi department until opening Sun Food Market in 2010. But it was when they added a small takeout menu featuring Japanese, Thai, Vietnamese, and Korean dishes along with two Burmese soups, that they really became an integral part of the dining scene. Within two years, it had become a

The Black Sheep

367 Connecticut Street, West Side, 14213

716-884-1100 | blacksheepbuffalo.com

Tue–Thu 5 pm–10 pm, Fri–Sat 5 pm–11 pm, Sun 11 am–2 pm

Let's start at the end of the meal and get this out of the way: Even if you're too full to eat anything else, you're going to The Black Sheep. They say there's always room for dessert, and the sticky toffee pudding *is* that dessert. Salty, sweet, and made with what has to be at least three sticks of butter, it's bonkers delicious. Like book-a-trip-to-Buffalo-just-for-pudding good. And that's just the cherry on top of chefs Steve and Ellen Gedra "global nomad" menu, one that features

daily seasonal specials and nabbed him a Best Chefs semifinalist nod for a James Beard Award in 2017. A meal starts with a bread basket with whipped seasoned lard that you won't want to let go of (don't, even if you finish the bread, you can always use a side of whipped, seasoned lard). If they haven't run out, you're ordering their signature smoked local pork chop with crispy potatoes, greens, and sausage jus, but you really could make a meal out of ordering from the dozen small plates whose star turns include barbecue pork nuggets, pierogi, potato gnocchi, burrata, roasted beets, fried clams, and pork liver deviled eggs. If you'd rather put yourself in the chef's hands, the tasting menu starts at $60

per person for three courses, and for something truly different, a pig head dinner is available weekdays for groups of six or more (requires two weeks' notice).

The Grange Community Kitchen

22 Main Street, Hamburg, 14075 | 716-648-0022
grangecommunitykitchen.com
Tue–Thu 7:30 AM–2:30 PM, 4:30 PM–9 PM;
Fri–Sat 7:30 AM–2:30 PM, 4:30 PM–10 PM,
Closed Sun–Mon

Some coffee shops and restaurants play lip service to wanting to be a community hub, but husband-and-wife team (and Hamburg natives) Brad and Caryn Rowell made efforts to celebrate the building they opened Grange Community Kitchen in. When they took over the space where Tina's Italian Kitchen had been for decades, they restored the building to make it look more like it did when it was built in 1892, and later served as a Grange hall, a place where farmers and families congregated when agriculture played a larger role in Buffalo. Brad was formerly the chef at Elm Street Bakery, so no surprise then that his seasonally-driven neighborhood bistro serves pizzas made in a wood-burning oven. There are usually about six pies, which beyond standard Margherita and pepperoni, feature seasonal ingredients like heirloom tomatoes and roasted corn. Starters and accompaniments get divided into cheese, oysters, and charcuterie. Garden and small plates include salads, soups, crudos, and dips, while mains like a pan-roasted porterhouse, pan-seared swordfish, confit chicken and clams in a saffron-tomato broth fill out the large plates section. And they're open mornings, serving housemade pastries and seasonal breakfast sandwiches, and for lunch where in addition to a limited pizza menu the requisite burger (a double) is joined by sandwiches like grilled cheese and house pastrami.

Toutant

437 Ellicott Street, Downtown, 14203 | 716-342-2901
toutantbuffalo.com | Thu 5 PM–12 AM,
Fri–Sat 5 PM–2 AM, Sun Brunch 11:30 AM–2:30 PM,
5 PM–12 AM, Sun 5 PM–12 AM, Closed Tue–Wed

The New Orleans dishes and southern classics served at Toutant (pronounced *too-tawnt*) are too long to list. Suffice it to say you'll find oysters Rockefeller, gumbo, hush puppies, jambalaya, po'boys, muffulettas, and fried chicken on the menu, all executed as well as you'll find them in The Big Easy—and better in many cases. For that, you can credit chef-owner James Roberts. The chef, who landed in Western New York in 2007 to work in a country club and never left, grew up surrounded by Louisiana's coastal shrimping and fishing community. I know, I know, like tacos and Chinese, good southern food deep in Yankee country can be something

to be skeptical of. The only thing to be skeptical of at Toutant though, is your willpower to stop at just one Sazerac or French Quarter frozen daiquiri while sitting at the downstairs bar. Yes, there are candied yams with marshmallow meringue, collard greens, and hot buttermilk biscuits better than grandma ever made, but don't mistake this for just being a comfort food joint. The food may be familiar, but it's also fantastic. The charred ribeye's as good as if not better than the one you had at the last steakhouse you visited, and the weekly barbecue selection is probably the best in town (when they're out, they're out). Speaking of out, Roberts does a fried bologna sandwich that's part homage, part reinvention. It's an in-house made bologna that's salty and meaty with cheese oozing out over every bite. But it's sometimes not listed. If that's the case, park yourself at the bar, and just keep ordering rounds of flavored pork cracklings and daiquiris, and let it be known you're not going anywhere 'til you have one.

Food Truck Tuesdays

Larkin Square | 745 Seneca Street, Larkinville, NY
14210 | 716-362-2665 | larkinsquare.com
April–October, 5 PM–8 PM

Anyone with a profligate palate who's interested in making a meal out of a wider array of flavors need look no further than Food Truck Tuesdays in Larkin Square. Said to be Buffalo's first business district, this site was once home to the Buffalo Hydraulic Association and the Larkin Soap Company. After renovation and remodeling, Larkin Square's reincarnation launched

in 2012. And now on Tuesdays from late spring to early fall, there are (mind-bogglingly) more than 50 participating trucks, with some 30 or so showing up most Tuesdays to serve more sweets, fried treats, and street meats than you can imagine, including mobile versions of classic Buffalo foods like pierogi and pizza. But there's everything from Greek, Hawaiian, and Australian grub to fried chicken and hot dogs. Beer, wine, and other beverages are available at several spots throughout Larkin Square, more trucks are parked a short walk away at Flying Bison Brewery, and The Hydraulic Hearth Restaurant & Brewery is across the street to catch you if you need to kick back with a proper meal and a beer (though they'll let you bring truck fare there too).

CHAPTER NINE

BOOZING UP BUFFALO

Last Call, 4 AM

In Nevada and Louisiana, bars can technically serve 24 hours a day, and some do. And Alaska's last call is 5 AM. But unlike Fairbanks, Buffalo never gets 22 hours of daylight, and its last call is one of the latest in the country: 4 AM. Every so often in Buffalo, the idea of rolling it back comes up, the claim being that it contributes to increase alcohol-related violence, health issues, and a toll on law enforcement.

The 4 AM last-call tradition is often attributed to Buffalo's history of having a large number of factory and industrial workers, some of whom worked third shifts that let them out at off hours. These folks, common lore goes, deserved to drink too. But there are also those who say that years earlier, hours were pushed back as a tactic of control, the idea being that the police could keep better track of after-hour clubs. It's all a little difficult to document.

What's clear, while reading author Timothy Bohen's *Against The Grain: The History Of Buffalo's First Ward*, is that bars have always played a *very* central role in the Buffalo community. "I have always been told that it was because the evening shift employees of the local factories and grain mills who got off of work at midnight needed more time to unwind in a saloon," Bohen told me, adding that, "In all of my research I never came across any stories about the 4 AM last call."

Bohen does note that saloons weren't just places to drink, have fun, look for (and control) votes for upcoming elections, and hear news. They were workers' cafeterias, sometime employment offices, and even lodging. You can easily imagine the importance that late hours would be to all of these endeavors.

However it originated, Buffalo's bars and bartenders get downright Shakespearean when the idea of closing at 2 AM is proposed. Brief candle and tale told by an idiot, it's all typically full of sound and fury, signifying nothing, then heard no more. Yup Macbeth, Buffalo's a drinking town (maybe, like Billy Currington says . . . with a football problem).

In recent years, people have been drinking Molson, Genny, Labatt Blue, and Budweiser. But Visit Buffalo Niagara reports that before Prohibition, there were nearly 30 breweries in Buffalo. According to *Buffalo Beer: The History of Brewing in the Nickel City*, in the early twentieth century, Buffalo had more breweries "than any city in the country except possibly New York and Chicago." The book goes on to note that, "In 1908, Buffalo breweries produced 31 million gallons of beer, most of which was consumed locally, making the per capita consumption approximately 77.5 gallons for every man, woman, and child in the city of Buffalo."

No surprise considering the role it played in America's grain trade, right? Unfortunately, its last two breweries, the Iroquois Brewing Company (the city's all-time greatest brewery) and William Simon Pure Brewery, closed in 1971 and 1972, respectively, leaving the city to big beer.

But Buffalo hasn't been left out in the cold in the decades since the craft beer movement has taken hold across America. Pearl Street Grill & Brewery and Flying Bison Brewing Com-

pany, founded in 1997 and 2000 respectively, are widely credited as the pioneers of Buffalo's craft beer revival. They've been followed by others, including Lafayette Brewing Company (2012), Resurgence Brewing Company (2014), and RiverWorks (2017), the world's first brewery inside a grain silo. And more craft breweries and distilleries are on the horizon.

In 2016, nascent craft brewer Community Beer Works was even paying customers $1 for every bottle or can of Budweiser turned in, just to get "them off our streets," no questions asked. "You don't even have to pretend someone left it in your fridge after a party," its chief operating officer Chris Smith stated. And in the everything-old-is-new-again vein, in early 2018, the *Buffalo News* reported that Community Beer Works had teamed with a descendant of former Iroquois owner William Weigel to work on a million-dollar West Side brewing operation that would bring *back* a retro version of one of the brewery's old standards.

Things are just as bright for the cocktail scene. It's no longer just a shot and whiskey-Coke kind of town (not that there's not a time and a place). A great bar program is becoming fairly expected. As some of its local publications are

fond of saying, after their kitchens close, many of Buffalo's best restaurants become its best bars. Asked who she thought had one of the most profound changes to the dining scene, Christa Glennie Seychew pointed to Jon Karel and Cameron Rector for bringing the craft cocktail movement to Buffalo, "That was the most obvious and broadly felt sea change I can pinpoint aside from the farm-to-table movement."

Which is all to say, there are enough great, storied bars in Buffalo to fill a book. These are 15 of the best—good enough to get any night more than off to an epic start.

Best bar debates are best debated at one of the bars *subject* to debate, preferably over several drinks, and taken from contender to contender. They rely on an endless list of criteria: encyclopedic knowledge of beer menus, wine lists, inventory, classic cocktail execution, ice and juice programs, innovation, and clever names otherwise usually only associated with boats and horses. And that doesn't even account for the bars' history, ambience, or the personality of either the folks behind them or the ones with whom you bend elbows in devotion. Buffalo, a

A "Jam Session" at Ballyhoo.

city full of great bars, makes this even more difficult. It is, in fact, a beautiful and impossible debate. And yet ...

This list of 15 places is bound to cause consternation because of the obvious bars missing. Let's note off the bat that you won't find some of the city's classic spots. Forget the awesome drinks at Dapper Goose, which could easily contend for the city's craft cocktail crown, classics like McPartlan's that could rank on a list of Buffalo's old-school spots; and the Old First Ward Brewing Company at Gene McCarthy's. All of these are mentioned elsewhere here, be it for one signature dish, overall food, or other determining factors. In the interest of providing a larger overview of great places, let's not repeat. Besides, the bars with great wings and weck aren't always necessarily the best *bars*, right?

5 Best Old-School Bars

What are the criteria for a great old-school bar? They can be places that are exacting with their execution of classic cocktails, sure. But they're not typically temples to mixology. An excellent old-school bar should have some wear. It's got to have been around forever, or at least feel as though it has. It has to serve cheap drinks. And it has to have either (or both) people who drink there who are in their 50s, or an interior that you'd rather not look too closely at in the daylight.

#5 Del Denby's Pub

1553 Hertel Avenue, Hertel Avenue, 14216

716-837-5360 | Mon–Sat 8 am–4 am, Sun 12 pm–4 am

Places like Del's existed in every section of Buffalo 25 years ago, but they're getting to be increasingly harder to find. It's a hole-in-the-wall, old-school plastic-cup bar with a pool table, simple drinks, and a narrow but deep backyard (some of it covered) great for hanging with friends—the kind of place underappreciated by anyone but old men and broke college kids.

Recently, Del's got a refresh. Its graying awning and white panel facade were replaced by large glass windows, letting a little light in on the regulars inside—enough to see the twinkle in their eyes, but not enough to scare them away.

In fact, Del's has somehow managed to maintain its pre-Buffalo renaissance vibe despite being situated on Hertel Avenue in North Buffalo, one of the city's fastest growing and priciest neighborhoods. Whether that's because it goes relatively unnoticed by the press, or because it seems tame compared to the bars nearby with full menus and huge flatscreens, is anyone's guess. What's certain is that out-of-the-way bars that manage without a cocktail menu (and maybe even a shaker—all hail the free pour) and that still sell iced-down buckets of splits on a hot summer day are not without merit.

#4 Nietzsche's

248 Allen Street, Allentown, 14201 | 716-886-853
nietzsches.com | Daily 12 PM–4 AM

"Without music, life would be a mistake," says the mural on the building's river-facing side, quoting its namesake, German philosopher Friedrich Nietzsche. Nietzsche's isn't the only place in town for live music, but it's one of the most storied. Nietzsche's was founded in 1982 by Joe Rubino, who took over the spot. Previously, since the 1930s, it had been known as the Jamestown Grill. Live music started as a weekend thing, but grew to several days a week within the first year. In an interview with *Art-Voice*, Rubino recalls a conversation with a bartender who suggested, "Why don't we just do it every night?" Nietzsche's has had its ups and downs, and a few dark nights, but for the most part ever since, daily live music has been its raison d'être.

Inside, Nietzsche's is decorated from the floor to the ceiling with paintings, sculptures, and (on the ceiling) the autographs of famous performers who have played it. Ani DiFranco and the 10,000 Maniacs are routinely noted as among the artists who got their starts at the bar, and it has played a key role in the city's comedy scene with the help of Kristen Becker, who founded the bar's Doin' Time Comedy Showcase. Even the bathroom graffiti has had its moment, inspiring a play produced by Buffalo musician Susan Peters.

#3 Rohall's Corner

Amherst Street, Black Rock, 14207 | 716-939-2087
Tue–Fri 4 PM–4 AM, Sat–Sun 1 PM–4 AM, Closed Mon

Bartender Greg Rohall had worked around town at some classic dartboard and jukebox spots, and while there's nothing wrong with them, when he decided to open his own place, he wanted it to be the kind of bar *he'd* like to hang out in. That place, Rohall's Corner, it turned out, was a mild update of the early '80s, the kind of bar you can get a pint and still hear yourself think. In 2007, Rohall bought the old Our Grill bar, whose doors had been closed since 1984, but was still mostly as intact as the day the key last turned. After some repairs and a paint job, he brought in tables made from reclaimed bowling lanes, rescued some blue and red retro bar stools from a tavern in Niagara Falls, decorated with some beer steins, and opened the kind of place where you don't have to try to be someone you're not.

#2 Founding Fathers

75 Edward Street, Allentown, 14202 | 716-855-8944
foundingfatherspub.com | Mon–Fri 11:30 AM–2 AM,
Sat 4 PM–4 AM, Sun 4 PM–10 PM

For many of the delinquents among us (myself included), there were enough frustrating moments in classrooms to want to *escape* them to bars to *avoid* higher learning. And here we are flocking to former social studies teacher Mike Driscoll's dive *#becauselearning* and *#beer*. No, seriously, the bar frequently easily gets three deep and on trivia night? Better get there at 3 PM. Who'da thunk?

Driscoll, who has owned the bar since the late '80s, and is its key bartender, is fond of saying he retired when he bought the place, which probably proves that old guidance counselor adage that it isn't work when you love what you do. Regardless, the man has clearly found his calling, and has a knack for presidential paraphernalia and bric-a-brac. Over the decades, he's filled the walls of this 1874 livery (you can still find the old hitching posts in the brick) with presidential portraits, newspaper clippings, flags, and election slogans.

The tavern menu somehow manages to avoid nearly all Buffalo icons (hail to the bologna and onions) in favor of salads, pastas, sandwiches, and a well-regarded pub burger. And it's a great place to just drink, but Mike's proclivity to ask customers trivia questions, something he's been doing since he bought the place, adds a social element that's contagious.

Founding Fathers truly shines during trivia night, which Mike has held for nearly a decade. On the first Tuesday of every month, teams of five members try their hands at his written test (60 questions plus bonuses) covering any and all subject matter (how's that for a pop quiz) while snacking on free popcorn and nachos before getting to the shout-out rounds, with the winning team's members known to take home bottles of wine.

Hey, maybe we'd have studied harder if we'd known it would help at the bar.

#1 The Old Pink

223 Allen Street, Allentown, 14201 | 716-884-4338
Daily 11 AM–4 PM

There's no sign. No address. Nobody seems to know why it's called what it's called and when it stopped being called what it was before. It's been compared to a black hole, described as the kind of place that would survive the Apocalypse, said to serve one of the city's best late-night meals, and it could easily stand in for the definition of quintessential dive bar. But who needs a sign when the navy-blue building housing it has a roof covered with painted snowflakes, green and red flames licking up from the ground, and 30 smokers outside at 2 AM. This is The Pink. A place to

drink, to drink cheap beer, or as bartender Rob Fatta says, mimicking most of his interactions with customers, "What are you drinking? You're drinking Bud Light? Here you go." It's a place to do shots, drink whiskey and Coke, and to get up to no good. It's iconic, unmistakable, beloved, and deservedly so.

The Allen Street Bar and Grill, its real name, is a dead ringer for making you as from out of town. It's "The Old Pink," or just "The Pink." But this corner bar on Allen Street *was* once known as The Pink Flamingo, and was still at least into the early '90s. Molly Brinkworth bought the Pink Flamingo in 1990, from Mother's owner Mark Supples. (If you recognize the name, the late Dennis Brinkworth was behind the old Colter Bay Grill.)

You can start and end a night at The Pink if you have the stamina and your liver can handle it, but as any local knows, this is *the* late-night spot, the place any night worth remembering starts being forgotten. One in the morning is early, and by two, it's three deep. The clientele? Crusties who have been drinking since it opened that day, wedding parties that should long ago have called it quits, chefs, accountants, students, celebrities or musicians making the requisite stop when in town—all walks.

Inside, there's a long battered bar, an adjacent room with a pool table, bathroom doors that don't close, two dartboards in the back, sagging ceilings, and checkered linoleum floors barely-lit by cage-enclosed red lights. The décor? Let's call it "eclectic with Elvis." "Most of the 'look' came from our customers bringing in unique items," Molly told *ArtVoice*. "If I liked it, it went behind the bar. Now the back bar is jam packed and none of it came from me!"

And it just so happens to serve some of the best sandwiches made in town. The bartenders are also the cooks, tending grill behind the bar just long enough in between pours to make sure the four items on their unwritten menu are cooked just right. The burger is one of the best, most unheralded in town, there's grilled chicken, grilled bologna, and, of course, the epic 12-ounce center-cut New York Strip steak sandwich, covered with provolone and onions and peppers made in a crock pot at the start of the shift.

It's been said that there's only one way to properly experience this sandwich: after many drinks at about 2 AM. That's true. There's a late-night magic about this dive that only exists in select watering holes across America, and few of those also serve simple but soul-satisfying food that late. Count The Pink as among special bars like Earnestine & Hazel's in Memphis that do. And the drinks and delinquency both contribute a special sauce that make it taste even better; but a visit during the quiet hours when the sunlight peeks into the front of the bar reveal food that's just plain good. Simple, but delicious. Just be careful, that's how you end up anchoring The Pink.

Behind the Bar with Rob Fatta at The Pink

The Pink is a late-night volume place. From 2 AM to 4 AM, it's non-stop movement behind the bar. Boom, boom, boom, shots of Jameson, shots of Jack, quick mixed drinks, and cheap beer. But Rob Fatta calls his job there, where he's worked for five years, one of the premiere bartending gigs in Buffalo. Not that it's anything fancy. Whereas much of the city has gotten into craft cocktails and shaking two drinks at once, Rob says, "We do whiskey and Coke, vodka tea, vodka soda, beers. I mean nobody comes in and orders a martini or asks, 'Can I see your drink list?'"

The "Ron Jeremy" at The Pink.

I caught up with Rob during the quiet of the early afternoon (just before the day drinkers started their weekly soap opera drinking game) to delve into a few of The Pink's secrets (an off-off menu item?!) and to make sure the place didn't disappear in the daylight.

How'd The Pink become The Pink?

It used to be called The Pink Flamingo. When they didn't renew the lease, the first owner retained the rights to the name, so technically our name is Allen Street Bar and Grill, but he left with The Pink Flamingo and he opened up a spot on Main Street called The New Pink Flamingo. So people just started calling this the Old Pink. So it's not the official name of the place, but it is. Something like how we still call Rich Stadium, Rich Stadium. It's not Rich Stadium any longer. His new place on Main Street didn't last very long. It was in a tough area. Mollie, the owner, has been going strong here for 27 years since.

When did this first start as a restaurant or a bar or whatever?

Well it was a bar in the '60s. I'm pretty sure before it was called The Pink Flamingo, it was a place called Birdie's Nineteenth Hole. I think before it in the '60s it might've been something like the Allen Street Kitchen or the Allen Street Grill or something like that. Something like what we call it now.

Have the sandwiches always been here?

Only going back to The Pink Flamingo. I know that they were here then. I don't know that they were here at Birdie's Nineteenth Hole. Hey Dave [a regular], did Birdie's Nineteenth Hole serve sandwiches, the steak sandwich? Yeah.

How's the chicken done?

The barbecue chicken is a breast with its skin still on it, and it's done with barbecue sauce, peppers, onions, and cheese. The bologna is the same thing: peppers, onions, and cheese on a toasted Costanzo's roll.

How many sandwiches do you think you make a night?

On a Friday night or a Saturday night, just steaks? Maybe two or three dozen. That's by far the big seller. We have loyalists for the chicken. The burger is a really good burger for $6. People come just for that. They have their specific sandwich.

Are there any off-off menu sandwiches?

Sometimes we'll mess around and put some bologna on top of the burger. Screw around. One of the other bartenders here named it the Ron Jeremy. It's a burger patty with peppers, onions, and three slices of provolone—it's provolone or no cheese, we make it easy for everybody—then we top it with a thick slice of bologna with peppers, onions, and cheese on top of that too. It's decadent.

How late do you serve sandwiches until?

Until 3 AM. There's always people congregating on the patio after 4 AM. They can't do it like they used to though. Nowadays, the cops are on you. It's time to go. Get out of there. But we have a reputation as a late-night, after-hours type place. It's not quite like that any longer. It used to be a little act of subversion, a little after-4 AM subculture, but that's gone by the wayside.

Were there ever any other menu items?

For a while we toyed with doing roast beef here, and it was just too tough. We weren't set up right to do it, but those came out really good too.

But you've never done wings, right?

No, we don't have a fryer. We don't do anything like that. It's no frills. You get a burger and a pickle. We used to sell chips, but you end up losing money on those.

What about live music?

We've had the same DJ here Friday and Saturday night. He has been here longer than Molly has owned the place so he's kind of an institution. People come to see him. He's a draw because he's always on with the new music, and he has a nice blend of classic and old stuff. The DJ's Wednesday, Thursday, Friday, Saturday, we've had some rock stars come in and actually DJ. We've done a few shows. I don't know if this is actually true or not, but I think somebody told me that the Goo Goo Dolls may have played here.

In the back? Are there any more shows?

Yeah. No. The last time I can remember someone playing here was one of the former employees had a band, and they were scheduled to play something at a beach place, and it was raining, and he asked, "Can we set up in here?" And they played. There's only been maybe a handful. That was probably five years ago. That was the most recent band that's played here. It's just not set up for that.

What is it about this place that makes it an institution?

We don't judge. And you know what? There's never any trouble here, really. We're a very accepting bar. We don't care about your race, your creed, your orientation. Everybody gets along in here, and it's always been that way. Maybe that's what it is. It's a blend of all these people that come in, and somehow it works. A lot of them come for the music, they come for the steak sandwich, and they know that they're not going to be treated with disrespect. It's really not that special.

Any stories or star sightings you can share?

No specific stories. Things like that just come and they go. Funny things are always happening, but we've had people come and visit like Anthony Bourdain and the guy who eats all the food, Adam Richman. Famous people on tour stop in. Ian Gillan, the lead singer for Deep Purple, he was living in Buffalo for a while, he loved it here. He would be here all the time. He would just come down, nobody would bother him, he'd drink his pint and chill out and listen to music. [A photo of the Old Pink is the cover of Gillan's Inn, *his 2006 album.]*

What's the story with the Elvis?
You've got velvet Elvis there, Elvis over here . . .

Things we accumulated over the years. There's no particular reason. It's just, you know, kitschy things that accumulated. There's another velvet Elvis in the DJ booth. The red lights also have a certain kind of glow that happens in the bar when things get dark. It's almost pinkish so again with The Pink.

The bathrooms . . . they're pretty epic.

Mm-hmm (affirmative). They've always been like that even before I worked here. Those get painted, not too frequently, but they get painted every two years or so, and there's a fresh slate so they can start again. Within a year it looks the same as it always did.

What do you have to do to get kicked out?

Steal money off the bar. We're pretty tolerant, most of us, but at the same time, I would have to guess there's probably over 100 years of experience behind the bar on Friday and Saturday nights, so sometimes we have a little shorter wick than others, but we all know what we're doing.

Do you have a most epic Pink story?

I've seen it all. Nothing shocks me. But those are probably stories that are better left not told.

How has the neighborhood changed around The Pink?

The neighborhood has become quite gentrified. It used to be you could've bought that building across the street for $100,000 10 years ago. Now it's high-income apartments and guys probably made $100,000 off of it already just in rent. The housing market is jacked. You could've bought any of these houses around here for $50,000 to $60,000, and now they're $200,000 or over $200,000 for some of them. The people who have come in have started to take care of their properties more. It's become a little bit trendier, a little less rugged.

Does that cause any tensions for The Pink?

I'm sure it does with some people. The Allentown Association has said, "Oh you've got to clean up a little bit better, you're too loud at night." It's like we don't have any speakers outside, but they find a reason to bitch, and life goes on. It is what it is. We're here. We've been here.

Is there anything else even Buffalonians don't know about The Old Pink?

One of the best things about this place is we're open every day of the year. So for Thanksgiving, we always do a feast dinner: the Vagrant's Thanksgiving. I'll make a turkey. Somebody else will make mashed potatoes. We'll do stuffing. We have a whole setup and our boss will buy these turkeys that are like four or five bucks a pound—the real deal, never frozen. We really do it up.

People come in from off the street?

Yeah, just buy a drink, you know what I mean? But if you got nowhere to go, come in, have a drink, have a plate of food, watch some football, and enjoy your Thanksgiving. It's a nice thing that she does. She pays for everything pretty much.

You call it "Vagrant's Thanksgiving?"

Yeah, well, we also call it, "Desperate Scumbags Thanksgiving."

5 Best Craft Cocktail Bars

Familiarity with Prohibition-era cocktails. Fresh-squeezed juices. House-made syrups, infusions, and bitters. Quality ingredients. Ice that someone has taken care with. And good, really good liquor. These are some of the signs of a good craft cocktail bar. Frequently these days, they're made by someone who wears a vest, has multiple tattoos, or is in love with their handlebar moustache and six-inch beard (or all of the above). That's cool. It's even okay if they're in love with their own cleverly named concoctions. You want someone who cares. At the same time, you want a place where you can just order your favorite drink. The best of all worlds? Maybe someone who tries to steer you in a direction you might really like, but maybe wouldn't have chosen, who will also make you your go-to if you don't end up digging where they took you.

#5 Vera

220 Lexington Avenue, Elmwood Village, 14222
716-551-6262 | verabuffalo.com
Mon–Thu 5 pm–12 am, Fri–Sun 5 pm–2 am

The man behind the craft cocktail program that put Vera on the map, Jon Karel, moved on, but the reputation he and its owner, Cameron Rector established there hasn't. Vera, a pizzeria that opened in a former yoga studio across the street from The Place in 2011, is considered one of Buffalo's first craft cocktail joints, and still one of the best.

The toasted marshmallow-garnished cocktail "Some More What" (graham cracker bourbon, hickory smoked syrup, and chocolate bitters) may be the most Instagrammable on the menu. But the drinks feature the fresh juices and ingredients, classic technique, and carefully made ice, you'd expect from a craft program. Look for other ingredients to include anything from matcha and extra virgin olive oil to chocolate and kiwi banana syrup.

#4 Més Que

1420 Hertel Avenue, Hertel Avenue, 14214
716-836-8800 | mesque.com | Open 4 pm daily;
food service Mon–Sat 5 pm–11 pm, Sun 5 pm–10 pm

Més Que is Buffalo's football bar—European football bar that is. Opened in 2012 by partners Tony Christiano and his cousin, Left Bank owner Mike Christiano, Més Que is serious about its soccer (footy? fútbol?), featuring an updated list of upcoming games for the week ahead on their website. But Més Que means "more than" in Catalan, and the Hertel Avenue futbol spot is more than a welcoming shelter for Buffalo's growing number of soccer fans. Under beverage director and bar manager Rachel Wright, it has also become one of the city's strongest cocktail bars.

There's a great whiskey selection (Irish, single-malt, blended Scotch, Japanese, Canadian, and rye), a healthy selection of beer, and lauded Moscow Mule variations. And while the cocktails are seriously good, they're not so humorless as to forget how to have fun. Look out for the #PSL, their twist on the pumpkin-spiced latte with Rittenhouse Rye, madeira, and organic pumpkin purée; Taco-Flavored Kisses made with corn-washed tequila; or "'Twas Professor Plum in Més Que with roasted plums and the shaker tin."

#3 Buffalo Proper Plate & Pour

333 Franklin Street, Downtown, 14202

716-783-8699 | buffaloproper.com

Tue–Thu 5 pm–12 am, Fri–Sat 5 pm–2 am,

Sun 11:30 am–2:30 pm, 5 pm–10 pm

Mixologist Jon Karel and chef Ed Forster opened Buffalo Proper in 2016 on the edge of downtown, and the lively, two-story space quickly drew young crowds abuzz over craft cocktails and creative food made with locally sourced ingredients by an alum of restaurants bearing the names of Jean-Georges, Georges Perrier, and Paul Kahan. Forster has since moved on, but Buffalo Proper has gone on to become one of the most well-known spots in town beyond Anchor and Duff's. It's even been singled out by *Travel + Leisure* as one of the city's standout experiences.

Inside, expect the requisite Edison light bulbs, ceiling-high shelves filled with booze, exposed brick, and a copper-backed bar where nearly 20 craft cocktails are on the offer. If you'd like to go tried and true, opt for the Smoke Break (Scotch, mezcal, sweet vermouth, coffee liqueur, orange bitters, and cinnamon) or the Ginger Baker (cachaça, ginger-jalapeño cordial, lime, red grapes). Otherwise, look to one of the cleverly named drinks featuring anything from red wine, apple jack, Szechuan red peppercorn oil, condensed milk, and cinnamon.

#2 Ballyhoo

211 South Park Avenue, First Ward, 14204

716-240-9901 | buffaloballyhoo.com

Mon–Thu 11:30 am–12 am, Fri 11:30 am–2 am,

Sat 12 pm–2 am, Sun 12 pm–12 am

Merriam-Webster's three definitions of *ballyhoo* are 1: noisy attention-getting demonstration or talk; 2: flamboyant, exaggerated, or sensational promotion or publicity; and 3: excited commotion. But maybe we should propose a fourth: house-ground links and great craft drinks in the First Ward worth making a commotion about.

In 2013, Timothy Stevens and his wife Morgan moved to Buffalo from San Diego (in Tim's case, moved back), where he was generally considered one of its best bartenders. And after he instituted a craft cocktail program at Hutch's, the couple set out to open their *own* place in late 2014. They settled into a recently closed blue-collar spot called The Malamute behind Swannie, a few blocks from the KeyBank Center.

There's a back page of the drink menu featuring classic cocktails (all made to original specs), but the pages before almost read like a proud

inventory, noting some 40 whiskeys, a dozen scotches and similar lists of mezcal, tequila, gin, vodka, and amaro. A board features the craft beer selection (12 taps that change daily), and perhaps most fun for those who like to participate, Ballyhoo's "Jam Session," eight jam preserves you can match with any spirit for the bartender to rock out for you.

If you're having trouble choosing between the six house-ground sausages to build a base with (they range from Korean short rib and herbed chicken to curry lamb), skip the list for an off-menu style: Tim's favorite, the chorizo and bacon TJ Dawg link done "'Hoo Style" with house chili and topped with their killer three-cheese mac.

#1 Billy Club

228 Allen Street, Allentown, 14201 | 716-331-3047
billyclubbuffalo.com | Mon, Wed, Thu 5 PM–1 AM,
Fri–Sat 5 PM–2 AM, Sun 11 AM–3 PM, Closed Tue

Pulling up to the candlelit white marble bar as the sun sets and settling into one of 10 craft cocktails on the menu, the dimly lit, minimalist space somehow almost makes you feel like you're getting cozy by a fireplace. There is no fireplace, but that feeling of hearth is no happenstance. It's due to the care and thoughtfulness its owners have put into the place since opening it in 2016. And with recent accolades from *Buffalo Spree* that include best use of local ingredients and best new hangout, you could say Jake Strawser and Dan Hagen *have* been on fire.

Billy Club was opened in the Puritan building (built in the 1890s), which once featured a speakeasy in the basement during Prohibition. While it's a whiskey bar (there's some *really* good whiskey), the drink menu features 10 rotating cocktails made with a balanced roster of spirits. The one cocktail that's been there since the beginning (also the last one they came up with) is the Buck Wild, their take on a Bourbon Moscow Mule (bourbon, lemon, loganberry, and ginger beer). In addition to some really good whiskey, and a short list of canned beers for both locals and beer nerds, "We focus primarily on craft producers and try to offer a range of options stylistically," Jake explains. "We chose to go with cans only because it keeps the beers as fresh as possible."

The bar is a great contrast to the crustiness of other Allen Street nightspots like Nietzsche's and The Old Pink, of which the restaurant's drink rail at its picture window has a great view. But far from looking down on it, Billy Club has slipped in comfortably amidst it.

It's almost a shame to make it seem like an afterthought, but the food's great at Billy Club too. It's a one-page menu divided into two sections. Small plates include cheese, charcuterie, pierogi, roasted marrow, fried fingerlings, and mushrooms. And entrees go beyond a great burger (cavatelli with braised rabbit, and monkfish with cured egg and sauerkraut rice) and check routine proteins off in thoughtful, updated ways (chicken thighs with seared sushi rice and Parmesan-prosciutto crumbs).

5 Best Craft Beer Bars

Breweries, even ones with taprooms, don't *always* beat great bars that serve craft beer. These five spots provide comfortable environments (some a little more . . . lived in, and others with better snacks for sessioning), with a diverse array of craft brews that include beers made locally, elsewhere in New York State, as well as from across America.

#5 Mr. Goodbar

1110 Elmwood Avenue, Elmwood, 14222

716-882-4000 | mrgoodbarbuffalo.com

Daily 12 PM–4 AM

"Good times, good friends, Goodbar!"

It's dark enough that some suggest bringing a flashlight inside on a summer day, there's often a considerable bro contingency, and you don't go to Mr. Goodbar if you want smooth edges or a clean bathroom. In fact, you're maybe going next door to Cole's (whose beer list is fairly impressive in its own right) if you're hungry after a few beers. In any case, though, if you're looking for live music and a good selection of craft beers on Elmwood, you'll find few better spots.

Mr. Goodbar has been at this since opening in 1968. It's a two-story bar with a big patio and a performance space upstairs called "The Attic" that features frequent live local and national bands. They have more than 30 taps, a beer engine that pours micro and import cask conditioned ales, they usually carry another three dozen bottled and canned craft beers, and there will typically be more than a dozen local brews available. If you plan to do any serious session drinking, it's worth picking up a pint club card (after 10 different premium drafts you get one free), and at 7:30 PM on the second Wednesday of each month the Good Beer Club convenes (tickets are $25 each), taking beer-lovers through 10 different beers grouped by theme, style, or season.

#4 Hydraulic Hearth
Restaurant & Brewery

716 Swan Street, Larkinville, 14210 | 716-248-2216

hydraulichearth.com | Tue–Thu 4 PM–10 PM;

Fri 4 PM–12 AM; Sat 10:30 AM–2:30 PM, 4 PM–12 AM

Hydraulic Hearth is routinely named among Buffalo's best beer gardens and places for outdoor dining. And with its dog-friendly gravel patio, wooden booths, pergolas, and two shuffleboard courts, it's not hard to see why. The restaurant, opened in an 1890s building redeveloped by the Larkin Development Group, was opened by restaurateur Harry Zemsky in 2014. (Zemsky is the son of Leslie Zemsky, a partner in LDG, and Howard Zemsky, who was tapped by Governor Cuomo to be the state's economic development director.)

Hydraulic's in-house brewery is operated

by Community Beer Works, which launched in 2012 and refers to itself as Buffalo's first nano-brewery (commonly defined as a brewery that produces no more than three barrels of beer per batch). That translates to a menu featuring nearly a dozen draft beers. There are also shandies, and beer is known to make its way into the house cocktails, from straight-up boilermakers to drinks featuring hopped simple syrup and IPA. The spacious brick-oven pizzeria serves an assortment of small plates and apps, and about a dozen thin-crust, wood-fired pizzas (beer even makes an appearance in their Beer B.Q. pie with pulled pork, cheddar, apple slaw, and "beer B.Q." sauce).

#3 Thin Man Brewery

492 Elmwood Avenue, Elmwood Village, 14222
thinmanbrewery.com | 716-923-4100
Mon–Thu 3 PM–1 AM, Fri 3 PM–2 AM,
Sat 11 AM–2 AM, Sun 11 AM–12 AM

Elmwood Village's first brewery opened in 2016, a collaboration between Mike and Suzanne Shatzel (behind Buffalo Food and Drink's stable of restaurants) and developer Rocco Termini and his wife Bridget. The two-story project involved taking over two buildings in disrepair and turning them into a craft brewery (run by their respective wives) and restaurant (with a roof patio) on Elmwood Avenue just blocks from icons Kuni's, Vera, and The Place. Thin Man is named for Buffalo's own crash test dummy, created in 1949, by Cornell Aeronautical Laboratory (now Calspan), a precursor to the ones we all know. It's a theme that's been cleverly implemented throughout the joint in its décor, a muse that symbolizes "the ingenuity, innovation, and commitment to quality that have always had a home in this region," the brewery notes.

At last count, Thin Man was making three IPAs, two sours and ales, a pilsner, a saison, a stout, a porter, and a lager (all available in 32-ounce growlers to go). But they also feature a rotating assortment of some two dozen guest brewery bottles from across New York State and the country (from Anchorage, Alaska, to Stratford, Connecticut). Share plates were designed to pair with the beers, among them a charcuterie plate and a few beer-themed snacks (beer mussels and beer cheese among them), soups, salads, and sandwiches (from roasted carrots and tofu banh mi to burgers and beef on weck).

#2 Colter Bay

561 Delaware Avenue, Allentown, 14222
716-436-5197 | colterbaybuffalo.com
Sun–Thu 11:30 AM–2 AM, Fri–Sat 11:30 AM–4 AM

Buffalo's beer nerds fell into something of a funk in 2016 when the Blue Monk, a spot many credited for kick-starting Buffalo's craft beer scene, closed due to a lease dispute. But the 32 drafts The Blue Monk featured are dwarfed by the 44 served at the revamped Colter Bay after it opened later that year. Co-owners Mike Shatzel (of Cole's, Thin Man Brewery, and Allen Burger Venture) and Tony Martina purchased Colter Bay from the Brinkworth family that had run it since the late '80s. They opened up its layout and gave it a fresh look, adding to its Jackson Hole ski-lodge theme.

The revamp has been praised for serving beer-friendly food, but beers take center stage. They carry local ones from Buffalo and Rochester (Flying Bison Brewing, Thin Man Brewery, and Genesee Brewing Company for example), stouts, Goses, IPAs, lagers, porters, Pilsners—you name the style, they likely have it. Beer is even the first menu you come across on Colter Bay's website, each one listed with a description, usually a paragraph long, that includes tasting notes, percentage of ABV, and city of origin. If you're in Buffalo and you're serious about beer, you've been to Colter Bay.

#1 Big Ditch Brewing Company

55 East Huron Street, Downtown, 14203

716-854-5050 | bigditchbrewing.com

Mon–Wed 11 AM–10 PM, Thu–Fri 11 AM–12 AM,
Sat 12 PM–12 AM, Sun 12 PM–8 PM

Before there was the Big Dig in Boston, there was New York's "Big Ditch," skeptics' nickname for the Erie Canal before it was completed when it seemed like it would never happen. Owners Wes Froebel, Matt Kahn, and Corey Catalano believe the canal's entrepreneurial spirit is still alive today, noting "Those who are shaping the next 100 years of prosperity are the ones we brew Big Ditch beer for, a beer that celebrates our roots and serves as a reminder that the Buffalo of the future is being built with the same strength, pride and ambition that created the Erie Canal nearly two centuries ago."

The project started with Kahn and Catalano brewing in a bucket and a garage, before they met Froebel. From there they honed, experimented, and opened in 2014, expanding into their 15,000-square-foot brewery on East Huron, which now also includes a tap room and restaurant. Their four signatures include the Hayburrner (a 7.2 percent ABV India Pale Ale), Low Bridge (4.8 percent ABV hoppy golden ale), Excavator (6.2 percent ABV rye brown ale), and 100 percent NY Pale ale (6.0 percent ABV). But they also do a number of seasonal stouts, ales, and IPAs, and limited releases that range anywhere from a jalapeño cream ale to a smoked porter.

Buffalo's Winter Drinking Tradition:
The Tom & Jerry Cocktail

"**A** Tom & Jerry, you've come to the right place," the bartender at McPartlan's Corner says, priming a mug with hot water and ladling in the thick mix. "This is the best Tom & Jerry in town or my name isn't Neil. Only have them a few more days."

It's a Monday afternoon in February, and it's unseasonably warm but there's still a Tom &

A Tom & Jerry at McPartlan's Corner.

Jerry punch bowl on the back counter behind the bar at McPartlan's. It's covered with a plate, with a ladle sticking out. Drips have stopped at various places around the sides, but they're thick enough that not one has reached the counter.

It's already late in the year for this thick but airy winter drink that starts being served around Thanksgiving and tastes just like you'd hope Christmas would for an adult when you're a little kid. A creamy sweetness fills the mouth, your throat and belly warm up, and the healthy dose of rum and brandy does something to your brain that makes you squint slightly with happiness.

Buffalo didn't invent the Tom & Jerry. Neither did the folks in Wisconsin, Minnesota, Upper Michigan, or Detroit—or really in any of the cities near the Great Lakes—where it's also still popular. In fact, at least through the early '60s, the Tom & Jerry seems to have been a pretty nationally well-known drink. "Yes, Mr. Sheldrake—no, I didn't forget—the tree is up and the Tom and Jerry mix is in the refrigerator—yes, sir—same to you," Jack Lemmon says, playing C.C. Baxter in Gene Wilder's 1960 flick, *The Apartment*.

For one reason or another, most of the articles written about the cocktail by the national press including the *New York Times*, the *LA Times*, and *Food & Wine*, and online food sites, seem to overlook the love Buffalonians have for this classic cocktail. It's beloved in Wisconsin and Minnesota, sure. But there are few mentions of Buffalo. That's bizarre. It really is a thing here. And sipping one makes you feel like you're stepping back in time.

"This was always *the* place in the city to go for Tom and Jerry's, if not in the whole area," The Place's co-owner Jason McCarthy told me one afternoon, explaining that when they're serving the cocktail, they usually go through about six gallons of batter a day. "They're just crazy about it. The day after Thanksgiving when the doors opened there were lines around the corner. You just can't believe it."

Just as Buffalo didn't invent the Tom & Jerry, neither is The Place the only bar that makes it. It's just probably the most famous for it. Boomerang's Bar & Grill has been said to have Buffalo's most refined Tom & Jerry (less potent and not as sweet) and is one of several places said to be using The Place's original recipe. The Tom & Jerry at Schwabl's is made with dark rum and brandy then finished with hot water—though some call theirs minty, so maybe they have a *secret* ingredient. (Incidentally, Memorial Day through Labor Day, Schwabl's serves a much less famous signature cocktail they call Ebenezer Punch with orange and lemon juice, Southern Comfort, and a splash of lemon-lime soda.) McPartlan's Corner makes a great one that you can pair with one of their amazing pies, and Glen

Park Tavern, Rohall's Corner, and Cole's are all known for making delicious versions too.

The when-to-when of Tom & Jerry season can be hard to pin down though. Generally, it's a safe bet that you can grab one between Black Friday up to a few days before the end of the year.

If It's Not Eggnog, What Is It?

A Tom & Jerry *isn't* eggnog. At least it's not the thick, creamy eggnog most Americans know from buying it in cans or cardboard containers in the supermarket dairy section during the Thanksgiving and Christmas holidays. Eggnog, by definition, is a drink consisting of eggs beaten with sugar, milk or cream, and often alcoholic liquor. The Tom & Jerry is light and airy and topped with a thick, sweet egg white cloud that the hot water or milk rises to its top.

Both eggnog and Tom & Jerrys use yolks and whites whipped with sugar. For starters, eggnog *sometimes* gets booze while Tom & Jerrys always do. And eggnog *always* gets milk or cream, but Tom & Jerrys only *sometimes* do. Additionally, Tom & Jerrys don't get warmed over the stove like a cooked eggnog does, and they don't get the air whisked out of them like eggnog does.

One last difference may be due to the fact that Tom & Jerrys are being made for paying customers who expect enough rosy-cheeked liquid courage to make for memorable holiday office parties. Unlike most recipes for uncooked eggnogs, which typically call for the booze to be incorporated into recipe *before* the whipped-to-peaks egg whites are folded in, Tom & Jerrys at Buffalo's best spots for them get their brandy and rum added at the *end*.

Tom & Jerry, Like the MGM Cartoon?

I f Buffalo didn't invent the Tom & Jerry, who did? Which came first: chicken or egg? Bellissimo or Young? Tom or Jerry? Two gentlemen are generally credited. And no, not William Hanna and Joseph Barbera who created the cartoon for Metro-Goldwyn-Mayer. One is Jerry Thomas, the legendary New York barman of the 1800s, who boasted of inventing the cocktail—so much, apparently, that it even played a central role in his obituary in the *New York Times*!

"Jerry was of an inventive turn of mind and was constantly originating new combinations

"One day in 1847 a gentleman asked me to give him an egg beaten up in sugar. I prepared the article, and then . . . I thought to myself, 'How beautiful the egg and sugar would be with brandy to it!' I ran to the gentleman and, says I, 'If you'll only bear with me for five minutes I'll fix you up a drink that'll do your heartstrings good.' He wasn't at all averse to having the condition of his heartstrings improved, so back I went, mixed the egg and sugar, which I had beaten up into a kind of batter, with some brandy, then I poured in some hot water and stirred vigorously. The drink realised my expectations. It was the one thing I'd been dreaming of for months. . . . I named the drink after myself, kinder familiarly: I had two small white mice in those days, one of them I had called Tom and the other Jerry, so I combined the abbreviations in the drink, as Jeremiah P. Thomas would have sounded rather heavy, and that wouldn't have done for a beverage."

—Jerry Thomas

of drinks, some of which like the Tom and Jerry, which he named after himself, became very popular and as they could not be patented, were quickly adopted by other saloons for the benefit of their patrons," the *Times* noted.

Jerry's own version (quoted above) is a compelling story (and you knew there would be a mouse involved somewhere), but in his wonderful book, *Imbibe!*, David Wondrich dispassionately dismantles Jerry's claims, citing an article published in 1827, in the Salem (Massachusetts) Gazette, that recounted the trial of a 13-year-old boy accused of stealing a watch from a man who sold him, "under the name of 'Tom and Jerry,' a composition of saleratus [baking soda], eggs, sugar, nutmeg, ginger, allspice, and rum.' A female witness testified that the boy . . . appeared to be perfectly deranged, probably in consequence of the 'hell-broth' that he had been drinking."

Sounds like the shenanigans familiar to anyone who has participated in the Tom & Jerry drinking contests that have been known to happen in Buffalo. The boy was acquitted, by the way, but Thomas wasn't, not, at least, in Wondrich's court. Thomas, he reminds us, was born in 1830. "It's quite possible, therefore, that Thomas mixed his first Tom & Jerry in 1847, while he was learning the bar business in New Haven, in the heart of the Tom & Jerry Belt. But *the* first? No way."

Wondrich is mum on the other man generally credited with inventing the drink, Pierce Egan, the British nineteenth-century, best-selling writer, adding that if Thomas didn't invent the drink, "he certainly did more than any other man to promote it. "For his part, Egan is said to have invented the cocktail to help popularize his book *Life In London or, The Day and Night Scenes of Jerry Hawthorn, Esq., and his Elegant Friend*

Corinthian Tom In Their Rambles and Sprees Through the Metropolis (talk about writing long). The book was published in 1821, and in a publicity stunt, Egan is said to have named the drink for the two characters whose adventures offered a glimpse into high and low urban culture in London.

No word on what happened to the cocktail also assuming the name of the Egan's third protagonist, Tom and Jerry's friend Bob Logic "the Oxonian." The novel notes Logic "had been 'on the town' for several years; and no person had been more industrious towards destroying a fine constitution, or endeavouring to reduce a long purse, than he had." Sounds like a fun guy. But no Logic, and none apparent either when it comes to explaining why Tom & Jerry the cocktail stopped being popular.

Ted Haigh, author of *Vintage Spirits and Forgotten Cocktails*, suggests that central heating may be the culprit in Tom & Jerrys near extinction. It was, after all, something you drank to warm up on cold winter nights. For a time, it stuck around at Christmas, but then largely disappeared across most of America.

Not so in Buffalo!

When it Comes to a Tom & Jerry in Buffalo, There's No Place Like . . . The Place

Taking over The Place from Kenny Moriarty also meant taking over one of Buffalo's most beloved winter drinking traditions, something co-owner Jason McCarthy only *truly* understood after his first year making it in 2016. "There's a whole thing to it," he said he learned. "People won't come and have a Tom & Jerry unless it's a certain temperature. They've got all these weird, quirky things that factor into whether they can drink it or not. I'd ask, 'Can I get you a Tom & Jerry?' and it would be, 'Oh, no, it's not cold enough. It's not below 32 degrees. I only can have it after it's 28 degrees out, but then that's only for six hours.'"

But once Tom & Jerry season is on, it's on. Indeed, friends Sara Wallitt and Mike Adragna were profiled in the *Buffalo News* in 2016 for having drank Tom & Jerrys together in 2009, for 36 days straight! And it can take a toll on the staff. "Everybody gets tired of making them," Jason explained. "If you're not selling it, it falls apart. It can only keep its consistency and shape for probably five to eight hours."

But it wouldn't be winter in Buffalo without them. So I asked Jay to share details behind carrying on this annual custom.

Did Kenny sell you The Place's Tom & Jerry recipe?

He gave me the recipe but we crafted our own, something we felt was better, adding like a pinch of this or that.

So you're carrying on the tradition, but with a few of your own tweaks?

A really good friend of mine came in and said, "What you need to make the batter better is a little pinch of cream of tartar." So I did that and it changed it for the better. It helps with the peaks. They come to a thicker and more stable point with a little touch of cream of tartar.

Are you giving away a trade secret here?

Nobody's going to want to make them for any extended period of time, even during the holidays, because it's a royal pain in the ass.

Why?

You have to separate the egg. Then you whip the egg white and the egg yolk separately. Then you bring it in like a meringue. It's a lot.

You serve them from when to when?

Anywhere between the day after Thanksgiving, to maybe a couple of days before the end of the year. Kenny said, "Just stop it sometime after January 1st, the first week or so."

When did you stop serving it?

I did it almost to Valentine's Day. For two straight days it was below zero and we didn't sell one. I was like, "That's all."

You keep it behind the bar like everyone else, right?

You can't refrigerate it. Another key is you've got to heat the cup with hot water. Then you put the batter in so that doesn't cool the cup down because then you put the hot water on top and then the batter will cool the cup, so you won't have a really molten, hot drink. There's a whole process.

You're frequently cited as the place to get a Tom & Jerry, that makes the quintessential Tom & Jerry in Buffalo.

Because we do. Other people do it but we're known for it. We're the father of it in Buffalo.

Do you drink it? Some people who make these things . . .

I have one or two in the beginning. But they're sweet as hell! They'll make your teeth rot. There are competitions, though, about how many you can drink in a night. I think the record was 15 in one sitting. Could you imagine 15? There's like 500 to 800 calories in each cup! That's like 15,000 calories!

What's the secret to making a great Tom and Jerry?

Hot, hot, hot water. You have to have hot water. The batter you make. The rum and brandy never goes bad. Hot water is the one commodity that you need a ton of that, when you're busy, sometimes you just have to make people wait. You just say, 'We've got to wait for the water to boil because we don't have any more.'

Any tips for the home bartender?

I have the recipe that Kenny gave me, but it's basically something you could get off Epicurious. It's just a matter of tinkering with it. But it's not something you can make for the first time and do it perfectly.

Recipes cite a host of spices—cinnamon, nutmeg, allspice . . .

Just a dash of nutmeg. Fresh nutmeg.

What about the right *order* to assemble a Tom & Jerry?

Hot water to warm the cup. Then your booze, then your batter. Then you put hot water on top of the batter so it fluffs it and it pushes it up to the top. A little sprinkle of nutmeg and then you serve it and give them a spoon.

You're known for your special cups too, right?

It was our 75th anniversary in 2016, 1941 to 2016, so we had to commemorate it. Each year we'll change the cup a little. It's kind of a collector's item. Kenny had done it in the past so we plan to too.

Buffalo's Best Tom & Jerrys

If Christmas was a dessert, this would be what it tasted like. And trying to determine the best Tom & Jerry cocktail in Buffalo would be a little like *ranking* Christmases. They're all really great and hard to say which is better (unless we count the time Uncle Paul drank four and couldn't talk—that may have been the best Christmas ever). And what kind of Grinch ranks Christmas?

So let's not go there. Accurate judging could involve drinking at least one from each place as close to one after the other as possible and at that point, the criteria start to get, er, fuzzy. Everything just becomes, "Great!"

There are reports that former owner Kenny Moriarty didn't regard his recipe as much of a

secret, and the number of places around town that claim to have been given The Place's recipe may back that up. But if you only have time for one spot, consider that this is also a testament to The Place's facility with the drink and its renown for serving it. There's only one The

Place. Okay, technically, that's not true. Interestingly, there's another "The Place," an unrelated bar in Ogdensburg, New York, about a four-hour drive to the northeast, with its own Tom & Jerry lore. But as far as Buffalo Tom & Jerry traditions go, The Place's is the most famous.

All three of these places make excellent versions, executing on airy frothiness, booze to batter, and just the right balance of spice to drink. And in truth, the best Tom & Jerry in town just may be the one you're holding at the time.

Schwabl's may offer the biggest window for experiencing Buffalo's signature winter drink.

McPartlan's Corner

669 Wehrle Drive, 14225 | 716-632-9896
mcpartlanscorner.com | Mon–Thu & Sat 10 AM–11 PM,
Fri 10 AM–12 AM, Sun 10 AM–10 PM

On one of my several visits, Joe McPartlan finally explains the origins of McPartlan's Corner's Tom & Jerry recipe, telling me that they got it from The Place before it was taken over by its new owners. Given that The Place has tweaked their recipe since the changeover, technically, if you want a taste of The Place's "original" Tom & Jerry recipe, this may be where to look. Here, it's served with long drizzles dripping down the side of the mug. In between every few creamy sips there are patches of granulated sugar chunks that haven't dissolved completely into the mix. It's a slight, welcome crunch that melts pleasantly into the gulp as the drink gets thin and boozy at the bottom. You want another, but a second easily turns into a fourth and if you ask around these parts about how many is the

right number, someone you're rubbing elbows with is bound to recount a story about the time they didn't move from their barstool until they'd quaffed nine or ten, only to stand up and find themselves walking slantwise out the door.

Schwabl's Restaurant

789 Center Road, West Seneca, 14224
716-675-2333 | schwabls.com | Mon–Thu 11 AM–9 PM,
Fri–Sat 11 AM–10 PM, Sun 1 PM–8:30 PM
(Available 2nd Monday in October to March 17th)

Schwabl's may offer the biggest window for experiencing Buffalo's signature winter drink, keeping it available Columbus Day through St. Patrick's Day. They ladle the batter out of a pink covered punch bowl on the bar across from the slicer station. First, hot water from a steaming kettle is poured into a vintage carnival glass to warm it, then a ladleful of the yellow mixture, some dark rum and brandy, and more hot water to fill the cup to the rim. There's a shake of nutmeg over the crown, then it's served on a napkin with a spoon. It's frothy and spicy with the sweetness on top and the booze lurking *just* below the foam and a few sugary lumps toward the bottom to help you shake off the alcohol. Oh yeah.

The Place

229 Lexington Avenue, 14222 | 716-882-7522
theplacebuffalo.com | Mon 4 PM–2 AM,
Tue–Sun 11:30 AM–2 AM (Availability varies:
Black Friday to a few days before New Year's Eve)

The Place has been serving Tom & Jerrys since 1941 and when the season hits, it will serve hundreds a week with days where the cocktail makes up three-quarters of *all* drinks sold. The record for the most drunk, at least as of 2016, was 15 in one sitting. If you're thinking of going for it, consider that given it's served in The Place's signature Tom & Jerry mugs (they give away a certain number each year as a commemorative item, so the earlier you get there, the better your chance), they're significantly bigger here than in many places, like nearly three times the size, and known for their characteristic heavy pour of house rum and brandy. They're also known for being a bit sweeter than other places, but again, nobody would blame you for thinking it was sweeter after drinking more!

Uber It: Tom & Jerry Crawl

There's nothing like going on a cold weather Tom & Jerry crawl with a bunch of friends. But unless you have a designated driver, this is a job for Uber. If you're from out of town, keep in mind that start and end dates for Tom & Jerry season can be fuzzy. A few places start earlier and end later, but it's a safe bet that you can grab one at any of these places from Black Friday up to a few days before the end of the year. That being said, because some places make decisions on the season based on weather, demand, and sometimes even feeling, if you don't want to be disappointed, call ahead.

Boomerang's Bar & Grill

995 Niagara Street, West Side, 14213 | 716-883-0408
Available Black Friday through
"when the weather breaks in March."

Cole's

1104 Elmwood Avenue, Elmwood Village, 14222
716-886-1449 | colesonelmwood.com
Available "the Monday after Thanksgiving
until the first of January."

Glen Park Tavern

5507 Main Street, Williamsville, 14221
716-626-9333 | glenparktavernbuffalo.com
They start serving Tom & Jerrys on Black Friday
and keep them going through the first of the new year.
Though they added, "If it's cold or yucky
after that, we'll keep them going through at least
the first week of January."

McPartlan's Corner

669 Wehrle Drive, Amherst Street, 14225
716-632-9896 | mcpartlanscorner.com
Available from Black Friday to Ash Wednesday—which
technically, is always 46 days before Easter Sunday.

Rohall's Corner

540 Amherst Street, Black Rock, 14207
716-939-2087 | Available between Thanksgiving
and the day before New Year's Eve.

Schwabl's

789 Center Road, West Seneca, 14224
716-675-2333 | Available Columbus Day,
the second Monday in October,
through St. Patrick's Day, March 17th.

The Place

229 Lexington Avenue, Elmwood Village, 14222
716-882-7522 | theplacebuffalo.com
Available Black Friday up to a few days
before New Year's Eve.

CHAPTER TEN

SWEET BRRR-FFALO:

Frozen Desserts and World-Famous Sponge Candy

Cinder toffee, golden crunchers, seafoam, hokey pokey, honeycomb, fairy food, molasses puffs—you may have heard one of these words if you like to visit candy stores when you travel, but they're just as likely to be as unfamiliar to you as to folks from somewhere along Lake Erie's eastern shore, where for maybe a century, there's been one name for this love-it-or-hate-it confection: "sponge candy." And while other towns and cities, like Erie, Pennsylvania and Rochester may be outposts in this "Sponge Candy Crescent," Buffalonians, even those who fall in the hate-it camp, will likely agree with former *Buffalo News* restaurant critic Janice Okun, who says, "There is no doubt in my mind that Buffalo is the sponge candy capital of the world."

"Is it . . . spongy?" you're asking. Nope. There's no squishiness or give. "It's yellow inside, is it like . . . a Butterfinger?" Nuh-uh.

Sponge candy has been described by its makers and those who love it as a light, crunchy, delicate toffee, or a fluffy meringue crossed with a malted milk ball. Sure, but as the experience of

Aléthea's sponge candy

it goes, sponge candy is a contrast in appearance versus reality. There's this chocolate covering on the outside that the first time you're about to bite into it, you think will disappear as you crunch into the center. The opposite happens! The center isn't hard at all and crumbles, then melts and disappears, leaving you with a chocolate finish. Break one open and you'll find the airy center is sandy enough to be blown away by a light breeze but not gritty enough to be compared to sand.

Like beef on weck, the history of sponge candy intersects with the Pan-Am Exposition in 1901 (at least in some stories). That's where Joe Fowler, an English immigrant, is said to have experienced enough success selling his chocolate candies and other confections, to inspire opening his own candy store (incorporated in 1910). It's around then, the story goes, that Fowler introduced Buffalo to the candy that he first learned to make in England. According to Western New York's regional magazine, *Buffalo Spree*, other stories attribute the creation to a mistake that happened in the 1940s, or possibly earlier. In 2012, they quoted Sam Mancuso, an 80-something-year-old consultant for Merckens Chocolate in Cumberland, Rhode Island, saying it happened further north, in New England, perhaps Massachusetts:

"They were making sponge, but not in the fashion that it's made here today," he says. "They would use the bicarbonate of soda, but they didn't use it with heat—they put it on a cold table, marble or metal—so it would only rise a couple of inches. They would break it up with a hammer and sell it that way. One day, somehow, somebody confined it to a box, and the heat by itself made it balloon up, and that's how it started.'"

But the discovery didn't take off in New England, *Spree* reports, noting that Mancuso doubted they could even *sell* Buffalo's sponge candy. "They still call theirs sponge, but it's very hard and they don't chocolate cover it," *Spree* reported him saying. And while Buffalo may have an unquenchable hunger for sponge candy today, that may be a recent phenomenon. Antoinette's Sweets' fourth-generation owner, Peter Morphis, told *Spree* that in 1975, when he began working full-time there, sponge candy didn't greatly impact the company's bottom line, but "Today, he says, it's the store's bread and butter best-seller."

However it started and whoever started it, sponge candy gets eaten by itself, crushed up on ice cream as a sundae topping, stuffed into cannolis, and at Buffalo's Resurgence Brewing Co., even turned into beer (they make their 5.5 percent ABV Sponge Candy Stout with Watson's clippings). Sugar, corn syrup, and baking soda are the ingredients most frequently cited, with some recipes calling for vinegar or gelatin. Baking soda is added to sugar dissolved in corn syrup over heat (typically accelerated by the addition of vinegar) causing carbon dioxide to bubble up and get caught in the sugar mixture. Then it's cooled and the candy is dipped in dark chocolate, milk chocolate, or orange-infused chocolate. If that all sounds very anodyne, just watch a video of it being made at one of Buffalo's time-honored places for it, where the whole thing can seem more like the forging of one ring to rule them all.

If you're playing Buffalo food bingo, sponge candy is one of the city's iconic foods that may frustrate you. It's been said that, like oysters, sponge candy can only be eaten in months that end in 'r.' Or at least, that it's very sensitive to heat and humidity. When it's been affected, the crisp, airy center collapses into a chewy gum. Some confectioners, like Ko-Ed, which closes during the summer, contend that the season makes keeping sponge candy untenable. They simply won't make it. Places that do often may have a dehumidified shop, and those that ship it during the summer closely monitor five-day weather forecasts so that the candy doesn't spoil. In 2015, Buffalo Mayor Byron W. Brown proclaimed Sept. 21, "National Sponge Candy Day" in Buffalo, so you'd think that'd be a safe bet for being able to find some around town, but generally, look to October for the beginning of sponge candy season. (And if you think that's over the top, there's now even a three-day festival devoted to the candy that culminates with a 5K race.)

5 Best Spots for the Sweet, Spongy Stuff

Great sponge candy is completely covered with chocolate without it being too thick of an exterior layer. The chocolate should be of good quality, not waxy, and not overly sweet. There should be an ever-so-slightly burnt molasses flavor to the interior, but you should have barely enough time to taste it as it melts away upon biting into it. And it should be crispy and light inside, with a tightly aerated structure. Size can vary, with some stores making thicker pieces than others. If you're more of a chocolate fan, then maybe the sponge candy places that turn out the thinner stuff are more for you. From this vantage point, the shops that turn out rounded squares about an inch by an inch give more of that crunchy pillow to chase as you sink into the memory of its disappearance.

Aléthea's Chocolates

8301 Main Street, Williamsville, 14221
716-633-8620 | aletheas.com | Mon–Sat 10 am–10 pm, Sun 10 am–9 pm

Gust Tassy and his son, Dean, opened Aléthea's (*a-lee-thee-ah*) in 1967. They named the shop for Gust's grandmother, who was known for the confections she created in the town of Kozani, in northern Greece. The factory where they make their sweets by hand is adjacent to the shop, which also houses an old-fashioned ice cream parlor where they've been serving homemade truffle-hot fudge sauce for 50 years. Aléthea's sponge candy is on the taller side, but they're most distinguished by the "A" they brand every piece with. Their location, about 5 miles from the airport, makes Aléthea's the frequent first pit-stop for ex-pats who need their fix.

Antoinette's Sweets

5981 Transit Road, Depew, | 716-684-2376
antoinettesbuffalo.com | Mon–Sat 10:30 am–9:30 pm, Sun 12 pm–5 pm

Founder William Morphis arrived in Buffalo in 1910, took a job in a candy store, and five years later, opened his own shop. All practice for Antoinette's, which he named for the eldest of his eight kids, and opened at Sycamore and Fillmore in 1934 (supposedly, as *Buffalo Spree* reports, with the winnings from an Irish sweepstakes). Morphis moved Antoinette's and his family (they lived in the new building too) to the current location on Transit Road in 1958. If you haven't been to an old-school ice cream shop in a while, this is the one to visit—everything from the whipped cream to the hot fudge tastes homemade. Their chocolate selection may not seem as varied as some of the other candy stores in town, but you can count on sponge candy. Theirs has a thicker chocolate covering than most, the top coating is about a ¼-inch thick, and it's available year-round.

Fowler's

100 River Rock Drive, Suite 102, Riverside, 14207
716-877-9983 | fowlerschocolates.com
Mon–Fri 8 am–4 pm

If you're looking for Buffalo's first sponge candy, Fowler's stakes that claim. There are several locations around Buffalo making it an easy spot to check off your list, and their sponge candy can be found in the Buffalo International Airport. In recent years, Fowler's has gotten into celebrating National Sponge Candy Day by introducing a variation on their signature creation. In 2017, that meant the launch a 2.25-ounce Milk Chocolate Sponge Candy Bar featuring small bits of sponge candy throughout, which means sponge candy flavor with less of its crunch.

Ko-Ed Candies

285 Abbott S. Buffalo, South Buffalo, 14220

716-824-3489 | koedcandies.com

Mon–Fri 9 am–7 pm, Sat 10 am–5 pm, Closed Sun

Sponge candy is big business for Ko-Ed, with its milk chocolate, dark chocolate, orange chocolate, and peanut butter chocolate sponge candy reportedly accounting for about 60 percent of its sales, probably all purchased by proud South Buffalonians who wouldn't dream of going anywhere else. Ko-Ed has been a stalwart since Ed Kolher and Theodora Edington started it in 1947. And until recently, its tradition was carried on by just two other families: Charlie and Phyllis Whitt (who bought it in 1969), and Mr. Whitt's son Gary and his wife Sandy (who took over in 1985). But in 2015, there was news when Gary and Sandy retired, selling to John DiGiuseppe, owner of one of North Buffalo's most well-respected candy makers since 1938, Platter's. But South Buffalo was able to breathe a collective sigh of relief—the new owners have assured everyone they weren't planning on changing anything: "You just don't go into a neighborhood like South Buffalo and undo nearly 70 years' worth of tradition. The neighborhood wouldn't stand for it." But so far that hasn't been entirely true: They went a step further in demonstrating dedication to Ko-Ed's tradition by bringing *back* retired favorites like the Peanut Butter Smoothie, Chocolate Melt-A-Way Fudge, and Ko-Ed's Cupie Doll. Just remember, Ko-Ed's a no-no when it comes to summertime. They're only open from the beginning of October until the end of May.

Watson's

2916 Delaware Avenue, Kenmore, 14217

watsonschocolates.com | 716-875-1935

Sun–Wed 10 am–9 pm, Thu–Fri 10 am–10 pm,

Sat 11 am–9 pm

It may not be able to stake a century-old claim like Fowler's, but Watson's pedigree goes back to 1946. And along with that other famous candy store, Watson's is one of Buffalo's most prolific candy shops—there are eight locations (five that also serve ice cream). Founded by brothers Louis and John Watson and their wives Ellen and Mary, the business remains in the family, continued first by Louis and Ellen's son Jim, and today, their daughter Whitney Watson Beecher. They continue using the family recipes, made by hand, in small batches, and using only Fair Trade Certified Cocoa in their chocolate products. Watson's sponge candy has a tight bubble and a creamy coating, and is routinely noted among Buffalo's best. Getting your hands on some shouldn't be hard given that it's made in their Tonawanda factory year round. Watson's *also* does a sponge candy toffee dessert and ice cream topping. But obviously, no Watson's visit is complete without leaving with an order of Chocolates Buffalo Bites, or solid milk chocolate wings, complete with a side of white chocolate "blue cheese" for dipping.

Sponge Candy Standoff

We could debate the finer points of sponge candy over a sponge candy stout at Resurgence, but the truth is that there are a dozen or more adept sweet shops in Buffalo that make this delicacy, and most of them are really great (Wegmans even makes a decent version).

Bella Mia Chocolate Shop, 1096 Hertel Avenue, North Park, 716-447-0922

Henry's Candy & Gifts in Alden, 13237 Broadway, Alden, 716-937-3400

King Condrell's Candy & Ice Cream, 2805 Delaware Avenue, Kenmore, 716-877-4485

Landies Candies, 2495 Main Street #350, Parkside, 716-834-8212

Mike's Homemade Candies, 2110 Clinton Street, Kaisertown, 716-826-6515

Park Edge Sweet Shoppe, 325 Abbott Road, South Buffalo, 716-824-0228

Parkside Candy, 3208 Main Street, Lasalle, 716-833-7540

Platter's, 908 Niagara Falls Boulevard, North Tonawanda, 716-693-5391

Sweet Jenny's Ice Cream, 56 East Spring Street, Williamsville, 716-631-2424

Yia Yia's Chocolates, 3100 Transit Road, West Seneca, 716-656-9585

Ice Cream, Custards, and Sundaes

"The winters are worse in Rochester," some Buffalo natives protest. Maybe, maybe not. Either way, Buffalo enjoys its summers, and with them, old-school ice cream joints making their own whipped cream and homemade sundae toppings, small-batch artisan ice cream makers churning unique flavors from sponge candy to ice wine sherbet, and roadside frozen custard spots.

Custard at Anderson's.

This town has *strong* custard culture—roadside shacks are often operated by students as summer jobs, pulling twists, doing dips, and scooping homemade sherbets and sundaes. These are places open just part of the year, usually March through September. And it *is* "custard," not "soft-serve." If that's confusing, you're not alone. The terms are frequently used interchangeably.

Frozen custard is typically a high butterfat base enriched with eggs. It's usually dense and made with considerably less air than either regular ice cream or soft-serve. Soft-serve is usually made with cream and sometimes even a pudding mix. And it's often made in a way that results in half of it being air. To make things *more* confusing, they can both be made in the same machine! "People call all soft-serve custard even if it's not," Christa Glennie Seychew confirms. Can you blame them?

Luckily, there's no pop quiz required to eat great ice cream. And there's plenty of that in and around town. Whether you're stopping for roadside custard between wing stops or looking to cap off a day of eating up Buffalo with a sundae dripping with homemade hot fudge, these five spots won't steer you wrong.

A special mention must also go to Churn Soft Serve (a sister brand of lloyd Taco Factory), whose ice cream is made from grass-fed cows in Ithaca.

Buffalo's 5 Best Ice Cream Spots

Anderson's

2235 Sheridan Dr, Kenmore, 14223 | 716-875-5952
andersonscustard.com | Sun–Thu 11 AM–9 PM,
Fri–Sat 11 AM–10 PM

Buffalonians Carl and Greta Anderson actually opened their first shop in 1946, nearly 400 miles east, in the Bronx. Homesick for Buffalo, this son and daughter of Swedish immigrants, returned to open their stand on Kenmore Avenue in 1947. They capitalized on its success three years later by opening a larger spot on Sheridan Drive in 1953 (it's still there), and today, there are seven locations around Buffalo, still run by the family (brother-and-sister duo Keith and Holly Anderson).

Anderson's is famous for its lines, even in the winter. (The *Buffalo News* features waiting

on this line as one of its 100 things to do in the city.) They're open year-round—they sell half-price cones when it snows—making them the proxy spot for your roadside custard experience if you're in town visiting out of season. There's an extensive food and snack menu that's light on the hot dogs (a policy initiated to be good neighbors with Ted's, practically across the street from their flagship). But foodwise, they're perhaps best known for beef on weck, which they started offering in the '60s.

That said, there are two signature moves. "Chocolate vanilla twist outsells everything," Holly Anderson told the *Buffalo News*. With good reason. It's *super* creamy, with a malty chocolate flavor. "And we have our signature lemon ice. That was my dad's signature recipe from New York City in the 1940s."

Antoinette's Sweets

5981 Transit Road, Depew, 14043 | 716-684-2376
antoinettesbuffalo.com | Mon–Sat 10:30 AM–9:30 PM,
Sun 12 PM–5 PM

Fresh whipped cream, toppings and syrups that are *all* homemade, and 20 ice cream fla-

vors churned from scratch by fourth-generation owners—they don't make 'em like Antoinette's much anymore. Antoinette's Sweets history goes back about a century, and they're also known for making some of the best sponge candy in town. But ice cream is the *jam*.

There are 11 different kinds of thick frosty milkshakes and double-thick shakes with flavors like butter-rum, root beer, and pineapple, with the option to add bananas, malt, or whipped cream. And the 20 flavors get mixed and matched with about as many toppings to create nearly 30 different sundaes, which are topped with everything from cinnamon to the homemade candies from their shop. If that's all a bit overwhelming as you consider your selection at the counter, gazing at mirror-backed shelf upon shelf of sundae glasses and bowls (there's no table service), the "old-tyme sundaes" are a great place to start.

The two favorites are Mexican (vanilla ice cream, chocolate sauce, and Spanish peanuts) and the Chocolate Nut (vanilla ice cream, chocolate sauce, and chopped nuts). Both come on a tray in a wide, shallow tin bowl on a pedestal with a spoon and short glass of water. The ice cream is airy but creamy (almost like a Pla-

tonic version of Dolly Madison), heaped under delicious whipped cream and a chocolate sauce that's slightly salty and thin, studded with fresh, tasty peanuts.

Fran-Ceil Custard

3411 South Park Avenue, Blasdell, 14219
franceilcustard.com | Mon–Sat 12 PM–10 PM,
Sun 12 PM–10 PM (March 1–September 30)

"FranCeil," "Fran-Ceils," "Fran and Ceils," "Fran 'n Ceils," and some people even call this tight little booth with the blue awning "Frenchy's." However you call it, it's been a custard institution on the border of Lackawanna and Blasdell on U.S. Route 62, about 8 miles south of downtown since 1953.

"Fran and Ceils," as its current owner Joe Dzialak calls it, was originally opened by two brothers-in-law, Tony Pierino and Michael Bordonaro, who named it for their wives Frances and Celia. Though, back then, the Fran-Ceil sign said "French" custard to connote the amount of egg yolks they used. The seasonal ice cream business couldn't support both families, and a few years later, the Bordonaros sold their

interest to their partners, who continued running it until 1980. That's when Joe's mother Jacqueline Dzialak bought it (Joe took over in 2007).

Their hard ice cream is Akron, New York–based Perry's, of course (about 30 miles east). The recipe for homemade sherbet is the original, and Joe has expanded the rotation from orange, lemon, and lime to also include raspberry, watermelon, and pineapple. And the custard recipe was passed on through various ownerships too. These days, in addition to vanilla and chocolate, there's a rotating cast of a dozen flavors that include pistachio, tangerine, black raspberry, blueberry, coconut, cherry, strawberry, and coffee.

"Smooth and creamy" seem inadequate to describe Fran-Ceil's custard. So smooth? So creamy? How about this: on a summer day, that rich swirl of velvety custard drips sweet and thick, but it's so good, it's a wonder it could ever come to that.

Hibbard's Original Frozen Custard

125 Portage Road, Lewiston, 14092 | 716-754-4218

hibbardscustard.com | Mon–Fri 11 AM–9 PM,

Sat–Sun 11 AM–10 PM (April–September)

Hibbard's has been family-owned and seasonally operated since Harold Hibbard Sr. opened it in 1939. The small blue-and-white trimmed shack is in a parking lot set off Center Street about a dozen blocks from the Niagara River in Lewiston, 40 minutes north of downtown Buffalo and just 15 minutes north of Niagara Falls. You have to go looking to find it. But look for it you should.

Supposedly, Harold Hibbard learned his recipe from a friend while on vacation in Florida in the 1930s. The shack's claim, "Hibbard's custard will put your ordinary soft serve ice cream to shame," may sound a bit like bragging, but this is *scoopable* frozen custard, something you don't see all the time, made fresh twice a day and stored in containers in freezers. The shop attributes its deliciousness to the design of the custard machine, which allows less air to be pumped in.

Hibbard's started with eight flavors, but there are now 26 that they serve on a rotation (six flavors daily). One of their most famous is "Coconut Obsession," but the black cherry is a dark horse not to be missed. As for the standards, those would be chocolate, vanilla, and, somewhat unexpectedly, black raspberry, a once-a-week flavor that sold so well it made it to the daily menu.

Lake Effect Artisan Ice Cream

1900 Hertel Avenue, Hertel Avenue, 14214

716-201-1643 | lakeeffecticecream.com

Mon–Fri 1 PM–9 PM, Sat–Sun 11 AM–10 PM

Whoa. There needs to be another word for ice cream to decribe something this dense, this smooth, this interesting, this … good. "Ice cream"?

Lake Effect is the brainchild of two high school teachers, Erik Bernardi (biology) and Jason Wulf (art), who started it in 2008, in a former billiard hall on Lock Street in Lockport, about 30 miles north of downtown Buffalo. And not that it wasn't worth it (it was), but there's now another location, on Hertel.

Their motto: "We work hard to make amazing ice cream." Locally sourced ice cream with unique flavors (like lime cardamom, redrum, candy apple, cinnamon toast, banana pancakes, coconut lime), fun names (Flux Capacitor, Truffle Shuffle, and Come on Praline to name a few), and some uniquely Buffalo flavors (sponge candy, loganberry, Paula's glazed doughnut—yes, with real chunks of Paula's doughnuts), and icewine sherbet.

Try counting and you lose track when you see something else you want. I finally gave up after some seven tries somewhere in the '70s. And that doesn't account for their ice cream sandwiches, icicles (Lake Effect's take on Freeze Pops), ten standard sundaes, and six ice cream cakes.

Not to Leave Anyone Out in the Cold . . .

There's always room for ice cream. If you find that's true, here's a longer list of the area's well-worn, much-beloved spots for that unquenchable sweet tooth.

Jerk's Soda Fountain & Ice Cream, Downtown, 523 Main Street, 716-436-2395

King Condrell's Candy & Ice Cream, Kenmore, 2805 Delaware Avenue, 716-877-4485

Kone King, West Seneca, 865 Center Road, 716-675-8282

Nick Charlap's Ice Cream, West Seneca, 1203 Union Road, 716-675-3981

Parkside Candy, Kensington, 3208 Main Street, 716-833-7540

Sweet Jenny's Ice Cream, Williamsville, 56 East Spring Street, 716-631-2424

CHAPTER ELEVEN

FULL?

What to Do Between Meals in Buffalo

Do you eat to live or live to eat? If you're reading this book, probably the latter. Still, while it might not seem like it based on what we've been talking about, there *are* actually other things to do in Buffalo besides eat.

Obviously, Buffalo's a big sports town (go Bills, Bisons, and Sabres). It also has great architecture—in addition to several Frank Lloyd Wright structures, you'll find the legacies of Henry Hobson Richardson, Frederick Law Olmsted, and Louis Sullivan. There's plenty of history, interesting (the city was a stop on the Underground Railroad) and presidential: Buffalo gave America two presidents (Millard Fillmore and Grover Cleveland) and saw both the assassination and inauguration of two others (odd though that there's little more than a plaque noting McKinley's assassination). There are great parks to walk, art to see, music to hear, and activities to participate in. And we haven't even mentioned the big one, Niagara Falls, less than a thirty-minute drive away.

The local area's marketing organization, Visit Buffalo Niagara is a detailed resource for the city's core and newest activities. And you'll want to check out the *Buffalo News* and *ArtVoice*, the city's weekly periodical for art, music, and event listings. But this is a list of attractions that all make great pit stops in between meals, and ways to work off all the wings, wecks, and pizza.

Things to Do Downtown

Buffalo Double Decker Bus Tours

297 Fuhrmann Boulevard, First Ward, 14203

716-246-9080 | buffalodoubledeckerbus.com

While a double-decker bus may seem a little incongruous, it can still be a fun way to get an overview of a city. Buffalo Double Decker offers several tours a day a few days a week, with various focuses including best-of Buffalo, Canalside, paranormal, tavern, and "drunk Buffalo" tours. Tickets start at $20.

Buffalo Transportation / Pierce-Arrow Museum

263 Michigan Avenue, Downtown, 14203

716-853-0084 | pierce-arrow.com

Thu–Sun 11 AM–4 PM | Adults $10, Kids $5

Jim Sandoro and his wife, Mary Ann, have spent more than 45 years collecting antique vehicles and automobile memorabilia, and started exhibiting it here in 2001. The museum is full of vintage bikes and cars, but the centerpiece may be the 1927 Buffalo Filling Station by Frank Lloyd Wright.

Buffalo Wing Festival

Coca-Cola Field, 275 Washington Street, 14203

buffalowing.com | Labor Day Weekend

Admission: $5 per day, food tickets are $1 each

Launched by Buffalo native Drew Cerza in 2002, after he got the idea from the Bill Murray movie *Osmosis Jones*, Buffalo Wing Festival is a two-day wing-eating event involving wing icons from Buffalo and challengers from across America. Some might argue it's the Super Bowl of wings for restaurants, wing lovers, and competitive eaters alike.

Canalside

44 Prime Street, 14202 | 716-436-7100

canalsidebuffalo.com

Canalside is located on the Niagara River just off Prime Street by the Buffalo Skyway and next to the HARBORCENTER, Buffalo RiverWorks (complete with brewery, pickleball, and roller derby), and KeyBank Center, where the Sabres play. This walkable waterfront is a frequent site for concerts and other community activities (some seasonal) and is adjacent to The Buffalo & Erie County Naval & Military Park, which includes tours of the USS *Little Rock*, the USS *Croaker*, and the USS *The Sullivans*. There are a number of restaurants in the surrounding area and kiosks for tour boats and rentals including paddle and pedal boats, and water bikes you

can ride to the Buffalo Light lighthouse or into the shadow of silos or the General Mills plant. Canalside is also home to Buffalo's signature selfie-spot: the Shark Girl statue by artist Casey Riordan-Millard.

City Hall Observation Deck

65 Niagara Square, 14202 | 716-852-3300

Mon-Fri 8:30 am–4 pm

After viewing the murals in the lobby of this Art Deco building dedicated in 1932, you can take the elevator to the 25th floor, then walk three flights up for a panoramic view of Lake Erie and Western New York.

Colored Musician's Club

145 Broadway, 14203 | cmctheclub.com

When an all-white musician union refused to include African-American musicians, a separate union was formed, the Buffalo Local 533 in 1917. They found their current home in 1934, and got their charter a year later. These days, you can hear performances several days a week (check event calendar for details), but the most fun may be on Sundays at 6 PM, when they hold jam sessions. If you have any skills, that's when there's also an open invitation to join in.

Forgotten Buffalo

716-833-5211 | ForgottenBuffalo@aol.com
$50 per Person

Join Maxwell Truth (Eddy Dobosiewicz) of forgottenbuffalo.com on a unique tour of Nickel City oddities, or hit some of its time-honored spots for some wings, weck, and fish fries along with a little history. Includes meal, transportation, and a docent-led guided tour. Must be 21 years of age.

Shea's Performing Arts Center

646 Main Street, 14202 | 716-847-1410 | sheas.org

Shea's was originally opened in 1926 to show silent movies. But over the past 20 years, it's undergone a $20 million restoration, and currently shows touring Broadway musicals and other special events.

Silo City

Take a walking tour of a historic Buffalo grain elevator (explorebuffalo.org), do a little indoor climbing (buffaloriverworks.com/rock-climbing) see them from a river tour, paddle around them yourself (silocitypaddling.com), or catch a performance of poetry, live music, or immersive theater amidst them (silo.city).

Catch a Game: Buffalo Bisons

Coca-Cola Field, 275 Washington Street, Downtown, 14203 | milb.com/index.jsp?sid=t422
April–August

The Buffalo Bisons have existed in some form since 1877, and over the years, they've been affil-

iated with the Pirates, Indians, White Sox, and Mets. But since 2013, this International League team has been a Triple-A affiliate home to prospects for the Toronto Blue Jays. The stadium was designed by the same architectural firm that went on to design Camden Yards.

Catch a Game: Buffalo Bills

New Era Field, 1 Bills Drive, Orchard Park, 14127

buffalobills.com | September–December

The Bills are the only team ever to play in four straight Super Bowls and are still looking to win their first. But with the Cubs having recently won their first championship since 1908, why shouldn't the Bills be due? And since their 2014 purchase by Terry and Kim Pegula (just the team's second owners since 1959), they seem squarely positioned to remain a Nickel City icon.

Catch a Game: Buffalo Sabres

KeyBank Center | One Seymour H. Knox III Plaza, Downtown 14203-3096 | 716-855-4100

nhl.com/sabres

Also owned by Terry Pegula, who purchased the club in 2011, the Sabres, who were founded in 1970, have advanced to the finals twice (1975 and 1999), but are still looking to hoist their first Stanley Cup. That doesn't lessen the passion for them in this hockey-loving town.

Around and Outside Buffalo

Albright-Knox Art Gallery

1285 Elmwood Avenue, Delaware Park, 14222

716-882-8700 | albrightknox.org | Tue–Sun 10 AM–5 PM

The Albright-Knox has been exhibiting art since 1862. The collection, housed in a neoclassical building at the edge of Frederick Law Olmsted's Delaware Park features art by Francis Bacon, Frida Kahlo, Roy Lichtenstein, Georgia O'Keeffe, Pablo Picasso, Andy Warhol, and oth-

ers. (On the first Friday of every month, admission to part of the museum is free.)

Buffalo Central Terminal

495 Paderewski Drive, East Side, 14212

716-810-3210 | buffalocentralterminal.org

This Art Deco terminal opened in 1929 and operated until 1979, serving more than 200 trains and 10,000 passengers daily. After spending years in disuse and neglect, there are now efforts to refurbish and repurpose the building, and there are occasionally cool tours of it.

Buffalo Olmsted Parks Conservancy

bfloparks.org

No visit to Buffalo is complete without visiting one of the city parks that are part of the Buffalo Olmsted Parks Conservancy. There are six parks spread out in the city over 850 acres that are connected by eight circles and seven parkways.

Buffalo Zoo

300 Parkside Avenue, Parkside, 14214 | buffalozoo.org

Daily 10 AM–4 PM | Adults $12, Kids $9

The Buffalo Zoo, which is near the northeastern tip of Delaware Park, is said to be America's third oldest. It dates back to 1875, when its first permanent building was erected five years after its first animals, a pair of deer, were donated. Today there are nearly 30 exhibits on almost 24 acres.

Japanese Garden

Delaware Park, 1 Museum Court, North Buffalo, 14216

716-873-9644 | Mon, Wed–Fri 9 AM–8 PM,

Closed Sat–Sun, Tue

This six-acre garden along Delaware Park's Mirror Lake gifted by Buffalo's Japanese sister city of Kanazawa in 1972, provides a contemplative setting to think about who makes the city's best wings.

Niagara Falls

Niagara Falls State Park Visitor Center,

332 Prospect Street, Niagara Falls, 14303

716-278-1796 | niagarafallsstatepark.com

Every second, 3,160 tons of water flow over the three waterfalls that straddle the border between Canada and the United States (Ontario and New York state). It's an impressive site, America's oldest state park (established in 1885), and one of those things you have to check off your list. And it's just a half-hour drive north from downtown Buffalo. It's free to walk into the park and see the

falls, but a Discovery Pass (adult $45, child $34) gets you as close as you want to the roar, be that the Observation Tower, a poncho-protected loop on the *Maid of the Mist*, or a 175-foot descent into the Niagara Gorge to experience the power of the Falls from the Hurricane Deck.

Niagara Wine Trail

niagarawinetrail.org

Take a self-guided tour of the more than 20 wineries that can be found off or along Rt. 18 or Rt.

104 in Niagara, Orleans, and Monroe counties between Niagara Falls and Rochester. Information about the wineries, their hours, lodging, restaurants, nearby breweries, distilleries, and wine shops can all be found on the Niagara Wine Trail website.

Slow Roll Buffalo

slowrollbuffalo.org | May–Oct

(plus monthly Snow Roll winter rides)

Slow Roll is a great way to see (and learn about) Buffalo. It started in Detroit, but it has caught on hard in the Nickel City where each week, on Monday at 5:30 PM, hundreds of cyclists meet at different venues and ride a unique route through the city. Slow Roll is open to everyone, with riders from ages 4 to 94 participating, usually riding about 10 to 12 miles at about 8 to 10 mph over an hour and a half. You just need a helmet and a bike, which you can rent through Reddy Bikeshare (reddybikeshare.socialbicycles.com).

Theodore Roosevelt Inaugural National Historic Site

641 Delaware Avenue, Allentown, 14202

716-884-0095 | trsite.org | Mon, Thu–Fri 9 AM–5 PM, Tue 9 AM–8 PM, Sat–Sun 12 PM–5 PM

Learn about Teddy Roosevelt and experience an audio reenactment of his inauguration in the room inside the Ansley Wilcox House where he was sworn in after President William McKinley was assassinated at the Pan-American Exposition in 1901.

Frank Lloyd Wright

The Martin House is the most well-known of Buffalo's Frank Lloyd Wright architecture, but that wasn't always the case. Unfortunately, the world-famous Larkin Administration Building at 680 Seneca Street was demolished in 1950. Still, Martin House is only one of several places in town to appreciate his work.

1927 Buffalo Filling Station

Pierce-Arrow Museum | 263 Michigan Avenue,
Downtown, 14203 | 716-853-0084 | pierce-arrow.com
Thu–Sun 11 AM–4 PM | Adults $10, Kids $5

The architect is said to have called his filling station, complete with copper and overhead gravity-fed gas distribution system, "an ornament to the pavement."

Blue Sky Mausoleum

Forest Lawn Cemetery, 1411 Delaware Avenue,
Elmwood Village, 14209 | 716-885-1600
blueskymausoleum.com | Daily 10 AM–4 PM

Plans commissioned by Darwin Martin for the Blue Sky Mausoleum were completed by Frank Lloyd Wright in 1928, but went unexecuted after Martin experienced losses in the stock market crash in 1929. The design was revived and completed in the Forest Lawn Cemetery in 2004, as part of a plan to build on visitors' Wright experience in Buffalo.

Fontana Boathouse

1 Rotary Row, Buffalo, NY 14201 | 716-362-3140
wrightboathouse.com | Tours: Thu 1:30 PM,
April–Oct, $10 per person

The designs for the "Boathouse for the University of Wisconsin Boat Club" were included in Wright's Wasmuth Portfolio, the first publication of any of his work. It would take until 2007 to be built overlooking Buffalo's Black Rock Canal and the Niagara River thanks to the efforts of rowing and architecture enthusiast Charles Fontana. Today, the first floor is a working boathouse and the second floor features a clubroom, locker rooms, balconies, and diamond-paned windows.

Graycliff Estate

6472 Old Lake Shore Road, Derby, 14047
716-947-9217 | experiencegraycliff.org
Tours by appointment

The summer house on the shore of Lake Erie was built for Darwin and Isabelle Martin and completed in 1931. Unlike the Martin House, Graycliff was built so as to let in lots of light. Some see the house as an important representation of Wright's transition from his Prairie period to his famous Fallingwater house in Mill Run, Pennsylvania. The Graycliff Conservancy offers a variety of tours, all docent-led and by reservation.

Martin House Complex

125 Jewett Parkway, Parkside, 14214 | 716-856-3858
darwinmartinhouse.org | Tours by appointment

The famous architect designed this house for wealthy Buffalo businessman Darwin D. Martin (Chief Operating Officer for the Larkin Soap Company) and his family between 1903 and 1905. The house received National Historic Landmark status in 1986, and is considered one of the finest achievements of Wright's Prairie period. Over the years, the house suffered damage, with three of its original five buildings destroyed, but it has undergone extensive restoration since 1997. You can walk around outside by yourself, but the three daily tours inside (10 AM, noon, and 2 PM, $19 to $37) are docent-led and pre-paid reservations are recommended.

William R. Heath House

76 Soldiers Place, Elmwood Village, 14222

The Heath House is a private residence today, and there are no tours. But you can walk by and check it out. It was commissioned by William Heath, an attorney at the Larkin Soap Company, and completed in 1905. While smaller in scale, it's similar in design to the Martin House.

A Special Stay

Hotel Henry Urban Resort Conference Center

444 Forest Avenue, Elmwood Village 14213

hotelhenry.com | 716-882-1970 | From $160 per night

Without question, Buffalo's coolest hotel. How often do you get to stay in a 191,000-square-foot luxury boutique hotel and conference center that used to be a psychiatric hospital? It's true, this 88-room full-service hotel sitting on 42 acres of the Richardson Olmsted Campus on the outskirts of Elmwood Village features all the dramatic landscape and Victorian and Romanesque architecture of a horror movie but without any of the scariness. The building was designed by Henry Hobson Richardson (who along with Wright and Louis Sullivan make up the trinity of American architecture) and completed in 1880. And it sits on grounds and gardens designed by Frederick Law Olmsted. Vastly high ceilings, huge windows, dramatic hallways, and a great bar.

Hotel @ The Lafayette

391 Washington Street, Downtown 14203

716-853-1505 | buffalobrewerydistrict.com/lafayette
From $139 per night

This refurbished French-Renaissance building is situated just across the street from Lafayette Square and a few more blocks away from Niagara Square. And it has the distinction of having been designed by Louise Blanchard Bethune, the first woman known to have been a professional architect in the United States. The hotel features 57 one- or two-bedroom suites, a small coffee and pastry counter, and brewery on site.

InnBuffalo

619 Lafayette Avenue, Elmwood Ave, 14222

716-867-7777 | innbuffalo.com | From $159 per night

InnBuffalo is the former home of H. H. Hewitt, said to have been a Buffalo brass industrialist.

Husband-and-wife team Joseph and Ellen Lettieri.

His 18-room, 11-fireplace mansion on Lafayette was built in 1898, and purchased at a city auction by husband-and-wife team Joseph and Ellen Lettieri in 2011. They've turned the mansion into a nine-suite boutique hotel with super comfortable beds, wifi, and all modern conveniences. In fact, spend a few nights sipping a beverage on the inn's comfortable covered porch and you just may decide you have no interest in leaving it and the complimentary breakfast, complete with Mickey Mouse shaped pancakes, behind.

Roycroft Inn

40 South Grove Street, East Aurora, 14052

716-652-5552 | roycroftinn.com | From $145 per night

The Roycroft Inn was opened to accommodate visitors of the Roycroft community, an American Arts and Crafts Movement created in 1897, in response to the industrialization of the Victorian age. The century-old inn was reopened in

1995, and features restored murals, handcrafted furniture, and an environment that lowers the blood pressure. It's just a 20-minute drive southeast of downtown, and also just so happens to be a few blocks walk from Bar Bill Tavern, Charlie the Butcher, and Elm Street Bakery.

The Curtiss Hotel

210 Franklin Street, Downtown, 14202

716-954-4900 | curtisshotel.com

From $169 per night

The Curtiss, an Ascend Hotel, which opened in 2017, has quite a bit of history and flare. This early 20th-century terra cotta building was built for Harlow C. Curtiss, a prominent Buffalo attorney and real estate investor who never could have imagined it would someday host high-speed elevators to 68 hotel rooms, a men's grooming salon, a rooftop lounge, and the only revolving bar in Western New York.

The Mansion on Delaware Avenue

414 Delaware Avenue, Downtown 14202

716-886-3300 | mansionondelaware.com

From $225 per night

Admit it, you've always dreamed of having a butler. Well, along with the gas remote-controlled fireplaces and multi-head showers, Buffalo Niagara's only AAA rated Four Diamond hotel offers "butler transportation" within a three-mile radius of the hotel.

CHAPTER TWELVE

ICONIC FOOD DAY TRIPS FROM BUFFALO

Famous Foods of New York State

According to at least one new St. Louis–based food festival, Flavored Nation, it's not bagels, pizza, or pastrami, but the chicken wing that's New York State's most iconic food. And there are enough iconic wing spots in the 716 to keep your eating itinerary occupied for a month. But New York has many other unsung and celebrated food pilgrimages and creations.

Consider the following foods and their New York State birthplaces:

Jell-O—LeRoy
Potato Chips—Saratoga Springs
Shredded Wheat—Niagara Falls
Thousand Island Dressing—Clayton
Philadelphia Cream Cheese—Lowville

And that doesn't even get into the claim that the first hamburger in America was made at the Erie County Fair in Hamburg in 1885, *not* at Louis' Lunch in New Haven, Connecticut, in 1895.

Whether we're talking Rochester's garbage plate, Naples' grape pie, Binghamton's spiedies, Utica's triad (greens, riggies, and tomato pies), or Oneonta's chicken and cold cheese slice, Buffalo makes a great beginning or final destination on an epic food road trip across New York State.

Here are some of the most iconic food day trip musts outside Buffalo ranging from just over 75 minutes to four hours driving time.

Rochester: Wings and Garbage Plates

Rochester, just a little more than an hour east of Buffalo on I-90 or Route 33, has its own wing culture and other food destinations worth exploring. Nick Tahou's is definitely the most famous place in town—they've trademarked their signature "Garbage Plate"—but a bunch of other places do riffs on this Rochester icon, calling it among other things, a "Trash Plate," "Rochester Plate," "Junkyard Plate,"

"Trasher Plate," "Trash Plate," "Compost Plate," and "Sticky Icky Plate." And there's more to Rochester than garbage (make sure you get a Zweigle's white hot somewhere, otherwise you're going to be cooking them yourself), including great wings.

Some would have you believe that true wing creativity is to be found outside Buffalo. Rochester's thought to be close enough to Mecca to know how to make them right, while not being beholden to the tradition of mild, medium, and hot. Here are a few beloved places to put that theory to the test.

Angry Goat

938 S Clinton Avenue, Rochester, 14620

585-413-1125 | theangrygoatpub.com

Mon–Wed 4 pm–2 am, Thu–Fri 3 pm–2 am, Sat–Sun 12 pm–2 am

Beyond wings with house sauces like blueberry barbecue, Cajun Buffalo, tangy gold, garlic Parmesan, or honey hot sauce, the Angry Goat does something rarer: duck wings, made with honey hot sauce.

ButaPub

315 Gregory Street, Rochester, 14620

585-563-6241 | butapub.com | Mon–Sat 11 am–2 am, Sun 10:30 am–4 pm

Korean-style chicken wings sprinkled with sesame seeds and scallions, and your choice of gochujang, soy-garlic, or sweet-sambal sauces. Make sure to get sides of both the house blue *and* miso-buttermilk dipping sauces.

Jeremiah's Tavern

1104 Monroe Avenue, Rochester, 14620

585-461-1313 | jeremiahstavern.com

Sun–Thu 11:30 am–2 am (kitchen closes at 12 am); Fri–Sat 11:30 am–2 am (kitchen closes at 1 am)

In addition to smoked wings and classic Buffalo heat levels, Jeremiah's does at least eight other

sauces, including these two must-orders: Pow Pow (a creamy sauce with a peppery garlic kick) and Nawlins Blues (Buffalo, Cajun, *and* Garlic Parm studded with crumbled blue cheese).

The Distillery

1142 Mt. Hope Avenue, Rochester, 14620

585-271-4105 | thedistillery.com | Sun 11 am–1 am, Mon–Sat 11:30 am–2 am

The Distillery has been doing their wing thing since they opened in 1980. Try one of their signature rubs, which include "barbacoa" and Brazilian piri piri, and wings made with a roster of sauces that includes basics like garlic Parm along with house specialties like smoke and fire and "Still's" butter garlic.

Nick Tahou Hots

320 W. Main Street, Rochester, 14608 | 585-436-0184

garbageplate.com | Mon–Thu 8 am–8 pm, Fri–Sat 8 am–12 am, Closed Sun

The garbage plate may be an icon of Western New York, but its origins, while college kid-popularized, are decidedly proletariat if not downright indigent. Echoes of the practicality and desperation that inspired it can ripple through the dining room within the first five minutes—before even going fork to mouth, someone might ask, "Can you help me with my Nick Tahou's Garbage Plate today?"

The business was started by Alexander (Alex) Tahou in 1918, and named for his son Nick, father of current owner (also Nick). The original business started just down the street from today's location, and moved to the present building on West Main Street just west of I-490, which once housed the Rochester terminal of the Buffalo, Rochester, and Pittsburgh Railway, in 1968.

"We started out as West Main Texas Hots," Tahou tells me. "Hamburgers didn't come on the menu until the '50s. We had rectangular hamburgers so they wouldn't have to have two types of buns. In 1968, when it moved, the name became Nick Tahou's Texas Hots. My father always said that his father was one of the first to call them Texas Hots, but everyone has their own story."

According to Nick Jr., the Garbage Plate was around since the beginning, created to feed construction workers "who needed the calories," though not with that name. The original featured two hot dogs, cold beans, and home fries, but the hamburger version is today's most common plate. As for the name, it came out of the early '80s, when college kids, seeing other people ordering it, would say, "Give me a garbage plate."

Nick Jr. said it was an appellation they fought,

Nick Tahou, Jr.

but decided to trademark when others started copying them. "They've copied it around the world, but you can't say you've had it unless you have it here," he said, adding, "If you have the Garbage Plate somewhere else, that's like buying a Chevy and putting a Caddy emblem on it and saying you have a Cadillac."

It's an interesting analogy for an underseasoned plate of hot and cold food that ranges from $4.50 to $6, served in what feels like a company cafeteria awash in cleaning fluids, but you have to admire the pride. Let's be honest, this is checklist item for ardent foodies, but it's a dish that's *just* meant to fill you up.

It's a heaping plate, but maybe not as big as

you'd expect. There's a chili coating that has a slight burn of a back-of-the-mouth bite (is that cinnamon?) and underneath, a pile that's half hash browns and half underseasoned, cold macaroni salad that in turn tops an underseasoned double-patty cheeseburger dressed with mustard. It's a culinary trainwreck that you can't help rubbernecking, bite after bite, chasing something you never quite find…and then you're full.

Nick Tahou's got the trademark on the "Garbage Plate," but what's the movie line in *Inception*? "The most resilient parasite is an idea." That's right, you can't keep a good trash plate down. Wait, that doesn't quite sound right, does it? They may not be able to use the term, but there are plenty of places that do their own versions and call them something similar.

DogTown

691 Monroe Avenue, Rochester, 14607

585-271-6620 | dogtownhots.com

Mon–Thu 11 AM–11 PM, Fri–Sat 11 AM–12 AM, Closed Sun

There are five different ways you can take your Junkyard Dog Plate (with combinations of hot dogs, cheeseburgers, and sausages) and a choice of home fries, macaroni salad, French fries, baked beans, or coleslaw. "Everything" here means mustard, onions, and DogTown sauce (Cincinnati-style chili).

Effortlessly Healthy

1921 South Avenue, Rochester, 14620

585-254-0078 | ehmeals.com | Mon–Fri 11 AM–5 PM

Effortlessly Healthy does what they've trademarked as "Healthy Trash Plates," all gluten- and dairy-free, served with roasted sweet potatoes and coleslaw and topped with avocado sauce. You also have the option to build your own, choosing from steak, burger, chicken, portobello, tofu, and veggies, and a bunch of add-ons, among them a few ways to make them a little less healthy (bacon and a meat hot sauce).

Mark's Texas Hots

487 Monroe Avenue, Rochester, 14607

585-473-1563

facebook.com/Marks-Texas-Hots-113324795363826

Daily 24/7

Mark's Sloppy Plate Special at this 24-hour diner includes two cheeseburgers or two hot dogs over fries (you can substitute steak or sausage), macaroni salad or beans and comes with two pieces of French bread.

Naples: Grape Pie

Naples is a tiny town in Ontario County (considered part of the Finger Lakes Wine Region) that's almost a straight shot east of Buffalo via New York State Route 400, U.S. Route 20A, and New York State Route 390. Naples is about halfway between Buffalo and Binghamton, a little under two hours from both.

According to Monica Schenk, during the Grape Festival she'll make 1,000 pies in two days.

"The Grape Pie Queen"

Seeds, skins, and the seasonality of Concords have to be the three things that have held back grape pie from national culinary acclaim. It's hard to imagine any other reasons why this delicious, and otherwise easy-to-make pie has largely remained a local treat since Irene Bouchard started making them for the Redwood Restaurant in Naples, New York, in the 1970s.

Bouchard had been running a bakery business out of her home since the '50s, and had a little bake shop across the street from the Redwood. At some point, the restaurant started selling Concord grape pies that they found were being eaten as quickly as they could make them. Al Hodges, the Redwood's owner, asked Bouchard if she'd help supply him. At her peak, Bouchard's obituary reports she was making some 17,000-plus grape pies a year, 10,000 just during the fall, when Concords are available!

The Grape Pie Queen passed away in 2015, at the age of 98. But her legacy lives on. The small Ontario County town features the World's Greatest Grape Pie Contest every year in the last week of September as part of the Naples Grape Festival, and two pie spots, Cindy's and Monica's, have been anchoring Naples' grape pie production for decades.

Monica's Pies

7599 State Route 21 Naples, 14512 | 585-374-2139
monicaspies.com | Jan 1–April 30, Daily 9 AM–5 PM;
May 1–Dec 31, Daily 9 AM–6 PM
(Cash or check only, ATM on premises)

Monica Schenk said she started baking grape pies in 1983, "My mother knew how to cook and I grew up watching her and learning how to cook, so I knew I could make a good pie." They grew their own grapes, put a picnic table on the side of the road, and it was self-serve. "It worked most of the time," Monica said smiling.

These days, Monica's just *slightly* busier, going through 10 tons of grapes a year (she no longer grows her own). She has a convection oven, several freezers so they can keep grapes to make the pies year-round, and a kitchen downstairs from her roadside shop on the outskirts of town where they also make summer pies and chicken pot pie. "During the Grape Festival we'll make 1,000 pies in two days," she said. "They move. We can do 48 pies at once if I have to."

You can buy the pies both frozen or fresh (the fresh pie has a "floating top" put on after the filling is cooked separately and placed inside). Monica also does versions topped with Graham cracker crumbs, oats, brown sugar, butter, and cinnamon, and sells jars of filling and bags of pie crust mix if you'd like to make her pie yourself at home. She's also published her recipe on her website and is pretty open about the process if you want to try your hand at making one from scratch. "There's one thing I do, just one thing I don't tell people," Monica says.

Other than that, for the filling, they just pinch the grapes to remove and reserve the skins, cook up and press the pulp, throw out the seeds, and add the lemon juice and sugar. "The pie crust is just a good old Crisco recipe with not too much water, just enough to give a feel to it," Monica said, and the crust is cooked separately, because otherwise, "You don't always get the crust cooked if you cook the crust and the grapes together because it's so wet."

Utica: Chicken Riggies, Utica Greens, and Tomato Pie

You think the origins of *Buffalo's* food icons are difficult to track down? Drive three hours east on I-90 to Utica. This city, with some four to five times fewer people has three food icons with origins at least as cloudy. (We're not even going to get into fried meatballs, half-moon cookies, and pasties.)

The Riggie-toni Awards

What is it about chicken, food creativity, and hazy origin stories? That's what you have to ask when delving into the birth of chicken riggies, an Utica rigatoni dish said to have originally been made with just cubed chicken, cherry peppers, wine, marinara, and cheese.

If you've never had chicken riggies and don't understand the appeal, try to imagine a smooth, spicy sauce made with so much grated cheese that you'd think it was made with cream. It's tangy, silky, sweet, hot, and just a little vinegary—one of those truly satisfying, overindulgent Italian-American dishes you know is nowhere near "authentic Italian" but too good to refuse.

Fortunately for riggies afficionados, Bill Keeler seems to have reported a pretty definitive account of the dish's origins on the radio for WIBX950 AM. It seems to have started in Clinton, just out of town at an Italian restaurant called Clinton House owned by chef Richie Scamardo with chef Bobby Hazleton. Chef Michael Geno, who worked there at the time, told Keeler it was invented on a Monday night in 1979. "The doctors, lawyers and union guys would come in on Monday nights to play cards and we would make them the 'riggie dish' with chicken, tomatoes and cherry peppers," he said. "When they came back the next week, they wanted the same thing we made them the week before. And there you have it—the birth of chicken riggies."

It does seem though, that another chef, Mike Schulz, may have had a hand in putting riggies on the map. He says he was washing dishes at the Clinton House in the 1980s when chef Hazleton used to make riggies, or a dish like it, for the dishwashers. Schulz worked his way onto the line, then left Clinton House to follow Hazleton to The Fisherman's Wharf, where he also made riggies with the chef. Schulz went on to become head chef at the Chesterfield Restaurant, where in 1989, after about six months cooking the same recipes, he decided to add new dishes like chicken riggies to the menu. "The rest is history," he told Keeler, noting that he didn't invent them, but probably did help make the dish famous. Chesterfield is routinely noted by many as serving the best chicken riggies.

There are about as many versions as restaurants in Utica. Many have strayed beyond the initial recipe, adding onions, mushrooms, black olives, and garlic, and tweaking the sauce by adding heavy cream, or as at Teddy's, an alfredo sauce (which, in many places, involves cream too). Some places offer shrimp and sausage riggies as frequent swaps for chicken. And at Bella Regina in Utica (where they serve nearly 6-pound buckets full of riggies to-go), the "Riggie Fest" section of the menu includes 13 different versions going beyond sausage and shrimp to also offer steak, pepperoni, meatballs, various vegetables, any *combination* of three meats, and even, wait for it . . . Buffalo-style riggies.

And if you think that's riggie-diculous (sorry), like "Buffalo flavor," chicken riggies has a life of its own. At Teddy's, another beloved riggies institution, they do a grilled chicken riggie *pizza*, and to get truly meta, Carmella's Cafe does wings with riggies sauce. A recent contest hosted by the *Post-Standard* in Syracuse and voted on by the public included 62 nominees. It's only a matter of time before the whole world goes mad for riggies.

A riggies quest could be its own book, but these four places are frequently noted as serving some of Utica's best.

Bella Regina

239 Genesee Street, Utica, 13501 | 315-732-2426
Tue–Fri 11:30 AM–2 PM, 4:30 PM–9 PM,
Sat 4:30 PM–9 PM, Closed Sun–Mon

Rigatoni and your choice of mushroom and peppers tossed in a creamy riggie sauce with: chicken, seafood, shrimp, pepperoni, vegetables,

sausage, eggplant, meatballs, steak, "Buffalo", trio (any three meats), or Sicilian (sausage, peppers, cherry tomatoes, mushrooms, and black olives). You can also level-up any riggie dish with black olives or onions.

Carmella's Café

8530 Seneca Turnpike, New Hartford, 13413
315-797-3350 | Mon–Thu 11 AM–12 AM,
Fri–Sat 11 AM–1 AM, Sun 9 AM–12 AM

The menu describes their version as "Utica's Best Chicken Riggies," served with fresh mushrooms, marinated peppers, onions, olives, three hot cherry pepper slices, and chunks of chicken tossed in their secret recipe.

Chesterfield Restaurant

1713 Bleecker Street, Utica, 13501 | 315-738-9356
chesterfield1713.net | Tue–Thu 4 PM–10 PM,
Fri–Sat 11:30 AM–11 PM, Closed Mon

Chesterfield's riggies are made "with diced chicken, red onion, hot and sweet peppers, grated Romano tossed with rigatoni in a spicy marinara sauce."

Teddy's Restaurant

851 Black River Boulevard, Rome, 13440
315-336-7839 | teddysrestaurantny.com
Mon–Sat 11 AM–9 PM, Closed Sun

Teddy's makes theirs with sweet peppers, mushrooms, onions, black olives, and chicken with rigatoni in a light wine sauce (with or without hot cherry peppers). They also do sausage riggies.

Utica Greens: Just "Greens" in Utica

Most restaurants would kill to be at the center of one iconic dish like riggies. Somehow, with Utica greens, the Chesterfield Restaurant has managed to be in the middle of two. Like wings in Buffalo aren't Buffalo wings, these are just "greens," "fried greens," or greens that are then named after the restaurant or chef making them.

The dish? A little spicy, a little cheesy, a little crunchy—altogether, more than a few incentives to eat your (bitter) greens. Escarole cooked with garlic, prosciutto, hot cherry peppers, Parmesan, and breadcrumbs, that's then topped with more cheese and breadcrumbs, broiled, and topped with a bit more grated cheese, for luck. Why not?

According to an interview given to the *New York Times* in early 2017, Utica greens—sorry, "greens"—started being served there in 1988 (a year before riggies), when chef Joe Morelle put them on the menu. The dish, a riff on one Morelle had seen another chef make while working at a restaurant (now closed) called Grimaldi's, was a runaway success. And like the Chesterfield's other hit, chicken riggies, greens can now be found in many area restaurants, sometimes with variations. Georgio's Village Cafe makes one variation called "Georgio Greens" with potatoes, and swaps salami for the prosciutto, and another called "Greens Spinelli" with artichoke hearts, mushrooms, broccoli, sugar snap peas, potatoes, melted mozzarella, and marinara.

Utica Tomato Pie

When it comes to tomato pie, there's Trenton tomato pie, Philadelphia tomato pie, and the latter's lesser-known sibling separated by birth, *Utica* tomato pie. (Let's sideline any talk of southern tomato pie, which is actually a pie, the kind made with a pie crust, not a pizza pie.) And while we'll get into the nuances, it's probably easiest to get one thing taken care of right away: only the first is technically pizza.

The Trenton tomato pie is a reverse-sauce pizza where the dough is topped first with cheese, then with toppings, and finally, sauce. It's a practice executed at select pizzerias elsewhere in the Northeast, often referred to as "upside-down pizza" (Frank Pepe's The Spot in New Haven, CT has been known for doing one). L&B Spumoni Gardens in Brooklyn, and New York Pizza Suprema in Manhattan are two other well-known practitioners. But unlike at *those* two, Trenton's tomato pies are round.

Then there's the Philadelphia tomato pie, a bready dough baked in a rectangular sheet pan where it rises to near Sicilian slice-thickness and is topped with a thick tomato sauce, usually heavily-seasoned. It's often finished with grated cheese. Tomato pies can differ depending on the region (or place) you find them, at times featuring a cloyingly sweet sauce with a dough that can range from just-cooked to well-done. It's *this* kind of tomato pie you'll find in Utica.

Two of Philadelphia's oldest tomato pie joints date back to the early twentieth century—Ianelli's to 1910, and Sarcone's Bakery to at least 1918. One of the oldest places in Utica known to make tomato pie, O'Scugnizzo's, traces *its* history to 1914, when owner Eugeno Burlino would sell an entire tomato pie for just five cents). Even given those dates, it's hard to credit one or the other with having invented the style, especially given that it's likely both were just riffs on *sfincione*, a similar flatbread topped with anchovy and breadcrumbs.

Whoever invented it, it's proliferated in Utica enough for many more places there to make it than in pizza-crazy New York City and Chicago, and for these spots to frequently be noted as the ones to have perfected it.

O'Scugnizzo's

614 Bleecker Street, Utica, 13501 | 315-732-6149
uticapizza.com | Daily 9 AM–11 PM

It's not on the menu, and you need to call a day in advance, but the oldest pizzeria in Utica (and some say the second oldest pizzeria in America) will still make you the tomato pie they started with in 1914.

Roma Sausage & Deli

2029 Bleecker Street, Utica, 13501
facebook.com/Romatomatopie
Mon–Fri 7 AM–4:30 PM, Sat 7 AM–3 PM, Sun 7 AM–1 PM

Roma, which started out in 1999, as a sausage maker, has been making a carefully constructed version of tomato pie since the early 2000s. They've been known to sell out, so the earlier you get there, the better chance of snagging your tomato pie.

Napoli's Italian Bakery & Deli

412 Culver Avenue, Utica, 13501 | 315-798-8709
napolisitalianbakery.com | Thu–Fri 6 AM–4 PM,
Sat 6 AM–3 PM, Sun 6 AM–1 PM, Closed Mon–Wed

Napoli's has been at tomato pie since 1964. They do a 15-slice small pie and a 30-slice large pie (they also do a 48-slice party cut).

Binghamton: Spiedies

Binghamton's about the same distance from Buffalo as it is from Manhattan, making it a good food pitstop on any road trip between the two. It's a three-and-a-half hour drive in a southeasterly direction from Buffalo via New York State Route 400, U.S. Route 20A, and New York State Route 390.

No, Not Speedos, the Banana Hammocks ... *Spiedies*

Who invented the Binghamton-beloved cubed, herb-marinated meat spiedies sandwich? It's all in the family—Camillo Iacovelli or his younger brother, Agostino—at least, according to Binghamton lore. A 2005 account in the Press & Sun Bulletin traces spiedies' Binghamton roots to a marriage proposal and a recipe that originated in the small town of Civitella Casanova, 20 minutes west of the Italian port city of Pescara on its eastern coast. The story goes that Camillo Iacovelli proposed via mail to his childhood sweetheart back in Abruzzo after immigrating to Endicott to open a restaurant. "Young Josephine said 'yes,'" the Press & Sun Bulletin reported, "and soon came to the States for her wedding—bringing with her a cherished family recipe of spiedis [sic]: cubed, marinated, broiled lamb, served on long metal skewers."

The spiedies (from the Italian *spiedo*, for "spit") were then supposedly drizzled with a sauce called "zuzu," which is said to have originally been made with water, wine vinegar, lemon juice, mint, and garlic. From there, some accounts credit the first Iacovelli to serve spiedies to Agostino (Augie) at Augie's Grill in the village of Endicott outside Binghamton while others say it was Camillo's Restaurant in the neighboring hamlet of Endwell. According to the *Press & Sun Bulletin* and Agostino's son Anthony Iacovelli, both Camillo and Augie deserve the credit. "Back in the 1930s," he said, "Camillo owned a restaurant called The Parkview Terrace on Endicott's North Side. My father (Augie) worked there. He was the one who prepared the spiedies and cooked them on the stove. They sold them for a dime apiece. It wasn't until later that my uncle (Camillo) opened Camillo's on the George F. Highway and my father (Agostino) opened Augie's."

Supposedly, as a kid, Anthony would run out to the men playing bocce on the court behind the Parkview with 10 spiedie skewers, wrap the bread around the meat, and make the transactions. So maybe that's the origin of the bread? Who knows. That doesn't even delve into Sharkey's claim that then owner Peter Sharak popularized spiedies at a cookfire in the window by his bar opened in 1947 (lamb then, but now chicken).

These days, spiedies are served everywhere in Binghamton. The meat, frequently chicken because it's less expensive, is soaked overnight in an olive oil, vinegar, herb, and mint marinade reminiscent of Italian dressing, charcoal-grilled, unskewered in soft Italian bread and hit with a bit of fresh marinade. In addition to Sharkey's, Binghamton's other spiedie titans include Lupo's (opened 1951), and the more recently established Spiedie & Rib Pit (1993).

There's enough spiedie passion to support Spiedie Fest (spiediefest.com), every year since 1985. The three-day festival draws 100,000 people, features spiedie cooking contests, live performances by the likes of Blue Öyster Cult and Eddie Money, and claims to be one of the top three hot air balloon rallies in America. Three places to try them:

Lupo's S&S Charpit

6 West State Street, Binghamton, 13905
607-723-6106 | spiedies.com | Mon–Thu 9 AM–9 PM,
Sun 9 AM–8 PM, Fri–Sat 9 AM–10 PM

Sharkey's Bar and Grill

56 Glenwood Avenue, Binghamton, 13905

607-729-9201 | sharkeysbarbinghamton.com

Mon–Sat 11:30 AM–1 PM, Sun 12 PM–1 AM

Spiedie & Rib Pit

1268 Upper Front Street, Binghamton, 13901

607-722-7628 | spiedieandribpit.com

Mon–Thu 10:30 –10 PM, Fri–Sat 10:30 AM–10:30 PM,
Sun 11 AM–9 PM

Oneonta Eats: Brooks' Chicken and the Cold Cheese Slice

Take I-90 east, pass Rochester, go through Syracuse, and make a right on New York State Route 8 before you get to Utica, and you'll hit Oneonta (the "City of the Hills") in southern Otsego County in about four hours. Once in town, you have two missions, about an 8-minute drive apart: Brook's for chicken and the cold cheese slice at Tino's.

Brooks' House of BBQ

State Highway 7, Oneonta, 13820 | 607-432-1782

brooksbbq.com | Tue–Thu 11 AM–8:30 PM,
Fri–Sat 11 AM–9 PM, Sun 11 AM–8:30 PM

This famous Oneonta spot serves a charcoal-barbecued chicken hand-basted and flicked on with their famous tangy sauce. It claims to be the home of the largest indoor charcoal barbecue pit in the East, and has been cluckin' at its present location since 1965. But the family-owned business has a history with chicken that goes back to a poultry farm started in 1912!

Griffith and Frances Brooks bought the farm from her parents in Stamford, New York, in the 1940s. After struggling a little, and learning the Cornell method published in 1950, they started supplementing their income by catering in 1951. That led to a concession stand at the Del-Sego Drive-in movie theater in 1958, and an 80-seat restaurant in 1961. When that was a hit, they opened the 300-seat restaurant you can still visit today.

The restaurant is now run by its third generation of the family, having passed to the Brooks' son John and his wife Joan in 1975, and to their son Ryan and his wife Beth in 2005. There are sandwiches and salads, and other barbecue including St. Louis-style ribs and pulled pork, but the half-chicken BBQ Chicken Dinner is the house specialty.

Tino's Pizza & Restaurant

180 Main Street, Oneonta | 607-432-0008
tinosoneonta.com | Mon 11 AM–10 PM, Tue–Sat
11 AM–3 AM, Closed Sun

The cold cheese slice exists in the pizza diaspora. There's a cold cheese colony at Little Vincent's in Huntington on Long Island. But contrary to what the teenagers indulging in this uncommon sight might think, it didn't originate there. Little Vincent's manager Daniel Rossi told me that they started doing it in 1986 or 1987, when kids returning home from college in Oneonta started asking for it. As to which pizzeria in Oneonta first invented it?

Some claim Joe Ruffino's Pizzeria and The Italian Kitchen were doing cold cheese slices in the '70s (both opened in 1972). Others nominate Mosca's Pizza and Mama Nina's. Unfortunately, they're all closed, and while it may not mean they didn't have a hand in inventing this unique practice, that makes it difficult to dethrone the pizzeria that makes the loudest claim: Tino's.

Tino's was opened by Agatino and Nancy Garufi as an extension of their Pizza Land business, inside a bar called the Black Oak Tavern, in 1985. And Mr. Garufi's son, Tino Jr., said that's the same year the cold cheese slice started.

Asked how, Tino Jr. said, "This guy came up to the counter and asked for a slice. But it was too hot so he said can you put some cold mozzarella cheese on top so he could eat it right away."

Tino Sr. shrugged his shoulders and acquiesced. It quickly became the routine best-seller to drunk students from SUNY Oneonta and Hartwick College between midnight and 3 AM on Friday and Saturday. Because cheese isn't free, they started charging for extra, and because business was so good, they moved it out of the Black Oak into its own storefront next door. Tino Jr. sold Tino's in 2002, and moved the business to Cooperstown, but returned to reopen in Oneonta in 2009. So you can still get a cold cheese slice in the town that invented it from the joint with the strongest claim.

If you're wondering what the appeal is, consider the following: more is better, excess oil gets absorbed by cold cheese, and last, the interaction of the different temperatures of cheese create a unique taste and texture experience. There isn't enough heat to melt all the extra cheese, but it does introduce three cheese stages: melted, starting to melt, and cold cheese. And of course, oven-fresh slices can immediately go: oven, peel, pan, plate, mouth.

It doesn't take much to become a convert.

ACKNOWLEDGMENTS

There are three people without whom this book, or its companion, *The Buffalo New York Cookbook*, would literally have not happened. Thank you to my agent Stacey Glick for having wanted to do a Buffalo-related book for years and for channeling my enthusiasm to The Countryman Press. Thanks to Michelle Buffardi, author of *Great Balls of Cheese*, for being a vegetarian and asking my wife if a wing-related book would be something I'd be interested in working on.

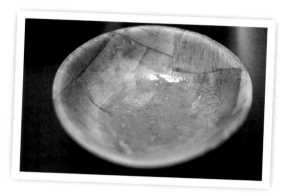

Last of the three, and most importantly, thank you to my wife, Angela Moore. Not just for bringing Buffalo adventures into my life and being supportive throughout the year I spent writing two books and for going solo for a month at home while I was away getting fat, but for enduring the months after our son Gus was born when *this book* still wasn't, and for suffering through endless Buffalo-themed dinners (okay, that last part was actually delicious and not hard at all). I love you. Thank you for everything.

Thank you to my parents, Rosmarie and Arthur Bovino, for doing read-throughs and for always believing in me, and to my sister, Emily, for advice on all things authentically Italian.

Thank you to our friend Deb Perelman of Smitten Kitchen for patiently answering questions about photography and other how-to details that came up in the course of trying to write a cookbook, and for suggesting a few really fun recipe ideas that should have been included from the start.

Thank you to all the writers, chefs, pizzaiolos, restaurateurs, bloggers, and bartenders I interviewed during the month I spent eating and drinking my way through Buffalo, and hassled afterwards with endless questions. Thank you to George Schaeffer, Cynthia Van Ness, Urner Barry, Bill Roenigk, Drew Cerza, Janice Okun, Anthony Kulik, Peter Dimfle, Mark Gress, Dr. Paul Bosland, Bill Metzger, Crazy Legs Conti, Calvin Trillin, Dale Talde, José Andrés, Ken Oringer, Andy Ricker, Philip Dorwart, Kristine Szczech, Donnie Kutzbach, Larry Santora, Jim Pacciotti, Anthony Kulik, Steve Cichon, and from the German department of the UB Department of Linguistics: Jean-Pierre Koenig, David Fertig, and Juergen Bohnemeyer.

In particular, thanks to Donnie Burtless of Buffalo Eats, my anonymous pizza paesano Sexy Slices, Andrew Galarneau, and above all, Christa Glennie Seychew, who was generous with her time *in* Buffalo but also thoughtfully responded to all of my questions, emails, and texts about the inane, arcane, minute, and crucial details of all things Buffalo, food-related and not.

Thank you to Visit Buffalo Niagara and its communications manager, Brian Hayden, for answering questions and providing some logistics and support. Thanks to its marketing manager, Drew Brown, and his fiancée (now wife!), Bernice Radle, for hosting me, some great tips on places to hit, for letting me keep pizza in their freezer, and not telling me I could never come back after leaving much of it there. (Please tell me I can claim credit for pizza being served at your wedding.)

Thank you to The Countryman Press, specifically editorial director Ann Treistman, my copyeditor Jenny Gropp, and production manger Devon Zahn. And thank you to my senior editor Róisín Cameron for her patience and dedication.

Thank you to my former *New York Times* bunker mate and boss Dan Okrent (public editor #1) for making some fun connections, and Colman Andrews for always seeming to know the answer to arcane food questions and connecting me to people who could answer the rare questions you couldn't. Thank you to my former word people at Mouth.com, Nancy Cohen, Jenny Acosta, Kaitlin Orr, and Josie Adams. If I hadn't worked with you, this book would not have been as punny. Any good puns I'll attribute to you. The bad ones are my fault.

Thank you to Barak Zimmerman for a long walk in April that helped dislodge the words. Once they started, they wouldn't stop.

Lastly, thank you to the city of Buffalo and everyone there who welcomed me with open arms.

INDEX